We The People's
Guide to
Estate Planning

We The People's GUIDE TO Estate Planning

A Do-It-Yourself Plan for Creating a Will and Living Trust

Ira Distenfield and Linda Distenfield

WILEY

John Wiley & Sons, Inc.

This book is printed on acid-free paper. ∞

Published by John Wiley & Sons, Inc., Hoboken, New Jersey.
Published simultaneously in Canada.

For general information on our other products and services please contact our Customer Care Department within the United States at (800) 762-2974, outside the United States at (317) 572-3993 or fax (317) 572-4002.

Wiley also publishes its books in a variety of electronic formats. Some content that appears in print may not be available in electronic books. For more information about Wiley products, visit our web site at www.Wiley.com.

Library of Congress Cataloging-in-Publication Data:

Distenfield, Ira, 1956–
    We the people's guide to estate planning : a do-it-yourself plan for creating a will or living trust / by Ira and Linda Distenfield.
        p.   cm.
    Includes index.
    ISBN 0-471-71667-7 (pbk.)
    1. Estate planning—United States—Popular works.   2. Wills—United States—Popular works.
3. Living trusts—United States—Popular works.   I. Title: Guide to estate planning.
II. Distenfield, Linda, 1942–   III. Title.
    KF750.Z9D57 2005
    346.7305—dc22   2004065765

Printed in the United States of America
10   9   8   7   6   5   4   3   2   1

CONTENTS

FOREWORD

Bill Lockyer
California Attorney General

A ccess to information is essential to life. Access to the legal system often supports a *successful* life. As Attorney General of California, I am a great admirer of We The People and the progress this enterprise has made to significantly improve access to the legal system for all Americans. We The People has led the way by being dedicated to arming people with the information to understand difficult legal situations and the roles that certain legal documents can play in their lives.

My ability to access quality information has allowed me to make good decisions throughout my personal and professional life. That's the whole point of information: It permits you to solve problems and be a smart and confident decision-maker. Information educates, trains, prepares, and opens new doors. It imparts knowledge; and it can also console, warn, and advise. I like to think of access to information as a basic necessity alongside food and water, and therefore it should be easy, inexpensive, and inviting. Unfortunately, it's not always that way. When it comes to the legal system, the gap between those privileged to access and use the law to their advantage and those who cannot is real for many Americans. Crafting documents that allow families to plan their future and leave the things they own to the people they love should not be an opportunity available only to a select few. Wills and living trusts are among the most powerful documents anyone can create, and anyone who wants to create these documents ought to be able to do so if they can. And with the right help, most people can.

As Attorney General I have witnessed the law's positive impact on people's lives, but I've also watched the legal system grow more complex and expensive every day. For too many Americans, the legal system is an 800-pound gorilla that sits on the other side of the table. One can have all the technology that money can buy and yet still feel completely cut off from the legal system, or the opportunity to execute documents, such as a will or living trust, that must meet specific legal standards to be enforceable when you need them most.

Every day, millions of Americans need to complete and file basic legal documents with the courts. Many of these documents don't require an attorney or a fancy degree to complete. I understand the need for competent independent counsel when necessary, but I also support the right to manage one's own legal affairs. Ira and Linda Distenfield founded We The People with a simple mission: to serve people who need to make uncontested legal transactions but who don't know how to approach the legal system and who neither have the resources nor desire to hire a lawyer. What I like best is seeing people served regardless of wealth or privilege.

This book helps you navigate the complex and daunting task of estate planning while providing do-it-yourself assistance for document preparation. Whether you can afford an attorney or estate planner or not, this book equips you with the knowledge and skills you need to control the creation of your own will or living trust. Good information and competent advice are the two most important ingredients for all legal documents, and here you'll find the information you need to understand how wills and living trusts work, and what you need to do to prepare intelligently for your family's future. Wills, and especially living trusts, are unfamiliar territory for most of us, but We The People has managed to map it out for you and tell what you need to know about every point of interest along the way.

Creating a will or living trust is a very important responsibility, and a task I hope more and more individuals and families will consider doing every year. It's easier than you think.

Twenty years ago few people had personal computers; no one had heard of the Internet; no one had e-mail or a way to carry a library of information on a computer chip that you keep in a hand-held device the size of your wallet. Fast-moving technology has given us ever more access to more information, has changed our expectations, and has changed our way of thinking. The impact that widespread information has had on Americans is evident: Americans feel better equipped and comfortable making pivotal life decisions, such as entering the housing market, changing careers, or starting a small business. Why? Information empowers people to change their lives for the better and make hard decisions. It is the ultimate equalizer.

My experiences have taught me about responsibility, leadership, and the value of being an independent thinker. I prepare relentlessly and always encourage others to do the same through studying, reading, and learning independently. My advice for anyone thinking about a will or living trust is to gather as much information as you can—seek the knowledge you need to be in charge of the decisions you need to make. Only then will you find the right advice to assist you in your endeavor. Only then can you be sure you're doing your absolute best to plan for and safeguard your future.

Success is not measured by status or wealth, but by how we deal with the challenges we face, by how we overcome those challenges through the decisions we make, and by the steps we take to move forward in our lives. This book allows you not only to access and gain information, but also to use the information to make sense of a difficult topic and take control of your family's future. You are entitled to create a will or living trust just as much as anyone else. Be well prepared for whatever course you take—with or without estate planning professionals by your side—and you'll move forward with greater peace of mind for you and your family.

ABOUT THE AUTHORS

Ira Distenfield is the Cofounder, Chairman of the Board, and Chief Executive Officer of *We The People Forms And Service Centers USA, Inc.,* a company he started with his wife in 1993. *We The People* is presently the largest independent paralegal company in the nation with offices in more than 150 cities and 31 states. Before his involvement with *We The People,* Mr. Distenfield was a Senior Vice President with Gruntal & Co., Inc., and a First Vice President with Smith Barney. He is a former President of the Port of Los Angeles, which, under his leadership, became the largest revenue producing port in the United States. He is an active member in his community and was named among the Outstanding Young Men of America by the U.S. Chamber of Commerce. He presently serves on the Santa Barbara County Sheriff's Council and is a member of the Santa Barbara County Parole Board.

Linda Distenfield is the Cofounder, President and Chief Operating Officer of *We The People Forms And Service Centers USA, Inc.* Before her involvement with *We The People,* Mrs. Distenfield served as Santa Barbara County's first full-time Film Commissioner. She also served as the Scheduling Director to the Honorable Tom Bradley, former Mayor of Los Angeles and gubernatorial candidate for the State of California. Mrs. Distenfield is active in several Santa Barbara organizations, and is a founding member of the Santa Barbara Firefighters Alliance.

The Distenfields live in Santa Barbara, California, but travel extensively throughout the country as they expand their company and support the franchise's growth. They enjoy seven children and three grandchildren.

ACKNOWLEDGMENTS

We owe our success to the thousands of customers we have helped through the years regain control of their lives or simply access the information they need to move forward and plan smartly. They continue to inspire, teach, and challenge us. Without them, this book would not have been possible.

Thanks to our supervising attorneys for their guidance and support of We The People, and especially Jason Sears, Esq. and Brant Jackson, Esq., who graciously reviewed the manuscript and offered their own expertise. Also, to Kenneth G. Gordon, Esq., of Laski & Gordon, LLP who answered many tax-related questions; to Creig Alan Dolge for helping us bring all this information down to everyday language; and to Bonnie Solow and Kristin Loberg for their direction and help through the writing and publishing process.

Finally, we'd like to dedicate this book to the millions of people out there who seek sound knowledge and have the courage to take charge of their own legal affairs—with or without the support of attorneys and professionals—and use what they learn to enhance their lives.

Introduction

If you are not a lawyer, and do not have access to one through family, friends, colleagues, or coworkers, facing a legal dilemma is a challenge—and mighty intimidating. Many transactions in life require legal documents, from a blissful marriage to an ugly divorce; from the birth of your children to the death of your parents *and you*. In fact, most all transactions in life that we experience involve legal documents at some point. *What's a legal document?* you ask. Legal documents are nothing more than papers that state a contractual relationship (example: marriage) or grant a right (example: trademark). Some are filed in a court, while others are kept between two agreeing people. All legal documents provide information of an official nature, and they are as prevalent as the air you breathe and the water you drink.

Life Is a Series of Transactions

The most significant transitions in life are punctuated by legal documents; you can think of life as a series of transactions for which you leave a paper trail of official and unofficial records: birth (certificate), education (degrees), work (employment permit or contract), marriage (certificate), major purchases (titles, deeds), minor purchases (receipts), travels (passport), maybe divorce (agreement), retirement (investment portfolios), and death (certificate, will, or living trust). Dozens more also come to mind. If you gathered up all the legal documents that you've amassed since birth, your collection would impress you. And you'd wonder how you managed to accumulate so many importance pieces of information (about you!) without really thinking about it along the way.

Some transactions are easier to make than others. Some require sticking to specific laws and seeking the approval of courts or government agencies. Examples include agreements, guardianships, child custodies, prenuptials, small claims, incorporations, trademarks, copyrights, evictions, and so on. But even the more common transactions of everyday life often involve legal documents. When you buy a house, secure a loan, finance a car, obtain your baby's birth certificate, purchase insurance, rent an apartment, hire a general contractor for home improvements, renew your driver's license, get a new credit card, or even accept the risk of parking your car in the mall lot, you deal with special legal documents without even realizing it. Planning for your death with a will or living trust also involves specific sets of documents.

Why Some Transactions Are Easy, Others Are Not

The difference between the seemingly mindless transactions and the complicated ones is clear: Someone else does most of the work in executing the simple transactions, and those transactions frequently don't involve the courts or a remote agency. For example, the document you sign when you lease a car is a legal document—a contract—between you and the car dealer, which will be upheld in a court of law (if you don't live by the contract's rules, such as making those monthly payments). You don't think so much about this contract as being a legal document, though, because the car dealer does all the work. Such a contract does not involve attorneys or filing with the courts, either, so the process is much less intimidating. You fill in the blanks, sign or initial your name on dozens of lines, and eventually drive off in a new car.

But for other, bigger transactions in life, such as setting up a living trust or writing a will, it's hard to find someone to guide you through the process at a low cost. On the outside, the process seems complicated, requiring a set of skills or knowledge you are not likely to find or understand easily. You know that if estate planning were so easy and uncomplicated, there would be no need for estate lawyers, tax lawyers, financial planners, and specialized accountants. (You're probably wondering, *What's estate planning? Do I have an estate?* The answer is yes, everyone has an estate, but we'll answer both of these questions in detail later in this book.)

Estate professionals deal with technical, mundane issues for a living. And while estate professionals come in handy for the complex and potentially problematic families, the majority of Americans do not fall into this category. You can do your own estate planning and learn as much technical information on the topic as you like—or focus on the basics and still get what you want out of it. If you dislike mathematics, tax matters, and the jargon that comes with the territory of property and ownership, you can still do your own estate planning successfully. Should you need to seek the advice from professionals to assist you, you'll have the foundation from which to approach these people, understand what they are talking about, and know exactly what you need.

Unfortunately, however, you don't even know how to begin this process without contacting one of these expensive professionals. You don't know where and how to craft these documents, and you lack the language for making these documents legally effective. So you don't know whom to trust and where to seek sound help. And to make matters worse, there are just as many shady, unreliable, and money-hungry estate attorneys out there as there are non-attorney estate planners with little experience in the drafting of these important documents.

Help! I Don't Know How to Do This

Welcome to We The People. We are a company that specializes in legal document preparation without the high costs related to lawyers. We are the first and only nationwide legal document preparation service in the country. Over the past decade, we have successfully served more than 500,000 consumers, including 13,000 people who simply needed to write a will. With 150 offices nationwide and growing every month, we have researched the requirements at

This book is one in a series of We The People books that give you the information you need to complete the trickier transactions in life that make most people cringe. They make people cringe because people don't know the how-tos to these complicated transactions, and the guidance they need is not so obvious in the real world. So you're not alone if you're reading this book and searching for help.

both state and local levels for a variety of legal documents. We know exactly what is required to make a will or living trust valid in all the states where we have stores. If you live in a state where we do not have an office, this book can provide essential information for you regardless (and chances are, we will reach your state soon).

By the time a publisher approached us to put our valuable information into a book, we were the nation's number one expert in the ins and outs of legal document preparation. And as founders of We The People, we felt exceedingly equipped to share our knowledge and experience. We've empowered hundreds of thousands of people over the past 10 years and we hope to empower millions more by sharing with you all the information that we've gathered. As you'll soon find out in the next few pages, **knowledge is power.**

In particular, this book explains the process of creating those important documents for transferring money and the property (things, such as your personal possessions and any real estate) you have accumulated in your lifetime. It's about wills, living trusts, powers of attorney, and other financial tools put in simple, practical language. These tools also help you make important decisions about your death and the disposition of your body. The will or living trust you set up ensures that certain transactions go according to *your* wishes. It's good to think of wills and living trusts as the means to secure future transactions that must take place when you no longer can make decisions for yourself and your family. So, in a sense, wills and living trusts prepare families for future transactions. In addition, a living trust is active while you are alive (hence "living"), and you can manage your own living trust for your own benefit during your life. At your death, your living trust continues to live (another reason for the "living" label) and benefit the people whom you name in your living trust.

If you don't think you are wealthy enough for a will or living trust, you are wrong. People who live modestly and save little still should think about a will or living trust. Why? Wills and living trusts command forward thinking and help you overcome even the smallest complications that can arise out of the smallest estates when you die.

The Purpose of Estate Planning

As we will show you in the first chapter, wills and living trusts are not only for the rich and famous. They are powerful documents that put you in the driver's seat even when you are physically unable to be there yourself—and when it has nothing to do with money or your assets. For example, smart estate planning can name guardians for minor children in the event you die before they reach adulthood. Moreover, you can plan for children to receive assets only at a certain time, when they are old enough to manage the assets. You can determine where your most prized but worthless possessions go (think of your bug collection), as well as your most valuable assets. Including other essential documents in your estate planning package can make the decision to take you off life support less troubling to make, as every state has laws that permit individuals to sign documents stating their wishes about health care decisions when they can no longer speak for themselves. And estate planning can prevent your family from incurring enormous fees related to probate (namely, executor and attorney fees) that turn any fortune you have amassed into dust. By having an estate planning package that prepares your family and minimizes the potentially negative consequences to your death, you can rest assured that you have done all that you can to keep your family safe. Wills and living trusts offer the same advantages to single people, too. You do not need to have children or a spouse to benefit from having a will or living trust.

In This Book

This book explains the process of executing wills and living trusts that won't be ignored or forgotten when you can no longer make decisions for you and your family. As unique as your family situation might be, we have heard a version of your story walk into one of our offices, and we know how to treat each and every situation successfully. We know how daunting the task of creating a will or living trust can be; it entails accepting your own mortality and planning for your family's future. It also entails reviewing your assets and deciding who you want to make responsible for the decision-making when you are gone or, in some instances, when you cannot act on your own behalf. Despite the initial fears, customers feel relieved once we guide them through the paperwork and help them create these important documents. We see it every day with smiles, gifts, notes of thanks, and grand sighs of relief from our customers. We hope this book becomes your friend, a lifeline similar to the way our offices become lifelines to the people courageous enough to walk in and ask for help.

If you find yourself having to help settle the estate of a deceased family member, this book also provides the information you need to get through the process. For example, if you have been named as an executor in a will, you'll find the must-have checklists and pointers that can help you successfully open, administer, and close an estate. Many of our customers do not start planning their own estate until they have gone through helping someone else settle an estate, so they understand how useful and effective good estate planning can be. They know that the better one plans for death in advance, the easier it is on the survivors.

Throughout the book, we answer questions you have about the kinds of dilemmas you may be facing: *Do I need a will? What about a living trust? What's the difference, and how do I know I've got enough assets to even bother considering these things? If so, how do I go about writing a will or setting up a living trust?* In addition to examples that bring technical legal language down to simple, everyday language anyone can understand, we provide step-by-step instructions on how to plan for and complete your will or living trust. We are your guiding light through this sometimes psychologically challenging process.

The Story behind *We The People*

Before we begin, let us explain how We The People came to be. We are Ira and Linda Distenfield, the founders of We The People who both came from different experiences that, conjoined, made for a perfect union in our new venture. It all began in the early 1990s. As senior vice president of a major New York Stock Exchange member firm, and president of the Los Angeles Port Authority, Ira frequently hired attorneys to handle his affairs. But something always struck him as odd. Why was he charged the same hourly rate for document preparation—primarily a clerical function—as for high-level legal advice?

Considering a career change, Ira began to research the paralegal field. He uncovered some surprising facts: The legal industry is a $100 billion business. At least half of a typical attorney's practice involves the processing of simple legal documents, often performed by non-attorneys. And if consumers hired independent paralegals rather than attorneys, their legal bills could be cut by as much as 90 percent.

While the marketplace offered an array of alternatives to attorneys, such as do-it-yourself legal software and court-run Internet web sites, Ira saw an untapped niche. He believed that legal forms were designed to confuse—created for lawyers and not the average consumer. Even though people can pick up legal forms at a drive-through courthouse kiosk or download them from the web, they still needed help filling them out.

We knew we needed marketing, organizational and legal expertise to succeed in our venture. As far as marketing, Ira capitalized on his 25 years as a stockbroker and experience traveling around the world encouraging countries to export their goods via Los Angeles Harbor, as president of the L.A. Port Authority. Linda took advantage of her administrative skills honed during her tenure as scheduling director for former Los Angeles mayor Tom Bradley. Together we attended paralegal school for a year to learn how to process legal documents, and hired an attorney to supervise our work.

In 1994, we opened our first We The People office in Santa Barbara, California. We knew this kind of service made sense in our lives, but we wondered if it would make sense for others. Was there a market for this type of service? Within three months, we got our answer.

Gifts started appearing at our door. "You got me through this bankruptcy for $199, and my lawyer wanted $3,000. Here, we bought a little box of candy for you," read a typical note. In Ira's 25 years of business experience, he had never witnessed such a personal gesture.

Our tiny one-room office in an executive suite filled a huge consumer need. For prices as much as 90 percent less than lawyer fees, customers who didn't require the advice of an attorney got help with more than 80 kinds of legal documents, such as divorce, bankruptcy, incorporation, living trusts, and wills. Customers provided information in simple workbooks. That information was then typed into the appropriate forms.

The Future of *We The People*

Ten years later, customer enthusiasm has fueled the launch of 150 offices in 30 states. In 2003, our company handled approximately 20,000 bankruptcies, 13,000 wills, and 38,000 divorces—more than any single law firm in the United States. We The People's multi-million dollar revenues continue to rise as more stores open and meet the needs of more people. Under the guidance of former New York City Mayor Rudolph Giuliani's consulting firm, Giuliani Partners, we plan to open 31 stores throughout the five boroughs of the City of New York this year and expand into additional markets nationwide. As testament to our careful research of the rules of local jurisdictions, We The People has helped more than half a million people successfully complete their legal matters. What makes us exceptional: We The People not only has become experts in the preparation of documents, but we know what many local courts require. Our company's expanding markets continue to afford us greater power in getting more information for fulfilling our customers' needs. An attorney can have only so much information. A robust company operating in more than half of the United States, however, can supply a wealth of information from the broadest of help to the most localized.

No Lawyers Means You Save Money

More and more people are seeking alternatives to the high cost of attorneys. According to an American Bar Association study in 1996, each year half of all low- and moderate-income households need legal help but must forgo it—in part because they can't afford a lawyer. As attorney fees rise to an average of $200 per hour, the number of people forced to navigate the system on their own has also climbed. In fact, fees have risen to such a point that even some lawyers privately say that, should they need it, they might be priced out of the legal market!

> According to the U.S. Bureau of Labor Statistics, the legal forms business is one of the largest growth industries in the nation, second only to home health care.

Whether it's buying bulk at Costco or trolling the Internet for the best deal on a printer, consumers are driven now more than ever to get the most for their money. Legal services are not immune.

The challenge, however, lies in accessing competent, qualified, and affordable legal document services. In our strategic alliance with Giuliani Partners, one of our goals is to streamline this industry so that every consumer can approach any legal document company and feel that he or she is getting superior results. At We The People, we aim to bring high-quality information and services to all consumers and minimize costs so that no one has to forgo accessing the legal system.

The simple truth is that lawyers are not necessary for many legal services. The head of one non-profit that provides legal help for low-income folks has estimated that only about 5 percent of its typical clients actually require a full-range, high-cost lawyer. As a result, a growing number of Americans are choosing to represent themselves in legal matters. In California, for instance, more than 50 percent of bankruptcies and 60 percent of divorces are now filed without an attorney. And when it comes to estate planning, attorneys are notoriously expensive for their services because of all the monies they potentially can collect from even a modest estate (the assets and liabilities, real and personal property left to descendants or others). They tend to generate enormous fees that eat away at the value of your estate. According to a survey published by the American Bar Association in 2001, trust and estate lawyers sustain malpractice claims twice as frequently as do criminal lawyers.

You have three choices for getting legal documents completed:

1. Type them yourself.
2. Go to a reputable legal document assistant (such as We The People).
3. Go to a lawyer.

This book is useful for any of the above options. Even if you decide to hire a lawyer or other professional to help you through your estate planning, you still need to educate yourself about the process and be as knowledgeable and prepared as possible. *No one should rely on one person alone to make such critical life decisions.* The more you know, the better you can plan and the more successful your plan will be. Wills and living trusts are extremely personal documents that reflect your wishes and possessions; you would not want just anyone to make

In its March 1991 issue, the American Bar Association *Journal* reported a study in which it was estimated that consumers can save more than $1.3 billion annually by representing themselves in just four routine legal transactions: uncontested divorces, wills, bankruptcies, and incorporations. When you represent yourself in a legal matter, it's referred to as doing it *pro se* (for yourself).

important decisions for you when it comes to these wishes and possessions—especially once you can no longer make them.

While some do-it-yourself legal resources provide general information, few provide guidance at the state-specific or local level. By reading this book, you set yourself up to complete your entire transaction. We know the details to setting up and maintaining an enforceable will or living trust in most states across the nation. You won't need to search high and low for the right forms to use and the right language to choose to clearly express your instructions for after you are gone. You can use the instructions contained in this book to begin the process of creating your own documents, and you'll know when and where to go to tailor your documents to reflect any state-specific requirements. For example, any We The People store near you can help you understand your state's specific requirements.

None of this book's contents can substitute the person-to-person contact you can get when you walk into one of our offices (see Appendix C for a listing of We The People stores by state), but this book is an excellent companion for those who do not have access to one of our locations or who prefer to complete the process as independently as possible. Backed by We The People's expertise, this book reflects years of experience and stands at the top of the self-help legal document market. No organization can claim that they have assisted 500,000 people over the past decade in filling out and filing basic legal documents. Having We The People's information in one comprehensive book that won't become outdated anytime soon is like having a universal tool tucked away in your pocket. You can draw on this reference for years to come. And it will add to your peace of mind, too.

Your Future

When you're considering a will or living trust, the first questions that rush through your mind are: *What's the big deal about wills and living trusts? What if I die without a will or living trust? What are the steps I have to take to get a will and living trust? How much is it going to cost? How long will it take? What is expected of me?*

Few people like to consider their own death, no matter their age. It's not a topic of conversation at cocktail and dinner parties, and it's certainly not something people are enthusiastic about planning. But death is a reality we all face, and knowing how wills, living trusts, and power of attorney documents can assist you and your family is important.

You don't have to possess enormous assets, live in a beachfront mansion, or be an heir to a family fortune (think Hilton or Rockefeller) to plan strategically for your death—or just a time when you are incapacitated. One of the reasons people avoid writing a will or setting up a living trust is this myth that you have to be wealthy or own lots of property. Not so. Middle-class and even lower-middle class people can and sometimes do leave money to their children or other loved ones, thus enhancing the lives of their survivors. If you don't prepare for your death with a will or living trust, the state in which you reside will ultimately make decisions for you with regard to your personal belongings and assets. Being in control of what happens at your death and helping your family avoid costly, unnecessary procedures involves having a will or living trust. You should decide what happens at your death—not the state.

People also don't realize how easy it is to create a will or living trust. You do not need a hotshot lawyer or estate planner for either of these transactions. And you do not have to go before a judge or file your papers with a courthouse. All you require is the courage to think about your death and how you'd want to distribute your assets, and the completion of the proper documents to reflect your wishes. In a matter of days, you can create these documents that have the potential to save your family thousands of dollars, plus unnecessary pain and anguish.

Wills, living trusts, tax issues, and power of attorney documents all sound like big words for big people, but they shouldn't be. They are the vehicles by which you can leave the things you own to the people you love. They are the tools you need to protect your family and prepare for its future. Planning now will save your family time, money, and a lot of emotional distress later on.

Finally, having a greater sense of control over your personal affairs by doing most of the work yourself is an empowering experience. With this book, and the knowledge you gain from it, you will pave a winning path of succession.

So let's begin.

CHAPTER 1

What Happens When Somebody Dies?

Death is a costly event. Just when you think living is expensive, consider dying. Without going into the details of funeral preparations, burials, and the cost of getting a person to rest in peace—which generally costs more than $6,000—plus end-of-life medical care, death itself trips a sequence of events that can cause unnecessary agony and frustration for a family. If you die without a will (called dying intestate), or problems emerge understanding your will or living trust and the distribution of your assets, your estate (that is, your stuff or assets) will end up in probate, a court process of distributing those assets. The value of your estate will diminish considerably in this expensive and time-consuming process. And you won't have much left over to give to your family. You may have *nothing* to pass on to your survivors, even if you considered yourself rich before you died.

This scenario is one you want to avoid. We hope to show you through this book that no matter how much (or how little) you own or owe, wills and living trusts are useful family planning tools. Wealth is a relative term, and an inventory of how much you already own or are responsible for—including children under your care—might surprise you. If you die tomorrow, how well would your family be prepared? Death has both administrative and emotional consequences; by minimizing these inevitable burdens you can save your loved ones undue distress. If you have ever had to deal with a death in your family, you may know what we mean. Chances are, you have a lot to protect physically, financially, and emotionally.

Look around you and think about all that you have accumulated thus far in your lifetime. You have worked hard to get to where you are today. You continue to work hard for yourself and your family. You set goals and achieve them, and you keep planning for you and your family. But as much as you carefully plan your future every day on small and large scales, having a will or living trust in addition to these plans can significantly complement your life. Think of wills and living trusts as the master keys to your lifetime goals. They are the means by which you protect your most precious possessions, people included.

According to a national survey conducted by the AARP, probate costs run on average 2 to 10 percent of a person's estate. But on a $300,000 estate, that can still cost $6,000 to $12,000. And in some cases, the costs can go much higher. Large estates obviously have a lot to lose;

Probate refers to the court's supervision of distributing your assets and handling any legal issues related to the settlement. It's the legal proceeding by which a person's assets are distributed after death. You can think of probate as a legal holding cell where assets and debts are accounted for, taxes are paid, and what's left is distributed to the beneficiaries named in the will or, if there is no will, to the heirs specified by state law.

but the smaller your estate, the more you have to lose—because less will be left to pass on to your loved ones.

An honest and revealing look at what happens when somebody dies, the focus of this chapter, begins our journey into estate planning (defined on page 12). While estate planning is generally a topic people don't like to discuss or think about, having the courage to plan for the what-ifs and sure things (because no one gets out of this world alive!) is the best way to make your family's future safe and secure.

The High Cost of Dying

Funerals and memorial services are daily occurrences. Unlike weddings and baby showers, however, they typically are not planned well in advance and are accompanied by grief, shock, and sometimes utter despair. But they can require the same amount of resources and effort as weddings and other grand events. You probably have an idea of what a wedding can cost these days (a lot!), but do you know how much it costs to die?

The average American funeral costs roughly $6,500. A full-service funeral with a viewing (a funeral service that allows survivors to see the embalmed body of the deceased, usually in an open casket) can cost upwards of $20,000. This does not include burial or cremation (nor the burial plot that can run more than $25,000 in some towns!). This does not include the emotional and physical cost of dealing with a death and moving the family forward. And this also does not factor probate fees into the equation, which can eliminate one's fortune—big or small—in a blink, but take years to resolve officially. So your family is left with nothing but expenses to pay for getting you to rest in peace.

To understand the impact of dying without a will or living trust, we want to show you how one family's arduous struggle through the probate process resulted in a devastating, almost unbelievable loss, to everyone. This is an unusual story that does not reflect most families' situations, but because of its extremes, it sets an example of what can happen when good plans go bad. The story starts with a very wealthy couple with riches beyond most people's dreams. The couple's family—including extended family—became so divided over the couple's dream-come-true assets when they died, that the litigation over the estate languished in the courts for more than a decade. Once the probate court took control to settle all the disputes involved, little remained to be distributed. The following is based on a true story:

Following the American dream, Willaim and Emma Banks bought real estate in Malibu, California, a long time ago—long before it became choice real estate. Their land covered 3.4 acres on beachfront property, and by the early 1980s, they believed it was valued at more than $10 million. In 1983, the Banks created a living trust funded by their Malibu property. Through this trust, they intended to leave $1 million to their daughter; $300,000 to a personal friend; $200,000 to a cousin; $100,000 to each of their seven great-grandchildren; and the remainder to the principle beneficiaries, their four grandchildren. The trust would not get distributed, of course, until all debts, taxes, and administration expenses related to the property had been paid.

Sounds like a lot of money. Sounds like the Banks could not have done better for themselves nor planned better for their family. Unfortunately, the story doesn't have a happy

Probate is designed to prevent fraud and abuse, as well as settle disputes and clear titles to property. The more arguments emerge among family members after the death of an individual, the longer it takes for probate to settle the estate and distribute assets to family members. Many estate planners like to argue that probate is an inefficient and expensive system that zaps the life out of a family's fortune, whatever that might be. True, probate takes longer to distribute one's estate than had the person set up a living trust. But probate exists to protect what the dead person left behind. It attempts, although sometimes does not always achieve, to also protect the wishes of the dead person—or what they would have wanted.

ending. After William and Emma passed away in 1987 and 1988 respectively, managing their estate and executing their wishes proved harder than they planned in their living trust. When complications arose out of the sale of the Malibu property, the beneficiaries of the trust got tired of waiting and took their frustrations to court. The only way to settle the disputes was to go to the probate court, which punctuated the beginning of a long and costly end.

How long did it take for the beneficiaries of the trust to get their money? By 2001—13 years after Emma died, lawsuits related to the estate were still moving through the probate court. All the meanwhile, the estate—which once had been worth millions—had dwindled to the point that there was not enough to distribute per the Banks's wishes. All that remained were angry family members (but happy lawyers) who never talked to one another again. Imagine how hard William and Emma must have worked their entire lives to maintain their land and prepare for its proceeds to benefit their descendants.

Bottom line: If you do not plan your estate as best you can with a will or living trust before you die, then your family may not receive all that you had intended them to receive. Your family may be left with hard decisions to make, more expenses to pay to help settle your affairs, and a long, drawn-out process that fails to distribute your assets in a timely manner. With a will, you can tell your family who gets what and when. You can also name guardians for minor children. You can do a lot more, however, with a living trust that is designed to avoid the probate process, distribute your assets quickly, and minimize taxes through built-in features (as we will see with an AB living trust).

You Don't Have to Be Rich

A huge misconception about wills and living trusts is that they are documents for wealthy people to worry about, but not for the average Jane and John Doe. As stories of heirs and heiresses splash the covers of magazines, you continue to make ends meet through hard work and deft planning. You worry about how you are going to send kids to college, pay for renovations on your house, stay healthy, finish paying off your car loan and mortgage, get out of debt, lose 10 pounds, and make enough money to retire someday. If you worry about these things, you are normal. But you do need to think about a will or living trust, too. Despite what you might think, a modest family with minimal assets has a lot to protect.

As members of the World War II generation pass their assets on to Baby Boomers, and the Baby Boomers, in turn, pass their assets on to their children, more money will pass from one generation to another in the first half of the twenty-first century than the rest of American history combined.

What Is Estate Planning?

You want to leave as much as you can to the people you love, as well as help them make important decisions related to your death and the events shortly thereafter. Prevent your family from experiencing the anguish and frustration of probate. Minimize how much your family will pay for your estate's distribution by making plans now and setting up a living trust. This kind of planning is called estate planning.

In the simplest terms, estate planning involves two actions while you are still alive:

1) Putting in writing the names of the people you would want to take care of your children, your finances, and your health care if you couldn't do so anymore (and telling them what you would want them to do); and

2) Using the appropriate legal documents so that in case of death or complete disability, the money and things you've worked so hard to acquire go to whomever you wish instead of being divided among family according to state law.

Estate planning can be an extremely lucrative business for savvy attorneys, financial planners, accountants, and the like. It's lucrative for these professionals both before you die (fees for setting up wills and trusts) and after you die (fees for managing what you leave behind). If estate planning intimidates you because you picture suited professionals and believe only they can do it for you, reconsider this view. Minimizing the cost of your death entails doing as much planning as you can before you die, as well as being informed about your options and the ways in which you can plan successfully. There is nothing wrong with creating your own will or setting up your own living trust without the help of an attorney. An experienced legal document assistant can help you navigate the language and terms you need to use to create good documents. An expert in tax laws and accounting can help you deal with tax issues and planning your estate accordingly.

Gaining knowledge and seeking competent advice are the keys to good estate planning. The more you know and the greater your foundation in estate planning techniques is, the better you can seek outside help with confidence. You'll know what to ask and how to take action on any advice you receive. Estate planning you do on your own pays off when you seek the help or advice from a professional and can tell the difference between a good one and a not-so-good one.

What Is an Estate?

The word estate confuses a lot of people. And the notion of estate planning leaves much to the imagination. Instead of picturing Beverly Hills and East Hampton mansions, butlers, and vast vineyards, think of your estate as everything you own and owe. Think of estate planning as financially preparing your assets and liabilities for when you are no longer alive. Everyone has an estate, no matter how big or small. Everyone has a right to set forth plans for his or her estate, too. Surprisingly, the least-complicated task to preparing one's death—the writing of a will, no matter how archaic—is only done by one-third of Americans. What happens to the other two-thirds of Americans who die without a will? Their families hopefully work together to deal with their beloved's body as the deceased would have wanted and pray no disputes arise over their beloved's estate. Either way—disputes or not—the probate court may control the process.

The death of a loved one is always sudden. If you were to go today, your family would have to deal with a lot of logistical stuff before even getting to your last will and testament (assuming you have one). Such logistics can include notifying family members and friends, physically moving your body from the place of your death to a funeral home; planning a funeral and memorial service; and carrying out organ, tissue, or body donating arrangements.

In most states, if you own real estate worth more than $10,000 or if your total estate (including personal possessions) is more than $30,000 to $60,000, your estate will go through probate—regardless of a will. In California, an estate needs to go through the formal probate process if the gross value of the estate is more than $100,000. It doesn't matter if there is a will. The probate process will ensue and it will take at least eight months to one year. For many cases, the complex process takes as long as three or four years or more. An attorney can charge as much as six percent of the gross value of the estate. Studies have shown that the probate process costs Americans anywhere between $25 billion and $50 billion annually.

Finding your will or letter of instruction is farther down the checklist. (We'll see how letters of instruction differ from wills in the next chapter.) You should hope that your family members, and in particular your named executor, find your will and letter of instruction at some point, in case you've made clear how you want your final arrangements done and it's not too late to carry out those wishes. Examples: You want to be cremated and have your ashes scattered over the ocean. You want Uncle Emil to give a eulogy. You don't want your Chihuahua to get into the hands of little Susie.

What Is a Will?

Simply put, a will is a statement that indicates your desire about the distribution of your wealth following your death. Don't let the word "wealth" intimidate you, either. Wealth is a relative term and can mean whatever you want it to mean. Whatever you've accumulated in your life thus far—by inheritance, luck, or hard work—is your wealth. Your wealth can equal a few used books, $100, and a rock collection; or it can equal a 10-acre parcel of land, a million dollars, and a country home. Later in this book we'll help you take inventory of your wealth so you have an idea of what you need to divvy up for purposes of your will.

A will not only gives you decision-making control over who gets what, but it also gives you control over how and when they receive it. It conserves and distributes your assets and money according to your wishes, it names guardians for your minor children, and generally minimizes the chances that things get screwed up. Wills, however, could be subject to probate. In other words, having a will alone cannot protect your estate from the probate process. This is why living trusts are important vehicles for transferring wealth.

What Is a Living Trust?

A living trust is the alternative to a Last Will and Testament that must go through probate to be proved. The nature of a living trust eliminates the probate process.

Trusts in general can be difficult concepts to conceive because they are not easy to visualize. When you think of a will, you picture a piece of paper with instructions written on it. But when many people think of a trust, their minds draw blanks. Is it a piece of paper? A bank account? A safe deposit box? Something mysterious inside a safe deposit box? Can you physically touch a trust? People also wrongly assume that trusts are created for the purposes of financially protecting children or for setting up a child's financial cushion for his or her future (trust fund baby). Not so. Trusts are for single people and families alike.

In basic terms, a trust is a relationship between people and property. One person (the trustee) is given legal ownership of assets to be managed or invested for the benefit of someone else (a beneficiary). Trusts are private contracts or agreements but are recognized by the laws and courts as independent legal entities—like people or corporations.

There are many different kinds of trusts. A trust may be created when you die (through your will). Or, a trust may be created while you are alive (a living trust). You can be the trustee of your own living trust. This allows you to maintain control of your property. At death, most property must pass through probate before it can be inherited. However, property owned by the living trust does not. This is why most people prepare a living trust—to avoid probate.

While we detail some other types in Chapter 5, our focus remains on living trusts. When you set up your living trust, you transfer all or most of your assets into it, then administer it yourself as the trustee. It is a "trust" because it creates an entity into which assets can be placed for normal use during your lifetime (you can sell or paint your house) and then be available for distribution to anyone you select after your death. It is "living" because you set up the trust while you are alive and you manage it while you are alive. A living trust is active during your lifetime, unlike a will, which is dormant until you die.

A living trust should also include a will, which serves a particular function in the living trust package. You can have a Last Will and Testament, but not necessarily a living trust; on the other hand, a living trust provides for both a will and a trust. And, while living trusts don't prevent your family from paying any estate tax (an ugly topic we discuss in Chapter 6), living trusts can dramatically reduce that estate tax.

A Will and Living Trust as an Estate Planning Package

Wills and living trusts are not only for the distribution of assets, which is why everyone should consider these documents. Other documents in your estate planning package should include

- A living will that states what kind of extraordinary medical efforts you do or do not want at your death; and
- Power of attorney documents for making medical decisions and financial decisions if and when you cannot make such decisions during your life.

These documents have little to do with money and assets. They set the stage for the what-ifs that you may encounter in life. They answer important questions that may arise at some unknown point in the future—hopefully not tomorrow.

Living Will. The so-called living will is a separate document that could be included in your health care power of attorney document (such as is the case in California) or as a separate document. This document states you do or do not want to be kept alive on machines at the end of your life. Living wills give clear instructions to your loved ones (and your doctors) on how to proceed once you cannot speak for yourself and must rely on others to take care of you. You do not want to force your family into making quick, unprepared decisions about your medical care, or the family's resources.

Powers of Attorney. Naming powers of attorney means you allow someone else to make decisions in your behalf for either medical or financial reasons—or both. For example, let's say you are in a ski accident and have no use of your arms or legs while you lay in a full-body cast (and heavily medicated), but important financial transactions must occur in your name. If you have an agent for durable power of attorney for financial decisions, you can rely on that person to carry out your financial wishes and make decisions on your behalf.

Although living wills and durable powers of attorney are optional documents to add to your living trust (if you leave them out, your living trust remains valid), we include living wills and durable power of attorney documents in our living trust packages because they are such excellent and powerful documents to have. We will revisit these documents in Chapter 5.

> A living trust has more meat and power to it than a standard will alone. Living trusts do contain wills, but they serve different functions than a Last Will and Testament.

Pour Over Will. The will part of a living trust is not the same as a Last Will and Testament. In a living trust, the will part is called a pour over will. This is because the trust contains your property as well as instructions about where your property goes after you death (it can remain in the trust, too, for a period of time). Because you are not likely to put everything you own into your living trust before you die (such as your household goods, rocking chair, music collection, knick-knacks, and so on), the pour over will transfers your remaining assets into the trust at your death. We will explain pour over wills in detail in Chapter 3.

Misconceptions About Last Wishes

Sometimes people think that they can scribble their notes down on a piece of paper, call it a letter of instruction, and give it to someone they know who can carry out their wishes. Such

 I Don't Understand What You Mean By . . .

Estate. The total of your assets and liabilities, real and personal property.

Assets. Everything you own, including real estate and personal possessions. *Assets* and *property* are interchangeable words.

Intestate. Dying without a will. Intestate is the state or condition of dying without having made a valid will, or without having disposed of a part of your property by will or a trust.

Testate. Dying with a will.

Will. A document that formally expresses your will—your intents, wishes, and decisions about financial matters—into the future of your family for their benefit.

Trust. A legal contract by which one party—the trustee—has legal ownership of some property (real or personal) to manage or invest for the benefit of another. A *living trust* is a specific kind of trust you set up while you are alive and serve as trustee for during your lifetime.

Trustee. The person appointed to manage a trust. The boss of the trust.

Probate. A court-directed review of a person's will, its validity, and how it can be enforced.

Probate assets. Any and all assets that must go through probate. Assets owned by a living trust do not normally have to go through probate. Assets jointly owned normally do not have to go through probate. But assets outside of a living trust or not jointly owned usually go through probate and are thus called probate assets.

a note is not a document that a court can easily enforce. Neither can a spoken statement about your wishes hold up well in court or prevent your family members from fighting over your assets. Moreover, should you become incapacitated or unavailable to make critical decisions for your benefit, without the right documents in place, your family may have a hard time carrying out your wishes.

By forcing yourself to create a will or living trust, you prevent your family (and possibly the court) from doing a lot of guesswork when you are gone. Clearly laying out your instructions for when you die lifts an enormous burden that your family members would otherwise have to bear at your death. Without these instructions, your family (and the court) has to settle your estate and wonder how you would have wanted to distribute your assets (this is assuming, of course, that your family managed to get through burying you and memorializing you as you would have wanted). This is where wills and living trusts take center stage: They are the means by which you can leave the things you own to the people you love without extraneous hassles and frustration. Moreover, if you choose to use a living trust, you can transfer your assets even more quickly, easily, and inexpensively.

While not necessarily part of your formal will or living trust document, the special instructions you leave with your will or living trust are the roadmaps that your survivors want to have at your death. They articulate how to dispose of your body, whether or not you want Last Rites, for example, and what songs you want played at your funeral.

An estate planning package makes you the director of your life both during and after. Although having a will can direct the traffic of your assets after your death, it may not transfer your assets easily to your beneficiaries without the court's direction. And a Last Will and Testament's instructions may not be as extensive and detailed as a living trust's directives. Ultimately how you choose to plan your estate is up to you. We give you all the tools you need to start that planning.

Living Trust Package–At a Glance

If you want your heirs and other survivors to receive your assets quickly and free of the high cost of probate, then you create a living trust. A typical living trust package includes:

- The articles of the trust that avoid probate
- A pour over will
- A living will, including a section that states you do or do not want to be kept alive on machines
- Two powers of attorney, one for health decisions and one for financial decisions (sometimes the living will contains the power of attorney for health care decisions)

A living trust can be called a revocable living trust. It's revocable because you can change your plan anytime during your lifetime—including revoking the entire plan if you choose.

A living trust is among the more enduring documents you can have to direct your posthumous wishes. Unlike a basic Last Will and Testament, a letter of instruction, or even a holographic will (a handwritten will), living trusts are designed specifically to avoid probate. That means living trusts don't incur probate fees and don't take a ridiculously long time to execute. You can think of a living trust as a special kind of last will and testament—one that keeps your estate out of probate.

Revocable Living Trusts

Revocable living trusts are living trusts that allow you to control your assets during your lifetime but pass them directly to your beneficiaries upon your death. You fund your living trust during your life by transferring your assets into it, which is a simple process that involves a few documents and having some of them notarized, witnessed, signed, and recorded. At your death, assets in your living trust are distributed according to your provisions, without supervision of a court. A properly designed living trust makes the hand-off of assets clean and private.

As we will see in Chapter 3, living trusts have five main advantages: (1) they avoid probate, (2) they allow for privacy, (3) they allow for flexible management, (4) they have the potential to save families money, and (5) they allow for easier and quicker transfers of assets at one's death.

This book contains all the information you need to set up and create your own living trust package. We call it a package because it includes not only the basic elements of a living trust, but also several optional documents that complete your living trust and comprise your entire estate plan.

If You Die Intestate

If you die without a will, you are said to have died intestate. This is one of the worst things you can do. The word itself sounds ugly, close to "intestines." Dying without a will may necessitate probate. The court will make all of the decisions for you, including appointing someone to be responsible for wrapping up your affairs. This person might not be the one you would have picked. The court may also appoint a neutral lawyer, who gets paid out of your estate and who has no intentions of making the process move along quickly. What's more, your family is at the mercy of state law, which means your estate gets distributed according to statutes (laws) that may not reflect your wishes. Imagine working hard and slowly building wealth over the course of your life, only to lose all that you've gained in expensive proceedings that don't guarantee your assets will end up in the hands of the people you had hoped!

Every state has a set of intestacy laws (rules) that govern what happens when someone dies without a will in that state. Here's what usually happens if you die without a will under different family circumstances:

> Only one-third of all Americans die with a will. No wonder all the people linked to the probate process make lots of money!

You're Married with Children. The law in most states gives only one-third to one-half of your assets to your spouse. The rest goes to your children, regardless of age.

You're Married with No Children. Most states give only one-third to one-half of your estate to your spouse. The remainder generally goes to your parent(s), if they are alive. If both parents are dead, many states split the remainder among the dead person's siblings.

You're Single with Children. State laws uniformly provide that your entire estate goes to the children.

Single with No Children. Most state laws favor your parent(s) in the distribution of your estate. If both parents are dead, many states divide your estate among your siblings.

How you own property, or hold title, to assets also determines how property gets distributed to family members. For example: If you own a house in joint tenancy with your spouse and you die, the law says that your spouse gets the entire house (your half of your interest in the home goes to your spouse). If, on the other hand, you owned an apartment in joint tenancy with your son, then at your death the apartment would go to your son.

You ask, what about friends, old mentors, old lovers, your distant pen pal, or current soulmate? The laws that govern probate cannot extend to include such people, so if you don't set up your estate properly before you die, important people in your life won't get any of your pie. What you think is family and what the state thinks is family are probably two different things. There is no one definition of family in today's world of relationships. You might consider your best friend as family, even though he or she has no blood or legal relation to you.

People die without wills and trusts in place every day. The probate court is always busy. People avoid making wills and setting up living trusts because they fear death or don't want to waste time thinking about things that happen after they are gone. People who also don't plan on dying anytime soon—either because they are young or just young at heart—don't consider a will or living trust. But no one knows the fate of one's own mortality, so there's no good or bad time to create a will or living trust. There's no guarantee you will live for another 20 years. Another way to think about it is this: Would you rather set up a will or living trust today or wait and have to go through the process when you are much older? It's easier to take care of your family's future while you are young and not 90 years old.

Who's Involved In a Living Trust?

Lots of people with special titles are involved in a living trust. By setting up a living trust, you get to name these people and place these titles on them. If you don't do it, the court (read: probate) will do it for you. Here's a list of the principle people involved in a living trust:

Trustee. The boss of the trust. The person appointed to manage a trust. For living trusts, you would serve as the trustee (boss) for the duration of your lifetime. Because you are the one setting up the trust, you also have the title of *grantor, settlor,* or *trustor,* depending on the state in which you reside. These all mean you are the creator of the trust.

Successor Trustee. The person who takes over your duties as the boss of the trust in the event of your death. This person may also be the executor of your will. (This person can also be a beneficiary.)

Executor. The person you name in your will to carry out your wishes at your death and distribute your assets. This person is typically a friend, relative, bank or trust company.

Administrator. The person given the authority to settle your estate at your death. The term *administratix* can also be used interchangeably. Both these words usually refer to court-appointed people for when there is no will specifically stating someone.

Personal Representative. The person who is responsible for carrying out your wishes as defined by you. A personal representative of your will is your *executor.* A personal representative of your living trust is your *successor trustee.* Should that person be unable to perform his or her duties at your death, you also name an *alternate personal representative* in your documents.

Beneficiary. The person entitled to profit or benefit from a trust. You name your beneficiaries in your will or living trust, instructing who gets what and when. You are also a beneficiary (of your own living trust) during your lifetime if you have a living trust.

> Generally speaking, *executors* are named in wills; *administrators* are named by courts. They perform the same duties and have the same responsibilities.

Note that a beneficiary isn't necessarily the same as an heir. An *heir* is anyone who inherits assets based on the rules of descent and distribution, namely, being the child, descendant, or other closest relative of the dear departed. It also has come to mean anyone who takes (receives) something by the terms of the will. So, while beneficiaries get named in wills and trusts, beneficiaries also become heirs when they receive assets from the instructions in a will.

Alternate Beneficiary. The person entitled to profit or benefit from your living trust upon the occurrence of a specific event, such as the death of the primary or lifetime beneficiary.

Conservator. The person appointed to act on behalf of another person. This term is generic, and can refer to anyone given the power to take charge of making decisions for someone who is incapacitated and unable to perform his or her duties.

Agent of Durable Power of Attorney. The person named to make certain decisions for you in the event you become incapacitated or unavailable (or just don't want to make decisions). In your living trust, you name two powers of attorney: one for financial decisions (often called *durable power of attorney for finances*) and one for medical/health decisions (often called *durable power of attorney for health care*). One person can hold both of these powers. "Durable" simply means that if you do become incapacitated, your agent can still make decisions for you.

Guardian/Custodian. The person you name to take care of minor children or disabled people under your care in the event you die.

There are lots of terms and titles related to trusts. The above ones are the basic, most important terms that you'll encounter. As we come across more, we'll define and explain.

Where Does the Money Go?

We've already explained how probate is scary because it diminishes the value of estates. But we've also hinted at the high cost of dying regardless of family planning and preventive tactics to avoid probate. (Despite the existence of a living trust, any estate is subject to probate if problems occur or someone decides to challenge a trust.) In addition to the price tags attached to your end-of-life events, such as your final medical expenses, mahogany casket, wake, lavish funeral and memorial service, and so on, here's a checklist of costs that your family might have to bear no matter what:

- Administrative fees to your executor and/or attorney (executors often hire attorneys to handle necessary paperwork, and both are allowed to charge reasonable fees such as $10,000 on an estate worth $400,000, if not more)

- Appraisal fees to any assets that must be appraised, such as a home that will be sold and whose proceeds will go to beneficiaries

- Legal and accounting fees

- Court fees (the filing fee to the probate court)

- Fees for publishing a probate notice in a newspaper

- Taxes and debts

The taxes and debts part of the equation can be enormous—especially the tax burden, which includes estate taxes, inheritance taxes, income taxes, and property taxes. An estate that appears to be worth millions can shrink to pennies on the dollar once debts and taxes have been paid. The so-called death tax, or federal estate tax, is the tax levied on estates worth more than $1.5 million and has been a source of debate in Congress for years. At its top level (of a tiered system based on taxable estate values), the death tax is nearly 50 percent.

In 2001, Congress finally passed legislation that repeals the federal estate tax incrementally until 2010, when it stands at zero. However, Congress could change that plan and reinstate the tax in some form before 2010. In 2011, the estate tax will return unless Congress votes to extend the repeal. Meanwhile, though, estate tax rates will go down and exemptions (what you can exclude from being taxed) will go up.

Even though this estate tax affects a small percentage of the population (about two percent), taxes still loom large for people concerned about family money. Families who own small businesses or farms can easily qualify for the estate tax. You'd be surprised how quickly a modest family's estate can add up to a lot of value. A gross estate includes the total value of all owned assets or property in which a person had interest at the time of his or her death. But, as we'll see in Chapter 6, it also includes life insurance proceeds, certain annuities, and certain kinds of assets transferred out of the estate within three years before the person died.

Moreover, Mr. Taxman wants to be paid every time someone inherits anything of substantial value. Later in this book we'll give you tips for minimizing taxes and using particular types of trusts, gifts, and other tax-eliminating strategies to reduce the value of an estate down to a value where taxes cannot take such a large bite.

Your Named Executor

When you set up your will or living trust, your named executor is the person who carries out your wishes. In a living trust, your successor trustee is your executor. He or she executes your wishes. The executor of your estate has the most important role in your life (and afterlife, so

There are two times to move money effectively to others: before you die and after you die. *Inter vivos* transfers are made while you are still alive; *testamentary* transfers are made after you die. These transfers can be made a number of ways: wills, gifts, trusts, and policy ownership under rights of survivorship. We will discuss each of these types of transfers throughout this book.

> Word to the wise: Well-crafted and clear living trusts and wills ensure that your wishes are carried out in a timely and successful manner. Disputes over ambiguity or unreasonable conditions can invite lawsuits that take a long time to resolve in the probate court. Similarly, an estate plan constructed too loosely or too rigidly can encourage unwise decisions among the people they're intended to benefit.

to speak!). The person you name as executor bears an enormous responsibility. He or she is responsible for carrying out your wishes—and the initiation, administration, and management of your estate until it is closed (your estate is closed when all of its debts have been paid and its assets have been distributed). This process can take anywhere from a few days to a few years, depending on the size and complexity of the estate.

Choosing a good executor is essential. Your executor could bear the following duties:

- Arranging for funeral services and burial
- Preparing an inventory of assets, investments, and debts (including pension assets, bank accounts, and insurance policies that name the estate as the beneficiary)
- Collecting legal documents (including wills, trusts, powers of attorney documents, bank account information, Social Security information, birth certificate, marriage license(s), citizenship papers, employee benefits, and recent tax returns)
- Determining the status of titles or deeds to property in the estate (did you own all you said you owned?)
- Making sure that all insurance policies are gathered and dealt with (notifying life insurance companies, keeping some premiums current in payment)
- Alerting your employer's benefits department and the Social Security Administration
- Contacting creditors and approving or disapproving their claims
- Collecting and arranging for payment of debts
- Making sure estate taxes are calculated, forms filed, and tax payments made
- Scheduling a reading of your will
- Filing for probate, if necessary

Your executor has a lot to do. A good executor needs to know the complete picture of what resources are flowing through which channels. He or she also has to be sure all debts are paid; distribute your personal possessions; collect and deposit any income that comes into your estate (example: from rents, licenses, partnerships); and determine the value of personal assets to be sold for the benefit of the estate. If you are an executor, you can hire assistants to help you with your duties.

In later chapters we'll give you more details on executors and provide tips for naming one in your official documents. The term executor can mean different things in different situations. Some wills give the executor broad discretion to make decisions that resolve conflicts or distribute assets; other wills make those decisions and only want the executor to fill out required documents. You will decide what role you want your executor to take.

Right of Survivorship

Survivorship is a buzzword in estate planning. You hear its root in obituaries: "He is survived by his wife, his four sons, and the family dog." Survivors are the people who outlive the deceased. If you survive the death of a loved one, you might assume you get something as a reward. The sense of entitlement people feel when someone close to them dies is a bit over-estimated. True, survivorship involves the passage of assets down to survivors of someone's death. But it's more complex than it appears.

Survivorship is a legal term that identifies who gets your assets at your death. It means that a person has the right to receive full title or ownership of an asset (including real estate) due to having survived you. Survivorship is particularly applied to people who own assets in joint tenancy, another buzzword in estate planning. Joint tenancy typically relates to the ownership of real property, which provides that each party owns an undivided interest in the entire parcel, with both having the right to use all of it, and the right of survivorship, which means that at the death of one joint tenant, the other has title to it all. The one who dies cannot leave his or her share to anyone but the joint tenant. The best example: You and your wife share joint tenancy in your home. When you die, your wife gets the home (your interest in the home passes automatically to her at your death). You cannot will your share of a joint tenancy property to someone else—other than your other joint tenant.

Procedurally, on the death of one joint tenant, title in the survivor is completed by recording an "affidavit of death of joint tenant," which describes the property and the deceased tenant and includes a death certificate—all of which is sworn to by the surviving joint tenant. When the second spouse dies, the estate must go through probate. As we'll see in a later chapter, holding the assets in an AB or C living trust can significantly reduce the amount of taxes owed and protect more money in the estate.

Rights of survivorship can make complicated money and estate issues simpler at the death of an individual. An automatic transfer of ownership from one party to another upon a death through survivorship laws can prevent having to go through the probate process. For example, in some states you can name your spouse or adult children as "joint tenants with right of survivorship" in the title to your home. When you die, the house passes to the co-owners (your spouse and children) easily, without going through probate. Survivorship rights can become muddied by complex families dynamics, however, such as multiple marriages and second wives who hold survivorship deeds, thus leaving out children from first marriages. We'll explore these issues and give you more information about the rules of survivorship throughout this book. Some of the complications become simplified through the creation of a living trust.

You may additionally want to set up a life estate for your spouse, which means you allow your spouse to continue living in the house for the rest of his or her life, but he or she cannot sell the home. At his or her death, the home goes to your children. You can do this through an AB living trust easily. (However, under certain circumstances the spouse may be able to sell such property. We will explore more about this later.)

How you decide to distribute your assets will depend on how many layers you have in your family. Have you been married once? Twice? Is your significant other not a legal spouse? Do you have children from more than one marriage? Dysfunctional heirs? Estranged relatives or siblings whose well-being you place second to close friends? As we said earlier, everyone's definition of family is different. Having a will or living trust allows you to define

NANCY'S STORY

It's hard to be the oldest child in the family. I have two younger sisters, and they always left the family planning up to me when it came to our parents. I lived in California, close to our parents, while they both lived in New York, which sometimes felt like the other side of the world. As our parents got older and needed more of my help and attention, I was there for them. I didn't mind caring for them and being available for them when my other sisters could not, but when our parents were killed in a freak car accident, everything changed.

I wasn't prepared for their untimely death. The grief was overwhelming, but dealing with the business end of their death made it even harder. I handled all of the initial arrangements (funeral, burial, and such) and my sisters were happy that I took on much of the responsibility. There was so much to do—organizing; arranging; notifying people; sorting through paperwork; getting the death certificates; calling the banks, postal service, and credit card companies; and searching for my parents' last will and testament.

One thing I deeply regret now: During all those years I spent time with my parents, I never had that talk with them about their financial affairs. They were in their late 60s when they died, and I had always assumed that they would live well into their 80s. I didn't know about a will or living trust, and neither of these things was ever found. Trouble started after the funeral. My parents had lived modestly, but they still had accumulated a decent amount of assets, including a home. My sisters and I argued over everything, and because there was no living trust, we had to go through probate. Selling the house and paying those taxes took two years, and I think my sisters thought I was somehow trying to cheat them out of their inheritance. One of my sisters (whose husband is a lawyer) even filed a petition demanding that I distribute her portion of the inheritance right away. If they only knew what I was going through! It was ridiculous, and there wasn't much I could do. I was at the mercy of the probate process and constantly dealing with more and more paperwork. The fees kept mounting.

When all was said and done, there wasn't much left for any of us to take. The probate process, administrative fees, taxes, and the lawyer bills zapped the value of the estate in a blink of an eye. It's been five years since the death of my parents. I barely talk to my sisters, and I have fears of another remaining fee or bill to come through to be paid. I don't want my children to have to go through this when I die. After things started to settle down, I did some research on wills and trusts. I learned that a revocable living trust eliminates the probate process. My husband didn't like talking about the possibility of one or both of our deaths, but after watching what I went through, he gladly filled out the forms and helped set up a living trust for our family. It was easy. As morbid as talking about death can be, it felt incredibly good to know that I've got my affairs in order should something happen to me and/or my husband. Our three children will be protected. We're not rich, and we don't have a ton of assets, but even a small amount is enough to protect. Once my husband and I created our living trust, I felt this great sense of relief. I looked at my daughters and thought, "If you only knew. . . ."

that word and have control over who gets what and when. Planning your will or setting up a living trust gets you thinking about your inner circle of family and friends, and how far out you want to distribute your assets to outer circles. Even if that means you leave everything (that you've secretly amassed over your lifetime) to a Hollywood actor whom you've never met. This actually happened, and the family left out of her fortune wasn't happy.

Conclusion

We've given you a lot to think about in this first chapter. We cannot talk about wills and living trusts without talking about death and the hereafter for your family, which is hard for many to consider. It's especially hard to plan for your death strategically when you're young (or young at heart), hard-working, productive, carry some debt, and worry more about immediate goals and problems than what lies way ahead of you at your deathbed. Building and keeping family money requires early planning, however. You may stress over paying tuition bills for your children or buying a first home after renting your entire life. The whole notion of a will or living trust just isn't on your radar. But the sooner you start thinking about wills and trusts, the more your family stands to gain in the long-run, for family money is the means of comfort, education, and freedom for you and the people who will come after you.

One important aspect to dying to keep in mind: Nothing can happen automatically at your death. You cannot assume that because you've told little Lisa that she gets your elaborate costume wardrobe, that she will get that easily and quickly. Lots of paperwork follows a death, and every transfer of assets from a dead person's estate to someone else—whether named or not by will or trust—must be accompanied by pieces of paper that follow certain laws. Wills and trusts are what help set up the paperwork and allow for this transfer.

The first step in planning your family's financial future is considering a will. Can you write it on a piece of toilet paper and hope that it passes muster in court? Can you speak your will into a recorder and hope that tapes are still readable when you die? How do wills work within a living trust?

We begin our journey by discussing wills in detail in the next chapter.

CHAPTER 2

Do I Need a Will?

A will is perhaps the most important document an average American will ever sign. It's hard to believe so few people write wills—only one-third of all Americans. The reasons are two-fold: People generally don't like thinking and planning for their death; and people simply don't know how to create a will. Those that write wills do so for a variety of reasons. Chief among these reasons: to prevent family conflicts from occurring once they die. You wouldn't want your family members to file lawsuits against each another and become estranged because of your death, so avoiding family disputes is a big reason to create wills, as well as trusts. (At least one-third of all wills are successfully contested by heirs, so while having the best written will won't prevent problems, it will decrease the likelihood of problems emerging.)

Another reason to create a will is that all of your assets will get distributed as you wish rather than according to your state's laws. Every adult who has assets—whether it's a home, a rocking chair, or a priceless art collection—should make out a will. And every parent with a child under the age of 18 should name a guardian for that child in a will. Creating a will is your opportunity to make your intentions clear and to keep important decisions in hand. Hence the word "will"—to will your decisions and intents into the future of your family for their benefit.

As we'll see in this chapter, wills are limited on many fronts, but they are the most common way people leave instructions for what to do when they die. No one is too young or too poor to write a will.

Next of Kin

The chart below (see Figure 2.1) shows you who gets your assets if you die and don't leave a will. Next of kin refers to your descendants by blood. Each state has its own rules for this procedure (called state intestacy laws), but this exemplifies what happens in most states. If there are no next of kin, the assets go to the state. Usually, somebody exists to accept the asset from an estate, even if it means contacting a far-off relative. States prioritize your relatives based on the assumed relationship you have with them; thus, a spouse is at the top of the list,

IF YOU DIE WITHOUT A WILL		
SURVIVOR(S)	COMMUNITY PROPERTY	SEPARATE PROPERTY
A spouse, no child, no parent, no brother, sister or child of brother or sister	all to spouse	all to spouse
Spouse and one child, or child of a deceased child	all to spouse	½ to spouse; ½ to only child
Spouse and more than one child, or one child and child of one or more deceased children	all to spouse	⅓ to spouse and ⅔rds to children
Spouse and no children or their child but a parent or parents	all to spouse	½ to spouse and ½ to parent(s)
Spouse, no children or their child, no parent, but brothers and/or sisters or child of deceased brothers and/or sisters	all to spouse	½ to spouse and ½ to brothers and/or sisters
No spouse but child	N/A	all to children
No spouse, no surviving child, but parent or parents	N/A	all to parent(s)
No spouse, no surviving child, no parent, but child of parents (brothers/sisters of decedent, or their child if they are deceased)	N/A	all to brothers and sisters
No spouse, no surviving child, no parent, no brother or sister or their child, but one or more grandparents or child of grandparents	N/A	all to grandparents or their surviving children, and predeceased spouse's next of kin
No spouse, no child, no parent or child of grandparent, but a spouse who died previously and has a surviving child or children	N/A	to children of predeceased spouse

Figure 2.1

and children will come before any siblings, parents, or distant cousins. We created a simpli-fied, cartoonish version of the chart that also shows how states divvy up your assets at your death when given no direction. (See Figure 2.2.) As you can see, an estate flows downward—to children and grandchildren first. Your siblings and parents are lower priority on the list.

If a married couple holds joint title to assets, those assets pass automatically to the surviv-ing spouse. But, if your spouse dies without a will, his or her individually-owned assets are subject to state intestacy laws. Depending on which state you live in, these laws normally divide the estate between a spouse and any children, using a predetermined percentage based on the number of children and martial status.

States may vary on their rules of intestacy, but they all have one common thread: They favor blood relatives and do not make room for leaving assets to a best friend, a confidant, or a long-lost lover. States also vary on rules of domestic partners. In California, for exam-ple, a domestic partner registered with the state can share the same rights to inheritance as a bona fide spouse. But domestic partner laws are subject to change, as this is an evolving

INTERSTATE SUCCESSION - WHO'S NEXT

⊚ DECEDENT
⊚ SPOUSE
⊚⊚⊚ KIDS
⊚⊚ PARENTS
⊚⊚⊚ BROTHERS/SISTERS

A spouse and children are the first to inherit
assets from a deceased person.
If there is no surviving spouse and there are no children,
then those assets typically get passed to the decedent's
parents, siblings, and grandparents—in that order.
Other relatives, such as cousins, nieces, and nephews
are less likely to inherit anything, unless there are no
immediate family members. Refer to your state's specific
laws of intestasy to find out more about how your state
deals with the distribution of assets among family members.
When the decedent didn't leave a will, certain exceptions to
the above depiction may apply.

Figure 2.2

In the eyes of the courts, inheritance typically flows downward—not sideways—with regard to family. So children would receive an inheritance before a sibling, parent, cousin, or nephew. If the deceased has no spouse or children, then the intestacy laws typically divide the assets among other relatives—and even the state.

field of law across the nation. Domestic partner laws are not common across the United States. If you wonder how domestic partner laws in your state work—or if there are any—you should do some research. To that end, if you are in a nontraditional relationship (that is, your partner is not your legal spouse), you have more reason to create a will or living trust to make sure your partner is not left out when it comes time to distribute your assets.

If you want to leave all of your assets to a friend and give nothing to your children, you need a will to specifically say so; otherwise, the state will pass your possessions down to your children. (However, if you do leave everything to someone other than your spouse or children in your will, your survivors will raise their discontent in probate and may have a legal right to a share of your estate under something called family protection allowances. All states have a minimum family protection allowance that guarantees the spouse and dependent children receive at least some funds for support from the estate—even if they weren't named as designated beneficiaries. We'll discuss what this means in Chapter 7.)

General Parts to a Will

You want your will to stand up in court and be clear and concise about your wishes. True, some people write wills down on scrap paper and some courts recognize the scrap as a formal will. But the more you have to leave to family and friends, the more you should formalize your will by using certain language and by having it typed and witnessed properly. Wills can vary, but most generally include the following elements:

- Your full name and city or county
- The date
- A declaration that the document is a will
- The names of your executor and alternate executor
- The names of guardians and successor guardians for children or disabled people in your care
- Bequests ("I give my goldfish to Mary Jane"; "I give 20 percent of my estate to the March of Dimes")
- Where you want to have your funeral, burial, cremation, and so on—or whether you don't want these ceremonies at all
- Your signature in the presence of at least two witnesses and their names and places of residence. In some states, you may need a notary

Some people do not prefer to list assets and, instead, speak in general terms about their assets and to whom they go. You can be more specific and personal in a Letter of Instruction (see "Letter of Instruction" below). In your will, if you do not leave everything to one person (such as your spouse or a child), you should allow your estate (in percentages of your total assets) to direct the distribution of your assets. For example: "I give . . . my entire estate . . . at my death 30 percent to my mother, Judith Strong; 25 percent to my nephew, Zachary Strong; 25 percent to my nephew, Jacob Strong; and 20 percent to my friend, William Kappenhagen." Wills are not difficult to create; they are more difficult to think about because of what they imply: that you will die someday.

A Will's Introduction

The sample will in this chapter (see Figure 2.3) is a basic will: Mr. Brown wants his estate to go to his wife, Caroline, and if his wife is already dead, then his daughter gets his stuff. If both his wife and daughter predecease him, Sandra Smythe is an alternate beneficiary. Each article (specific section) clearly lays out his intentions.

Being of Lawful Age. An individual of lawful age is 18 years or older. An individual under the age of 18 cannot write a legal will. Any minors who have accumulated sizeable assets (such as pop music stars and actors) must have their parents or named guardians manage their estates until they reach legal age.

Being of Sound Mind and Memory. This phrase means you know what you are doing when you create your will. Many wills face challenges in the court when family members who are upset about what they did—or, more likely, did not—get as a result of your death try to prove you were not of sound mind and memory when you made your will. A person of sound mind and memory understands that he or she has four children and six grandchildren, for example, and understands clearly who is getting the assets after his or her death. Although descendants would naturally be the people to whom a person would leave an estate, that's not a requirement!

You are not required to be smart, wise, reasonable, or fair in your will. You only have to know what you are doing. The law will respect your wishes so long as any lawful claims (example: debts and taxes) get paid and any rights to your surviving spouse are met. Courts do not easily accept claims that you were mentally-impaired or under restraint when you wrote your will. Wills that get thrown out become invalid, and your estate is handled as if you had never written a will.

Under No Restraint. No one put a gun to your head or forced you to write your will a certain way. Another phrase that means the same as "under no restraint" is "under no undue influence or duress."

Revoke All Other Wills and Codicils. Creating this will automatically cancel any previously composed wills and codicils. (A codicil is an amendment or change to a will. More on those below.)

Assets and Obligations to Think About

Before making your will, you should think about your assets and liabilities, even if you are not going to specifically list them out. Taking inventory of what you own gets you thinking about your estate and what you need to consider when you're dividing up your assets among your beneficiaries (unless you are leaving everything to one person).

LAST WILL AND TESTAMENT
OF
GREGORY BROWN

I, GREGORY BROWN, of San Luis Obispo County, being of lawful age, sound mind and memory, and under no restraint, do publish this, my Last Will and Testament, and revoke all other wills and codicils heretofore made by me.

I am married to CAROLINE BROWN. I am the father of CORY BROWN.

ARTICLE 1

1.01   All expenses, fees, costs, and taxes related to this estate shall be paid from the probate estate assets, and all gifts and bequests shall be paid from the net distributable estate.

ARTICLE 2

2.01   I give, devise, and bequeath my entire estate, real or personal, or mixed, of every kind and nature, and wherever situated, which I may own or hereafter acquire or have a right to dispose of at my death to my wife, CAROLINE BROWN.

2.02 If CAROLINE BROWN predeceases me, I give, devise, and bequeath my entire estate, real or personal or mixed, of every kind and nature, and wherever situated, which I may own or hereafter acquire or have a right to dispose of at my death to my daughter, CORY BROWN. If CAROLINE BROWN and CORY BROWN both predecease me, I give, devise, and bequeath my entire estate to SANDRA SMYTHE.

ARTICLE 3

3.01   I nominate and appoint my wife, CAROLINE BROWN, to be the Executrix of this my Last Will and Testament, granting unto her full power and authority to sell and convey any or all of my estate, real and personal, or mixed, upon such terms and prices as she may deem proper, without obtaining any prior order of the court. I also grant her full power and authority in the settlement of my estate, to compromise,

Page 1 of 2   ____GB

Figure 2.3a

adjust, and settle any and all debts and liabilities due to or from my estate, for such sums, and upon such terms and conditions as she shall deem best.

3.02   In the event that CAROLINE BROWN shall for any reason decline to serve, or fail to qualify for any reason, or having qualified and been appointed, fail to complete the administration of my estate, then I nominate my daughter, CORY BROWN, to be the Alternate or Successor Executor.

3.03   I direct that no bond or surety shall be required of any Executor named herein. If any beneficiary in any manner, directly or indirectly, contests or attacks this instrument or any of its provisions, any share or interest given to that contesting beneficiary under this instrument is revoked, and shall be disposed of in the same manner provided herein, as if that contesting beneficiary had predeceased me.

IN WITNESS WHEREOF, I have hereunto subscribed my name, and acknowledge and publish this instrument as my Last Will and Testament, consisting of two pages including this page in the presence of the undersigned witnesses, on _____, 2005.

_____
GREGORY BROWN

We hereby certify that the above named GREGORY BROWN subscribed his name thereto this day in our presence, and to us declared the same to be his Last Will and Testament, and that we subscribe our names hereto as witnesses, at his request, and in his presence, and that at the time of the signing, that he was of sound and disposing mind and not under any restraint, to the best of our knowledge and belief. We declare under penalty of perjury that the foregoing is true.

WITNESS our hand and signature in San Luis Obispo, California, on _____, 2005.

Witness signature_____
Print name_____
Residing at _____
_____

Witness signature_____
Print name_____
Residing at _____
_____

Page 2 of 2

Figure 2.3b

The following is a personal inventory checklist to use prior to writing your will.

Total Assets (what you own)

Basic bank accounts (checking and savings)

Money market accounts

Certificates of Deposit

Treasury bills or notes

Safety deposit boxes

Retirement accounts

Brokerage accounts (stocks and bonds)

Government bonds and securities

Insurance policies, including life insurance proceeds

Real estate

Automobiles, boats, airplanes, other recreational vehicles

Household items, jewelry, clothing (that mink coat)

Artwork, antiques, and collectibles

Tools and equipment

Valuable animals or livestock

Money owed you

Other investments or valuable property

Total Liabilities (what you owe)

Mortgage or home equity loans

Credit card balances

Auto leases/loans

Tax obligations

Other personal loans or debts

Don't worry about coming up with exact or even approximate values to the above items. The goal of this exercise is to realize what you own and what you still owe. If you are young, you are still building your estate, so you may not have some of these items; if, on the other hand, you are older or have retired, you probably have amassed many of these items.

Reciprocal Wills

Married couples use reciprocal wills (separate wills that leave their assets to each other) to ensure that assets from one spouse who dies transfer easily to the surviving spouse. Whether married or not, each partner writes a separate will that is the mirror image of the other's will. It is best to have separate wills that make reference to each other but are not part of the same, or joint, will. Your specific state may have rules for reciprocal wills, such as whether any changes you make to the wills can only be done to one of the wills.

A Word About Unmarried Domestic Partners

Unless you are in a common law marriage (which is a legal recognition of marriage in some states if you have been living together for a certain period of time and intend to be husband and wife), unmarried couples have no automatic legal right to inherit any of each other's assets. However, some states have passed domestic partner laws that can allow gay and lesbian couples to register with the state for these rights. (Note that the passage of these laws is a hotly contested issue and may change.) If you are in a relationship that your state may not recognize as legal for purposes of benefits and rights of survivorship or inheritance (or you worry that your state may recognize your relationship today and not tomorrow), a will or a living trust that spells out your exact wishes can avoid the problems you face trying to leave your estate to your partner. For example, domestic partners who do not have wills or living trusts but have children from other marriages can encounter many problems in the probate court when one dies and the other tries to claim survivorship rights to the deceased's property. The probate court may rule that the assets must go the children, leaving nothing for the surviving domestic partner—especially if the children present lawsuits. Moreover, if you wish to disinherit any blood relatives at your death and leave assets to someone other than a family member—who may or may not be a legal spouse—this is reason enough to create a valid will or living trust. If you create a valid will or living trust, you generally can leave whatever you want to whomever you want.

How do reciprocal wills handle the order of death? Usually, people phrase it this way: "If I die first, everything goes to my spouse. If my spouse has already died, everything goes to my descendants, in equal shares, *per stirpes.*" *Per stirpes* is Latin for "by roots or stock," or "by representation." Put simply, if a child dies before the parent, that deceased child's *children* split the share that would have gone to their parent. Another way to understand it: Substitute *per stirpes* with ". . . to his or her children, by right of representation, share and share alike." Including *per stirpes* language in your will ensures that your assets continue to get distributed downward.

What if a couple with reciprocal wills dies at the same time? If a couple dies together in a car or plane crash, for example, what happens? This can create problems. Wills usually include language to deal with such a situation, called a common disaster or simultaneous death clause. Such language can be: "All of my property goes to my spouse, if he/she survives me by at least 30 days." There is nothing special about the 30 days, but the period should be less than six months. If it is longer, the tax-free status of the property transfer to the surviving spouse could be lost.

Complications revolving around who died first when a couple dies in the same accident or event can create problems of a technical nature. The executor of the husband's will finds that the wife did not survive for 30 days after her husband's death, so she inherits nothing. The husband's estate is divided among *his* children, some of which could be from a previous marriage. They pay inheritance tax. On the flip side of the coin, the executor of the wife's will finds that the husband did not survive for 30 days after his wife's death, so he inherits nothing. The wife's estate is divided among *her* children, some of which could be from a previous marriage. If a couple has the same, and only the same, children, this language doesn't matter because the assets eventually get passed down to the children. But, if one or both of the spouses have children from a previous marriage, managing their wills gets tricky.

When children from a previous marriage are involved, a husband's and wife's reciprocal wills are not true mirror images to one another. Each will has a parallel section that articulates the differences. Each spouse has probably brought individual (separate) property into the marriage. And each might want the current spouse to have use of that separate property, too—if the current spouse survives. If the current spouse is already dead, though, each parent might wish to leave that separate property only to his or her previous children. The section of the will that lists separate property and attaches an alternate beneficiary to that asset or assets solves this problem.

Most states have adopted the Uniform Simultaneous Death Act to avoid the "who died first?" question when considering where the assets go. The law dictates the order of death when parents die together. It is used only when the spouses' wills say nothing about who survived whom—or if there are no wills at all.

You can include such clauses in your will. Example: "If we die together, and the order of our death cannot be determined, my wife [or my husband] is presumed to have survived me." This may sound crazy to articulate, but in some tax situations it's a good idea. Assets must be left to the surviving spouse in order to take the unlimited martial deductions for calculating federal estate taxes. We will go into tax details in Chapter 6. Suffice it to say, incorporating simultaneous death clauses into your documents ensures a quicker passage of assets to beneficiaries if you die together with your spouse. Simultaneous death clauses remove an administrative step that could prolong the distribution of assets to a couple's final beneficiaries.

What You Need to Write a Will

Names and addresses are what you primarily need when preparing your will. Besides your own name and place of residence, your will includes the following:

- The names and addresses of everyone named in the will (including your executor, beneficiaries, and any guardian or custodian for your children), even if some are not getting anything
- The names and addresses of children left out of the will
- Your marital status
- Deceased children and/or children of deceased children
- How you intend to distribute your estate, whether you make special gifts ("Connie gets my grand piano") or refer to the residue of your estate ("Billy gets 25 percent of my estate")

The residue of your estate is what's left after taxes and debts or obligations are paid, and any other specific bequests have been made. For example, if you give your stamp collection to Sammy, but you make no other specific bequests, the remainder of your assets comprises the residue of your estate.

You can indicate which people are minors and which people are adults (of legal age) in your will, and you must have two different people named as witnesses to your signing. Your witnesses' names, addresses, and places of residence are also indicated. Having witnesses to your will makes your will an attested will.

A self-proven will takes an attested will one step further. In addition to having two witnesses, you and the witnesses sign an affidavit that becomes attached to your will. That affidavit "proves up the will." When your will reaches the probate court, the affidavit is used to prove all of the necessary execution requirements. This eliminates the need to find the witnesses and to bring them to court unless there is a challenge to the will. Even if the witnesses are dead, the will can be proved up without much ado.

> States vary as to how they like to see wills and what makes a will proved. In California, for example, two witnesses must sign under penalty of perjury, but no notary is required. Other states may not require wills to be notarized or signed under penalty of perjury. In Vermont, you need to get at least three credible witnesses, but no notary. In Louisiana or Iowa, a witness can be 16 years old. Because each state has its own rules for proving a will, you should find out the rules in your specific state and follow them as best you can.

If a will is not self-proved, there can be substantial expense—and delay—in locating the witnesses to attest that they, in fact, did sign the will. If they cannot be found, or if they are dead, then alternate procedures must be used to prove up the will and get it admitted to probate.

Use the sample will in this chapter to draft your own version. Choose competent, clear-headed adults to witness your will signing. They must be 18 years of age or older; should not be a recipient of any of your assets (although some states do allow a witness to inherit property); and should be easy to locate when you die. Your witnesses are witnessing the signing of your will, but they don't need to have read it or know exactly what's in it. Your witnesses must assemble in one place—you cannot have each one sign on a different day.

Use plain, 8½" × 11" paper. Neatly word process it using an easy-to-read professional font, such as Times New Roman or Courier, 12-point, and avoid fancy formatting and styling (no pie graphs, charts, boxes, or borders). You can also type your will the old-fashioned way with a typewriter if you choose. Your will should appear clean, professional, tidy, and most of all, cogent. You can use all capital letters and bold-faced type when designating people in your will. Create a simple title page or cover for your will that states what the document contains. Example: Centered in the middle of Gregory Brown's cover sheet it reads: Last Will and Testament of Gregory Brown. Staple the cover sheet to the will.

If you find errors or typos after you've completed it, redo it by reprinting or by retyping the document. Never make handwritten changes to your will, even if you initial them. If you need to make changes to your will, rewrite your will and get it witnessed again.

Find a safe place to keep your will, such as in a desk where you keep other important documents or in a fireproof box at home. Make a copy of your will and give one to your executor if you want. The person responsible for carrying out your wishes in your will should also know where to find your original document. He or she may find your Letter of Instruction first, which provides more logistical and practical details that must be handled immediately at your death.

Codicils and Updates

Keep your will current by making the necessary changes as time goes on and circumstances change. You may, for example, name someone in your will who dies before you do. If you have not named an alternate beneficiary, which is someone who takes the place of another named beneficiary in such a situation, then you should create a codicil, an amendment, or change, to your will that specifically spells out the change.

A sample codicil is on the next page. (See Figure 2.4.) Use this sample codicil as a template for drafting any codicils you may need to create. As you can see, codicils clearly state the following:

- Your name, the date, place of residence
- Referral to your previously-composed will and its signing date
- The exact article you are changing
- The change you are making, including everyone affected by the change
- Your signature
- The signature of two witnesses and/or notary if required in your state, with their addresses included.

Codicils are best used to address legal technicalities or typographical errors in the original document. Any substantive changes, such as the addition or deletion of beneficiaries, would best be done by drafting a whole new document. Because wills are relatively easy to create and less extensive than trusts, drafting another will that inherently revokes previously created wills is the better option to creating multiple codicils.

If you are young and are creating a will, you likely will have to create a new will in the future as changes to your estate occur. Young people continue to build their estates over time, and their relationships change with the birth of children, the death of family members, and other events that change the circumstances of their lives. If you move to another state, your will remains valid and your new state will recognize it, as long as it meets that state's minimum requirements. You should make the proper changes to your will that reflect your new state's requirements or laws. It's best to comply with your new state's rules and preferences so your executor can carry out your wishes more easily.

When you create your will, you do so with the knowledge and estate you have today. But because circumstances change over time, keeping your will up-to-date and aligned with those circumstances makes your will stronger and more enforceable once you die. On the other hand, if you are older and have acquired most of your estate already, you may not need to make many amendments or overhauls to your will in the future. No matter your age, make a practice of revisiting your will occasionally to confirm that you are still happy with it and that it reflects your current wishes. You may want to check your will once a year at a time you do other annual routines, such as paying your taxes.

Prevent the need for codicils by making sure your will is clean and error-free when you first sign it. It's foolish to use codicils to correct editing mistakes. You want your will to stand alone, so read it thoroughly before signing.

If you find that your will is not up to par with your current situation, you can do something about it. Don't file your will away and let it go unchecked for 20 years! (It will definitely be out of style by then in the sense that it won't be in

CODICIL TO THE WILL
OF
DEBRA CLOSE

I, DEBRA CLOSE, a resident of Santa Barbara County, California declare this to be the first codicil to my will dated December 1, 1988.

It is my wish that Article 3 be amended to delete THELMA JONES as Alternate Personal Representative and substitute in her place and stead JOYCE J. JOHNSON.

In all other respects I confirm and republish my Will dated December 1, 1988.

I subscribe my name to this codicil this _____ day of _____2004, at Santa Barbara, California and do hereby declare that I sign and execute this codicil willingly, that I execute it as my free and voluntary act for the purposes therein expressed and that I am of the age of majority or otherwise legally empowered to make a codicil and under no constraint or undue influence.

_____
DEBRA CLOSE

On this _____ day of _____, 2004, declared to us, the undersigned, that this instrument was the codicil to the Will dated December 1, 1988 and requested us to act as witnesses to it. DEBRA CLOSE thereupon signed this codicil in our presence, all of us being present at the same time. We now, at Santa Barbara, California, request, in the presence of each other and in the presence of DEBRA CLOSE, subscribe our names as witnesses and declare we understand this to be DEBRA CLOSE's codicil and that to the best of our knowledge DEBRA CLOSE is of the age of majority, or is otherwise legally empowered to make a codicil and is under no constraint or undue influence.

We declare under penalty of perjury that the foregoing is true and correct, this _____ day of _____, 2004 at Santa Barbara, California.

Witness _____
Residing at _____
_____

Witness _____
Residing at _____
_____

Figure 2.4

synch with your life anymore nor your assets and wishes.) A person can write three or four wills over again in the course of a lifetime. The wills that get contested successfully are typically the ones authored a long time ago—the ones the will-writer never went back to review and update.

Sidenote: Similar to the cover sheet or title page you created for your will, do the same for your codicil, stapling it all together.

Holographic Wills

Holographic wills are unwitnessed, handwritten wills that make movies and mystery novels more exciting. They are valid documents, but contrary to popular belief, they are not accepted as legal documents in many states. This is because they were not witnessed by competent people who can testify that the will—including the signature and date—was written entirely in the handwriting of the person whose will it purports to be. So while courts can approve and execute a holographic will's instructions, holographic wills can easily be contested and voided as well. Here's a good example:

In 1997, a Kentucky woman died and caused quite a stir when her family realized she had left everything to the actor Charles Bronson, whom she'd never met. In a handwritten will dated April 1996, Audrey Joan Knauer wrote her wishes on a list of emergency phone numbers to leave all her money to the "talented character actor" and added that if Bronson didn't want the money, it would go to the Louisville Free Public Library. At first, the family wasn't too concerned because they didn't think Audrey had much money by the time she died (in fact, they assumed she was broke). But when the family discovered that $300,000 remained after taxes and legal fees had been paid, the family didn't want that money to go to Mr. Bronson. Finding another clause in her will must also have stirred ill will: "Under no circumstances is my mother, Helen, to inherit anything from me—blood, body parts, financial assets."

This case went through probate, and the woman's sister filed a lawsuit claiming that Audrey was not of sound mind at the time she wrote her will. The sister wanted the will declared illegal and the money distributed to the family. In the end, the lawsuit was settled out of court and Bronson agreed to pay the sister an undisclosed sum. The library got nothing. This story illustrates how families can easily contest holographic wills, and the will-writer is no longer available to provide a defense or explanation. For Audrey Knauer, maybe Mr. Bronson meant more to her than her own family members, and thus she should have been able to leave whatever she had accumulated to whomever she liked. But her handwritten will wasn't enough to ensure that transfer. Her wishes were too quirky for her will to uphold.

When you think of holographic wills, you imagine relatives visiting a dying, old—but incredibly wealthy—man on his deathbed, trying to get him to write down his wishes in a last ditch effort to secure their inheritance before he goes. Does this work? Sometimes, but the courts scrutinize any such effort with skeptical eyes, just as the court did in the Bronson case. Audrey's sister could have disputed the will even if were a typed, signed, and witnessed will (thus, not holographic). But the mere fact the will was holographic made it even easier to contest.

To make a holographic will, you still need to meet two criteria: You must be of sound mind at the time you create your holographic will (otherwise known as having testamentary capacity); and you must be executing your holographic will out of your own free will—and not under any restraint or duress to do so (hence, the deathbed holographic will-making with

---

Questions to Ask Yourself

- Does my will include everyone I wish to cover?
- Is my will current, or does it need an update to reflect births, deaths, changes in tax laws, and changes in my state of residence?
- Does my will address any bequests (gifts) I wish to make, especially bequests that involve personal assets that have sentimental value? What about charitable bequests?
- Does my will take into account items that will pass outside of my will, such as insurance policies and retirement plans?
- Does my will make plans for my children's future in the event I die before they reach legal age (18)?

---

your greedy heirs forcing you to make specific bequests to them won't work). Use plain paper. The clearer and more reasonable your handwritten will is, the greater chance you have that it will work.

Bottom line: Avoid holographic wills, and for that matter, nuncupative wills, which are oral (spoken) deathbed wills. If you can create a typed, formal will and meet your state's requirement for getting it signed, witnessed, and possibly notarized, you minimize the chance of someone challenging your will.

Letter of Instruction

A letter of instruction is a bit different from a will, and you should think about writing one to accompany your formal will (you keep it separately, however, from your official will). Sometimes, letters of instruction are found sooner than wills, as they contain time-sensitive information. A letter of instruction is where you can make specific instructions as to the disposition of your body and whether you want to donate any of your body parts to medicine or a donor program. Because a letter of instruction is not technically a legal document, whereas a will goes through probate, this letter can remain private. You allow your named executor to have access to this letter of instruction so he or she can execute your wishes as soon as possible.

Instead of including your assets and liabilities in your will, you list them in your letter of instruction, specifying their location and identifying their form of ownership (solely, jointly, in a trust, or payable to a beneficiary). Your executor will need this information in order to settle your estate. Include all types of other information that will be helpful to survivors, such as computer passwords, where keys and important papers are hidden, the contact information for the gardener, the plumber, the mechanic, and so on. The letter may also contain any personal messages that are not appropriate to include in a will. (Remember: Your will, once filed in probate court, becomes a public document, accessible to anyone.) In addition to funeral arrangements, the letter sometimes expresses wishes, such as how to divide personal property—clothes, plants, photos, pets, birds, and odds and ends—that are not included in the will. Big-ticket items—such as real estate, jewelry, stocks, and bonds—are part of the estate and subject to probate if not held jointly.

After you write your letter of instruction, give copies to the individuals you intend to take care of your wishes at your death, namely your executor and substitute executor. Keep your original in a safe place, and tell your executor where it's located (example: desk, fireproof box in your den, behind the living room wall art in a hidden safe, etc.). It's best to avoid safety deposit boxes for letters of instruction, as such boxes can take time for family members to access after your death. This is why wills and letters of instruction are not always located in the same place. You may want to lock your will in a desk, but have your letter of instruction more readily available (not locked up).

Because a letter of instruction is not a legally enforceable document, it can be in almost any format, from an informal letter to a computer disk. We reiterate: It should be immediately accessible to the executor after the death. That's the most important part.

The following is a checklist of items to include in your letter of instruction:

Letter of Instruction Checklist

- ☑ Full legal name
- ☑ Maiden name
- ☑ Date of birth
- ☑ Place of birth
- ☑ Citizenship
- ☑ Social Security number
- ☑ Military service information (dates of services, rank and service number, branch of service, location of discharge papers)
- ☑ Marital status
- ☑ Name of spouse/partner, address, and phone number
- ☑ Names, addresses, and phone numbers of children and dependents
- ☑ Names (including father's legal name and mother's maiden name) and birthplaces of parents; if living, their addresses and phone numbers
- ☑ Names, addresses, and phone numbers of brothers and sisters
- ☑ Names, addresses, and phone numbers of former spouses
- ☑ Names, addresses, and phone numbers of friends, employers, business associates, and others to be contacted
- ☑ Advanced directives: health care proxy or medical power of attorney, living will
- ☑ Organ/tissue or body donation information
- ☑ Names, addresses, and phone numbers of doctors
- ☑ Religious affiliation
- ☑ Designated agent for body disposition (funeral home or other)
- ☑ Type of disposition desired (body donation, cremation, burial)
- ☑ Type of funeral or memorial service (if any)
- ☑ Hymns/readings for service
- ☑ Where to make donations in his or her name

☑ Names of pall bearers (if any)

☑ Location of will

☑ Name and phone number of attorney and/or executor

☑ Location of keys to any safe deposit boxes and address of bank

☑ Location and account numbers for all checking and savings accounts

☑ Location of checkbooks, stock certificates, bonds, trusts

☑ Location of all credit cards

☑ Location of all insurance policies, policy numbers

☑ Location of property titles, deeds, leases, real estate

☑ Location of tax returns

☑ Name and phone number of accountant

☑ Debts owed to others

☑ Debts owed to deceased

☑ Memberships in professional, fraternal, social, and volunteer organizations

☑ High schools and colleges attended (dates and location)

☑ Where to run obituary

Other useful contacts to include in the letter of instruction include the following:

- Therapist
- Electric company
- Heating fuel company
- Telephone company/cell phone service
- Gardener
- Housekeeper
- Veterinarian

As you can tell, letters of instruction are much more elaborate than wills. They contain the personal information that your named executor needs to know in order to execute your wishes and submit your will to probate in a timely manner, if necessary. You can change a letter of instruction quickly and easily and whenever you want without the hassles of formalizing the letter with witnesses and signatures. Unlike a will that requires a codicil to make changes, the letter of instruction is an extremely flexible and multi-layered document; you can revisit it daily if you want. Because there are no requirements to this letter, you can choose how detailed you want to make it, and what kind of information you want to include.

As an informal document, a letter of instruction has no legal constraints in form or content. Your survivors are not legally bound to follow the instructions it contains, but they

> Your will is a legal document that may list money, property, and possessions that you want to bequeath to others. Your will should not list everything you own because it will need to be amended each time you buy, sell, or give away any assets listed. The letter of instruction is not a legal document but more like a map for those who may be left by your illness or death to navigate through your life.

will have something to guide them through tough (and some easy) decisions to make at your death. Finally, a letter of instruction does not become part of public record, so this is also the place where you can include any personal statements to family members or friends. You can tell people anything and everything about you, your possessions, and your life.

Community Property

You hear about community property a lot when it comes to estate planning. Community property is a form of asset ownership between a husband and wife. Under this form of ownership, all assets acquired prior to marriage and assets that one spouse receives either by gift of inheritance during the marriage are separate property. All other assets acquired during the marriage are community property. Each spouse owns one-half interest in the community property assets. Example: A married couple buys a home together; the husband is the breadwinner and pays the mortgage while the woman is a stay-at-home mom. If they live in a community property state, the wife still owns one-half of that home—regardless of the her husband's responsibility for paying the bills. The community property states are: Arizona, California, Idaho, Louisiana, Nevada, New Mexico, Texas, Washington, and Wisconsin. Alaska has an optional community property system.

Specific community property laws differ greatly among these states, but they all share one defining feature: Irrespective of the names on title documents, ownership of all assets acquired during the marriage are split equally. Each spouse is free to do whatever he or she wishes with his or her half of the community property in a will. This also means that one spouse's half of the assets would not pass automatically to the survivor, as they would if owned jointly with right of survivorship. However, there are many tax advantages to owning community property as opposed to owning property in joint tenancy. And in some states, you can own community property with right of survivorship, so at the death of one spouse, the surviving spouse automatically gets the other half of the community property. Married couples can also create agreements that create this designation.

For example, a married couple can use a community property agreement to ensure complete forgiveness of capital gains tax at the death of one spouse. So, if you have your community property in a living trust and leave your half of the property to your surviving spouse, your family can avoid probate and may avoid some costly taxes. We'll see how this works in upcoming chapters. How you can plan your estate around these tax advantages can get complicated, but we'll show you the basics of how it works and how you can deal with your assets appropriately in your living trust.

Because of the difference between holding property in joint tenancy versus community property can be great—especially with regard to taxes—you should consider seeking the advice of an accountant or financial planner who is knowledgeable about the tax advantages of a living trust. Moreover, how your state treats marital property can play a big role in how you can distribute your assets. People who move from non-community property states to community property states—or vice versa—may find that their assets get re-classified as a different kind of ownership. How you own property, either separate or as community, is not always obvious. If you and your spouse (or someone with whom you share property) have any doubts about how you own property and any possible restrictions placed on willing away your share of the property, it's wise to consult with someone knowledgeable about your state's laws and the kinds of property you own. How you hold title becomes even more important when it comes to living trusts. You need to know what property is owned by each person and what property is held in shared ownership. This affects how you can transfer your property into a living trust (more on this in the next chapter).

The Limitations of a Will

We've already said that wills do not avoid probate. But there are many other issues related to wills of which you should be aware. Wills have limits to what they can do, and what they can control.

First, assets that pass through your will are collectively called probate property, referring to the probate process that carries out the terms of your will. But you may have other types of legal contracts or documents that must be taken care of at your death that do not relate to your will. They are described below.

Life Insurance Proceeds. Proceeds from any life insurance policy go directly to the beneficiary named on the policy—without passing through your will. This person who receives the proceeds does not have to pay taxes on them, but if you own and control the life insurance policy, the proceeds are part of your estate and may be subject to tax. Moving life insurance proceeds out of your taxable estate is key.

Because of the unlimited marriage deduction (to be discussed in Chapter 6), payments to your spouse incur no liabilities (such as taxes). However, for payments to your children or others, you will want to

- Have someone else buy and own the policy on your life; or
- Irrevocably transfer the policy to a life insurance trust at least three years before you die and name someone you have faith in—either an adult family member, friend, or an institution—to serve as trustee.

These tactics prevent your family members from paying estate taxes on your policy's proceeds (particularly if those proceeds are high at your death). Life insurance trusts are legal entities that you create for the purposes of owning life insurance. It's an irrevocable trust that reduces death taxes, especially federal estate taxes. If you don't want someone else owning your life insurance policy, you create this kind of trust and specify that the trust remains in effect during your life. After you transfer the policy to the trust, you cannot change the beneficiary or borrow money from your policy (more on buying life insurance on page 44).

Retirement Plans. Proceeds from retirement plans, such as SEPs, IRAs, 401(k)s, pensions and profit-sharing plans also pass directly to the beneficiary. However, those assets are subject to estate and federal income tax (although you get deductions for estate taxes paid), in a manner similar to life insurance proceeds. You may also be subject to a large tax if you have a large estate.

Assets Owned in Joint Tenancy. Assets owned by you and someone else, such as houses, bank accounts, and brokerage accounts, can be held in joint tenancy with right of survivorship, which means that if one of you dies, the other person has legal rights to the assets. If your spouse is the surviving person, usually half of the value of the asset is taxed in your

> The largest limitation of a will is that it cannot avoid probate. Anyone who owns anything of value and has a spouse and/or children should consider a living trust.

estate. If it's someone else, such as your adult child, the IRS will look to who actually paid for the assets and decide who will pay. As we've mentioned previously, the community property versus joint tenancy issue is a complex and important topic that we will discuss in Chapters 3 and 6.

Note that owning anything with your adult children in joint tenancy is generally a bad way to avoid taxes. While joint tenancy avoids probate on the first death of a married couple, it does not avoid probate on the second death or on a simultaneous death. After a first death, using joint tenancy with your adult children can lead to unwanted results, such as having to split the value of your house with your child's ex-spouse on your child's divorce, having to sell your house to pay your child's creditors after a car accident, or having to deal with your child's gift tax problems when he or she gives part of the house to his or her siblings after your death. Before putting any property in an adult child's name, we suggest that you speak with a tax professional first who can tell you want you can expect and warn you about any potential consequences as a result of this kind of ownership.

Buying Life Insurance

A discussion about estate planning without a mention about life insurance would be missing an important piece of information. People buy life insurance for the same reason they plan their estates: to protect certain things in the event of their death. Life insurance is a great way to help pay for some of the death-related expenses, such as funeral and burial, or to help the surviving spouse pay for raising children, sending them to school, or to pass proceeds directly to beneficiaries without having to go through probate (unless you have designated your own estate or its personal representative as the beneficiary).

An insurance agent can advise you about life insurance based on your age, the age of your children, and your financial goals. If your children are young, have special needs, or plan to attend college, their financial needs for the future are greater than if your children are already grown and living on their own. Life insurance can help take care of your family at your death. The proceeds do become part of your taxable estate for federal estate tax purposes, but you can get around this by transferring ownership of the policy while you are alive to a beneficiary on the policy, as mentioned above. A life insurance policy can also help pay when those estate taxes come due. A life insurance agent or tax advisor can best assist you in learning how this works and which kind of life insurance suits your circumstances.

> In Chapter 6 we go into detail about how gifts work. Briefly here: A gift of life insurance is subject to the same federal gift tax if its value exceeds the annual exclusion ($11,000 in 2005, $22,000 per couple). Premiums on policies you have transferred also count as gifts but are not likely to exceed the annual exclusion. If the gift of an insurance policy is made within three years of your death, the IRS will consider the full death benefit as part of your taxable estate.

Keeping Your Life in Check

Some people may find a will most appropriate for their current life, but as life changes and future events happen, they must revisit their plan to be sure 1) that their will is updated and reflects their current life; and 2) that a will is the best vehicle for transferring what they currently own should they die today. Taking an occasional inventory of your assets and liabilities is a great way to take stock of your financial goals. You may realize, for example, that you need to buy more life insurance in order to protect your family in the event of your death. Or, you may realize that you can easily keep your estate from probate by shifting some assets to joint ownership or that your estate will be subject to tax at your death unless you make some lifetime gifts.

If you periodically inventory your estate as it grows throughout your life, you may find that setting up a living trust, family annuity, or other such vehicle for transferring your assets is beneficial. Whichever way you choose to plan your estate, always keep your financial goals, your family goals, your expectations, and your circumstances in tune with your plan. If you can meet the needs of you and your family through careful planning, you have achieved success.

Pre-planning a Funeral

How many people like planning their own funeral? Not many. You have to at least think about your own funeral if you choose to make special provisions or give certain instructions regarding it in your will. But if you have ever been in the position of having to plan someone else's funeral and related events following his or her death, and you didn't have any instructions or plans to follow, you know the value of setting up *some* plans before you die. This is an area where you can plan as much or as little as you like. You have the freedom to make plans, change them, get rid of them, or redo them at any time—and without ever having to get anyone's approval or signature.

A funeral typically refers to the service (example: church service, cemetery memorial service, wake) and the disposition of the body (example: cremation, burial). And there are dozens of options in both the type of service you can have and the manner in which your body is put to rest. This book does not focus on the how-tos of planning a funeral and memorial service—or how to scatter the remains of a body over a mountain or ocean (which sometimes requires permits!)—but below are a few questions to ask yourself when crafting your special instructions. Alternatively, you can discuss these wishes with your executor (and not include all of them in your letter of instruction) and rely on your executor to carry them out.

- Do you want your family to use a funeral director?
- Do you want cremation or burial?
- Earth burial? Entombment? Burial at sea?
- Bury cremains? Place cremains in a niche within a columbarium? Scatter cremains? Keep cremains at home?
- Do you want to be embalmed? Or not?
- What kind of casket do you want?
- Have you selected a cemetery or received permission to use private property?

- Have you purchased a plot, crypt, or niche?
- Have you purchased a vault or grave liner or found a cemetery that does not require any?
- Have you ordered a gravestone, plaque, or market?

Making Those Arrangements Ahead of Time

If you are the detail-oriented type, if you begin to think about how you want your family to deal with your body at your death, other questions naturally surface. This is just the beginning of the decision-making process. Nothing can happen following your death without someone making a decision for you, and chances are there will be multiple decisions to make. Other things to think about include:

- Exact type of service you want
- The setting—formal or informal
- The invites (who gets invited and how they learn of your death—public newspaper, written mailing, phone calls, and so on)
- Who leads the service
- The content of the service
- The readings of the service (Bible, poetry, something you've written, a eulogy)
- The music
- Use of photographs, memory books, videos
- Use of flowers or a fund set up for charities or survivors in lieu of flowers
- The food and refreshments
- The memorial notice (where to place obituary and how to contact others who may not see the obituary)

When you pre-plan your funeral arrangements, you provide the opportunity for open discussion of your personal preferences, feelings, and values. In the event of your death, your family will be comforted knowing that they are carrying out your wishes. Pre-planning also allows you to do some comparison shopping and helps you know what you want, or how your family can avoid costly expenses related to death.

Paying for Your Funeral in Advance. While you can plan in depth your funeral, as well as share your wishes with your family, it's generally not a good idea to pay for them ahead of time. The funeral industry may say you should pre-pay for your death-related expenses, but this is not necessarily for your benefit. The pre-need funeral industry has grown exponentially in the past two decades to become a multi-billion dollar industry; a million pre-paid funeral contracts are sold each year for billions of dollars. However, you can get the same—or better— security by placing any funds you'd use to pre-pay your funeral into an interest-bearing savings account or trust for funeral purposes so the funds remain under your control and can be transferred to another location, changed, or withdrawn without any penalty and interest.

The pre-need sales pitch locks in present day prices, but in actuality your survivors may be manipulated into paying more for cash advance items such as flowers, an organist, soloist, and minister, as well as the funeral director's fee for arranging such items. If you are seriously considering paying for your funeral now, seek advice and help from a trusted expert in this field—and preferably not someone tied to the funeral industry who may only share one perspective. New laws likely will emerge in the future to help protect consumers from the hazards in the funeral industry, and until that happens, you can stay abreast of developments or learn more about pre-purchasing goods and services from this industry by contacting the Federal Trade Commission (www.ftc.gov). The FTC, for example, recommends that you get answers to specific questions before paying for anything, and it can provide you with an unbiased look at your options. You may also want to contact a funeral consumer group or memorial society. You can start by finding a list of non-profit funeral consumer groups and memorial societies recommended by the Funeral Consumers Alliance at www.funerals.org.

Conclusion

If you don't write a will, the state in which you reside (and presumably die) decides how to distribute your assets and settle your estate. But it might not be the way you would have wanted. The purpose of a will is to make sure your assets and liabilities get taken care of when you die. We've been hinting at the disadvantages of a Last Will and Testament over a living trust, but for some, starting with a will (Last Will and Testament) and letter of instruction is the only option a person wants to consider. And that's okay, too.

Among the limitations of a will that we have not mentioned is the time frame involved. When you die and your will goes through probate, all that remains must get distributed at that time. Assets that were part of your estate cannot be held anywhere for future distribution. Here's an example: You have kept a savings account with $200,000 in it for your grandson's college tuition. You don't want him to access those funds until he turns 18 or matriculates in a university or college. But if you leave that bank account to your grandson in your will— without any specific instructions about when that money can reach him—and you die well in advance of his needing the money, he will likely get that money as soon as your estate has gone through probate. However, if you specify in your will that the money cannot go to your grandson until he turns 18 or enters college, your executor should set aside that money and create a special trust or other legal entity that can hold the money (and accrue interest) until the time is right for him to get it.

A living trust, on the other hand, usually avoids this situation entirely. By setting up a living trust, you create a legal entity into which you can place assets and set your own instructions for the use of those assets after your death. So, you can place that bank account into your trust and articulate in your trust papers that those funds are not to be made available to your grandson until he applies for college or has matriculated. (As we'll see later, you can also create children's trusts within your trust.) In other words, a trust allows you greater control— where and when it all goes—over your estate.

Living trusts are powerful financial vehicles for transferring family money. A living trust can also include a version of a letter of instruction. If you think you need a will, you most definitely do, and you can probably do even better with a trust. Read on.

CHAPTER 3

Do I Need a Living Trust?

The simple answer to the question, "*Do I need a living trust?*" is "*Yes.*" If you have asked the question, then you have assets you want to protect and you don't plan on dying broke. A living trust is the optimal way to pass on your assets as best you can, and prevent your family from dealing with costly, painstaking, and emotionally troubling legal procedures, notably probate. If you plan your estate right, your heirs won't have to go to court. You've worked hard your entire life, and you continue to work hard, live well, and build your family's wealth. Don't lose all that you've created to the attorneys when you are no longer living. Preserving your estate and making sure you protect your family's future entails setting up a living trust today. What's more, living trusts keep your family affairs private, unlike probate that exposes families to a public legal process. Fewer people have living trusts than wills—only about 20 percent of Americans have a living trust—and you should be part of that 20 percent.

A living trust has five big advantages over a Last Will and Testament or no will at all:

- Avoids probate
- Avoids some post-death income taxes
- Has estate-tax savings for married couples
- Has flexibility in the distribution of an estate
- Maintains privacy

Additionally, a living trust avoids having to go through the court to set up a conservatorship for someone who cannot manage his or her estate due to advanced age or illness. A court-directed conservatorship proceeding can add expense and, often, embarrassment and psychological grief to both the conservatee (the one needing help) and the conservator (the person petitioning for the conservatorship). Also, many transactions undertaken by a conservator, including most sales of property, require court approval. An alternate trustee, or cotrustee under a living trust, however, can manage financial matters without the necessity of a conservatorship. And, because a living trust is revocable, its creator (the settlor) who disputes his or her incapacity will not have given up any control. In all, a living trust package (that also includes some optional documents for greater management) can be the saving grace to a lot of hassles and heartache related to death or the state of one's incapacity.

A living trust is a probate-avoiding tool for anyone—young, old, wealthy, middle-class, and even lower-middle class. If you are young, healthy, and see yourself as asset-poor, you can still set up a living trust, and as you course through your life and accumulate more assets, you can add those assets to the trust and build your family's wealth. Plus, if you have minor children, the living trust allows you to make detailed plans for them in the event you suddenly die, including setting up separate trusts within your living trust for each child (see Chapter 5). Until the formal probate process changes, or gets an overhaul of astronomical proportions, the living trust is the answer. There are enough costs related to death; no family needs the added cost of probate piled on top of the other inevitable expenses. Some estate planning experts say that the greatest impact of probate costs is on smaller estates (those valued at $100,000 or less)—the estates that can least afford it. In a worse-case scenario probate case, if the process drains half of the value of a very small estate away from the heirs, that can mean very little—if anything—is left to give. Living trusts are such versatile documents that it's hard to find reasons *not* to have one.

In later chapters, we will explain how a living trust has some tax-related advantages, as well as greater flexibility in the distribution of one's assets. For example, with a living trust, property need not pass immediately at the death of an individual. Instead, it can be held to benefit a number of beneficiaries according to particular written instructions or at the discretion of the trustee. While children reach the legal age of adulthood at 18, many are not mature enough to wisely use a lump sum. A living trust can help solve this problem.

In this chapter, we give you an overview of the living trust, and prepare you for creating an actual living trust in Chapter 4. If you come across any words that confuse you, refer to Chapter 9 for a list of definitions. Once you understand the basics of living trusts, reading one won't be difficult. They are not intimidating documents with foreign language. They do not require endless management. To the contrary, living trusts are among the easiest, most flexible entities to manage in your life. When you realize how effective our living trusts are, you will wonder why it took you so long to consider one.

A Brief History of Living Trusts

Two questions you might wonder right away: How long have trusts been around? And, if they've been available for a long time, then why don't I hear that much about them from attorneys and tax planners?

Living trusts have been around for more than 1200 years, since about 800 A.D. (Roman Empire) when English peasants adopted a system to protect their lands from abusive kings and nobles. The probate system is also very old, dating as far back as medieval times, but the system used in the United States today is antiquated, outdated, and unnecessarily complex. When the probate system was set up in America's early days, we took the most complex type of probate system out of England and set it up here. Today, the probate system in some states is an agonizing process that does nothing but ensure that lawyers reap the rewards from private estates—you!

The reason why living trusts are not freely discussed in attorney–client meetings, at your annual tax meeting with your accountant, or across dining room tables among friends, is two-fold:

WARNING: Watch out for advice that suggests you don't own enough to have a living trust. Even if your estate does not meet the criteria for the formal probate process or the federal estate tax ($1.5 million in 2005, $2 million in 2006), the costs and pain of probate can be burdensome enough to justify having a living trust. Small estates enjoy the same benefits of having a living trust as large estates—namely, the estates avoid probate and your beloved survivors have fewer hassles to deal with and can receive their inheritance relatively sooner. Moreover, careful planning through living trusts can help you minimize estate taxes.

- People generally don't know much about living trusts and how they work (or they don't like talking about them because they seem complex and they imply death).
- The very people who make a living by probating estates do not want everyone to have a living trust that limits his or her paycheck. Sounds ludicrous and unbelievable, but you'd be surprised by how much money probate can generate for the players involved. Your family, unfortunately, is the *last* player paid on this list.

Another point to make: Not every attorney knows a great deal about estate planning. Estate planning is a specialized field, so should you decide to employ an attorney's services for creating your will or living trust, we hope that you find an honest and well-versed attorney who has done many such living trusts in the past for families.

The costs of probate are often undervalued or misrepresented by the professionals who make a fine mint by the process. In other words, they won't tell you exactly how much probate will cost. They cannot know, of course, because each estate is different and there's no telling how many actions (lawsuits) will get filed in the probating process from family members. And the longer those family members have to deal with the process, the more likely they are to get disgruntled, angry, and frustrated to the point they begin filing lawsuits that do nothing but further delay the process. Living trusts allow for the transfer of assets to beneficiaries to happen considerably faster than if the estate were in probate. Through a living trust, small estates can avoid probate just as easily as large estates.

The time involved in probate is the most agonizing part of the process. Just when your family members are trying to move forward and overcome your death, they have to deal with the exhausting and time-consuming process that can loiter around the courts like a resident rat in an old building. In many states, it is almost impossible to complete the probate of an estate in less than six months, and it may take years. Once someone decides to create more trouble and file more lawsuits in relation to your estate, the probate process lengthens. Amusingly, probate courts frequently hear motions about excessive probate fees when families finally realize what probate did to their beloved's estate and they don't get much in the end. So they accuse the probate courts of taking too long and draining the estate through excessive fees and legal expenses. These motions are never wins for families. Probate courts have no problems justifying probate fees (of executors and

Probate does not just have the potential to drain a family's money and rightful inheritance. Probate can drain good emotions and build ugly ones—anger, frustration, disappointment, stress and worry. These non-monetary costs can be so high as to be incalculable. When you combine the monetary and personal costs, that's the real cost of probate—and you cannot put a price tag on that. (There are exceptions, however, to this experience. Probate isn't all that bad in some states—it just depends where you live.)

attorneys)—in the millions for some estates! Unless they agree to take less, executors and attorneys are usually entitled to fees set by law and calculated from the size of the estate (without reduction for mortgages or other debts). For example, for a $100,000 estate in California, an executor's and attorney's fee would total $6,300. For a $1 million estate, their fee would total $42,300.

Other problems associated with probate that go unnoticed until the family reaches its trenches include the following:

- The probate process, once started, cannot stop. It only takes a poorly planned death for the probate process to start, and once it gets going, it keeps going and going and going—and no one can stop it (nor speed it along).

- The probate process is a public proceeding. Your family cannot maintain its privacy in probate. Public notices of probate are published every day in papers around the world. Anyone may view the court's probate file, which normally contains the name, address (and sometimes age) of each relative and heir, and a description of all property in the estate and its disposition.

- The probate process includes lots of red tape. Court approval and extensive notice requirements are still required in many situations. For example, some sales of real estate may require court approval and an auction. This further delays the probate process.

- The probate process must be conducted in every jurisdiction where a dead person owned real estate at the time of that person's death. So if you write a will, leaving a home in Virginia and some land in California, then reside in Florida when you die, your family may have to endure three independent probate proceedings. The more land or real estate you own in different states, the more probate proceedings your family must tolerate. These duplicate proceedings may sound redundant and tiresome, but they are necessary.

So, you know that probate has a bad reputation. Yet so many people go through probate every year. (We should say that probate is far easier in some states than in others. And there are ways to get through simple probate procedures.) We'll go into the details of the probate courts in Chapter 7. For now, let's turn to the elements of a living trust that can detour your family around probate.

The Elements of a Basic Living Trust

A living trust is designed to do certain tasks and alleviate the tax and probate burdens related to wills. Because it necessitates specific kinds of transfers that must be done a particular way (example: using a quit claim or warranty deed to transfer ownership of your real estate to your living trust), you need to know the correct language for the transfers, which assets should or should not be transferred into your living trust, and the different methods for transferring different assets into your trust. Not transferring assets into your living trust or transferring assets incorrectly can be worse than having no living trust at all.

How a Revocable Living Trust Works—Review

A living trust can also be called by its common name, a revocable living trust. It is called "revocable" because you can alter your estate plan anytime during your lifetime and even revoke the entire trust if you choose. It is described as "living" because you create it and manage it while you are alive; and the living trust estate survives you at death and will distribute your assets per your request in contrast to a Last Will and Testament, which only comes into existence at your death. It is a "trust" because it creates an entity into which assets can be placed for normal use during your lifetime and then be available after your death for distribution to anyone you selected.

To avoid probate, a person or a married couple can place assets in trust while keeping full control over their property. The living trust has actual ownership of the property although you own the trust throughout your lifetime. The living trust holds all of your main assets. Anything you leave out of your trust will get dumped into it with your pour over will, another part of your living trust package.

The Parts to a Living Trust

The living trust is a set of documents, some of which are part of the living trust's inherent framework and others that you can include as optional additions. In the least, a living trust should contain the following documents:

- Declaration of Trust and Articles of the Trust
- Pour Over Will

As optional documents to complete your estate planning package, we suggest that people include the following with their living trust:

- Living Will
- Durable Power of Attorney for Finances (financial affairs/decisions)
- Durable Power of Attorney for Health Care (medical affairs/decisions)
- Any documents personalized for you

Your Articles of the Trust contains a variety of important information, such as an Incapacity Clause, Definitions, Trustee Designations, Separate and Community Property, and very specific instructions for dealing with your estate. In the next chapter, we will show you a sample Table of Contents that makes for a complete living trust package, and then we'll take you through the most commonly executed living trusts that We The People orchestrates.

Beneficiaries Named in Your Living Trust

As we've said, you are a lifetime beneficiary of your living trust. When you die, the people you have named in your living trust to receive assets from your trust are called the benefici-

A living trust avoids probate because, unlike a Last Will and Testament, it is a fully effective document that exists now, during your lifetime. Equally important, your living trust continues to exist after death as a separate entity. Since there is no probate, there are no fees to be paid to attorneys, executors, appraisers, courts, and so on. Everything you leave goes directly to whomever you have chosen. When you designate your successor trustee, you give that person the responsibility of administering your living trust after you die, which includes managing and distributing the assets placed in your trust.

Although it may sound complicated at first, the person who sets up a living trust wears three hats:

1. Settlor

2. Initial trustee

3. Lifetime beneficiary

You remain in control of your living trust for the duration of your life. This means you can do any of the following without any penalties or restrictions:

• Sell, loan, or give away assets in your living trust

• Change ownership of assets from the living trust back into your name

• Add assets to the living trust

• Change beneficiaries, successor trustee, personal representatives, agents for powers of attorney, alternates, and so on

• Revoke (cancel) the living trust in its entirety

aries. Remember, you are entitled to make any kinds of changes during your life. This can include adding new beneficiaries, removing existing beneficiaries, changing the distribution of assets or even selling the assets and revoking the trust. As the settlor (creator) of the living trust, the trust belongs to you. You also manage the assets that are placed into the trust. Thus, the settlor is also called the trustee (the boss) of the living trust. After your death, your successor trustee takes over the management of the living trust's assets. Since you have created the living trust, managed its assets, and benefited from the trust, you are called the settlor, trustee, and life beneficiary of the living trust.

In the example below, Bob Smith established a living trust. He will pay no probate fees and his estate will not go through probate at all because he created a living trust during his lifetime.

When Bob dies, his wife, Jane, takes over the administration of his living trust because Bob designated Jane to be his successor trustee. Bob also designated Jane to receive his assets

	During Bob's Life	*After Bob Dies*
Settlor	Bob Smith	None
Trustee	Bob Smith	Jane Smith (Successor Trustee)
Beneficiary	Bob Smith	Jane Smith (Bob's Wife)

after his death. As the example illustrates, Jane is a contingent beneficiary of Bob Smith's living trust. During his lifetime, Bob Smith is the only person who benefits from the trust. At Bob's death, the designated successor trustee takes over and distributes Bob's assets according to his wishes.

Types of Living Trusts

Basic Living Trust for Individuals and Couples. If you are single or married, you can create your own single living trust and place your share of your assets into the trust. You get to name your successor trustee(s), distribute your assets as you wish, and make plans for children, including naming a guardian or a custodian under the Uniform Transfer to Minors Act (UTMA; more on this Act in Chapter 5).

Couples can also create a shared, basic living trust in which each spouse is named as cotrustee and both have control over their shared property. This type of trust, however, has tax consequences that make the AB Trust a better option for traditional families. All of our joint living trusts for married couples at We The People are AB living trusts.

AB Living Trust for Married Couples. Married couples often create an A/B, or joint, living trust. In a joint trust both spouses put their property into the living trust. When one spouse dies that spouse's property does not have to pass through probate. At one spouse's death, the entire trust gets split into two: trust A (sometimes called the marital deduction trust) and trust B (the bypass trust, or as some planners joke, the below-the-ground trust). The B trust bypasses probate and taxation (if it's below the federal exemption limit). The surviving spouse—the one with the A trust now—can use the property while he or she is alive, but the decedent's property remains in the B trust and becomes irrevocable. That means the surviving spouse can *use* the property (such as his boat that he has willed to his good friend Charlie) for living, but not sell, transfer, or give it away. This is called creating a life estate. The B trust is designed for the ultimate benefit of heirs, as it is designed to conform to the federal estate tax shelter limit, which we'll discuss in Chapter 6. Shelter limit refers to how much value an estate can have before it becomes subject to federal estate taxes. We often refer to this also as the tax threshold, or the point at which taxes are due because the estate's value has reached the threshold.

When the second spouse dies, the property passes to the trust beneficiaries, usually the couple's children. Because of the tax-planning benefits to AB trusts, they are typically used by married couples who intend to leave their estate to their children. During their lives, they have an initial living trust that's totally revocable and in their control. But when the first spouse dies, their joint living trust splits into two. This gets the money out of the couple's combined estate, so that it escapes estate taxation after the second spouse's death. (More on this topic in Chapter 6.)

ABC Living Trust. Married couples with estates worth more than $2 million can set up an ABC trust to assure that beneficiaries of the first spouse's trust (after that spouse has died and thus prompted the creation of the B trust) receive their designated share of the estate. The ABC trust is similar to the AB trust, but it includes the C trust, which is also called a qualified terminal interest property (Q-TIP).

When the first spouse dies, $1 million stays in the B trust and the excess flows down into the C trust, which the surviving spouse cannot change in terms of beneficiaries or allocation and distribution of its assets. Although the excess could flow into the survivor's A trust tax-free under the Unlimited Marital Deduction provision, using a C trust preserves the assets in the B trust for those beneficiaries and may have some tax-saving benefits in the long run. A surviving spouse can choose to postpone paying any estate taxes at the death of his or her spouse. The surviving spouse has a right to the income generated by trust C's assets for life—regardless of remarriage—but may not necessarily have the right to those assets' principal. Example: A couple decides to leave their Los Angeles apartment to the husband's son of a first marriage. Their estate is worth $4 million. The husband dies in 2005, when the tax exemption is $1.5 million. The overage that can be taxed is $500,000, or the value of the apartment. This $500,000 asset goes into the C trust and the son is named as the final beneficiary.

We will discuss more about this type of trust in Chapter 5. For now, think of the ABC trust as the one you want to use if you've got an estate worth $2 million or more. (Some planners suggest setting up a C trust at $1 million.)

How You Hold Title

Before you transfer title into your living trust, you need to know what kind of ownership you have in some assets, especially real estate. You have five possibilities:

Joint tenancy. (or joint tenancy with right of survivorship). A holding of property by more than one person in such a way that any one person can act as owner of the whole and take the property by survivorship.

Tenancy in common. A holding of property by more than one person in such a way that each person owns an individual share.

Community property. A holding of property between a husband and wife in a state where community property laws are enforced. Each spouse owns one-half interest in all assets acquired during the marriage. The following states have some form of community property laws: California, Arizona, New Mexico, Texas, Nevada, Idaho, Washington, and Louisiana. In Alaska, a couple can sign an agreement that designates certain assets as community property.

Community property with right of survivorship. The same as above, but when one spouse dies, the surviving spouse automatically owns all the property. This kind of property ownership is only available in some states, including Arizona, California, Nevada, Texas, Washington, and Wisconsin. Some of these states require particular agreements to specify this type of ownership.

Tenancy by the entirety. A holding of property similar to joint tenancy, but for married couples only. If you hold property in tenancy by the entirety, you cannot transfer your portion of the property without your spouse's consent, whereas with joint tenancy you can. At your death, your portion of the property goes to your surviving spouse. Tenancy by the entirety is available in only a handful of states.

If you don't know how you own your property, look at the paperwork related to your property and it should indicate the type of title you have. How your state views shared property (that is, whether you live in a community property state or not) also affects how you can own property. As noted above, if you live in a non-community property state, for example, any property owned between a husband and wife can create a tenancy by the entirety. But to be sure, check with a local real estate expert or attorney who can help you make sense of your property. You may also want to consult with a tax specialist about this type of ownership's tax advantages—or disadvantages—when you transfer it to the living trust.

Notes about Joint Tenancy

People talk a lot about joint tenancy because it is a way to own property and avoid probate. If you own property in joint tenancy, with right of survivorship, at your death your interest in the property automatically goes to the other joint tenant or tenants, no matter what your will says. While joint tenancy has some advantages—it avoids probate, so this is an easy way for married couples (who own property in joint tenancy) to ensure their share of a home goes directly to a spouse at their death—the disadvantages of joint tenancy can be serious:

- Joint tenancy is not very flexible. The interests of all joint tenants must be equal and they are distributed immediately and automatically at the death of a joint tenant.

- Joint tenancy might not give the advantage of a stepped-up basis (see Chapter 6), which the community property form of ownership gives a married couple. This is how a living trust can provide some income tax savings.

- Property in joint tenancy can be reached by the creditors of each joint tenant. For example, if you hold property in joint tenancy with your children so that they will get the property at your death, an underinsured automobile accident in which they are involved could jeopardize the asset during your lifetime.

It's generally a bad idea to own property in joint tenancy with your children; if you want to create a way to avoid probate, a living will can accomplish this goal but also give you greater flexibility over the control of your assets. In most cases, the most advantageous form of ownership is to hold assets in the name of your living trust. We will revisit joint tenancy throughout this book; how you can transfer assets held in joint tenancy may depend on whether you live in a community property state or a noncommunity property state.

How to Fund Your Trust

Establishing a living trust enables an individual or family to transfer property to the living trust without giving up management or control. Unlike an irrevocable trust (which can't be changed), the living trust gives you all the benefits of a trust instrument but does not take away control over the assets or benefits from those assets.

Transferring assets to your trust is called funding your trust. A funded living trust is one in which you (the settlor) have transferred ownership of your major assets to the trust. Major assets to consider placing in your trust include the following:

- Houses, land, and other real estate, including mobile homes and partial interest in real estate

- Boats, cars, airplanes, other objects of value

- Money markets, savings accounts, and other financial accounts

> **WORD OF CAUTION:** Better, more efficient vehicles for managing certain retirement accounts, such as Individual Retirement Accounts (IRAs) and other so-called Qualified Plans (traditional IRAs, Keoghs, qualified annuities, or 401(k) plans) may be available, so discuss the tax and potential legal consequences with a professional before placing them in your living trust. Consult your retirement account manager. Also, there are pros and cons to adding life insurance policies to your trust, which we will discuss in Chapter 5.

- Stocks, bonds, treasury bills, securities, investments, and other brokerage accounts
- Valuable heirlooms, jewelry, antiques, furs, furniture, or other valuable household goods
- Precious metals
- Valuable works of art or other collectibles
- Business interests, such as majority stock in a company
- Patents, copyrights, or royalties

It is not always recommended to name your living trust as the beneficiary to your life insurance proceeds, and any consideration of doing so should be done with the help of a professional who understands your particular circumstances and can guide you in making the right decision for your family.

You want to place as many assets into your living trust as you can. Anything you've insured due to its value should go into the trust. In most instances, transferring major assets entails contacting the agent or company with whom you deal for that particular asset (example: calling your banks and brokers to transfer accounts and using their official transfer forms; or calling your business partners with whom you share business interests). To transfer titles to homes, you simply create new deeds and register them with the county land records office where the property is located. Below are more specific instructions for funding your trust with the most common assets. For items that you don't have attached paperwork proving ownership (example: you don't have a deed to your antique doll collection), you merely need to fill out an Assignment of Interest document (also called a Notice of Assignment, described below) and list them as assets in your trust papers that organize your assets into lists (that is, your schedule).

> A living trust cannot be a legal owner of an insurance policy, so while you are alive you remain the legal owner of your policy. If you name your living trust as a beneficiary of your life insurance policy, you do not need to re-register the title to the policy, nor transfer ownership of the policy into the trust's name. But you can designate the living trust to receive the proceeds of the policy at your death and the trust becomes the entity into which those proceeds go at your death. This means you do not list the policy in your schedule. You name your trust as the beneficiary of the proceeds and you name one or more beneficiaries in the trust documents to ultimately receive those proceeds. If you have minor children, children's trusts can be set up to hold the proceeds until a certain time. The death benefits thus can be invested, managed, and distributed (at the right time), rather than paid out in a lump sum, which may or may not be used for the purposes you had in mind.

If you still owe money on an asset you want to place into your living trust, such as a house, boat, car, or large-ticket item, you can still transfer the asset and your beneficiary will inherit the debt as well (the mortgage or loan); however, you can plan for paying for those debts through your estate—typically by selling certain assets and using those proceeds to pay off other debts.

Items you may *not* want to place in your trust include the following:

- Small assets you buy and sell frequently, or that you don't intend to have forever
- Your personal bank accounts that you use frequently, such as a checking and savings account from which you draw money
- Small items that would be too cumbersome to list, and that can be handled by your Pour Over Will
- Insurance policies, including life insurance and annuities
- Individual Retirement Accounts (IRAs, 401(k)s, and profit-sharing plans)
- Pay-on-death bank accounts

Vehicles can be tricky to transfer into a trust if you still owe a decent amount on the loan. People do not always put their cars into their living trust. If your car has little value, your pour over will captures this asset and adds it to the trust at your death. However, if you own a car that has considerable value, such as a luxury or an antique car, you may elect to place it in your living trust.

Insurance companies can be cranky when it comes to insuring a vehicle that's owned by a trust and not a person. If you have a hard time getting your vehicle transferred into your trust, you can use other maneuvers to protect that asset from probate, such as registering the vehicle in joint tenancy or filling out a transfer-on-death form with your Department of Motor Vehicles (which says that your car goes to Joey, for example, at your death, and it avoids probate). Only some states allow these types of maneuvers, but it's worth investigating if you want your car in your trust and your insurance company will not allow it.

Your trust does not take effect until you have executed it by signing all the necessary papers and obtained witness signatures and notarization. However, your trust remains unfunded until you transfer your assets into it. Transferring your assets into your trust is important and actually quite simple. With a deed, for example, you transfer your real property from your current ownership into your new trust. The law does not consider such a transfer to be a sale for the purpose of reassessing your property for tax reasons. Simply contact your bank or other institution where you hold assets and ask them to rename your assets and accounts as now belonging to your trust.

CDs, Savings Accounts and Checking Accounts

Go to your bank with your trust documents and tell the customer service representative that you have created a trust and you need to change the name on your accounts to reflect the trust name. The representative will have the proper forms for you to fill out. Keep in mind that it's best to exclude active accounts that you use daily, such as checking, from your living trust. The living trust cannot hold cash unless it is held somewhere concrete. In other words, you cannot simply list $10,000 on the schedule. Instead, you will list the location of the cash, such as a bank account or a safe-deposit box or an in-home safe.

> **CAUTION:** Technically, you are not selling your home to your living trust. Some mortgage documents contain so-called due-on-sale clauses, which are provisions that give the lender the right to demand payment of the remaining balance of the loan when the property is sold. It is a contractual right, not a law. This means that if you transfer the title to the property, the bank may (or may not), at its option, decide to call the loan due. Do not worry about these clauses for purposes of placing your real estate into your living trust.

Stock or Mutual Funds

Your account executive will give you the papers needed to transfer your current name to your trust name.

Real Estate

While the general procedure for transferring real estate to your living trust is similar across the states, each state may have its own version or style of the process. The paperwork may differ across the states as well. You will need to fill out and sign a Quit Claim or Warranty Deed form for transferring the title to your trust name. Use deed forms for your state. You can sometimes find these forms in stationery or office supply stores or at a title company. A local We The People store near you can also help you deal with these forms and find the exact one you need. Be sure to have your exact property description, which is how the property is described on the previous deed. The deed needs to be witnessed and notarized. If you are transferring the title from a co-owned property with your spouse into your joint living trust, your spouse must also sign the deed.

The Quit Claim or Warranty Deed is then taken to the county office that houses property records. This is the county office that files property records. Land records offices in different states may have different names: Office of the County Recorder, Land Registry Office, or Country Clerk's Office. Call your local land records office for information about mailing in your new deed. Also ask about transfer taxes, although these are rare because you are not selling your property.

You may need to file other forms alongside your deed, such as a Transfer of Property form, which can be picked up at the land recorder's office. In filling out this form, you will need the parcel identification number, which can be found on your most recently recorded deed (it may also be on your property tax papers). Ask your local recorder's office exactly what you need to transfer your property to your living trust. It shouldn't be that difficult, and the forms are easy to fill out. The hardest part to transferring ownership of property from you to your trust is making the time to do it.

If you have a mortgage, you do not need to prepare any documents for that liability—as it follows the asset into the trust. If you have real property in a state other than where you set up your trust, find the deed form for the state where the property is located and transfer it as you would any property: You complete the deed form and record it with the county land records office where the property is located. The county land records office can tell you if any extra paperwork is required to make the transfer.

You do not need to notify your mortgage lender that you are transferring ownership of your real estate into your living trust. Keep in mind that transferring titles to your living trust is *not* a sale. Your mortgage lender may ask for your title if, for example, you decide to refinance your home. In such a case, you may have to transfer your title out of your living trust, complete the refinance, and then transfer that title back into the living trust. Yes, we know it sounds like a peculiar, circular action to take, but we do it all the time for customers. You will not have to pay off your mortgage just because you have a living trust own your real estate.

Record any so-called deeds of trust that you have as well. Deeds of trust are types of assets similar to a mortgage. Example: You loan money to a start-up company that puts up interest in real estate as security for the loan. The company gives you a deed of trust for the loan. Transfer this interest in the real estate by transferring your deed of trust to your living trust.

For Property Owned as Joint Tenancy in Noncommunity Property States. If you live in a noncommunity property state, you may have to complete an extra step in transferring your property to the living trust. If you hold a deed to property in joint tenancy or tenancy by the entirety, you should create a new deed that transfers your property from joint tenancy (or tenancy by the entirety) to tenants in common. Then you prepare another new deed that transfers your tenants in common deed to the living trust. That way, you don't risk your property going into the living trust and retaining its joint tenancy label. This gives you more flexibility for leaving your share of the property to whomever you want. If you do not know how you share property with others (you don't know if you own property in joint tenancy or by tenants in common, for example), check with a local attorney who can help you understand your deed and the laws of your state. Your current deed may not mention what kind of ownership you have, and it may simply list names. In some states, any deed shared by a husband and wife automatically creates a tenancy by the entirety.

Mobile Homes

You will need to change the title on your mobile home from your name to the name of the living trust. Find the registration for your mobile home and contact that agency. This may be the Department of Housing or the Department of Motor Vehicles in the county where the mobile home is located. There is a small fee, and this might take some time to complete.

Once you establish your living trust, maintaining the trust is relatively simple. It is always a wise idea to discuss with your accountant the tax advantages of your living trust. We give a general overview of how taxes work in Chapter 6; having a basic understanding of taxes will allow you to get the best advice possible when seeking professional help.

Businesses

If you are the sole proprietor of a small business, you can (and should) transfer it to your trust by listing the business in the schedule of assets. Example: "Optical Illusions Optometry" or "Right from the Oven Corner Bakery." Fill out a Notice of Assignment form and attach it to your trust. Be sure to list the assets related to your business on the schedule. A sample of an Assignment of Business Interest is provided here. (See Figure 3.1.) Note that you must meet your own state's Notice of Assignment requirements. The sample notice here is from California.

The trust is a ghost at tax season for income tax purposes. You continue to deduct your mortgage interest from your income taxes, even though your home is now owned by the trust and under the control of the trustee (you).

ASSIGNMENT OF BUSINESS INTEREST

The undersigned, NAME OF ASSIGNOR, (herein called the "Assignor") hereby assigns, pledges, transfers, and delivers to THE NAME OF ASSIGNOR LIVING TRUST, UTD _____, 20___ (herein called 'the Assignee') the following:

All of [his/her] right, title, and interest along with any and all profits, money, or funds due or to become due to Assignor of whatsoever description or character presently or hereafter derived from that certain business known as "BUSINESS NAME," located at BUSINESS ADDRESS, (herein called the "Business").

Assignor further represents, warrants, and agrees as follows:

1. That Assignor has full legal right and authority to execute and carry out the terms of this instrument; and that as of the date of the execution of this instrument, Assignor is not in default in the performance of any of the obligations existing with respect to the Business.

2. That Assignee shall not be liable to any person or persons for damages sustained in connection with the Business or such other contract into which the Assignor may have entered in connection therewith.

3. That Assignor will execute and deliver any additional instruments which Assignee deems necessary to carry out the purport and tenor of this instrument and to better secure the payment of the liabilities.

4. This Assignment of Business Interest shall be governed by and construed in accordance with the laws of California.

This Assignment of Business Interest is binding upon and inures to the benefit of Assignee and any holder of any of the liabilities and is binding upon Assignor.

IN WITNESS WHEREOF, XXX has executed this Assignment of Business Interest in CITY, California, as of _____, 20___.

_____

XXX, Assignor

State of CALIFORNIA

County of_____

On _____, 20___, before me,_____, Notary Public personally appeared NAME OF ASSIGNOR, proved to me on the basis of satisfactory evidence to be the person whose name is subscribed to the within instrument and acknowledged to me that [he/she] executed the same in [his/her] authorized capacity, and that by [his/her] signature on the instrument the person, or the entity upon behalf of which the person acted, executed the instrument.

WITNESS my hand and official seal.

_____

Figure 3.1

For corporations in which you hold stock, contact a broker to complete stock transfer forms. Or consult with the corporation's advisors for completing this transaction. You may have to meet requirements in the corporation's bylaws or articles of incorporation. If you are a partner in a company, speak with your fellow partners about transferring your interest in the partnership. The partnership agreement and possibly a certificate of partnership must be revised.

For any business you want to transfer into your trust, contacting the person at that business (unless it's just your own) who knows how to complete this transfer is the place to start. This person can be an internal accountant, general partner, owner, or attorney.

Copyrights, Patents, Trademarks, Royalties

Registered trademarks and service marks should be re-registered. Contact the United States Patent and Trademark Office (www.uspto.gov) for this information. The Office can also give you the information for transferring a patent to your trust. You will have to fill out an assignment document, pay a small fee to the Patent and Trademark Office, and record your transfer with the Office. You can also transfer copyrights to your trust by listing the copyright on your schedule of trust assets and by filling out a document provided by the Copyright Office (www.copyright.gov).

For any royalties you receive, you can transfer those rights by listing them on your trust schedule. In addition to listing your royalty rights clearly on your schedule of assets, it's wise to fill out an assignment form and give a copy to the company or person that pays you the royalty. Keep the original with your original living trust.

All the Things You Own that Don't Have Titles or Other Official Paperwork

The bulk of your estate, in terms of number of items, is probably comprised of little things—the small assets of your daily life. You cannot transfer a title to your living room set, your antique armoire, or your telescope. Your goal in setting up and managing your living trust is to transfer your major assets into it and allow the pour over will at your death to take care of those remaining little assets that get left out. For valuable assets that do not have titles or other official paperwork attached, you should transfer them officially to your living trust by using a Notice of Assignment document. A sample of one is included here. (See Figure 3.2.)

For example, you would create an Assignment of Interest to transfer an original art collection, a valuable set of china, or your fancy racing bicycles. You may create an Assignment of Interest for "furniture, furnishings, and personal effects" without creating a detailed inventory, and this assignment can take care of any future personal property that you acquire. Examples of personal property include furniture, appliances, pictures, china, silverware, glass, books, jewelry, clothing, and so on. These are typically the contents of a home.

Keep your focus on your major assets—assets that have legal identities, such as titles, deeds, and account numbers—because your small assets are likely to change throughout your life. You want your trust set up in a way that is easy to manage, and less of a strain on your daily life for all that you buy, sell, trade, and give away. Remember: If your living trust owns all of your valuable assets, the little things will get poured into it at your death through the pour over will. If you think that your little things will add up to a lot of value (that can trigger the formal probate process), you may want to consider using Assignment of Interest

ASSIGNMENT OF INTEREST

The undersigned, NAME OF ASSIGNOR, (herein called the "Assignor") hereby assigns, pledges, transfers, and delivers to THE NAME OF ASSIGNOR LIVING TRUST, UTD _____, 20___ (herein called "the Assignee") the following:

All of [his/her] right, title, and interest along with any and all profits, money, or funds due or to become due to Assignor of whatsoever description or character presently or hereafter derived from that certain asset known as "(DESCRIBE ASSET)," located at ADDRESS, (herein called the "asset").

Assignor further represents, warrants, and agrees as follows:

1. That Assignor has full legal right and authority to execute and carry out the terms of this instrument; and that as of the date of the execution of this instrument, Assignor is not in default in the performance of any of the obligations existing with respect to the asset.

2. That Assignee shall not be liable to any person or persons for damages sustained in connection with the asset or such other contract into which the Assignor may have entered in connection therewith.

3. That Assignor will execute and deliver any additional instruments which Assignee deems necessary to carry out the purport and tenor of this instrument and to better secure the payment of the liabilities.

4. This Assignment of Interest shall be governed by and construed in accordance with the laws of California.

This Assignment of Interest is binding upon and inures to the benefit of Assignee and any holder of any of the liabilities and is binding upon Assignor.

IN WITNESS WHEREOF, XXX has executed this Assignment of Interest in CITY, California, as of _____, 20___.

_____
XXX, Assignor

State of CALIFORNIA

County of_____

On _____, 20___, before me,_____, Notary Public personally appeared NAME OF ASSIGNOR, proved to me on the basis of satisfactory evidence to be the person whose name is subscribed to the within instrument and acknowledged to me that [he/she] executed the same in [his/her] authorized capacity, and that by [his/her] signature on the instrument the person, or the entity upon behalf of which the person acted, executed the instrument.

WITNESS my hand and official seal.

_____

Figure 3.2

documents to transfer some of your smaller assets formally into your living trust. But for the most part, this is unnecessary and creates a lot of extra paperwork.

See Chapter 4 for examples of how to list your assets in your living trust schedules.

Homestead Rules

Homestead laws exist in most states to protect the equity in your home (the amount you actually own in your home) up to a certain amount. Homestead rules prevent creditors from forcing you to sell your home to pay debts, unless those creditors are the actual mortgage lenders. Your specific state sets these rules, amounts, and methods for administering this protection. In some states, the protection is automatic and you don't have to do anything; in others, you may have to visit your county land records office and record a Declaration of Homestead. Only worry about the homestead rules and qualifications in your state if you do carry enough debt to justify the forced sale of your home.

Transferring your home into a living trust should not affect any homestead rights you have; however, you can include specific language referring to this protection in your trust. You do this by stating that you remain eligible for your state's homestead exemption just as you would without the home being in your trust.

Homestead Rights. Do not confuse homestead rules that relate to protection against creditors and a homestead right of a surviving spouse and dependent children to remain in a home that has been bequeathed to someone else. As we'll explain in a later chapter, a spouse may claim a *homestead right,* which allows the spouse and minor children to stay in the deceased's home for a specified period. Example: A man has bequeathed his home to his son from a previous marriage. When he dies, his surviving second wife can remain in the home for a specified period of time, sometimes for the rest of her life, at which point the son inherits the house. Refer to Chapter 7 for more discussion on this topic. Homestead rights and family protection allowances go hand in hand and can affect how your survivors inherit your assets (some may be entitled to a statutory share regardless of how much you leave them through a will or living trust).

Storing Your Trust

Protecting your trust so it's available in the event of your death is extremely important. In some states, you can register your trust with a government agency; but in others, you have to store it in a safe place and tell the proper people—your successor trustee—where to find it.

States where you can register your trust include the following: Alaska, Colorado, Florida, Hawaii, Idaho, Maine, Michigan, Mississippi, Missouri, Nebraska, and North Dakota. You can register your trust by filing a statement with the court where you (the trustee) reside. You cannot register your trust in multiple states. Not to worry, however. Registering a trust is not very common. Your living trust remains equally as valid if you do not register it; the goal is to create a valid trust at the start and store it in a safe place.

Keep your trust in a place where you normally keep other important documents, such as birth certificates, passports, insurance policies, financial papers, and so on. A fireproof box at home or in your office is a good choice; if you place your trust in a safe-deposit box, be sure your successor trustee can access it easily after your death. Trust documents have no monetary value to them, so the point in finding a safe place is to ensure they don't get destroyed or lost. And you may not want just anyone to find your trust and read its private contents. If you keep a copy in your home office, lock it away in a desk, filing cabinet, or safe.

Make copies of your original living trust. You can write or stamp "COPY" on the duplicates, but it's not necessary. Do not make any copies of unsigned living trusts. You may want to give your successor trustee a copy to keep so he or she can prepare for the job of administering your estate. (But you must also tell your successor trustee where to find the original if you die or become incapacitated.) Avoid giving anyone else copies of your trust, including your beneficiaries. Only you, your cotrustee if you have one, and your successor trustee even need to know about your living trust.

Moving to Another State

Although every state may have its own unique way of drafting living trusts, rest assured that your living trust remains valid when you move to another state. When you declare the state in which you reside and create your original trust, that state's laws govern your trust while you live in that state. When you move, your new state governs the trust and settles any disputes over your assets. If you move to another state and know that you will live in that state for a long period of time (perhaps the rest of your life) it's wise to acquaint yourself with your new state's laws and make any minor changes to your trust in relation to those laws. The states vary on the following issues:

- Whether you can register your trust
- How property can be owned (example: moving from a noncommunity property state to a community property state)
- The rights of a surviving spouse to inherit
- State death taxes
- How you can leave assets to minor children or set up custodians

Become familiar with the above legal issues in whichever state you reside. You can achieve this by visiting your state's government web site, a local law library, or a trusted attorney or estate planner.

Changing Your Living Trust

Making changes to your living trust at any time is easy. You simply create another document (an official "Amendment To . . .") that clearly states what you are changing, making specific references to the original living trust. An example of such an amendment is shown here. (See Figure 3.3.)

In this particular amendment, the trustees (The Millers) have changed the names of their beneficiaries. The Millers have axed their initial list of beneficiaries and listed Don Charles

AMENDMENT TO
THE GEORGE M. MILLER and ILENE MILLER LIVING TRUST
UTD _____, 2005

GEORGE M. MILLER and ILENE MILLER, Settlor/Trustees of THE GEORGE M. MILLER and ILENE MILLER LIVING TRUST, UTD _____, 2005, hereby amend the Trust as follows:

Pursuant to Article One, Section 1.06(a), "At any time and from time to time during the life of the Settlor, the Settlor may alter, modify or amend the Trust created by this Agreement in any respect by a duly executed instrument in writing delivered to the Trustee." GEORGE M. MILLER and ILENE MILLER now choose to establish this Amendment to the above referenced Declaration of Trust to the GEORGE M. MILLER and ILENE MILLER LIVING TRUST effective _____ _____, 2005.

AMENDMENT

NOW THEREFORE, the said Declaration of Trust is amended as set forth hereinbelow:

ARTICLE THREE, Section 4.03.(b): Delete list of beneficiaries in its entirety and replace with the following: "DON CHARLES ADAMS 100%."

TRUST INSTRUCTIONS: Delete the Trust Instructions in their entirety and replace with the following: "It is my wish that DON CHARLES ADAMS shall receive 100% of the condo and antique rocking chair."

All other terms and conditions of the Trust remain the same.

Dated: _____

                        _____
                        GEORGE M. MILLER, Settlor/Trustee of THE
                        GEORGE M. MILLER and ILENE MILLER
                        LIVING TRUST, UTD _____, 2005

Dated: _____

                        _____
                        ILENE MILLER Settlor/Trustee of THE GEORGE
                        M. MILLER and ILENE MILLER LIVING
                        TRUST, UTD _____, 2005

111 A

Figure 3.3a

Declaration and Acknowledgment of Notary Public

STATE OF CALIFORNIA

COUNTY OF (COUNTY)

    On _____ before me, _____,
personally appeared JOHN DOE and JANE DOE, _____ personally known to me -OR- ____
proved to me on the basis of satisfactory evidence to be the person(s) whose name(s) is/are
subscribed to the within instrument and acknowledged to me that he/she/they executed the same
in his/her/their authorized capacity(ies), and that by his/her/their signature(s) on the instrument
the person(s), or the entity upon behalf of which the person(s) acted, executed the instrument.

        WITNESS my hand and official seal.

_____
Signature of Notary Public

111 B

Figure 3.3b

Adams instead as the beneficiary of 100 percent of the condominium and rocking chair. This is a major—formal—change to a trust (it is a change in the plan), so the amendment is witnessed by two people and notarized.

To keep your living trust valid, you want to be extra careful and formal in making any amendments. Generally all amendments need to be executed formally in the same way as the original document, so they all should be witnessed and notarized. Very minor, informal changes, however, may not need to be witnessed and notarized. Examples of informal changes include adding or taking away assets from the trust that do not affect the legal body of the trust document (the legal body of your living trust document is the Articles of Trust where your beneficiaries and successor trustees are named). Any changes you make that have an effect or change the legal body of your trust document require a formal amendment to be completed, signed, witnessed, and notarized.

Caution: Never cross out or change the legal body of your living trust (or will, for that matter) informally by handwriting changes or crossing out sections. This can invalidate the entire document. When in doubt about how to make a simple change, do it formally by creating an amendment and getting it witnessed and notarized. Alternatively, speak with someone about your particular change and how to go about making the change correctly. Never risk invalidating your documents by handwriting in changes or creating amendments without getting the proper signatures from witnesses and a notary public. If you are uncertain about handwriting and initialing changes to any documents outside of the legal body of the living trust (in your Trust Instructions, for example), ask for help. In most cases, you can make informal changes to your Trust Instructions because these changes may not affect the body of your trust document. However, follow all formal rules of execution when in doubt. Your living trust is not a rough draft for the duration of your life. Keep it formal, official, and valid. Err on the side of caution—always.

People typically make the following amendments to their living trusts:

- Change successor trustees and alternates

- Change beneficiaries and alternates

- Change guardians for minor children

- Change custodians for a minor's property, or an alternate custodian

- Change instructions for distribution of property

- Change the trust's contents (adding and deleting assets)

Some of the above changes are changes to your overall plan, while other changes are not. For example, changing your successor trustee, beneficiaries, or how your assets get distributed are changes to your overall plan, while simple changes to your living trust's contents through the buying, selling, or transfer of assets are not really changes, but how you *manage* your plan. Changing names is usually formal, while changing assets is usually informal. You manage your living trust through its Trust Instructions, which is not part of the legal body of the document. Thus, changes to your Trust Instructions normally do not require formal amendments.

> **You must formally amend your living trust for any of the following reasons: changing beneficiaries, changing the percentages for a beneficiary, and changing a successor trustee. Informal changes made in your Trust Instructions do not require formal amendments.**

Don't be afraid to make changes—minor and significant ones—to your living trust once you execute it. The whole point of having a living trust is to create a flexible, manageable plan for your assets now and in the future. You can make as many changes as you want whenever you want. The way the Trust Instructions work, you can make many changes that do not necessarily change the legal body portion, but you can change the trust's contents and who gets what.

It makes sense also to revisit your living trust occasionally, as you would a will, to make sure it remains up-to-date and that it continues to reflect your current wishes, circumstances, and future plans. Try to review your plan at least once every five years. If you marry, re-marry, have children, survive named beneficiaries who die, or even change your official name, you need to make the proper changes to your trust. In some circumstances, you will need to revoke your living trust and create an entirely new one (although this is rare).

Another reason to review your plan occasionally is to ensure it matches current laws and tax rules. If, for example, Congress passes a new law that affects the Tax Code or estate tax, you will want to incorporate that change into your trust, hopefully for the benefit of your overall plan. Any major changes to laws that affect estate plans should call for a review of your trust.

Adding Assets to Your Trust

Any asset of value that you acquire after you've set up your trust should be added as soon as possible. You accomplish this by transferring any title or, if there is no title, by creating an Assignment of Interest. You also revisit the schedule where that new asset should be placed (recreating a new schedule and removing the old, outdated schedule) and amend any other trust documents related to your new asset. You only need to create an amendment to your living trust document if your new asset affects the legal body of your trust.

For example, if you buy an antique automobile you plan to leave to a grandson, you amend the paperwork that designates your grandson as a beneficiary. This requires creating a formal amendment with signatures from not only you, but a witness and notary public as well. Your beneficiary for the car must be added to the trust documents (if not already). Because computers make it easy to retype a schedule, it's in your best interest to redo the entire schedule. Avoid handwriting anything onto your living trust document. However, you may handwrite notes that are included in the unofficial areas of your living trust package, such as in your Trust Instructions where you leave your successor trustee detailed information about the contents and administration of your living trust. For any handwritten notes you make, initial and date them. If you have to add or take out assets listed on your schedules, err on the side of caution and retype the entire schedule. Do your best to keep your living trust package as clean and professional as possible.

Reminder: For assets you add to your living trust that relate only to the management of your trust and do not affect the legal body of it, you do not need to create an official amendment. Example: You buy, sell, and give away assets throughout your life. You can change the list of your current assets in your schedules, which are part of your Trust Instructions, at any time.

Selling or Giving Away Assets in Your Trust

You have no restrictions in doing away with assets in your trust, whether you choose to sell them, donate them, or give them away. All you have to do is amend the schedule where that asset is listed (creating a new schedule to attach to your trust papers and removing the old one), and complete a formal trust amendment document that states your changes to the living trust's contents, if necessary. This is the same procedure for adding an asset to the living trust by redoing the schedule and creating an amendment with proper signatures if your new situation changes the legal body of your living trust. Example: You own an antique rosewood desk that you originally had going to your older sister when you died, but you've decided that you want your eldest daughter to have it now because you no longer want your older sister as a beneficiary. You simply give your daughter the desk, and when you make your amendment, you formally remove your sister as a beneficiary (unless you have her receiving other assets).

Reminder as above: For assets you remove from your living trust and that relate only to the management of your trust (that is, their removal does not affect the legal body of the living trust by requiring changes to it), you do not need to complete an official amendment form. As you buy, sell, and give away assets throughout your life, you can change the list of your current assets in your schedules, which are part of your Trust Instructions, at any time.

Revoking Your *Revocable* Living Trust

The beauty of a revocable living trust is how flexible and easy it is to control and manage. You can cancel (revoke) your living trust at any time, although few do. And the process can be easier said than done. Only under certain circumstances would a person want to revoke a living trust, and those circumstances can include getting a divorce or wanting to make extensive changes to a living trust that call for a new one. However, it's not so easy to revoke a living trust because it entails transferring ownership back to yourself (or others) from the trust. The assets in the living trust cannot remain in the trust once it has been canceled. Revoking a living trust requires filling out more transfer forms and a Revocation of Living Trust document. (See Figure 3.4.)

If you need to revoke your trust, consult an attorney or estate professional about doing so. He or she can help you complete the transactions of transferring titles back again and guide you through reversing the process. For example, if you are getting a divorce and you have a joint (AB) trust with your spouse, you will want to revoke that trust and set up another one as an individual. Unfortunately, you cannot "roll over" an AB or joint trust into a new, single one—nor can you split a joint trust into two single ones. You'll have to transfer titles, revoke, then start all over again. But your state may have a certain way of doing this, so check with a local estate professional.

Instructions for Your Successor Trustee or Alternate

Preparing your successor trustee for the task of administering your estate can be challenging. It requires having a conversation about the what-ifs. More to the point: It requires *initiating* a conversation with someone who may or may not want the task of serving as successor trustee. If you are creating a joint living trust with your spouse and you name each other as cotrustees and successor trustees in the event of one's death, this conversation is part of setting up your

REVOCATION OF TRUST

We, **GEORGE M. MILLER** and **ILENE MILLER**, as Settlor/Trustees of **MILLER FAMILY TRUST,** UTD, September 21, 2005, do hereby revoke the **MILLER FAMILY TRUST,** UTD, September 21, 2005, Executed at Santa Barbara, California.

Dated:

_____
GEORGE M. MILLER, Settlor/Trustee of the **BENSON FAMILY TRUST**, UTD, September 21, 2005.

Dated:

_____
ILENE MILLER, Settlor/Trustee of the **BENSON FAMILY TRUST**, UTD, September 21, 2005.

Declaration and Acknowledgment of Notary Public

STATE OF CALIFORNIA

COUNTY OF SANTA BARBARA

On _____ before me, _____,
personally appeared **GEORGE M. MILLER** and **ILENE MILLER** personally known to me -OR-
_____ proved to me on the basis of satisfactory evidence to be the persons whose names are subscribed to the within instrument and acknowledged to me that they executed the same in their authorized capacities, and that by their signature on the instrument the person, or the entity upon behalf of which the person acted, executed the instrument.

WITNESS my hand and official seal.

_____
Signature of Notary Public

Figure 3.4

living trust. But if you are an individual and choose someone to be your successor trustee, or if you are a couple choosing an alternate successor trustee, this assignment can be an emotional experience.

In Chapter 2 we talked about a Letter of Instruction that you give to your executor or that is found at your death, which details certain instructions for what to do with you and your estate. Providing a similar document to include in your living trust will help your successor trustee or alternate successor trustee better and more efficiently settle your estate. These documents are called final instructions or special instructions. In them, you can give your successor trustee a checklist of things to do and take care of at your death. You can include where your trust documents are located and give a copy of these instructions to your successor trustee in a sealed envelope. When we go over our living trust package in the next chapter, you will see how these instructions become part of your living trust, even though technically they are not part of the legal body of your trust. Much of this information gets incorporated into the optional and additional documents you add to your living trust.

The following is a checklist of items you may want to include in your final or special instructions:

- A primary list of people to contact first, with names and phones numbers: immediate family, friends, business associates/employer, extended family, physician, hospital (if donating body parts), religious representative

- A secondary list of people to contact eventually: creditors, utility companies, post office (to redirect mail), Social Security Administration, insurance companies, any advisors or attorneys (financial or otherwise), housekeeper, veterinarian, gardener, therapist

- How you want your body to be disposed of (burial, cremation, donation) and what kind of memorial service or funeral you want, if at all. Include hymns, readings for service and names of pall bearers

- Where to make donations in your name

- Where your safe-deposit box is located, and how to access it

- Where to place an obituary

- Passwords, PINs, or security codes or locations to personal accounts that will need to be opened. Provide location of all necessary keys

- How to distribute some of your prized, personal possessions that may not be specifically assigned to someone in your trust (example: your pooch, photo albums, baseball card collection, or bottle of Chateau Petrus)

- Location and account numbers for all checking and savings accounts

- Location of checkbooks, stock certificates, bonds, trusts, etc.

- Location of all credit cards

- Location of all insurance policies, policy numbers

- Location of property titles, deeds, leases, real estate

- Location of tax returns

- Debts owed to others

- Debts owed to you

Choosing Your Executor or Successor Trustee

The people you name in your will (executor) or trust (successor trustee) to ultimately take care of your affairs when you (and if you are married, your spouse as well) are gone, must be responsible and trustworthy individuals. They will play a vital role in the future of your family. It's more important that your executor or successor trustee be diligent, dependable, and honest than good with math, tax rules, or the law, or have some special academic degree. If your executor or successor trustee needs to employ the help of professionals (such as an accountant, tax, or estate lawyer), he or she can do so and use funds in your estate to pay for it. Pick someone who you know is up to the task and won't create problems for your family. This goes to say you should choose someone that your family likes and trusts as well. Selecting the outcast or mean Aunt Ruthie will not make for a smooth ride for your family. Finally, we always tell our customers to inform their chosen executors or successor trustees beforehand that they have been named in a will or trust. You don't have to show them the actual documents, but at least give them the heads up. No one wants to suddenly discover that he or she has to take on such a big role immediately and with no warning.

- Membership in professional, fraternal, social, and volunteer organizations
- High schools, colleges/universities attended (dates and location)

The above is a partial list. You can tailor your instructions as you see fit. Some of the above information will be contained in your living trust, but there's no harm in repeating time-sensitive instructions in a separate document you create and give to the person responsible for settling your affairs.

As hard as it may be, consider yourself dying today and think of all that you leave unsettled or "up in the air." If you could come back to inform others that you will no longer be living to take care of things, whom would you call first, second; and what would you need to do in order to cut your ties to this world? We know, it sounds morbid. But this is exactly what people have to deal with every day as loved ones die and don't prepare for it.

Conclusion

Creating a living trust is the first step in planning for your family's future. Even if you have another 50 years of joyful living, a living trust will be your companion that provides you with a sense of security and assurance that things will be okay when you are gone. At We The People, our attorneys have created excellent frameworks for setting up living trusts, which we will share with you in the next chapter. They include the most important pieces to any living trust, as well as some ancillary documents that we feel complete the living trust package. The goal of any living trust package is to preserve the estate and prevent probate. Tactics to avoid excessive taxation are also part of the goal. You want your possessions to get distributed in an orderly and quick fashion—to whom you intended them to go.

Once you have the basic documents completed in your living trust, you may opt to place them in a binder or folder for protection. You will also want to include copies of other important papers in your estate plan binder or folder:

- Military papers (example: discharge papers)
- Adoption papers
- Vehicle registration certificates
- Birth certificates
- Marriage certificates
- Divorce or separation papers
- Citizenship papers
- Any documents of personal interest

Having a personal data sheet that lists the names of your family's most recent lineage, such as you and your wife's parents' names, places of birth, and mothers' maiden names, can be helpful as well (for when anyone asks). You never know what kinds of questions might arise that must be answered by one of your survivors.

Next, we take you through an actual living trust. We'll show you a typical trust for an individual, as well as one for a married couple.

CHAPTER 4

The Living Trust Up-Close

This chapter takes you through the mechanics of a living trust, its parts, its powers, and what it means for you and your family. The previous chapters have given you a strong foundation for understanding the actual documents and absorbing their language. Throughout this chapter, we excerpt parts from two sample living trusts and explain each article and all sections of the trusts we use for our customers. We think one of the best ways to understand a living trust is actually seeing what one looks like and getting general explanations of exactly what it is you are signing and setting up. It looks hard, but the more you understand about these pages, the more confident you will feel about executing your own living trust.

These living trusts were specially planned and drafted by our attorneys. They contain all the legal mumble-jumble that you need to have in a solid, credible living trust. If you want more information about living trusts in your state, visit a local We The People (check Appendix C). You can also visit a law library or consult with an attorney who is experienced in estate planning. The Internet can be a good source of information, but you do have to be careful about any information you retrieve. Always double-check information you get off the Internet, and be especially prudent about obtaining up-to-date data. Laws and rules are always subject to change. You may also need to consult with an accountant or tax specialist to learn how you can plan your living trust to minimize tax burdens and maximize what goes to your beneficiaries. For example, if the value of your spouse's and your gross estate is more than what you can exempt from federal estate taxes, an estate planner can work with you and may be able to design ways of lowering your taxable estate. By reading this book, and seeing how an actual living trusts reads, you'll be better prepared to deal with a lawyer, accountant, or planner (or coming in to see us!).

If you use our living trusts as templates for creating your own and you omit any of the sections or articles used in these trusts, you risk invalidating the entire trust, so be careful about selecting any parts and doing away with them. Also avoid changing words or sentences around to make them sound better. This means don't insert or take out words, shorten sentences, or use a thesaurus to make substitutions. The IRS sets rules for exactly how a living trust should read, or else it may lose its structure and become a mess for your family legally. We know that much

This book contains only one full-length sample living trust—the Miller Family Living Trust, which is an AB joint living trust for a married couple. We have posted the sample single living trust—the Susan Allen Living Trust—on our web site at www.wethepeopleforms.com for you to view.

of the language in a living trust isn't how you'd talk to your friends and family. Living trusts don't read like the morning paper, magazine articles, mystery novels, or a good Stephen King bestseller. (You can't make movies out of these documents, either!) Living trusts use peculiar words, long sentences that lose you by the end of them, and legal jargon that means nothing to you but everything to the validity of a living trust. The living trusts we have here reflect what must be on paper to make any living trust legal. (Most of the terms in these living trusts reflect California's state laws; you should do your homework when matching your living trust to your own state's requirements.)

If you have your own attorney or planner set up your living trust (from scratch using his or her own style of a living trust and in light of your state's particular laws), you can still use this chapter to understand the basic framework of what your trust means. Your actual living trust may not read or appear exactly like these living trusts, but the general concepts outlined here are common to most living trusts. We think one of the best ways to explain living trusts is to show you one and go through it. The sections and articles may not match up to one you create with your lawyer or estate planner, but you'll get a good idea of what a living trust should contain, and be able to compare. The goal is to have a general understanding of a living trust's structure and the language it may contain. Exposure to this language and the concepts will prepare you for whatever living trust you ultimately create—with or without an attorney.

One living trust, the Susan Allen Living Trust, is a living trust for an individual. The other living trust, the Miller Family Living Trust, is an AB joint living trust for a married couple. For purposes of this chapter, if we say "joint trust" we are referring to a joint AB living trust.

Because some of the parts to these living trusts are lengthy, we focus on the key points, giving you general explanations to all sections. Only occasionally do we include the entire excerpted section from the sample trust. In places where we don't include the entire section from the living trust, you can refer to Appendix B to see the full and complete language used. Visit our web site (www.wethepeopleforms.com) to view more samples that you can use as templates. Simply enter WTPEP as your password to gain access to useful forms. Any additional documents to the living trusts can also be found in the Appendix. Should you need the advice of an attorney or estate planner to understand more or get some advice tailored to your situation, we suggest you find a professional to assist you. Everyone's circumstances vary.

Setting up a living trust requires three important steps:

1. Completion of the proper paperwork and creation of your living trust package

2. Obtaining all the necessary signatures, witnessing, and notarizing

3. Funding your living trust by renaming assets to the trust's name and thus, transferring assets into it

Living trusts are important for single persons, widows, widowers, and divorced individuals; however, they are especially important for married couples. The following example illustrates a typical mutual or joint living trust: The husband is the first spouse to die (called the deceased spouse), and the wife survives him (called the surviving spouse). During their life together, they establish a living trust and transfer their property to their living trust. After the husband dies, his remaining separate property is transferred to the trust and the trust, in turn, becomes the property of the wife. At the time of the wife's death, the designated successor trustee continues to manage the trust and/or distributes the assets according to the specific instructions contained with the trust.

Unlike a will, setting up a living trust requires you to deal with your banks, brokerages, and other financial outlets that relate to your assets. You must create new deeds, complete transfer documents, and notices of assignment in order to have your assets officially transferred into your living trust. For some transfers, you may have to record your documents with the county Recorder. It's not that hard, however, to accomplish these tasks and have everything set up within a couple of days. So let's take a look at two sample living trusts.

I Forgot What You Mean By . . .

Grantor. This is the person who sets up a living trust, so it's you (or you and your spouse together). Two other ways of saying grantor are *trustor* or *settlor.*

Settlor. The creator and boss of the living trust. Same as grantor or trustor. We use the term settlor in our trusts. Settlors are the original creators of the trust—and the bosses of their trusts during their lifetimes.

Trustee. Anyone who has power over the trust. In the following samples of living trusts, that person is not necessarily the same throughout, because when an original trustee dies or becomes incapacitated, someone else—another trustee—must take over. A *successor trustee* is the person the settlor names to take over as trustee after the settlor's death (or, with a joint trust between a husband and wife, after the death of the second spouse).

Principal. This is not the head of your grade school or high school. In living trust terms, the trust principal refers to the assets that you place in the trust. Other terms that mean the same thing include *trust property, trust estate,* and *trust corpus.*

Estate. All that you own at your death. All of your assets, whether they are in your living trust or not, at the time of your death.

Taxable estate. How much your estate (all of your assets combined) is worth at your death minus all debts (what you owe) and liabilities (what you are responsible for) in terms of your assets.

Beneficiaries. The people and/or organizations named to benefit from the trust at your death. During your lifetime, however, you are a beneficiary of your own trust.

The Table of Contents

Whether you are creating a single living trust or a joint trust with your spouse, your Table of Contents is very similar. The Contents for the joint (AB) living trust, however, will have additional information regarding what happens to the estate of the first spouse who dies. Because this is an AB living trust, at the death of one spouse, the mutual living trust gets split into two separate trusts—the A trust (also called the Survivor's Trust) and the B trust (also called the Decedent's Trust). An additional article exists in the joint trust to explain and detail the terms of the joint trust, which is more complex simply because two people's estates are combined. You'll see that the contents of Article 4 in the Miller Family Living Trust are not found in the Susan Allen Living Trust. Therefore, the single living trust has 10 articles, while the joint trust has 11 articles. But most of the articles in each type of trust follow a comparable pathway. Let's take a look.

Contents for a Single Living Trust

ARTICLE 1
1.01 Trust Estate Defined and Trust Purpose
1.02 Definitions
1.03 Trustee Designation
1.04 Additions to Trust Properties
1.05 Separate and Community Property Remain As Such
1.06 Amendment and Revocation

ARTICLE 2
2.01 Trust Income
2.02 Protection of Settlor in Event of Incapacity
2.03 Incapacity
2.04 Principal Invasion
2.05 Residence

ARTICLE 3
3.01 Death of Settlor
3.02 Payment of Death Expenses
3.03 Trust Income and Principal Distribution
3.04 Principle of Representation

ARTICLE 4
4.01 Non-Income Producing Property
4.02 Trustee Powers
4.03 Power to Borrow
4.04 Power to Loan to Trust
4.05 Purchase of Securities
4.06 Manner of Holding Title
4.07 Settlor's Residence

ARTICLE 5
5.01 Direction to Minimize Taxes
5.02 Power to Waive Recovery of Taxes

ARTICLE 6
6.01 Incontestability
6.02 Disinheritance

Contents for a Joint Living Trust

ARTICLE 6
6.01 Direction to Minimize Taxes
6.02 Power to Waive Recovery of Taxes

ARTICLE 7
7.01 Incontestability
7.02 Disinheritance

ARTICLE 8
8.01 Accrued Income on Termination of Beneficial Interest
8.02 Distribution in Kind or Cash
8.03 Spendthrift Provision

ARTICLE 9
9.01 Trustees

ARTICLE 10
10.01 Perpetuities Savings Clause

ARTICLE 11
11.01 Governing Law
11.02 Invalidity of Any Provision
11.03 Successor Trustee

We'll take a look at each of the above Articles in turn. But, before we even get to the first article, a statement generally prefaces Article 1 that gives the name of the living trust, the settlors' names, their place of residence (county and state), and the date. Centered in the middle of the page, this statement declares the living trust and formally introduces the trust.

For the Single Living Trust:

THE SUSAN ALLEN LIVING TRUST
REVOCABLE LIVING TRUST AGREEMENT
DATED: _____, 2005
BETWEEN: SUSAN ALLEN, AS SETTLOR
AND: SUSAN ALLEN, AS TRUSTEE

SUSAN ALLEN, a resident of the State of California, County of Los Angeles, establishes a Trust upon the conditions and for the purposes hereafter set forth.

For the Joint Living Trust:

THE MILLER FAMILY LIVING TRUST
REVOCABLE LIVING TRUST AGREEMENT
DATED: _____, 2005
Between: GEORGE M. MILLER and ILENE MILLER, as Settlors
And: GEORGE M. MILLER and ILENE MILLER, as Trustees

GEORGE M. MILLER and **ILENE MILLER,** residents of the State of California, County of Santa Barbara, establish a Trust upon the conditions and for the purposes hereafter set forth.

Naming Your Living Trust

Your living trust must have a name. While you can get imaginative with names, using your own family name or individual name is best. If you've adopted the use of another name but own assets in your original name, this can cause some confusion when you transfer assets into your trust. You may have to change the deed to reflect your current name and then transfer the asset into the trust.

If you set up more than one trust, use the label "UTD" (under trust dated) after the title to indicate the specific trust. Examples:

- The Ernest Hemingway Living Trust, UTD January 14, 1943.
- The O'Henry Family Living Trust, UTD August 10.
- The Ira and Linda Distenfield Living Trust, UTD June 22, 1995.
- The Nancy Reagan and Ronald Reagan Living Trust, UTD December 5, 1986.
- The Chateau Martel Living Trust, UTD October 14, 2004.

The date essentially becomes part of the living trust's name.

Unmarried couples and gay and lesbian couples can create living trusts, but our joint living trusts are specifically designed for married couples. If you are part of an unmarried couple, you each can create separate living trusts. If you prefer to set up a joint living trust together, go to an attorney who specializes in such trusts, as the laws can vary by state. In most states, partners cannot claim a legal right to inherit property in the absence of a will or living trust, so making sure your will or living trust is worded correctly to carry out your partner's and your wishes entails having a professional advise and assist you.

Article 1

Section 1.01. Trust Estate Defined and Trust Purpose

This section defines the trust by saying the trust holds assets for the purpose of providing for the "health, support and maintenance" of the people who set up the trust, and ultimately, for their named beneficiaries. The first paragraph in a single or joint trust is the same.

> All property hereafter transferred or conveyed to and received by the Trustee to be held pursuant to the terms of this instrument is herein called the "Trust Estate" and shall be held, administered, and distributed by the Trustee as provided in this Trust Agreement. The Settlor shall transfer and deliver to Trustee the property described in the various schedules accompanying this Trust. Such title and interests the Trustee has received or may hereafter acquire in that property and such other property as may hereafter be added to the Trust, shall be vested in the Trustee.

The second paragraph is slightly different between the single and joint trusts.

Single Trust's Version:

> The primary Trust purposes shall be to provide for the health, support and maintenance of the Settlor during his or her lifetime, in his or her accustomed manner of living. The secondary Trust purposes shall be to permit the Settlor to provide funds for the reasonable health, support, and education of the Settlor's designated beneficiaries.

Joint Trust's Version:

> The primary Trust purposes shall be to provide for the health, support and maintenance of the Settlors during their lifetime, in their accustomed manner of living. The secondary Trust purposes shall be to permit the Settlors to provide funds for the reasonable health, support, and education of the Settlors' designated beneficiaries.

Section 1.02. Definitions

This section defines the main people related to the trust, which are the trustees. If the trustees have children, they are all named, regardless of whether they will be beneficiaries or have already died. Various terms used throughout the trust also get defined here. The joint trust contains a few more definitions.

Single Trust's Definitions:

As used in this Declaration of Trust,

a) The term "settlor" shall refer individually to **SUSAN ALLEN.**

b) The term "trustee" shall mean the person appointed to administer the Trust.

c) The terms "child" and "children" as used in this Declaration shall mean the lawful issue of **SUSAN ALLEN,** and shall include children hereafter born to or legally adopted by **SUSAN ALLEN.** The terms "issue," "next-of-kin," "heirs," "child," "children" or any other class designation shall not include stepchildren, foster children, half-bloods or persons born out of wedlock, unless otherwise specifically designated as a beneficiary of this Trust. Said definition shall also apply to any testate or intestate beneficiary or potential beneficiary. The names of the Settlor's children are: **DAVID ALLEN, JUDY ALLEN** and **SALLY ALLEN.**

d) The Term "beneficiary" shall mean the person or persons for whose benefit assets are held in Trust.

Joint Trust's Definitions:

As used in this Declaration of Trust,

a) The term "husband" shall mean **GEORGE M. MILLER.**

b) The term "wife" shall mean **ILENE MILLER.**

c) The term "settlor" shall refer individually and collectively to Husband and Wife.

d) The term "trustee" shall mean the person appointed to administer the Trust.

e) The terms "child" and "children" as used in this Declaration shall mean the lawful issue of Settlor, and shall include children hereafter born to or legally adopted by Settlor. The terms "issue," "next-of-kin," "heirs," "child," "children" or any other class designation shall not include stepchildren, foster children, half-bloods or persons born out of wedlock, unless otherwise specifically designated as a beneficiary of this Trust. Said definition shall also apply to any testate or intestate beneficiary or potential beneficiary. The names of the children of the Settlor currently living are: **GEORGE MELVIN MILLER** and **SCOTT C. MILLER.**

f) The Term "beneficiary" shall mean the person or persons for whose benefit assets are held in Trust.

Section 1.03. Trustee Designation

This section is brief and simply names the trustee. Because these are living trusts, the trustees are the same people who are setting up the trust, or the settlors. They all serve as their own trustee for the duration of their lives, unless they become incapacitated. Notice that in the joint trust, each person is a cotrustee.

Single Trust's Designation:

SUSAN ALLEN is hereby designated as Trustee. Should **SUSAN ALLEN** become unable because of death, incapacity, or other cause, to serve as such Trustee, or should **SUSAN**

ALLEN resign as such Trustee, before the natural termination of this Trust, the Successor Trustee named herein in Article Eight shall thereafter serve as the Trustee.

Joint Trust's Designation:

GEORGE M. MILLER (Husband) and **ILENE MILLER** (Wife) are hereby designated as Co-Trustees. Should either **GEORGE M. MILLER** or **ILENE MILLER** become unable because of death, incapacity, or other cause, to serve as such Co-Trustee, or should either resign as such Co-Trustee, before the natural termination of this Trust, the remaining Co-Trustee, **GEORGE M. MILLER** or **ILENE MILLER,** shall thereafter serve as sole Trustee as provided for in this Declaration. Furthermore, the Co-Trustees shall have the authority to designate either Husband or Wife to deal with particular assets because of their special knowledge of that asset. This designation shall be evidenced by a written agreement signed by both the Settlors and Trustee, a copy of which shall be appended to this Agreement. The term "Trustee" as used in this Declaration shall refer collectively to **GEORGE M. MILLER** and **ILENE MILLER** so long as they shall serve as such Co-Trustees and thereafter to such of them as may serve as sole Trustee. This Paragraph is subject to the provisions contained in Section 9.01.

Section 1.04. Additions to Trust Properties

This section is identical in both single and joint trusts. It explains certain rights of the trustee with regard to adding assets to the trust. Basically, a trustee can move assets in and out of the trust as he or she sees fit; the trust can accept any assets designated to the trust; and the trust can be named as a beneficiary of any insurance, pension, or other death benefit.

a) At any time during the continuance of this Trust the Trustee, in the Trustee's sole discretion after consideration of the possible tax consequences thereof to all concerned, is authorized to receive additions of cash or other properties to the Trust, subject to any conditions to which the Trustee may agree, from any source whatsoever without limitation, whether by gift, will, or otherwise. However, the Trustee shall accept all assets which any person or persons may give, devise, and/or bequeath by last will and testament to this Trust hereunder as well as all assets which may be transferred to this Trust pursuant to the expressed provisions of any other Trust document or documents of any kind.

b) Furthermore, at any time any person or persons may designate this Trust as the beneficiary, primary or contingent, of any insurance, pension, or other death benefit, relating to the life of anyone (such designation to be presumed to be revocable unless it is expressly irrevocable) and, until such benefit matures by reason of death. The Trustee shall have no responsibility whatsoever with respect thereto, it being intended that, unless and until the Trust which is designated beneficiary of such death benefit becomes the owner of the insurance proceeds involved (or other source of such benefit), such Trust arrangement shall be operative only with respect to such net proceeds as actually become payable by reason of death.

Section 1.05. Separate and Community Property Remain As Such

This section states that when the trustees add their assets to their trust, they add both separate and community property. Because a joint trust may contain assets owned separately by both the husband and wife, those assets will be delineated and listed in a later part of the trust. Even though you set up a trust with your spouse, and have assets that you acquired outside of your marriage, all of your spouse's and your assets can go into the trust.

Single Trust's Language:

All property now or hereafter conveyed or transferred to the Trustee pursuant to this Declaration, which was community property, quasi-community property, or separate property at the time of such conveyance or transfer, shall retain its character respectively, as community property, quasi-community property, or the separate property of the Settlor transferring such property to the Trust.

Joint Trust's Language:

All property now or hereafter conveyed or transferred to the Trustee pursuant to this Declaration, which was community property, quasi-community property, or separate property at the time of such conveyance or transfer, shall retain its character respectively, as community property, quasi-community property, or the separate property of the Settlor transferring such property to the Trust.

For the purpose of devise or distribution to the beneficiaries of the Settlor who owns such separate property, all property listed on the accompanying "Husband's Separate Property Schedule" shall be allocated to the beneficiaries of the Settlor/Husband listed on his schedule. All property listed on the accompanying "Wife's Separate Property Schedule" shall be allocated to the beneficiaries of the Settlor/Wife listed on her schedule. Final distribution of the property listed on these accompanying schedules, if not otherwise noted herein, shall be at the death of the surviving spouse.

All other Trust property acquired during the Settlors' marriage, unless included in either the "Husband's Separate Property Schedule" or "Wife's Separate Property Schedule," shall retain the nature of its previous character and shall be distributed according to the terms of this Trust Agreement.

Section 1.06. Amendment and Revocation

This section lays out the rules for making changes to the trust, including canceling it. Joint trusts are more complex because while the two cotrustees are still alive, both can do whatever he or she wants to the trust, but once one spouse dies, the trust gets split into two, and the decedent's trust cannot be changed or canceled by the surviving spouse. The decedent's trust becomes irrevocable. However, the surviving spouse, who is typically the successor trustee to the dead spouse, controls, manages, and administers all of the decedent's trust. In our joint AB trust, the surviving spouse has a life estate in the decedent's trust, meaning he or she uses the assets in the decedent's trust for living.

Refer to Appendix B (or the web site) to see this section's language.

Article 2

Section 2.01. Trust Income

This section says that settlors can take income produced by the assets in the trust and use that income for living. Example: You have a rental property in the trust that produces monthly income for you from tenants, and you can use that money by freely taking it out whenever you like. This section only relates to primary trustees, and not successor trustees. It grants the settlors the right to use any of their trust's income.

Single Trust's Language:

During the life of the Settlor, the Trustee shall at least annually, unless otherwise directed by Settlor in writing, pay to or apply for the benefit of **SUSAN ALLEN,** all of the net income from the Trust Estate.

Joint Trust's Language:

During the joint lives of the Settlors, the Trustee shall at least annually, unless otherwise directed by both Settlors in writing, pay to or apply for the benefit of Husband and Wife, all of the net income from the Trust Estate in the same proportions as each of their respective interests in the Trust Estate.

Section 2.02. Protection of Settlor in Event of Incapacity

This section instructs what to do when a trustee becomes incapacitated. A successor trustee (or a cotrustee in the case of a couple) can use the trust to the benefit of the incapacitated trustee. Once a trustee becomes incapacitated, he or she loses the power to do anything to the trust, such as cancel it, make changes, or withdraw assets. A successor or cotrustee must take over at that point and make decisions for, but also to the benefit of, the incapacitated trustee.

Single Trust's Language:

During the life of the Settlor, should the Settlor become incapacitated as defined in Section 2.03 below, the Trustee may, in the Trustee's discretion:

a) Pay to or apply for the benefit of the incapacitated Settlor such amounts of the principal of the Trust Estate as the Trustee may, from time to time, deem necessary or advisable for his or her use and benefit.

b) Apply such portion of the net income, up to the whole thereof, of the Trust Estate as the Trustee may deem in his or her absolute discretion reasonable and proper for the benefit of the Settlor so adjudged to be incompetent or unable to manage his or her own affairs.

c) Declare void and without effect any attempt by the incompetent Settlor to exercise the reserved rights of revocation, amendment, withdrawal of assets, control over Trustee, etc., unless a court of competent jurisdiction determines otherwise or a Settlor's disappearance constitutes incapacity under Section 2.03 c) and the Settlor has reappeared.

Joint Trust's Language:

During the joint lives of the Settlors, should either Settlor become incapacitated as defined in Section 2.03 below, the Trustee may, in the Trustee's discretion:

a) Pay to or apply for the benefit of the incapacitated Settlor such amounts of the principal of the Trust Estate, up to the whole of the community estate and the separate property of such Settlor, as the Trustee may, from time to time, deem necessary or advisable for his or her use and benefit. However, the Trustee shall not make payments from the community estate without first obtaining the written approval of the Settlor not so disabled. Any payments made pursuant to this paragraph from the community estate shall be community property.

b) Pay the entire net income of the Trust Estate in monthly or other convenient installments to the remaining competent Settlor, or

c) Apply such portion of the net income, up to the whole thereof, of the Trust Estate as the Trustee may deem in his or her absolute discretion reasonable and proper for the benefit of the Settlor so adjudged to be incompetent or unable to manage his or her own affairs.

d) Declare void and without effect any attempt by the incompetent Settlor to exercise the reserved rights of revocation, amendment, withdrawal of assets, control over Trustee, etc., unless a court of competent jurisdiction determines otherwise or a Settlor's disappearance constitutes incapacity under Section 2.03 c) and the Settlor has reappeared.

Section 2.03. Incapacity

This section defines incapacity. The legal language is the same for both single and joint trusts. Incapacity can be determined in many ways: by a court order, by two physicians who acknowledge with a certificate that a trustee is incapacitated, by the physical disappearance of a trustee, or by circumstances that indicate a trustee is not able to look after his or her own best interests. When a trustee is declared incapacitated, the reversal of that denotation requires considerable proof that the person can make prudent decisions in his or her best interests.

Section 2.04. Principal Invasion

This section says that should the trustees not have enough money to support themselves from the trust's income, they can dip into the trust's principal (again, principal refers to the assets in the trust) to generate more income for the trustees. An example of invading the trust's assets would be when a trustee decides to sell an asset in the trust to make money. The language in both the single and the joint trusts are almost identical.

Single Trust's Language:

> During the life of the Settlor, should the net income of assets contained in this Trust be insufficient to provide for the care, maintenance or support of the Settlor as herein defined, the Trustee may, in the Trustee's absolute discretion, pay to or apply for the benefit of the Settlor such amounts from the principal of the Trust Estate as the Trustee may in the Trustee's absolute discretion, from time to time deem necessary or advisable for the care, maintenance or support of the Settlor. As used in this section, the term "care, maintenance or support of the Settlor" shall mean:
>
> a) The providing of proper care, maintenance and support for the Settlor during any period of illness, or other want or necessity;
>
> b) The maintenance of the Settlor in the manner of living to which he/she is accustomed on the date of this Declaration.

Joint Trust's Language:

> During the joint lives of the Settlors, should the net income of assets contained in this Trust be insufficient to provide for the care, maintenance or support of the Settlors as herein defined, the Trustee may, in the Trustee's absolute discretion, pay to or apply for the benefit of the Settlors, or either of them such amounts from the principal of the Trust Estate as the Trustee may in the Trustee's absolute discretion, from time to time deem necessary or advisable for the care, maintenance or support of the Settlors. As used in this section, the term "care, maintenance or support of the Settlors" shall mean:
>
> a) The providing of proper care, maintenance and support for the Settlors, or either of them, during any period of illness, or other want or necessity;
>
> b) The maintenance of the Settlors in the manner of living to which they, and each of them, are accustomed on the date of this Declaration.

Section 2.05. Residence

This section sets rights and rules regarding the homes of the trustees if homes are part of their trust (as listed assets). We will only show the joint trust's language here, which is identical to the single trust's language with the exception that the world "Settlor" is plural to refer to both spouses.

If the Settlors' residence property is a part of the Trust, the Settlors shall have possession and full management of it and shall have the right to occupy it, rent free. The Trustee shall be responsible for the maintenance of the property and for all taxes, liens, assessments and fire insurance premiums from the Trust to the extent such assets are available for such payment. At such time as the Settlors direct or when it is no longer used by the Settlors as a residence, it may be sold and the Trustee is hereby authorized to purchase another residence or a life tenancy in a retirement facility for use by the Settlors as the Trustee may select. The cost of the new residence or the retirement facility may exceed the proceeds from the sale of the former residence.

Article Three

Here is where the two types of trusts—single and joint—part ways and the remaining articles do not match. The joint (AB) trust must set forth the terms to what happens when one spouse dies. The single trust, on the other hand, is more straightforward. Thus, we will continue onward but focus on the joint trust only. You can refer to the web site to view the single trust in its entirety. You'll find that the remaining articles and sections of the single trust are also part of the joint trust but they do not take a spouse into consideration.

Section 3.01. Provisions After First Death

This section sets forth what happens upon the first spouse's death. In a joint AB trust, the death of the first spouse triggers the trust to split into two entities—the A trust (survivor's trust) and the B trust (decedent's trust). The surviving trustee must decide how best to divide the assets between the two trusts. If no decision is made, the two trusts are said to each contain half of the shared property between the spouses.

> On the death of either Settlor leaving the other Settlor surviving him or her, the Trustee shall collect all insurance proceeds payable to the Trustee by reason of such death, all bequests and devises distributable to the Trust Estate under the terms of the last Will of the deceased Settlor, and shall divide the entire Trust Estate into two or more separate trusts to be known and herein designated as the "Survivor's Trust" and the "Decedent's Trust."
>
> Whenever the Trustee is directed to make a distribution of Trust assets or a division of Trust assets into separate trusts or shares on the death of a Settlor, the Trustee may, in the Trustee's discretion, defer such distribution or division until six months after the Settlor's death. When the Trustee defers distribution or division of Trust assets, the deferred division or distribution shall be made as if it had taken place at the time prescribed in this Declaration in the absence of this paragraph and all rights given to the beneficiaries of such Trust assets under other provision of this Declaration shall be deemed to have accrued and vested as of such prescribed time.

Section 3.02. The Survivor's Trust

This section defines Trust A—the survivor's trust.

> The principal or Trust Estate of the Survivor's Trust shall consist of all the interest in each and every assets held by the Trustee pursuant to this Declaration on or by reason of the death of the deceased Settlor not allocated to the Decedent's Trust pursuant to Section 3.03 of this Agreement.

> Notwithstanding the provisions of this Trust Agreement regarding Trustee's powers:

> 1. The Settlor(s), by written instrument delivered to the Trustee, may require the Trustee of the Survivor's Trust to dispose of unproductive property or direct the Trustee's to convert unproductive property to productive property.

2. The Trustee shall invest and reinvest the assets of the Survivor's Trust in such manner that the aggregate return of all investments of the Trust shall be reasonable in light of then-existing circumstances.

Section 3.03. The Decedent's Trust

This section defines Trust B—the decedent's trust. The taxes referred to in this section will be discussed in Chapter 6. The key point: Trust B is a legal entity for sheltering assets from the tax burden. It's sometimes called the bypass trust, the exemption trust, the family trust, or the credit shelter trust because it allows a person to place many assets into it without taxation, based on the exemption amounts available. This section also adds more powers over the decedent's trust to the surviving spouse so that he or she can maximize that trust's money-making abilities.

> The principal or Trust Estate of the Decedent's Trust shall consist of assets equal in value to the maximum amount, if any, that can pass free of federal estate tax by reason of the unified credit available to the estate of the deceased Settlor, after considering any adjusted taxable gifts and bequests by will or other disposition which do not qualify for the marital deduction made by the Settlor, and all charges to the principal of the estate which are not deducted in computation of the federal estate tax of the estate of the deceased Settlor; provided however, that the allocation to the Decedent's Trust shall be satisfied with assets valued as of the date of allocation or distribution; provided further that any assets in the Trust Estate which do not qualify for the federal estate tax marital deduction shall be first used to satisfy the allocation to the Decedent's Trust.
>
> Notwithstanding the provisions of this Trust Agreement regarding Trustee's powers:
>
> 1. The Settlor(s), by written instrument delivered to the Trustee, may require the Trustee of the Decedent's Trust to dispose of unproductive property or direct the Trustee to convert unproductive property to productive property.
>
> 2. The Trustee shall invest and reinvest the assets of the Decedent's Trust in such manner that the aggregate return of all investments of the Trust shall be reasonable in light of then-existing circumstances.

Section 3.04. Last Expenses

This section explains how to pay for a trustee's end-of-life and death-related expenses, including any taxes.

> On the death of the first of the Settlors to die, the Trustee shall pay, either from the income or principal of the Decedent's Trust or partly from income of the Decedent's Trust, as the Trustee in the Trustee's absolute discretion may determine, the expenses of the deceased Settlor's last illness, funeral and burial expenses, and any inheritance, estate or death taxes, that may be due by reason of the deceased Settlor's death, unless the Trustee in his or her absolute discretion, determines that other adequate provisions have been made for the payment of such expenses and taxes. All estate, inheritance, transfer, succession and any other taxes, plus interest and penalties thereon (death taxes) which become payable by reason of the deceased Settlor's death, upon property passing under this instrument, shall be paid without reimbursement from the recipient and without reapportionment. All death taxes upon property not passing under this instrument shall be apportioned in the manner provided by law.

Section 3.05. Distributions from Survivor's Trust

This section explains how the surviving trustee uses his or her trust's assets. The surviving trustee has full use of any and all monies in his or her trust, whether that money comes from the trust's income or the trust's principal. The death of the first spouse does not change how the surviving spouse can manage his or her own trust (trust A).

a) Income

The Trustee shall pay to or apply for the benefit of the Surviving Settlor the net income of the Survivor's Trust in quarterly, or more frequent installments.

b) Principal

If the Trustee considers such income insufficient, the Trustee shall also pay to or apply for the benefit of the Surviving Settlor such sums out of the principal of the Survivor's Trust as the Trustee in the Trustee's discretion, shall consider necessary for the Surviving Settlor's health, support, comfort, enjoyment, and general welfare.

c) Right of Withdrawal

In addition, the Trustee shall pay the Surviving Settlor, as much of the principal of the Survivor's Trust as he or she shall request in writing.

3.06. Distributions from Decedent's Trust

This section explains how money can come out of the decedent's trust. This is where the notion of a life estate comes in to play. The surviving spouse can use assets held in the decedent's trust for living (referred to as "for the . . . health, education, support and maintenance" of the surviving spouse), but the surviving spouse has to use his or her side of the trust (trust A, or the survivor's trust) before using any of the decedent trust's principal.

a) Income

On the death of the deceased Settlor, the Trustee shall pay to or apply for the benefit of the Surviving Settlor and the net income of the Decedent's Trust.

b) Principal

The Trustee shall also pay and apply for the benefit of the Surviving Settlor such sums out of the principal of the Decedent's Trust that the Trustee, in the Trustee's sole discretion, considers necessary for the Surviving Settlor's health, education, support and maintenance in accordance with the Surviving Settlor's accustomed standard of living at the date of the deceased Settlor's death.

Payments out of principal to the Surviving Settlor shall be made first out of the Survivor's Trust until it is exhausted, and thereafter out of the Decedent's Trust.

Article Four

Section 4.01. Second Death

This section explains what happens when the second spouse dies. The trustee who takes over the surviving spouse's trust distributes the assets in the trust per the instructions left by the former (now dead) trustee. For example, the surviving spouse will distribute any special bequests made by the dead spouse right away and use the rest of the trust's contents for the "health, education, support and maintenance" in the rest of his or her life.

Upon the death of the Surviving Settlor, the principal of the Survivor's Trust and any accrued and undistributed income of the Survivor's Trust, shall be distributed by the Trustee in such a manner and to such persons, including the estate, the creditors, or the creditors of the estate of the Surviving Settlor, as the Surviving Settlor shall direct by specific reference in his or her special trust instructions.

Section 4.02. Payment of the Second Death Expenses

This section explains how to pay for the second spouse's death-related expenses. Similar to the first spouse's death expenses, payments come out of the survivor's trust (unless instructions were made for other resources to be used). Note that "trustee" here must refer to the successor trustee because both original trustees are dead:

> On the death of the Surviving Settlor, the Trustee shall pay either from the income or principal of the Survivor's Trust, as the Trustee in his or her absolute discretion may determine, the expenses of the Surviving Settlor's last illness, funeral, burial, and any inheritance, estate or death taxes that may be due by reason of the inclusion of any portion of the Trust Estate in the Surviving Settlor's estate, for the purposes of any such tax, unless the Trustee in his or her absolute discretion determines that other adequate provisions have been made for the payment of such expenses and taxes.

Section 4.03. Trust Income and Principal Distribution

This section details the distribution of the trust estate (including both deceased spouses' portions). Notice that beneficiaries are named here, as well as specific instructions about how and when they will receive their inheritance. Conditions can be placed on how beneficiaries of a young age can receive their inheritance, such as giving the trustee power to hold on to a beneficiary's inheritance in a separate trust until that beneficiary has finished school or has reached the age of 25. This section makes reference to another document—the Trust Instructions—that details more instructions and is part of the living trust package. We'll see this document a little later. Read carefully:

a) Upon the death of the Surviving Settlor, the Trustee shall distribute the tangible personal property of the Settlor set forth on the special trust instructions accompanying this Trust which are incorporated herein by this reference, to the beneficiaries designated therein. In the event that the Settlors have not deposited written instructions with the Trustee concerning disposition of personal effects or if such instructions do not concern the disposition of all the Settlors' personal effects, then the personal effects not otherwise disposed of shall be distributed among the Settlors' beneficiaries set forth below in subsection b), in such equitable manner as may be determined between them. The Trustee shall lend whatever assistance the Trustee deems advisable or appropriate to facilitate the distribution of personal effects. If the Trustee determines, due to a dispute or conflict among the beneficiaries, that a sale is in the best interests of the beneficiaries, the Trustee may, in the Trustee's sole discretion, sell the personal effects and distribute the sales proceeds as set forth below in subsection b).

b) Unless stated otherwise, the Trustee shall divide and distribute the net income and principal of the Trust Estate (consisting of the Decedent's Trust and Survivor's Trust(s) subject to Section 4.02) for the benefit of the Settlors' named beneficiaries as follows:

GEORGE MELVIN MILLER 50%

SCOTT C. MILLER 50%

If one of the beneficiaries named above is deceased at the time of distribution, the entire Trust Estate shall be distributed to the surviving beneficiary.

c) If any beneficiary, to whom the Trustee is directed in a preceding provision hereof, to distribute any share of the Trust principal, is under the age of 25 years when the distribution is to be made, the beneficiary's share shall vest in interest indefeasibly, but the Trustee may, in his or her discretion, continue to hold it as a separate Trust for such period of time as Trustee deems advisable, for matters including college or vocational training, but not after the time the beneficiary reaches the age of 25 years. In the meantime, the Trustee may use as much of the income and principal as Trustee determines to be required, in addition to the beneficiary's other income, from all sources known to Trustee, for reasonable support, comfort, and education. The Trustee has discretion to add any excess income to the principal. Unless otherwise specified in this Section, the Trustee may distribute income to a beneficiary at any time if, in the Trustee's sole discretion, such a distribution would reduce federal or state income taxes that would be paid on income produced by the trust estate and would be beneficial to the beneficiary entitled to receive said income.

d) When each beneficiary reaches the age of twenty-five (25) years, the Trustee shall distribute to each beneficiary One Hundred Percent (100%) of the then balance of the principal of his or her share of the Trust Estate.

e) Except as otherwise specifically provided above in subsection b), if any beneficiary for whom a share of the Trust Estate has been set aside should fail to survive the above distribution, then the Trustee shall distribute one hundred percent (100%) of the balance of such deceased beneficiary's share of the Trust Estate, in equal shares, to the issue then living of the deceased beneficiary, by right of representation, to be held in Trust for such beneficiary's issue until each such beneficiary attains the age of twenty-five (25) years. If there should be no such surviving issue, then all of the balance of such deceased beneficiary's share of the Trust Estate shall be added to the other shares set aside for the benefit of the Settlors' other living beneficiaries as hereinabove provided, including proportionately both the distributed and the undistributed portions of each such share, to be held, administered and distributed as part of other shares. If all beneficiaries fail to survive the above distribution, then their shares of the Trust Estate shall be divided equally among said beneficiaries' surviving issue to be held in Trust until each of said issue attains the age of twenty-five (25) years. Notwithstanding the foregoing, in the event of any distribution to issue of a deceased child, if in that child's estate plan a trust is established for the benefit of said deceased child's issue, the assets which would otherwise be distributed hereunder directly to such issue of such deceased child may, instead, be distributed to the trustee of such trust, to be held, administered and distributed as set forth therein for the benefit of such issue.

f) If all of the Settlors' beneficiaries and their issue should fail to survive final distribution of the Trust Estate, all of the Trust Estate not disposed of as hereinabove provided shall be distributed one-half (½) to the persons who would then be **GEORGE M. MILLER**'s beneficiaries and the other one-half (½) to the persons who would then be the beneficiaries of **ILENE MILLER.** The identities and respective shares of the aforesaid beneficiaries to be determined in accordance with intestate succession laws of the State of California then in effect relating to the succession of separate property not acquired from a predeceased spouse. If either of the Settlors has no such heirs, then all of the Trust Estate shall be distributed to the aforesaid beneficiaries of the other.

Section 4.04. Principle of Representation

This section says what happens if a named beneficiary dies before the second spouse dies.

Should a beneficiary predecease the Surviving Settlor's death that beneficiary's interest shall then be distributed to the surviving issue of such deceased beneficiary in equal shares on the principle of representation.

Section 4.05. Simultaneous Death

This section contains the simultaneous death clause, which determines the order of death for the spouses should they die at the same time. This language may sound stupid, but it allows for the distribution of the assets down to beneficiaries to occur free of legal complications caused by the question of who died first. In other words, it allows both spouses to do what they want with their assets held separately, no matter who died first.

> Should both Settlors die simultaneously or under any circumstances rendering it difficult or impossible to determine which Settlor predeceased the other, each Settlor shall, for the purpose of disposing of his or her separate property be deemed to have predeceased the other Settlor.

This language allows assets to go directly to beneficiaries without going through the estate of the spouse who died second; so, in a practical sense, this eliminates a step in the distribution of assets and the beneficiaries receive their stuff right away.

Article Five

Section 5.01. Non-Income Producing Property

This section relates to assets that do not produce income, such as an antique rocking chair or entertainment system. These assets can be placed in the trust, and upon the death of a spouse, the assets can either remain in the trust or be distributed to a named beneficiary per the trust's instructions.

> During the joint lives of **GEORGE M. MILLER** and **ILENE MILLER,** the Trustee is authorized to retain in the Trust for so long as the Trustee may deem advisable and in the best interest of such Trust, any property received by the Trustee from the Settlors, or from either of them separately, whether or not such property is of the character permitted by law for the investment of trust funds. After the death of the deceased Settlor, the Trustee may retain any such property in the Trust at his or her sole discretion (subject to Section 5.07 of Article 5 herein). Such property shall otherwise be distributed to those beneficiaries defined in Section 3.03.

Section 5.02. Trustee Powers

This section is lengthy, wordy, and heavily detailed. We chose not to include it here, and you can refer to Appendix B (or the web site) to see exactly how this section reads. A trustee holds many powers, much of them broad and sweeping. This section describes and lists all the powers that a trustee has over the trust to manage it responsibly and to the benefit of the trust and its final beneficiaries. It talks more about what a trustee *can* do, than what a trustee cannot do. It also mentions the state under which the trust is governed by law and reiterates specific instructions for how minor beneficiaries can receive assets, such as whether or not a distribution can be made under the Uniform Transfer to Minors Act and the maximum age of that distribution. We will discuss the Uniform Transfer to Minors Act (also the Uniform Gifts to Minors Act in some states) in Chapter 5, as well as explain the trustee's most important powers.

Section 5.03. Power to Borrow

This section says a trustee can borrow money for any trust purposes, such as paying taxes.

> The Trustee shall have the power to borrow money for any Trust purpose (including borrowing from the probate estates of the Settlors for the purpose of paying taxes) on such terms and

conditions as the Trustee may deem proper, from any person, firm or corporation, and shall have the power to repay such borrowed money.

Section 5.04. Power to Loan to Trust

This section gives the trustee permission to get a loan, place it in the trust, and repay that loan using the trust's assets.

See Appendix B (or the web site) for this section's language.

Section 5.05. Purchase of Securities

This section gives the trustee permission to purchase securities or other assets outside the trust (anything outside of the trust is called the probate estate). A creator of a trust can purchase securities, such as stocks and bonds, in his or her own name and not necessarily transfer them into the trust. If the settlor decides to transfer securities into the trust, he or she can do so, as well as transfer ownership of those securities back out, from the trust to his or her own name again. In a basic sense, this section merely gives the trustee more powers with regard to how he or she can manage securities; it prevents any limitations that the trust could otherwise imply.

> The Trustee is authorized to purchase securities or other property from the probate estates of the Settlors with or without security to the executor or other representative of the estate of the Settlor. The Trustee is further authorized to make loans and advancements to the probate estates of the Settlors, again, with or without security to the executor or other representative of the estate of the Settlor.

Section 5.06. Manner of Holding Title

This section says that a trustee who holds securities or other assets outside of the trust can do so without owning them in the name of the trust. We explained this above: A trustee can own securities in his or her own name and keep them out of the trust.

> The Trustee may hold securities or other property held by Trustee in Trust pursuant to this Agreement in Trustee's name as Trustee, in Trustee's own name without a designation showing it to be Trustee, in the name of the Trustee's nominee, or the Trustee may hold such securities unregistered, in such condition that ownership will pay by delivery.

Section 5.07. Settlors' Residence

This section explains how a surviving spouse can remain living in the same residence upon the death of the first spouse (the surviving spouse has a life estate in the decedent's half of the assets in the trust, which usually includes shared interest in a home). The surviving spouse is not bound to remain in the same residence, however, if another residence, including a retirement home or similar facility would be best. For example: Even though a wife, whose husband died, shared a home with her husband, which is owned by their trust, she can decide to sell that home and move to another state. She has a right to sell trust property and use those proceeds to buy new property in the name of the trust.

> After the death of the first Settlor, the Trustee is authorized to retain in any Trust or Trust for personal use of the Surviving Settlor, any property occupied by the Settlor as his/her principal place of residence at the time of death of the first Settlor to die, for so long as the Surviving Settlor may desire to occupy the residential property; during such retention, the Trustee shall pay, from either

the income or principal of the Trusts as the Trustee may deem in the best interests of such Trusts and their beneficiaries, all taxes and assessments levied or assessed against such property, and all costs of keeping such property properly insured, maintained and repaired. The Surviving Settlor shall not be obligated for the payment of rent. On written request of the Surviving Settlor, the Trustee may sell such property and replace it with other property, including a life tenancy in a retirement facility, to be retained in Trust in the same manner as the replaced residence property, suitable in the Trustee's judgment as a residence for the Surviving Settlor. The cost of the new residence or the retirement facility may exceed the proceeds from the sale of the former residence.

Article Six

Section 6.01. Direction to Minimize Taxes

This section explains that any and all tax-saving tactics can and will be used to minimize the amount owed in taxes. As we'll see in Chapter 6, the purpose of a trust is to avoid probate and minimize taxes. There are many tools a trustee can use to prevent costly taxes and maximize the use and inheritance of his or her estate.

Refer to Appendix B (or the web site) for this section's language.

Section 6.02. Power to Waive Recovery of Taxes

This section also relates to taxes, and how a rule in the Internal Revenue Code allows a trustee or personal representative to "waive the right to recover taxes paid." What this really means: If taxes were overpaid (yikes! You paid too much!), but the cost of recovering those overpaid taxes is too high, you don't have to recover those taxes.

> The Settlors' Personal Representatives and the Trustee shall have the discretionary power to waive the right to recover taxes paid pursuant to Internal Revenue Code Section 2207A or any successor statute.

Article Seven

Section 7.01. Incontestability

This section, also referred to as the no-contest clause, helps prevent costly disputes over the trust when a trustee dies. If, for example, beneficiaries raise any unnecessary disputes or try to void the trust and claim they are entitled to more than what you leave them, which jeopardizes the integrity of the entire trust, those beneficiaries risk losing their inheritance. If a beneficiary sues and loses, he or she gets nothing. The purpose of this section is to ward off any challenges to the trust that can result in expensive and long-winded legal battles.

Not all trusts have no-contest clauses, but we include them in our trusts. See Appendix B (or the web site) for this section's language.

Section 7.02. Disinheritance

This section names people to whom you do not intend to leave assets, but who would typically expect to receive an inheritance. If you leave someone out of your trust, you disinherit that person through omission. This AB living trust sets up a life estate for the surviving spouse, which means the surviving spouse receives a life interest in the dead spouse's assets. He or she can use all of the assets owned by the dead spouse's trust (minus any specific bequeaths distributed to beneficiaries) for "health, education, maintenance and support" for

Noncommunity Property States		
Alabama	Iowa	North Carolina
Alaska (unless the cou-	Kansas	North Dakota
ple signs a written	Kentucky	Ohio
community prop-	Maine	Oklahoma
erty agreement)	Maryland	Oregon
Arkansas	Massachusetts	Pennsylvania
Colorado	Michigan	Rhode Island
Connecticut	Minnesota	South Carolina
Delaware	Mississippi	South Dakota
District of Columbia	Missouri	Tennessee
Florida	Montana	Utah
Georgia	Nebraska	Vermont
Hawaii	New Hampshire	West Virginia
Illinois	New Jersey	Wyoming
Indiana	New York	

as long as the surviving spouse lives. If you want to disinherit a spouse in your living trust, state laws may limit your ability to do so. You cannot disinherit a spouse entirely if you live in one of the noncommunity property states. In these states, a surviving spouse is entitled to demand a set share of the property based on state laws. In the community property states, spouses who own property together are said to each own half of all the community property. A spouse cannot disinherit the other spouse's half. However, a spouse can leave separate property and his or her half of the community property to anyone.

> Repeat: If you live in one of the above states, if a surviving spouse does not receive one-third to one-half of the decedent's assets through a will or living trust, the surviving spouse is entitled to whatever the state law says he or she is entitled to. Some of these states may adopt community property-type laws in the future.

You can disinherit a child in a will or a living trust. You expressly state that you are not leaving the child anything. Or you can say that you have intentionally left out everyone who has not been named in the will or living trust. Because you have listed all of your children at the start of the living trust, as well as listed your beneficiaries, you can disinherit anyone outside of those listed people by stating something along the following:

> Except as otherwise provided herein, GEORGE M. MILLER and ILENE MILLER have intentionally omitted to provide for any other of their heirs living at the time of their deaths.

This statement leaves little room for people to emerge and contest that they should have been named in the will or living trust.

Article Eight

Section 8.01. Accrued Income on Termination of Beneficial Interest

This section says that if a beneficiary cannot receive his or her share of payments from the trust by reason of death (or other), the trustee must continue to manage those payments.

Example: A beneficiary who is receiving payments from a living trust dies. Those payments end and the trustee must decide whether to hold, administer, or distribute those payments to others. The trustee controls what happens to those payments that are no longer going to the deceased beneficiary.

See Appendix B (or the web site) for this section's language.

Section 8.02. Distribution in Kind or Cash

This section says that a trustee can use his or her discretion to distribute assets from the trust, which can entail dividing up assets into shares or partial shares. This distribution can also entail the trustee selling assets and using those proceeds to distribute cash or partly in cash and partly in kind (tangible goods, such as a physical asset).

See Appendix B (or the web site) for this section's language.

Section 8.03. Spendthrift Provision

This section sets conditions for how beneficiaries can use inheritance from a trust. For example, if you worry that your beneficiaries will squander their inheritance, you can set conditions in this section, such as saying they cannot use trust money to pay for their debts. One can imagine the situation: Grandparents don't want their living trust to allow their grandchildren to use any inheritance to pay for misbehaviors on their credit cards during their early adulthoods.

Article Nine

Section 9.01. Trustees

The section lists the names of the trustees in order of succession.

The following shall act as Trustees in the following order of succession:

a) The undersigned, **GEORGE M. MILLER** and **ILENE MILLER**

b) The survivor of the undersigned as Trustee of the Survivor's Trust, and Decedent's Trust.

c) At the death, incapacity, or resignation of the undersigned, then **GEORGE MELVIN MILLER** as First Successor Trustee. Should the First Successor Trustee fail or decline to serve, then **SCOTT C. MILLER** shall serve as Second Successor Trustee. They are to serve without bond.

d) A Trustee chosen by the majority of beneficiaries, with a parent or legal guardian voting for minor beneficiaries; provided, however, that the issue of any deceased beneficiary shall collectively have only one vote.

Article Ten

Section 10.01. Perpetuities Savings Clause

This section contains obscure language and does not seem to amount to anything but frustration for the reader. Don't worry about this section, or even bother asking what a "perpetuity" is. You need this section in your living trust, whether you like it or not. If you are truly curious, this clause relates to how long a trust can own assets with restrictions. It sets parameters for the lifespan of a trust, so as to avoid a single trust existing for 10 generations (hundreds of years!), or some such.

See Appendix B (or the web site) for this section's language.

Article Eleven

Section 11.01. Governing Law

This section allows for your trust to be governed by laws in more than one state. Although you execute a living trust under the laws of the state in which you set up the trust and live, you want your trust to be valid and enforceable in other states as well.

See Appendix B (or the web site) for this section's language.

Section 11.02. Invalidity of Any Provision

This section says that should provisions in your trust become invalid or unenforceable, the remaining provisions remain effective. You wouldn't want one flaw in your trust to jeopardize the entire trust. This is an important clause.

> Should any provision of this Declaration be or become invalid or unenforceable, the remaining provisions of this Declaration shall be and continue to be fully effective.

Section 11.03. Successor Trustees

This section lays out the rules for the successor trustee. For example, when a successor trustee takes on full responsibility as a trustee, he or she is not liable or responsible for any misdeeds or mistakes that the former trustee made. We'll discuss the role of the successor trustee in later chapters.

See Appendix B (or the web site) for this section's language.

Signatures and Declaration of Intent

The pages following the articles are where you must sign your documents and obtain a signature from a notary public. In our trust documents, a Declaration of Intent follows the general signature page, and you must obtain a notary signature here as well. To put simply, this Declaration of Intent is where you sign that you have signed the previous page. It's the extra signature to confirm that you have signed the actual trust documents. In most states, you do need to have witnesses sign your living trust. For joint trusts, both spouses must sign and appear before the notary. You may feel as you complete your trust documents, that you have signed in a million places. Don't worry about it. It's better to sign in too many places than in too few. If a page needs your signature (or a witness's or a notary public's signature), don't forget about it. Before you file away your living trust in a safe place, go through it again to ensure you have signed in every place required.

Refer to Appendix B for a peek at what these signature pages look like.

Pour Over Will

Since it is impractical to include everything you own in your trust by deed, account, or name, we set up pour over wills for our customers as part of their living trust package. Unlike the normal Last Will and Testament you may be accustomed to, the pour over will simply directs your named executor to "pour over" any assets that you failed to include in your trust for distribution under the terms of your living trust. Examples of such assets are jewelry, cars, active bank accounts, and household items you didn't officially include in your trust. Typically, a conscientious trustee of his/her trust will have already transferred all major assets into the living trust so that probate will not be necessary when distributing the remaining assets from the pour over will to the trust.

All assets that get placed into the trust using the pour over will, however, are subject to probate. The items that get poured into your trust are also referred to as the residue of your estate (it's the leftovers!). You must name someone to execute this will, and that person is called your personal representative. You also name an alternate should the personal representative be unable or decline to serve.

In our pour over wills, which you can see in Appendix B, there are three brief articles and two witnesses must sign a declaration.

Notice that pour over wills are written on an individual basis—there are no joint pour over wills for married couples setting up a joint living trust. In each spouse's pour over will, a statement at the beginning of the will mentions the state and marital status (name of spouse), and it lists all the children.

Each spouse must also obtain a Self-Approved Affidavit. Again, this is the document where you sign that you have signed in another place (in the will documents). It further confirms the validity of the will by clearly stating that the settlor/testator was of sound mind, of legal age, and under no duress when creating the will. Two witnesses and a notary public must sign this affidavit as well.

> Don't let the word "affidavit" confuse you. Affidavits are just pieces of paper that make something official. An affidavit is a sworn statement in writing. The affidavits in your living trust further formalize your documents and make them official, valid, and trustworthy (pun intended). Your successor trustee may have to use several affidavits in settling your estate at your death, as we'll see in Chapter 7.

Affidavit of Trust

This affidavit—the Affidavit of Trust—completes the main trust document set. Also called an Abstract of Trust or Certification of Trust, it proves your trust; if anyone ever requires proof of your trust, this is the page to show. This affidavit seals the deal and officially puts the stamp of approval on your trust. By now you may feel like you've signed in plenty of places, but the more you sign, the more you assure the world that your living trust is real and serious, and fully enforceable. This affidavit must be witnessed by two people and notarized.

Schedules

As part of your living trust package, you include the lists of the assets you have in your trust; this is an organizational tool to help your successor trustee know what your living trust owns and, sometimes, indicate where certain assets are located. "Schedule" is simply another word for list. In a joint living trust, three schedules are included. As trustee, you hold your assets in the trust (actually, the trust owns your assets) for your own benefit during your life. When you place assets in your trust you should identify those assets as belonging to "The Miller Family Living Trust, George M. Miller and Ilene Miller, Trustees." This simply means that your trust owns the assets and you own the trust.

- Schedule A: You and your spouse list all community or shared assets here.
- Schedule B: You list one spouse's sole and separate assets.
- Schedule C: You list the other spouse's sole and separate assets.

Understanding how property ownership works in your state will have an impact on your trust and how you can list your assets. Married couples need to know who owns what and whether the state in which you reside considers all that you acquire jointly as community property. States where community property laws rule are Alaska (if the couple signs an agreement), California, Idaho, Nevada, New Mexico, Texas, Washington, and Wisconsin. In these states, all assets acquired during the marriage are owned 50/50 no matter who paid or whose name is on the title. Any assets acquired *before* the marriage, however, or during the marriage by gift or inheritance to one spouse only, are called separate property. In common law states (all the states except for the community property states), property can be owned by one spouse or shared by both. Either one spouse's name appears on the title or both names appear. If there is a question as to who owns what, the person who paid for the asset or received it as a gift owns it.

How you own property will determine how you can transfer that property or do something with that property once it's inside the trust. In today's increasingly complex family situations, couples who clearly define who owns what and plan their estates smartly in consideration to all family members, are successful.

Funding Your Trust

Don't forget to fund your trust! The trust must own something, so you have to transfer at least one asset into it. We hope that you transfer all of your major assets into the trust by doing the proper paperwork and changing titles to reflect that the trust owns certain assets. See Chapter 3 about how to fund your living trust. It requires the time to make a few phone calls, complete some paperwork, and possibly visit your banks or other financial institutions. Anyone can do it—it's not that difficult.

If you set up all the documents, obtain all the proper signatures, and then never fund your trust by transferring ownership of your assets into the name of the trust, then you might as well not have a trust at all! An unfunded trust is meaningless. An unfunded trust is not an executable legal entity because there's nothing in it. Too many people do all the hard work of completing the paperwork and thinking about how they'd want to distribute their assets at their death . . . but then they never activate their trust by funding it. Don't be foolish in this regard. Transfer your most significant assets into the trust as soon as you can. It's not that difficult.

Listing Your Assets

You can transfer as many assets as you wish into your trust. Refer to Chapter 3 for instructions on how this works. In most cases, you have to deal with the financial institution that holds your assets, such as your bank, brokerage house, and so on, to officially transfer titles and account numbers from your name to the name of your trust. For real estate, you create new deeds and register them with your county land records office. You do not have to deal with your lender, as any debt tied to the property (as in a mortgage) goes with the asset into your living trust. For other assets of value that do not have an attached title to them, you create a Notice of Assignment to transfer them officially.

Examples of how to list certain types of property are below. Remember: Your schedules are an organizational tool for your successor trustee, so he or she knows what is in your living trust, and where items are located. This helps your successor trustee administer your estate and carry out your wishes. For household contents, you can be as general or as specific as you like. For personal property, you can categorize groups of possessions. You may want to itemize assets that you plan to give to specific people at your death.

Your Home:

- The house at 310 Maple Rd., Marblehead, Massachusetts, including all contents (personal possessions and household furnishings); and the adjacent (undeveloped) lot at 312 Maple Rd., Marblehead, Massachusetts.
- The 10 acres of undeveloped land in Santa Ynez, California.
- All of the household furnishings and contents at 805 Cantor Lane, Charlotte, North Carolina.
- The antique armoire in the master bedroom at 607 Malcolm Ave., Cooperstown, New York.
- Set of chinaware and silverware in basement at 33 Linden Ave., Eugene, Oregon.

Your Accounts:

- Money Market Account #123-4567-89 at ABC Financial, San Francisco, California.
- Savings Account #123-4567-89 at XYZ Bank of the People, Austin, Texas.
- Mutual Fund Account #123-4567-89 at Friendly Bank, Branch #5, Indianapolis, Indiana.
- 250 shares in Coca-Cola company.

Your Business and Partnerships:

- All assets of the settlor doing business as Lu-Lu's Kitchen, 210 Green St., Nashville Tennessee.
- All of the settlor's interest in Kathy's Wine Shop, 55 Merlot Ln., Napa, California.

Your Personal Property:

- First edition set of Encyclopedia Britannica kept in office at 341 Dover Blvd., Boston, Massachusetts.
- All machines, tools, and equipment kept in the garage at 89 Pine St., Phoenix, Arizona.
- The photograph albums kept in the living room at 266 Edgewater, Chicago, Illinois.
- The jewelry box and its contents kept in the master bathroom at 107 Prince Dr., Ft. Collins, Colorado.
- Two Cannondale road bikes kept at 767 Barnwood St., Billings, Montana.
- Two Dell computers (serial #123-4456789; and #987-654321) kept in office at 30 Santa Margarita, San Diego, California.

The clearer you are about listing your property in your schedules, the easier it will be for your successor trustee to manage your living trust. There are no standard rules for completing your schedules; they must indicate what is owned by the living trust. Listing assets on the schedules does not give those assets to beneficiaries, nor does it officially transfer those assets into your living trust. You are not designating who gets what—you are simply creating a document that clearly states what your trust owns for organizational and administrative ease. Do your best to be clear and thorough.

Optional Documents as Part of Your Living Trust

You'll find that in our sample living trusts, a segment of the package includes essential information for your successor trustee. These pages contain key information that your successor trustee may need to do his or her job efficiently and to the "T" of your living trust, but these

Reminder: Assets that have titles or other official paperwork to them, such as a home or a brokerage account, must be transferred to the trust via new deeds or by completing transfer forms with your brokerage house, for example. Simply listing the assets on the schedules does not automatically transfer to—or fund—your living trust. Think of your schedules as a table of contents for your living trust, but if you do not fund your living trust correctly, then you have a book with a table of contents and many blank pages.

are optional pages. They include your special instructions, or final instructions, and are not part of the legal body to your living trust, so you can change them at any time. The additional information you provide in these pages helps your successor trustee mechanically deal with many tasks, such as locating documents, contacting people, and knowing about any important information related to your assets. Examples of what to include in this section are as follows:

- Date and location of personal and real property
- Professional consultants and advisors (including doctors, clergy, and financial advisors)
- Location of documents and records
- Safe deposit box information
- Safe combination

The following are typical documents we include in our living trust packages. You'll find samples of these pages in the sample living trust in Appendix B (or by viewing samples on the web site).

List of Liabilities

After you list your assets and where important items are located, you get to list your liabilities, which are things you owe. You want to list names, addresses, related account numbers, balances, and dates for every liability you have. Examples of liabilities include loans, credit card debt, past and current taxes due, legal judgments, and child support. This page alerts your successor trustee to what needs to be taken care of.

Insurance Policies

A document that lists all of your insurance policies, including policy numbers, name of insured, beneficiary, and the premium, helps the trustee keep those items in check. Include all types of insurance policies: life, automobile, homeowners, real estate, equipment, disability, medical, and dental.

Burial Instructions

Here is where you detail how you want to be buried (if at all). You can give any special instructions that you wish here, such as having your ashes scattered in the ocean where you spent the summers as a child, or give the name of the mortuary you wish your family to use upon your death. Remember: This is an optional document, and you can change it at any time.

This is where you get organized and manage your living trust responsibly. This entails leaving important instructions for any successor trustee, such as where to find documents related to your estate and what specific items you intend to give to your beneficiaries. If you were someone's successor trustee, what would you need to know about his or her estate to settle affairs?

Documents and Records to Include in Itemized List of Locations

Trust Documents	Other Investment Records	Keogh Plan Records
Copy of Trust Documents	Birth Certificate	Safe-Deposit Box
Life Insurance Policies	Marriage Certificate	Information
Cemetery Plot Information	Citizenship Papers	Safe Combination
Bank Account Records	Divorce/Separation	Partnership Agreements
Deeds to Real Property	Documents	Notes and Loan Agreements
Rental Property Records	Military Discharge Papers	Record of Stored and Loaned
Motor Vehicle Registration	Adoption Papers	Property
Tax Records	Passports	Employment Records
Stock/Bond Certificates	Annuity Contracts	Educational Records
Broker Account Records	IRA Plan Records	Miscellaneous

Donation of Anatomical Gifts

If you want to donate specific organs to a hospital, you can pick the hospital and pick which organs you want donated. It's a good idea to sign your name and date this paper. Note that burial and organ donation instructions are done individually. Again, this is an optional document, and you can change it at any time.

Trust Instructions

The Trust Instructions detail how the successor trustee should carry out your wishes with regard to certain issues that need more direction. If specific instructions are not conveyed through the language of the actual trust articles, this is where you record that essential information and provide precise directions. Your Trust Instructions are informal and can be revised at any time without the hassles of creating formal amendments. (If, however, any of your Trust Instructions affect the information in your Articles of Trust, you will have to make formal changes.) Generally, your Trust Instructions make up your living trust notebook—a place to make important notes regarding the management of your living trust. Think of this part as the place where you can freely make notes because you cannot write in the textbook to which it correlates.

Especially important are the actions you take to designate what assets you wish directed to your identified individual beneficiaries. You may have requested in the body of your living trust that certain percentages of your estate should be passed on to specified individuals or members of your family. However, your Trust Instructions can be utilized to make specific gifts. For example, you may have indicated that your estate should be divided equally to "share and share alike" among your children at your death. You can use your Trust Instructions to pass specific assets of your trust to individual children. It can also nominate guardians for minor children or custodians for minor beneficiaries.

Examples of such information listed in this section are below:

In Our Sample Miller Family Living Trust:

> If at the time of my death, any of our children are minors and a guardian is needed, we nominate our good friend, Judy Sanders to be the guardian of their estate and their person.

Date: 3/5/05 Signed: George M. Miller

Date: 3/5/05 Signed: Ilene Miller

We give the antique rocking chair and our condo to our son, George Melvin Miller.

Date: 3/12/05 Signed: George M. Miller

Date: 3/12/05 Signed: Ilene Miller

Two notes about Trust Instructions:

* Anyone that gets a gift from you at your death is also a beneficiary, so he or she must be listed in the body of the trust at the beginning when you list your beneficiaries.

* If a beneficiary dies before receiving an asset, you have many options. You can name an alternate beneficiary for that asset or have it distributed equally among the remaining beneficiaries, for example.

Sign and date your Trust Instructions page. For every specific instruction you make, sign and date it. Don't leave too much white space, however, between your specific instruction and your signature/date. If you leave white space, someone else can insert new instructions that look like you signed and dated.

Emergency Information Sheet

While not a necessary part of your living trust package, having one sheet that lists the names and contact information for first and second successor trustees, an alternate conservator, and an alternate agent of health care decisions can come in handy. This sheet is good for emergency purposes, because people who hold powers of attorney for the management of the trust's assets, agents holding power to make health decisions, executors, and successor trustees need to be notified.

In your Trust Instructions, you specifically state how you want your successor trustee to distribute certain personal possessions, such as giving your piano to Annie or your electric guitar to Michael. Sign and date all of your entries.

Conclusion

This chapter went through the guts of a typical living trust document. We focused on a joint, AB living trust. Joint living trusts are complex by design because they must reflect two people's lives rather than just one. They also must contain all the right language and jargon so that they remain valid and enforceable for as long as possible. People who set up living trusts decades before their death want those trusts to be good when they need them most. This is true for families and individuals.

Note about naming guardians for children: You do not need a living trust solely for the purpose of naming guardians for minor children in the event you die before they turn 18. You can do this in a will and not have a living trust. When you name guardians for minor children, you nominate them. The court ultimately has to approve of the guardian you nominate. If you have a living trust, you can nominate your guardian (and custodian) in your Trust Instructions page.

We haven't discussed your powers of attorney and advanced health care directives. While these documents are optional additions to your living trust package, we urge you to include them. A living will can be included with these documents. You will determine now whether you want to be kept alive on life support machines. Including these additional documents is a necessary part to planning your estate responsibly and preparing your family for the future.

Pat yourself on the back for getting this far into the book. With the end of this chapter, the bulk of the legalese is behind you. You can refer to the Appendices or the web site at www.wethepeopleforms.com if you crave more legal mumble-jumble.

CHAPTER 5

Powers of Attorney, Successor Trustees, and Beneficiaries

We continue our review of a sample living trust by turning now to additional documents that our customers include in their living trust packages but are considered extra. In this part of your living trust package, you name your agents for power of attorney for both finances and health care and give any instructions they may need to carry out your wishes. These instructions might relate to a time when you cannot make certain decisions for yourself during your life, or it's the end of your life and someone needs to decide whether to withhold or continue life support, for example. The people you name in your living trust and additional documents to take care of your affairs—both asset-related and health care–related—have a huge role to play. In most joint living trusts, each spouse automatically assumes this role of being a successor trustee to a dead spouse's estate, but for individuals who set up living trusts, choosing someone to distribute their estate at their death can be daunting.

In the previous chapter, we stopped talking about the single living trust early on in our discussion of how basic living trusts work for married couples. Single trusts are simpler by design because they don't have to take a spouse's half of the estate into consideration. If you look at the sample single living trust we have on the web site, you'll find that most all of what's included in a single trust is also part of a joint living trust, but the single trust does not set parameters for splitting the trust into two separate trusts at the death of the individual. Once the person dies, the trust becomes irrevocable and the assets and liabilities of the individual are taken care of by the named successor trustee according to the individual's instructions.

Common to both single and joint living trusts (as supplemental documents) is the ability to name people to hold the durable power of attorney on your behalf, as well as give clear directions for how to deal with a situation whereby you are unable to make decisions about your health care and you must rely on someone else to do it for you. Your successor trustee cannot make (has no power to make) health care decisions for you if you become incapacitated, so if you want to name someone to make important decisions regarding your health throughout your life, you need to prepare this document. Additionally, if you want to die naturally and refuse any life support systems, you should prepare a living will. In some states, such as California, a document that names an agent with durable power of attorney includes a living will. In other states, this is a separate document.

Also, your successor trustee cannot manage any assets that are not in your trust if, for example, you go insane, get Alzheimer's, or are in another country and unavailable to make critical financial decisions for yourself. So if you fail to prepare a durable power of attorney for finances (sometimes called a durable power of attorney for property management), and you become incapacitated, any assets outside of your trust will need to be managed by a court-appointed conservator or guardian. Your successor trustee can be the same person as your personal representative and also have your power of attorney for finances and/or health.

Durable Power of Attorney

The first lesson in understanding durable powers of attorney is clear: They are alive when you are alive, and they are dead when you are dead. What does this mean? The sole purpose of having someone named to hold durable power of attorney on your behalf is to have someone available to make decisions for you when you cannot make them yourself during your life. If you lose your mind or become unavailable to act on your own behalf, your agent for durable power of attorney will do the thinking and decision-making for you. The person you choose to act on your behalf for financial and health care decisions is called your agent (also attorney in fact). People typically choose a close family member, a best friend, or a life partner.

You can execute two durable powers of attorney: one for managing assets (financial matters) and one for managing your health care. The term durable simply means that you name someone who will endure the state of your incapacity. Unlike a standard power of attorney, which becomes null and void in the event you are too ill to make decisions for yourself, the durable clause in these documents guarantees that the named person can act on your behalf if you become incapacitated. Example: You are in a coma and need someone to speak on your behalf for both medical and financial matters.

Your durable power of attorney documents may need to meet state law requirements, and they may have to be notarized. Every state makes its own rules for how these documents should appear and be formalized. In joint living trusts, spouses usually nominate each other to serve as agents of the estate or agents for health care decisions (which means they hold primary powers of attorney for each other). Each durable power of attorney document is separate, so each spouse will have his or her own set of signed and notarized documents naming an agent and an alternate.

Don't let the term "durable power of attorney" confuse you. A durable power of attorney is a written document signed by a person giving another person the power to act in conducting the signer's business, including signing papers, checks, title documents, and contracts; handling bank accounts; and other activities in the name of the person granting the power. The person receiving the power of attorney (the agent) is attorney in fact for the person giving the power and usually signs documents as "John Smith, attorney in fact for Jane Doe." This does not make the agent an attorney in the usual sense of the word. We know this term is odd and misleading, but you get used to hearing it.

An Especially Important Document for Single People. People wrongly assume that important decisions can be made for them at any time in the event of an incapacity or accident that prevents them from acting on their own behalf. For example, if you are in a car accident and reach the emergency room unconscious, the hospital and doctors would need someone to authorize your surgery. That person would have to legally hold the durable power of attorney for health care on your behalf. Or, let's say that while you are in the hospital recovering, you must sign a financial document that is critical to the lifeblood of your company, or your company may suffer greatly. You cannot physically do it yourself, so you would need to have appointed someone to hold durable power of attorney on your behalf to take care of that financial matter. Another example that puts this into perspective with regard to living trusts: Let's say you are an individual with a single living trust. You suffer a stroke and cannot do any more transfers of assets into your living trust. You have securities that you had not officially transferred into your living trust. Neither you—nor anybody else—can do that for you legally now. If, however, you have named someone to hold durable power of attorney for finances, that person can go ahead and complete the transfer.

Durable power of attorney documents are excellent documents to have—regardless of wills and living trusts. They are particularly important for single people who do not have spouses who may be able to make medical decisions legally under certain circumstances. Most people assume that their children could sign an authorization for them in an emergency situation, but that is not always true. Children do not have the authority to authorize a doctor, for example, to perform any life-saving surgery or treatment. (On the same token, parents may not be able to authorize such emergency treatment for their adult children.) Spouses can generally sign a medical release if their spouse is unable to sign those papers. Moreover, since spouses who set up a living trust together usually name the other as co- and successor trustee, each can manage the trust in the event one becomes incapacitated. However, it's wise for each spouse to also create power of attorney documents for both the medical and financial decisions. One can never be certain what set of circumstances leads to a moment when a decision must be made and no one can legally make it.

Married couples typically name each other as their agents for durable power of attorney, but they should also name alternates in the case where both become incapacitated at the same time (example: they are both in the car accident).

While most legal documents are uniform across the country, the durable power of attorney document can vary greatly. Each state has adopted its own version and approach to how these documents function. Following are two sample power of attorney documents for finances. (See Figures 5.1 and 5.2.) One is from Colorado and the other is from California. Notice how the California document allows you to specifically mark which powers you want your agent to have. You can limit what your agent can and cannot do. Or, you can allow your agent to have full discretion in making decisions on your behalf.

By showing samples of two different durable power of attorney documents for health care decisions, you can see just how no two are created equal from one state to another—but they serve the same purpose. (We show excerpts from these documents below.) Note also how these documents allow you to give specific instructions. You can define just how much power you want to give your agent by describing—in as much detail as you want—your desires, special provisions, and limitations.

As we noted earlier, a durable power of attorney for health care may contain right-to-die language, which states you do not want any extraordinary medical treatment if you become

GENERAL DURABLE POWER OF ATTORNEY

THE POWERS YOU GRANT BELOW ARE EFFECTIVE
EVEN IF YOU BECOME DISABLED OR INCOMPETENT

CAUTION: THIS IS AN IMPORTANT DOCUMENT. IT GIVES THE PERSON WHOM YOU DESIGNATE (YOUR "AGENT") BROAD POWERS TO HANDLE YOUR PROPERTY DURING YOUR LIFETIME, WHICH MAY INCLUDE POWERS TO MORTGAGE, SELL, OR OTHERWISE DISPOSE OF ANY REAL OR PERSONAL PROPERTY WITHOUT ADVANCE NOTICE TO YOU OR APPROVAL BY YOU. THESE POWERS WILL EXIST EVEN IF YOU BECOME DISABLED OR INCOMPETENT. THIS DOCUMENT DOES NOT AUTHORIZE ANYONE TO MAKE MEDICAL OR OTHER HEALTH CARE DECISIONS FOR YOU. YOU MAY EXECUTE A SEPARATE DOCUMENT FOR THAT PURPOSE. IF THERE IS ANYTHING ABOUT THIS FORM THAT YOU DO NOT UNDERSTAND, YOU SHOULD ASK A LAWYER TO EXPLAIN IT TO YOU.

KNOWN BY ALL PERSONS PRESENT, THAT:

I, **ROBERT J. SAMPLE,**

of 432 S. Palm St., Denver, CO 80236, "Principal", execute this Durable Power of Attorney and

do hereby make, constitute and appoint:

EDWARD F. SAMPLE,

of 432 S. Palm St., Denver, CO 80236,

"Agent" or "Attorney-in-Fact", as my attorney-in-fact **TO ACT IN MY NAME, PLACE AND**

STEAD in any way which I myself could do as if I were personally present and to the extent that

I am permitted by law to act through an agent, pursuant to the following provisions:

EFFECTIVENESS OF POWER OF ATTORNEY:

This instrument is to be construed and interpreted as a general durable power of attorney effective immediately.

GRANT OF POWERS: I grant to my Agent full power and authorization to do everything necessary in exercising any of the powers herein granted by this power of attorney as fully as I might or could do if personally present. My agent shall have full power of substitution or revocation. I hereby ratify and confirm all that my Agent lawfully does or causes to be done by virtue of this power of attorney and the powers herein granted. My Agent shall have the power to exercise or perform any act, power, duty, right or obligation whatsoever that I now have or may hereinafter acquire, relating to any person, matter, transaction or property, real or personal, tangible or intangible, now owned or hereafter acquired by me, including, without limitation, the following specifically enumerated powers:

Figure 5.1a

Powers of Collection and Payment:

> To forgive, request, demand, sue for, recover, collect, receive and hold all sums of money, accounts, annuities, bequests, bonds, certificates of deposit, checks, commercial paper, debts, deposits, devises, dividends, drafts, dues, insurance, interests, legacies, notes, pension, profit sharing, retirement, social security, stock certificates and other contractual benefits and proceeds, all documents of title, all property, real or personal, intangible or tangible, and property rights and demands whatsoever, liquidated or unliquidated, now or hereafter owned by, or due, owing, payable or belonging to, me or in which I have or may hereafter acquire an interest.

> To have, use, and take all lawful means and equitable and legal remedies and proceedings in my name for the collection and recovery thereof, and to adjust, sell, compromise, and agree for the same, and to execute and deliver for me, on my behalf, and in my name, all endorsements, releases receipts, or other sufficient discharges for the same.

Property Matters:

> To acquire, purchase, exchange and sell, or grant options to sell, mortgage, pledge, lease, sell and convey real or personal property, tangible or intangible, or interests therein, on such terms and conditions as my Agent shall deem proper, with full authority to sign, endorse, execute and deliver any sales agreement, deed, bill of sale and all other instruments or documents pertaining to the sale of any of my real or personal property; and to enter into bonds, contracts, mortgages and deeds connected therewith.

> To sell, assign, transfer, convey, exchange, deed, mortgage, pledge, lease, let, license, demise, remise, quitclaim, bargain or otherwise dispose of any or all of my real estate, stocks, bonds, evidences of indebtedness and other securities and other personal tangible and intangible or mixed property, or any custody, possession, interest or right therein at public or private sale, upon such terms, consideration, and conditions as my said attorney shall deem advisable and to execute, acknowledge and deliver such instruments and writings of whatsoever kind and nature as may be necessary, convenient or proper in the premises.

Management Powers: To maintain, repair, improve, invest, manage, insure, rent, lease, encumber, and in any manner deal with any real or personal property, tangible or intangible, or any interest therein that I now own or may hereafter acquire in my name and for my benefit, upon such terms and conditions as my Agent shall deem proper;

Banking Powers: To make, receive and endorse checks and drafts, deposit and withdraw funds, acquire and redeem certificates of deposit, in banks, savings and loan associations, and other institutions, execute or release such deeds of trust or other security agreements as may be necessary or proper in the exercise of the rights and powers herein granted;

Business Interests: To conduct or participate in any lawful business of whatever nature for me and in my name; to execute partnership agreements and amendments thereto; to incorporate, reorganize, merge, consolidate, recapitalize, sell, liquidate or dissolve any business; to elect or employ officers, directors and agents; to carry out the provisions of any agreement for the sale of any business interest or the stock therein; and to exercise voting rights with respect to stock, either in person or by proxy, and to exercise stock options;

Figure 5.1b

Safe Deposit Boxes: To have access at any time or times to any safe deposit box rented by me, wheresoever located, and to remove all or part of the contents thereof, and to surrender or relinquish said safe deposit box, and any institution in which any such safe deposit box may be located shall not incur any liability to me or my estate as a result of permitting my Agent to exercise this power;

Power to Hold Property and Make Investments: The power to hold or acquire any property, real or personal, or securities, regardless of whether such property or securities are a so-called "Legal" investment, where such course is, in the said Agent's opinion, for my best interest;

Power to Borrow: To borrow any sum or sums of money on such terms (including the power to borrow against the cash surrender value of any life insurance policy issued on my life), and with such security, whether real or personal property, as my Agent may think fit, and for that purpose to execute all promissory notes, bonds, mortgages, deeds of trust, security agreements, and other instruments which may be necessary or proper;

Disclaimer: To exercise or release powers of appointment in whole or in part and to disclaim or renounce in whole or in part any interest that I might otherwise have as a joint owner, beneficiary, heir or otherwise and in exercising such discretion, my Agent may take into account such matters as shall include but shall not be limited to any reduction in estate or inheritance taxes on my estate, and the effect of such renunciation or disclaimer upon persons interested in my estate and persons who would receive the renounced or disclaimed property;

Trusts: To transfer, assign and convey any property or interest in property, the legal or equitable title to which is in my name, to any trust of which I am the primary beneficiary during my lifetime and under the terms of which I expressly have the power to amend or revoke such trust, and to exercise any right of withdrawal of income and/or principal which I may have pursuant to the terms and conditions of such trust, whether such trust was created before or after the execution of this power of attorney;

Power to Change Beneficiaries on Any Insurance Policies on my Life: To change the beneficiaries on any insurance policies on my life; provided, however, that neither such right and power, nor any other rights and powers, shall be exercisable with respect to any policies of life insurance which may at any time be owned by me on the life of my Agent herein named.

Executing Government Vouchers. To execute vouchers in my behalf for any and all allowances, compensation and reimbursements properly payable to me by the Government of the United States or any agency or department thereof.

Depositing Money and Other Property. To deposit in my attorney's or my name, or jointly in both our names, in any banking institution, funds or property, and to withdraw any part or all of my deposits at any time made by me in my behalf.

Recovering Possession of Property. To eject, remove or relieve tenants or other persons from, and recover possession of, any property, real, personal or mixed in which I now or hereafter may have an interest.

Figure 5.1c

Litigation. To institute, maintain, defend, compromise, arbitrate or otherwise dispose of, any and all actions, suits, attachments or other legal proceedings for or against me.

Tax Returns. To prepare and execute any tax returns, including, but not limited to, Federal income tax returns, State income tax returns, Social Security tax returns, and Federal and State information and estimated returns; to execute any claims for refund, protests, applications for abatement, petitions to the United States Board of Tax Appeals or any other Board or Court, Federal or State, consents and waivers to determination and assessment of taxes and consents and waivers agreeing to a later determination and assessment of taxes than is provided by statute of limitations; to receive and endorse and collect any checks in settlement of any refund of taxes; to examine and to request and receive copies of any tax returns, reports and other information from the United States Treasury Department or any other taxing authority, Federal or State, in connection with any of the foregoing matters.

Automobiles. To execute and deliver to the proper persons and authority any and all documents, instruments and papers necessary to effect proper registration of any automobile in which I now or may hereafter have an interest, or the sale thereof and transfer of legal title thereto as required by law, and to collect and receipt for all monies paid in consideration of such sale and transfer.

MISCELLANEOUS: I grant to the Agent named herein the following additional powers of authority:

In the event any agent named herein should be of the opinion at any time that she or he does not have the expertise to manage all or any part of my assets, I grant to said Agent the right and power to delegate the management powers hereinabove granted over all or any part of my assets to any person(s) or firm(s), and to enter into any management or agency agreements with said person(s) or firm(s), pertaining thereto, with the right on the part of the Agent named herein to revoke and cancel any such agreement at any time upon ninety (90) days' written notice to said person(s) or firm(s).

I grant full and absolute authority to the Agent named herein, on a noncumulative, yearly basis, to make gifts to my children, in trust or otherwise, as well as to their spouses, and to their children, in trust or otherwise, with the amount of gifts to each such person each year not to exceed that amount which is excludable from the total amount of gifts made during such year under Section 2503(b) Internal Revenue Code of 1986, as amended from time to time.

I further authorize and empower the Agent named herein to use and apply so much of the income and principal of the assets comprising my estate as may be necessary or desirable, in the sole discretion of said Agent, for my maintenance and support. Any provision herein to the contrary notwithstanding, the Agent shall have no power or authority to use or apply the principal to discharge any legal obligation that the agent or any other person may have to support me or any dependent or beneficiary or mine, except to the extent that there are no assets reasonably available to the person having the obligation of support to pay the same.

I further authorize and empower my Agent to engage, employ and dismiss any agents, clerks, servants, attorneys-at-law, accountants, investment advisors, custodians, or other persons in and about the performance of these presents as my Agent shall think fit.

Figure 5.1d

Any decisions made by the said Agent with respect to the matters set forth hereinabove in sections 3(b), 3(c), and 3(d) shall be final, binding and conclusive upon all of the beneficiaries of my estate, and said Agent shall be released and discharged of and from all liability for any such decisions that she or he may make in good faith with respect thereto.

INTERPRETATION AND GOVERNING LAW: This instrument is to be construed and interpreted as a general durable power of attorney. The enumeration of specific powers herein is not intended to, nor does it, limit or restrict the general powers herein granted to my Agent. This instrument is executed and delivered in the State of Colorado, and the laws of the State of Colorado shall govern all questions as to the validity of this power and the construction of its provisions. This instrument is intended to be effective in all states of the United States and in all foreign countries.

INDEMNITY: I hereby bind myself to indemnify my Agent and any successor who shall so act, against any and all claims, demands, losses, damages, actions and causes of action, including expenses, costs and reasonable attorneys' fees which my Agent at any time may sustain or incur in connection with carrying out the authority granted her or him in this power of attorney.

NOMINATION OF GUARDIAN OR CONSERVATOR: In the event court proceedings are hereafter commenced to appoint a guardian, conservator or other fiduciary to take charge of my person, or to manage and conserve my property, I hereby nominate and appoint my Agent above-named, as my guardian, conservator, or other fiduciary, to serve without bond unless otherwise required by a court of competent jurisdiction.

REVOCATION: This general durable power of attorney may be voluntarily revoked by me by written instrument signed by me and delivered to my Agent. My guardian may also revoke this instrument by written instrument signed by him or her and delivered to my Agent. Any affidavit executed by my Agent stating that she or he does not have, at the time of doing any act pursuant to this power of attorney, actual knowledge of the revocation or termination of this power of attorney, is, in the absence of fraud, conclusive proof of the nonrevocation or nontermination of the power at that time.

DEATH: My death shall not revoke or terminate this agency as to my Agent or any other person who, without actual knowledge of my death, acts in good faith under this power of attorney. Any action so taken, unless otherwise invalid or unenforceable, shall be binding upon me and my heirs, devises, and personal representatives.

JOINT POWER: If I name two persons to serve as my Agent hereunder, it is my intent that the power granted to them shall be a joint power, which shall and must be exercised by them together as they may from time to time act on my behalf. No action or transaction requiring a signature will be effective or binding without both such persons' signatures affixed to the written instrument(s) reflecting the action or transaction.

FURTHER, I do authorize my aforesaid attorney to execute, acknowledge and deliver any instrument under seal or otherwise, and to do all things necessary to carry out the intent hereof, hereby granting unto my said attorney full power and authority to act in and concerning the premises as fully and effectually as I may do if personally present.

PROVIDED, however, that all business transacted hereunder for me or for my account shall be transacted in my name, and that all endorsements and instruments executed by my said attorney for the purpose of carrying out the foregoing powers shall contain my name, followed by that of my said attorney and the designation "attorney-in-fact".

Figure 5.1e

My agent is entitled to reasonable compensation and reimbursement for reasonable expenses for services rendered as agent under this power of attorney, if desired.

TO INDUCE ANY THIRD PARTY TO ACT HEREUNDER, I HEREBY AGREE THAT ANY THIRD PARTY RECEIVING A DULY EXECUTED COPY OR FACSIMILE OF THIS INSTRUMENT MAY ACT HEREUNDER, AND THAT REVOCATION OR TERMINATION HEREOF SHALL BE INEFFECTIVE AS TO SUCH THIRD PARTY UNLESS AND UNTIL ACTUAL NOTICE OR KNOWLEDGE OF SUCH REVOCATION OR TERMINATION SHALL HAVE BEEN RECEIVED BY SUCH THIRD PARTY, AND I FOR MYSELF AND FOR MY HEIRS, EXECUTORS, LEGAL REPRESENTATIVES AND ASSIGNS, HEREBY AGREE TO INDEMNIFY AND HOLD HARMLESS ANY SUCH THIRD PARTY FROM AND AGAINST ANY AND ALL CLAIMS THAT MAY ARISE AGAINST SUCH THIRD PARTY BY REASON OF SUCH THIRD PARTY HAVING RELIED ON THE PROVISIONS OF THIS INSTRUMENT.

THIS DURABLE GENERAL POWER OF ATTORNEY MAY BE REVOKED BY ME AT ANY TIME.

Signed this _____ day of _____, 2001

_____
Signature

_____
City, County, and State of Residence

STATE OF COLORADO

County of_____

This document was acknowledged before me on _____(date)

by_____ (name of principal)

who certifies the correctness of the signature(s) of the agent(s).

My commission expires:_____.

[Seal]

_____
Notary Public

Figure 5.1f

DURABLE POWER OF ATTORNEY FOR PROPERTY MANAGEMENT
(California Probate Code Section 4401)

TO PERSON EXECUTING THIS DOCUMENT:

NOTICE: THE POWERS GRANTED BY THIS DOCUMENT ARE BROAD AND SWEEPING. THEY ARE EXPLAINED IN THE UNIFORM STATUTORY FORM POWER OF ATTORNEY ACT (CALIFORNIA PROBATE CODE SECTIONS 4400-4465). IF YOU HAVE ANY QUESTIONS ABOUT THESE POWERS, OBTAIN COMPETENT LEGAL ADVICE. THIS DOCUMENT DOES NOT AUTHORIZE ANYONE TO MAKE MEDICAL OR OTHER HEALTH CARE DECISIONS FOR YOU. YOU MAY REVOKE THIS POWER OF ATTORNEY IF YOU LATER WISH TO DO SO.

1. DESIGNATION OF AGENT. I, **GEORGE M. MILLER**, of 714 Main Road, Santa Barbara, CA 93105 do hereby designate and appoint **ILENE MILLER**, whose address is 714 Main Road, Santa Barbara, CA 93105, to be my agent (attorney-in-fact) to act for me in any lawful way with respect to the following subjects.

2. TO GRANT ALL OF THE FOLLOWING POWERS INITIAL (#15) ONLY, FOR THE LIMITING OF POWERS INITIAL ONLY THOSE POWERS WHICH YOU ARE GRANTING TO YOUR AGENT.

_____ (1) Real estate transactions
_____ (2) Tangible personal property transactions
_____ (3) Bond, share, and commodity option transactions
_____ (4) Banking & other financial institution transactions
_____ (5) Business operating transactions
_____ (6) Insurance operating transactions
_____ (7) Retirement plan transactions
_____ (8) Estate, trust, & other beneficiary transactions
_____ (9) Claims and litigations
_____ (10) Tax matters
_____ (11) Personal & family maintenance
_____ (12) Benefits from Social Security, Medicare, Medicaid or other governmental programs, or civil or military services
_____ (13) Records, reports, and statements
_____ (14) Full and unqualified authority to my agent to delegate any or all of the foregoing powers to any person or persons whom my agent shall select
_____ (15) All of the powers listed above.

3. DURATION. This Power of Attorney shall exist for an indefinite period of time even though I become incapacitated, unless I have specified otherwise.

4. NOMINATION OF AGENT. I nominate, as the agent of the estate, **ILENE MILLER**, whose address is written herein above. In the event that **ILENE MILLER** is unable or declines to serve, I nominate **GEORGE MELVIN MILLER** to serve as alternate agent of the estate.

Figure 5.2a

5. RELIANCE. I agree that any third party who receives a copy of this document may act under it. Revocation of the power of attorney is not effective as to a third party until the third party has actual knowledge of the revocation. I agree to indemnify the third party for any claims that arise against the third party because of reliance on this power of attorney.

DATE AND SIGNATURE OF PRINCIPAL

I, **GEORGE M. MILLER**, sign my name to this Power of Attorney on this
_____ day of _____, 2005, at Santa Barbara, CA

_____
GEORGE M. MILLER
Social Security #

BY ACCEPTING OR ACTING UNDER THE APPOINTMENT, THE AGENT ASSUMES THE FIDUCIARY AND OTHER LEGAL RESPONSIBILITIES OF AN AGENT.

Certificate of Acknowledgment of Notary Public

STATE OF CALIFORNIA

COUNTY OF SANTA BARBARA

On _____ before me, _____,
personally appeared **GEORGE M. MILLER**, _____ personally known to me -OR- ____ proved to me on the basis of satisfactory evidence to be the person whose name is subscribed to the within instrument and acknowledged to me that he executed the same in his authorized capacity, and that by his signature on the instrument the person, or the entity upon behalf of which the person acted, executed the instrument.

WITNESS my hand and official seal.

_____
Signature of Notary Public

Figure 5.2b

terminal. This language is closer to what comprises your living will, where you indicate whether you do or do not want to be placed on life support, for example. Hence, your state may include a provision about end-of-life care in your durable power of attorney for medical care document, but you may also have a living will as an additional document to your living trust package. This may sound confusing, but think of it as a way to make sure all of your wishes are spelled out and any and all potential circumstances are covered. You do not want any holes in your estate planning package that limit the chance of your wishes being carried out according to *you.*

Living Wills

Living wills answer questions regarding your medical care and the decisions that usually emerge at the end of your life. For example, a living will can let the doctors know whether you want pain medication to hasten your death or surgery to prolong your life. It can also tell doctors whether you'd prefer to remain on life support for as long as possible (within the limits of generally accepted health care standards). These directives may also be subject to state laws, but today all living wills are legally accepted documents. You have a right to determine your own quality of life. As recently as 1990 the United States Supreme Court ruled that people have a "right to die" and that one can express his or her desires in writing about receiving medical care. For you to exercise your legal right to die, however, you must express these wishes ahead of time by creating a living will. You set up a living will while you are healthy (living) and are not terminally ill or incompetent. If you learn of a terminal illness today, you may not be able to create this document today. Some states have enacted laws that prevent a person from creating a living will within five days of learning that he or she has a terminal illness.

Your specific state may have a special name for this document, such as Medical Directive, Directive to Physicians, Advanced Health Care Directive, Health Care Proxy, Declaration Regarding Health Care, Designation of Health Care Surrogate, or Patient Advocate Designation. All of these documents are *living wills,* but they may vary stylistically across the country.

Generally, all living wills clearly state your wishes regarding end-of-life medical treatment—such as the use of ventilators and breathing and feeding tubes—in the event of a serious or irreversible illness when you can no longer communicate. In some states, however, you do not have to specify what your instructions would be if you designate someone to wear the hat of holding durable medical power of attorney and choose to rely on that person to make the right decisions for you. That person would have to know your personal values and be able to make good decisions that reflect your wishes. A living will usually goes into effect when you are not expected to regain consciousness.

Having a living will that specifies you do not want to receive extraordinary medical treatment does not mean, once you arrive in a hospital and cannot speak, that you will not be placed on life support or that the doctors will pull the plug the next day. Living wills are not direct orders. They are the means by which you can express certain wishes and help the doctors and your family members make those ultimate decisions if the time comes. You create a living will so it's available if and when these difficult decisions must be made. Only you or your family decides when a living will should be used.

Because not every medical crisis contingency can be covered by a living will, having a named durable power of attorney for making medical decisions is a good idea. A health care

A hospital or hospice may ask you to sign a Do Not Resuscitate (DNR) Order upon admittance, which provides medical staff with clear instructions not to perform any extreme lifesaving measures. This is your right-to-die document. As long you are aware of the risk, you have the right, unless you are mentally incompetent, to refuse treatment even when treatment will be provided. You will be made as comfortable as possible, given pain control medication, and allowed to die as peacefully as possible. If you are incapacitated, however, your agent with durable power of attorney for medical care may have to step in and sign the document. A spouse can sometimes sign this document.

proxy can be in lieu of, or as a back up to, a living will, depending on how your state deals with these two documents (a medical power of attorney and a living will). Written documents are subject to interpretation, whereas a human being can make critical decisions in minutes if necessary. The designated person, sometimes called the patient advocate, should have a clear understanding of your wishes and be willing to see them carried out in spite of any opposition from family or doctors. Most states do not allow the patient's doctor or health care provider to be the patient advocate. Other states do not allow a beneficiary to have medical power of attorney.

The living will must be signed in front of two qualified witnesses (no relatives, heirs, or doctors). The documents must be specific and make clear that the signer does not want doctors to use any extreme means—such as artificial nutrition, hydration, or ventilation—to sustain life if the condition is terminal or incurable, or if he or she is in a vegetative state.

You may want to deliver a copy of your living will to your doctor and/or hospital as a precaution. Letting your family members know about your wishes and your living will is also important. Emergencies can happen at any time, and as long as your doctor and family members know in advance about such wishes, they can ease the pain that naturally accompanies these decisions. Your living will can answer some of the most heartbreaking decisions a person must make at some point in your life.

Following are samples of living wills from two states— California and Colorado. California includes its living will language within the health care power of attorney document, which you can find in its entirety in Appendix B's sample living trust. Here we show you an excerpt from the document, which explains what the California Probate Code allows in an advanced health care directive. (See Figure 5.3.) The other sample is a power of attorney for health care in Colorado (see Figure 5.4) and a living will from Colorado. (See Figure 5.5.) Colorado uses a separate document for living wills. We repeat: These document vary across the states. We provide them here so you can see what these documents look like and how they can differ widely. Refer to Appendix B to view more pages. (California's Advanced Health Care Directive, which includes the durable power of attorney for health care document, has several parts to it and clearly covers all bases.)

Information about obtaining forms for each state is available from the American Bar Association at 740 Fifteenth Street, NW, Washington D.C. 20005-1022. You can call them at 202-662-8690, or visit their web site at www.abanet.org. Your local We The People store can also help you obtain your state's preferred form.

ADVANCE HEALTH CARE DIRECTIVE
(California Probate Code Section 4701)

Explanation

You have the right to give instructions about your own health care. You also have the right to name someone else to make health care decisions for you. This form lets you do either or both of these things. It also lets you express your wishes regarding donation of organs and the designation of your primary physician. If you use this form, you may complete or modify all or any part of it. You are free to use a different form.

Part 1 of this form is a power of attorney for health care. Part 1 lets you name another individual as agent to make health care decisions for you if you become incapable of making your own decisions or if you want someone else to make those decisions for you now even though you are still capable. You may also name an alternate agent to act for you if your first choice is not willing, able, or reasonably available to make decisions for you. (Your agent may not be an operator or employee of a community health care institution where you are receiving care, unless your agent is related to you or is a coworker.)

Unless the form you sign limits the authority of your agent, your agent may make all health care decisions for you. This form has a place for you to limit the authority of your agent. You need not limit the authority of your agent if you wish to rely on your agent for all healthcare decisions that may have to be made. If you choose not to limit the authority of your agent, your agent will have the right to:

    a)   Consent or refuse consent to any care, treatment, service, or procedure to maintain, diagnose, or otherwise affect a physical or mental condition.

    b)   Select or discharge health care providers and institutions.

    c)   Approve or disapprove diagnostic tests, surgical procedures, and programs of medication.

    d)   Direct the provision, withholding, or withdrawal of artificial nutrition and hydration and all other forms of health care, including cardiopulmonary resuscitation.

    e)   Make anatomical gifts, authorize an autopsy, and direct disposition of remains.

Part 2 of this form lets you give specific instructions about any aspect of your health care, whether or not you appoint an agent. Choices are provided for you to express your wishes

Figure 5.3a

regarding the provision, withholding, or withdrawal of treatment to keep you alive, as well as the provision of pain relief. Space is also provided for you to add to the choices you have made or for you to write out any additional wishes. If you are satisfied to allow your agent to determine what is best for you in making end-of-life decisions, you need not fill out Part 2 of this form.

Part 3 of this form lets you express an intention to donate your bodily organs and tissues following your death.

Part 4 of this form lets you designate a physician to have primary responsibility for your health care.

After completing this form, sign and date the form at the end. The form must be signed by two qualified witnesses or acknowledged before a notary public. Give a copy of the signed and completed form to your physician, to any other health care providers you may have, any health care agents you have named. You should talk to the person you have named as agent to make sure that he or she understands your wishes and is willing to take the responsibility.

You have the right to revoke this advance health care directive or replace this form at any time.

****

PART 1

POWER OF ATTORNEY FOR HEALTH CARE

(1.1) DESIGNATION OF AGENT: I designate the following individual as my agent to make health care decisions for me; **GEORGE M. MILLER** whose address is 714 Main Road, Santa Barbara, CA 93105, and telephone number is (805) 555-3772.

If I revoke my agent's authority or if my agent is not willing, able, or reasonably available to make a health care decision for me, I designate as my first alternate agent: **GEORGE MELVIN MILLER** whose address is 714 Main Road, Santa Barbara, CA 93105, and telephone number is (805) 555-3772.

Figure 5.3b

(1.2) AGENT'S AUTHORITY: My agent is authorized to make all health care decisions for me, including decisions to provide, withhold, or withdraw artificial nutrition and hydration and all other forms of health care to keep me alive, except as I state here:

_____

_____

_____

(Add additional sheets if needed.)

(1.3) WHEN AGENT'S AUTHORITY BECOMES EFFECTIVE: My agent's authority becomes effective when my primary physician determines that I am unable to make my own health care decisions unless I initial the following line. **If I initial this line _____, my agent's authority to make health care decisions for me takes effect immediately.**

(1.4) AGENT'S OBLIGATION: My agent shall make health care decisions for me in accordance with this power of attorney for health care, any instructions I give in Part 2 of this form, and my other wishes to the extent known to my agent. To the extent my wishes are unknown, my agent shall make health care decisions for me in accordance with what my agent determines to be in my best interest. In determining my best interest, my agent shall consider my personal values to the extent known to my agent.

(1.5) AGENT'S POSTDEATH AUTHORITY: My agent is authorized to make anatomical gifts, authorize an autopsy, and direct disposition of my remains, except as I state here or in Part 3 of this form:

_____

_____

_____

(Add additional sheets if needed.)

(1.6) NOMINATION OF CONSERVATOR: If a conservator of my person needs to be appointed for me by a court, I nominate the agent designated in this form. If that agent is not willing, able or reasonably available to act as conservator, I nominate the alternate agents whom I have named, in the order designated.

Figure 5.3c

MEDICAL DURABLE POWER OF ATTORNEY
(Colorado Revised Statutes 15-14-506)

THIS IS AN IMPORTANT LEGAL DOCUMENT. BEFORE SIGNING THIS DOCUMENT YOU SHOULD KNOW THESE IMPORTANT FACTS:

Except to the extent you state otherwise, this document gives the person you name as your agent the authority to make any and all health care decisions for you when you are no longer capable of making them yourself. "Health care" means any treatment, service or procedure to maintain, diagnose or treat your physical or mental condition. Your agent, therefore, can have the power to make a broad range of health care decisions for you. Your agent may consent, refuse to consent, or withdraw consent to medical treatment and may make decisions about withdrawing or withholding life-sustaining treatment. Your agent cannot consent or direct any of the following: commitment to a state institution, sterilization, or termination of treatment if you are pregnant and if the withdrawal of that treatment is deemed likely to terminate the pregnancy unless the failure to withhold the treatment will be physically harmful to you or prolong severe pain which cannot be alleviated by medication.

You may state in this document any treatment you do not desire, except as stated above, or treatment you want to be sure you receive. Your agent's authority will begin when your doctor certifies that you lack the capacity to make health care decisions. If for moral or religious reasons you do not wish to be treated by a doctor or examined by a doctor for the certification that you lack capacity, you must say so in the document and name a person to be able to certify your lack of capacity. That person may not be your agent or alternate agent or any person ineligible to be your agent. You may attach additional pages if you need more space to complete your statement.

If you want to give your agent authority to withhold or withdraw the artificial providing of nutrition and fluids, your document must say so. Otherwise, your agent will not be able to direct that. Under no conditions will your agent be able to direct the withholding of food and drink for you to eat and drink normally.

Your agent will be obligated to follow your instructions when making decisions on your behalf. Unless you state otherwise, your agent will have the same authority to make decisions about your health care as you would have had if made consistent with state law.

It is important that you discuss this document with your physician or other health care providers before you sign it to make sure that you understand the nature and range of decisions which may be made on your behalf. If you do not have a physician, you should talk with someone else who is knowledgeable about these issues and can answer your questions. You do not need a lawyer's assistance to complete this document, but if there is anything in this document that you do not understand, you should ask a lawyer to explain it to you.

The person you appoint as agent should be someone you know and trust and must be at least 18 years old. If you appoint your health or residential care provider (e.g. your physician, or an employee of a home health agency, hospital, nursing home, or residential care home, other than a relative), that person will have to choose between acting as your agent or as your health or residential care provider; the law does not permit a person to do both at the same time.

You should inform the person you appoint that you want him or her to be your health care agent. You should discuss this document with your agent and your physician and give each a signed copy. You should indicate on the document itself the people and institutions who will have signed copies. Your agent will not be liable for health care decisions made in good faith on your behalf.

Even after you have signed this document, you have the right to make health care decisions for yourself as long as you are able to do so, and treatment cannot be given to you or stopped over your objection. You have the right to revoke the authority granted to your agent by informing him or her or your health care provider orally or in writing.

This document may not be changed or modified. If you want to make changes in the document you must make an entirely new one.

You should consider designating an alternate agent in the event that your agent is unwilling, unable, unavailable, or ineligible to act as your agent. Any alternate agent you designate will have the same authority to make health care decisions for you.

Figure 5.4a

DESIGNATION OF HEALTH CARE AGENT.

I, **BETTY SAMPLE** of 407 State St., Golden, CO 80403,

do hereby designate and appoint **RODNEY A. SAMPLE** of 144 Elm Ave., Ft. Collins, CO 80521, as my attorney in fact (agent) to make health care decisions for me as authorized in this document. For the purposes of this document, "health care decision" means consent, refusal of consent, or withdrawal of consent to any care, treatment, service, or procedure to maintain, diagnose, or treat an individual's physical condition.

2. CREATION OF DURABLE POWER OF ATTORNEY FOR HEALTH CARE. By this document I intend to create a durable power of attorney for health care. This power of attorney shall not be affected by my subsequent incapacity.

3. GENERAL STATEMENT OF AUTHORITY GRANTED. Subject to any limitations in this document, I hereby grant to my agent full power and authority to make health care decisions for me to the same extent that I could make such decisions for myself if I had the capacity to do so. In exercising this authority, my agent shall make health care decisions that are consistent with my desires as stated in this document or otherwise made known to my agent, including, but not limited to, my desires concerning obtaining or refusing or withdrawing life-prolonging care, treatment, services, and procedures.

> *(If you want to limit the authority of your agent to make health care decisions for you, you can state the limitations in paragraph 4 ("Statement of Desires, Special Provisions, and Limitations") below. You can indicate your desires by including a statement of your desires in the same paragraph.)*

STATEMENT OF DESIRES, SPECIAL PROVISIONS, AND LIMITATIONS.

> *(Your agent must make health care decisions that are consistent with your known desires. You can, but are not required to, state your desires in the space provided below. You should consider whether you want to include a statement of your desires concerning life-prolonging care, treatment, services, and procedures. You can also include a statement of your desires concerning other matters relating to your health care. You can also make your desires known to your agent by discussing your desires with your agent or by some other means. If there are any types of treatment that you do not want to be used, you should state them in the space below. If you want to limit in any other way the authority given your agent by this document, you should state the limits in the space below. If you do not state any limits, your agent will have broad powers to make health care decisions for you, except to the extent that there are limits provided by law.)*

In exercising the authority under this durable power of attorney for health care, my agent shall act consistently with my desires as stated. Additional statement of desires, special provisions, and limitations:

[None or State limitations]

> *(You may attach additional pages if you need more space to complete your statement. If you attach additional pages, you must date and sign each of the additional pages at the same time you date and sign this document.)*

Figure 5.4b

5. INSPECTION AND DISCLOSURE OF INFORMATION RELATING TO MY PHYSICAL OR MENTAL HEALTH. Subject to any limitations in this document, my agent has the power and authority to do all of the following:

(a) Request, review, and receive any information, verbal or written, regarding my physical or mental health, including, but not limited to, medical and hospital records.

(b) Execute on my behalf any releases or other documents that may be required in order to obtain this information.

(c) Consent to the disclosure of this information.

Consent to the donation of any of my organs for medical purposes.
(If you want to limit the authority of your agent to receive and disclose information relating to your health, you must state the limitations in paragraph 4 ("Statement of Desires, Special Provisions, and Limitations") above.)

6. SIGNING DOCUMENTS, WAIVERS, AND RELEASES. Where necessary to implement the health care decisions that my agent is authorized by this document to make, my agent has the power and authority to execute on my behalf all of the following:

(a) Documents titled or purporting to be a "Refusal to Permit Treatment" and "Leaving Hospital Against Medical Advice."

(b) Any necessary waiver or release from liability required by a hospital or physician.

7. DESIGNATION OF ALTERNATE AGENTS.
(You are not required to designate any alternate agents but you may do so. Any alternate agent you designate will be able to make the same health care decisions as the agent you designated in paragraph 1, above, in the event that agent is unable or ineligible to act as your agent. If the agent you designated is your spouse, he or she becomes ineligible to act as your agent if your marriage is dissolved.)

If the person designated as my agent in paragraph 1 is not available or becomes ineligible to act as my agent to make a health care decision for me or loses the mental capacity to make health care decisions for me, or if I revoke that person's appointment or authority to act as my agent to make health care decisions for me, then I designate and appoint the following persons to serve as my agent to make health care decisions for me as authorized in this document, such persons to serve in the order listed below:

First Alternate Agent:

TODD A. SAMPLE, whose address is 642 Main St., Arvada, CO 80004

8. PRIOR DESIGNATIONS REVOKED. I revoke any prior durable power of attorney for health care.

DATE AND SIGNATURE OF PRINCIPAL

I sign my name to this Statutory Form Durable Power of Attorney for Health Care on

_____ at _____ ,
   (Date)   (City)   (State)

_____
       (You sign here)

(This Power of Attorney will not be valid unless it is signed by two qualified witnesses who are present when you sign or acknowledge your signature. If you have attached any additional pages to this form, you must date and sign each of the additional pages at the same time you date and sign this Power of Attorney.)

Figure 5.4c

STATEMENT OF WITNESSES

(This document must be witnessed by two qualified adult witnesses. None of the following may be used as a witness: (1) a person you designate as your agent or alternate agent, (2) a health care provider, (3) an employee of a health care provider, (4) the operator of a community care facility, (5) an employee of an operator of a community care facility, (6) your spouse, or (7) your lawful heirs or beneficiaries named in your will or a deed. At least one of the witnesses must make the additional declaration set out following the place where the witnesses sign.)

I declare under penalty of perjury under the laws of Colorado that the person who signed or acknowledged this document is personally known to me (or proved to me on the basis of convincing evidence) to be the principal, that the principal signed or acknowledged this durable power of attorney in my presence, that the principal appears to be of sound mind and under no duress, fraud, or undue influence, that I am not the person appointed as attorney in fact by this document, and that I am not a health care provider, an employee of a health care provider, the operator of a community care facility, an employee of an operator of a community care facility, my spouse, or my lawful heirs or beneficiaries named in a Will or deed.

Signature: _____

Print name: _____

Date: _____   Residence address: _____

Signature: _____

Print name: _____

Date: _____   Residence address: _____

(At least one of the above witnesses must also sign)

I further declare under penalty of perjury under the laws of Colorado that I am not related to the principal by blood, marriage, or adoption, and, to the best of my knowledge, I am not entitled to any part of the estate of the principal upon the death of the principal under a will now existing or by operation of law.

Signature: _____

Signature: _____

Figure 5.4d

NOTARY

State of COLORADO
County of JEFFERSON

On this _____ day of _____ 2001   before me personally appeared **BETTY SAMPLE** full name
of signer of instrument) to me known (or proved to me on basis of satisfactory evidence) to be the person whose
name is subscribed to this instrument, and acknowledged that he/she executed it. I declare under penalty of
perjury that the person whose name is subscribed to this instrument appears to be of sound mind and under no
duress, fraud or undue influence.

_____
Notary
Print Name of Notary: _____

My Commission Expires:
_____

Figure 5.4e

DECLARATION AS TO MEDICAL OR SURGICAL TREATMENT

I, **SHERYL SAMPLE**, being of sound mind and at least 18 years of age, direct that my life shall not be artificially prolonged under the circumstances set forth below, and hereby declare that:

1. If at any time, my attending physician and one (1) other qualified physician certify in writing that:

a. I have an injury, disease or illness which is not curable or reversible and which, in their judgment, is a terminal condition; and

b. For a period of seven (7) consecutive days or more, I have been unconscious, comatose, or otherwise incompetent so as to be unable to make or communicate responsible decisions concerning my person; then

I direct that in accordance with Colorado law, life-sustaining procedures shall be withdrawn and withheld pursuant to the terms of this declaration; it being understood that the term "life-sustaining procedures" shall not be interpreted to include any medical procedure or intervention for nourishment considered necessary by the attending physician to provide comfort or alleviate pain. However, I may specifically direct, in accordance with Colorado law, that artificial nourishment be withdrawn or withheld pursuant to the terms of this declaration.

2. In the event that the only procedure I am being provided is artificial nourishment, I direct that one of the following actions be taken:

(DECLARANT SHALL INITIAL ONE CHOICE BELOW)

_____ a. Artificial nourishment shall not be continued when it is the only procedure being provided; or

_____ b. Artificial nourishment shall be continued for _____ days when it is the only procedure being provided; or

_____ c. Artificial nourishment shall be continued when it is the only procedure being provided.

Figure 5.5a

I execute this declaration as my free and voluntary act on

_____, 2001.

_____

SHERYL SAMPLE

The foregoing instrument was signed and declared by **SHERYL SAMPLE** to be her declaration, in the presence of us, who, in the declarant's presence, in the presence of each other, and at declarant's request, have signed our names below as witnesses and we declare that at the time of the execution of this instrument, the declarant, according to our best knowledge and belief, was of sound mind and under no constraint or undue influence.

Dated at Denver County, Colorado, on _____, 2001.

Witness   Witness

_____   _____

Figure 5.5b

A durable power of attorney for either health or financial matters does not relate only to end-of-life decisions. The person you pick as an agent for health care decisions and financial decisions can make decisions for you at *any time during your life.* You may be temporarily incapacitated or unavailable to make important decisions during your life, at which time, having someone designated to make such decisions is important.

All of these documents give you many options. You can usually be as descriptive or as limiting as you want. You can request that your organs be donated, or not. You can also give little direction and simply allow your agent to make decisions on your behalf. The point of these documents—both durable powers of attorney and living wills—is to afford you the opportunity to remain in control of your own destiny, no matter what happens.

Some states may also require that a third special witness sign if you are a patient in a skilled nursing facility. In the absence of anyone being granted the power of attorney or a living will in place, medical professionals will consult in order of importance with the spouse, adult children, parents, adult siblings, or other close relatives or friends. They must adhere to any hospital ethics.

Choosing Your Financial and Health Care Decision Makers

How much power you authorize your agent to have should affect how you choose that person to act on your behalf. The more power you allow an agent to have, the greater you must trust that person; he or she should have intimate knowledge of your personal values and wishes. In the document that executes your durable power of attorney for financial matters, you can define how broad or narrow you want your agent's powers to be. For example, you may want your son to be able to sign checks on your behalf so he can take care of the bills but not be able to buy and sell in your investment portfolio. Being very clear about your wishes is perhaps the most important part to using these documents effectively. It's wise to discuss your wishes with your agent on all matters that your agent may have to face.

When choosing an agent to hold durable powers of attorney for finances, avoid naming any troublemakers in the family. Many people choose a child, or they name their children as coagents. You can have more than one agent holding durable power of attorney for either health care and/or finances. Example: You have two daughters and you name both of them as coagents for both health care decisions and financial decisions. Note, however, that this can lead to an inconvenience when a decision must be made and all of the coagents must appear together, at the same place and time. Having one agent may facilitate the decision-making process.

If you anticipate problems with the person you choose, gather your family together and explain why you've chosen this person. This is not when you want to pick people that disturb other family members, or who won't listen to any family members' advice. To that end, you can input a statement in your durable power of attorney documents that explicitly states that your agent has the final say. Your agents can also be named in other parts of your trust. As we said above, the same person can hold the title of personal representative, successor trustee, and agent of durable power of attorney. (He or she can also be a beneficiary.) Check your state's specific rules for any restrictions.

Naming Caretakers for Minors and Their Inheritance

In planning the event of your death, you may wish to make arrangements for minor children for two reasons:

- They will need to be taken care of because they are under 18 years of age.
- They may need help managing any assets they receive from your trust.

(You can make these arrangements also in a will by naming guardians for minor children and setting provisions for when they are to receive certain assets, but here we focus on the living trust.)

Living trusts can set provisions for when a beneficiary is old enough to manage his or her own inheritance. For example, you may not want to let a 20-year-old be in total control of a large inheritance. (Imagine inheriting millions of dollars at the tender age of 18; would you be able to manage that money wisely and still have some left over 10 years later?) Rich minors are frequently spotlighted in the media because they are either worth millions (think heiress Christina Onassis) or they make millions and sue their parents once they become adults and realize that their parents had abused their income for years.

Minors are not allowed to legally control significant amounts of assets, so it's your responsibility to set up this management unless you want the court to ultimately appoint someone. In our sample living trusts, we include the ability to name a custodian for minors who inherit assets. Custodians manage the assets that a minor inherits until that minor comes of age. You can choose—with a children's trust built into your living trust—when you'd want those minors to obtain control of their inheritance, too. Some choose 21, 25, or even 35 years old. When choosing an age, you should consider the type and size of the asset.

You can also set an age for when any beneficiary can receive an inheritance, whether that beneficiary is of legal age (18) or not. Example: You intend to leave your miniature pony farm to Johnnie, but believe he needs to mature to at least the age of 30—and learn how to care for such a farm—before he inherits it. You can set this provision in your trust. You can also say that all beneficiaries must receive their inheritance by a certain age, such as 30 or 35.

The Uniform Transfers to Minors Act

In every state except for South Carolina and Vermont, you can name a custodian in your living trust to manage assets you leave a minor, until the minor reaches a specific age. (Vermont and South Carolina use the Uniform Gifts to Minor Act (UGMA), which is essentially the same and has similar provisions.)

State laws set this age, either 18 or 21, but some carry it out to 25 years of age. If you want minors named in your trust to receive their inheritance at a later age, say 30, or if their inheritance is significant enough that a longer time frame is beneficial, then setting up a children's trust as a subtrust to your living trust may be best. Otherwise, unless you live in South Carolina or Vermont, the minors will receive their inheritance outright when they reach the statutory age under the Uniform Transfers to Minors Act (UTMA).

If you live in a state that has adopted the UTMA, but later move to South Carolina or Vermont, you should revise your living trust to reflect the change.

Children's Trusts

Within your living trust, you can create children's trusts. Your successor trustee manages these trusts and the assets you leave in them to children. Successor trustees use the trust's assets to take care of child's education, health, or other needs. In the case of a joint living (AB) trust, the surviving spouse would manage the assets in the children's trusts until his or her death, at which point the successor trustees takes control. Each child's trust ends at the age you designate in your trust. Children's trusts, however, tend to be less flexible than custodianships:

- Children's trusts are a bit more complex, whereas custodianships are part of state law, so institutions are familiar with them.

- Children's trusts are less flexible in the sense that a surviving spouse or successor trustee is the trustee for all of your children's trusts (whereas you can name different custodians for different beneficiaries under custodianships).

- Income tax rates on a child's trust may be more than if their inheritance had been handled by a custodian.

> Living trusts allow you to leave specific gifts and name alternate beneficiaries for each gift. For any of these gifts, children's trusts can be set up for minor recipients. If you need more complex children's trusts set up for your estate, such as trusts that place extensive controls over what you intend your children to receive from your estate, consult a lawyer or estate planner familiar with children's trusts.

Bottom line: If you are trying to decide between using children's trusts in your living trust and naming a custodian, consult an attorney or estate planner familiar with the laws in your state.

You create trusts for your children by inserting such clauses into your living trust where you list each child's name and the age at which he or she, as a beneficiary, is eligible to receive the asset outright. If you die before the child reaches the age of eligibility, a trust is automatically created for that beneficiary. However, if the child is of age at your death, then no trust is created, and he or she gets the asset. Children's trusts that become activated at your death require a separate taxpayer ID (for each trust) and tax returns must be filed separately. Your successor trustee (or the surviving spouse) must manage these trusts carefully. It's almost easier to think of children's trusts as separate entities that are housed within the body of your living trust.

Leaving Life Insurance Proceeds

We've hinted that life insurance policies can be tricky to manage. If you want your children to be beneficiaries of your life insurance proceeds at your death, but you die before they can manage those proceeds, you must prepare for this situation.

Naming your trust as the beneficiary of your life insurance proceeds is not always recommended, unless you have minor children. The living trust does not legally own the insurance policy, but it's the entity that receives those proceeds at your death. If you name your trust as the beneficiary of your life insurance, and then in your trust documents you name your children as beneficiaries of your life insurance's proceeds (saying exactly how you want those proceeds distributed percentage-wise among your children), you can create children's trusts and ensure that they receive those proceeds at the right time. By passing a life insurance's proceeds through a living trust, you avoid both probate and state inheritance taxes, if any. Federal estate tax will be paid, however, unless the proceeds pass to the surviving spouse who claims the unlimited marital deduction.

You can also deal with life insurance proceeds through a custodianship by naming your custodian as a beneficiary of a certain amount of those proceeds. But if you don't want your children to receive those proceeds until a certain age (which might be older than the age at which your state stipulates proceeds must be handed over), then this is not the approach to take. Most choose to leave life insurance policies out of their living trust.

Because life insurance proceeds can create complex issues regarding minor children and living trusts, consulting with an attorney or planner is wise. (More on this below.)

The C Trust

We began talking about the C trust (Qualified Terminal Interest Property) in Chapter 3. Q-TIPs are tax and accounting tools for couples who own a valuable estate. For example, if a couple's estate is worth $5 million and they die in 2006, $1 million of that estate is taxable under the allowable exemptions for that year. But they can use a Q-TIP to spread out their estate among three subtrusts (the A, B, and now C) to postpone the payment of certain taxes.

A married couple who sets up a joint AB trust can include the Q-TIP trust as a way of postponing payment of estate taxes otherwise due when the first spouse dies. The Q-TIP is a special type of marital life estate trust that can be used only by the surviving spouse (not a partner in an unmarried couple). The advantage of the Q-TIP is that it allows the surviving spouse to delay any estate taxes assessed on the assets of the first spouse who dies until the second spouse dies. One drawback to a Q-TIP is that the federal estate taxes eventually paid on the assets of the first spouse to die are assessed against what the assets are worth when the surviving spouse dies—not what the assets were worth when the first spouse died. So, in essence, the taxes due could be more.

Q-TIPs provide for the welfare of the surviving spouse. They are a good idea for any spouse in a marriage who has an estate valued over the estate tax threshold (over which the

---

ELIZABETH'S STORY

When I got married again at 55, my children were grown and I had a lot of assets to protect, such as a valuable home and lots of other items left to me from my late husband. My estate was worth $6.5 million, which was over the estate tax threshold. I almost didn't remarry because I was worried about how the marriage would affect my estate and what I could ultimately leave to my children. Christopher also came into the marriage with grown children, but he didn't have nearly the kind of assets that I had. He didn't own a home, and he still worked full-time to make ends meet. We were not a "balanced" couple from a financial standpoint.

We set up an AB trust that listed most of our assets as separate property, and we also created a Q-TIP trust to help absorb the assets that would flow out of my estate upon my death. I named my children as the ultimate beneficiaries of my assets, but with the Q-TIP, Christopher is allowed to live in the home and use my estate for the rest of his life. When he dies, all of my assets will go to my children. Best of all: Christopher won't have to pay any of my estate's taxes until after he dies, at which point my children will have to take care of those taxes using what's left in the estate.

estate is taxed) and who (1) plans to leave all of his or her assets to the surviving spouse tax-free until the surviving spouse dies, and (2) names beneficiaries of the trust's assets to ultimately receive the assets. There is no estate tax on property that passes between spouses because of the unlimited marital deduction. However, no marital deduction is allowed for property that passes into a trust for the benefit of a surviving spouse and then to someone else. However, property transferred to a Q-TIP trust, where the spouse is entitled to all the trust income for life, can still qualify for the marital deduction. The advantage of a Q-TIP trust, besides qualifying for the marital deduction, is that it allows the decedent to determine who will ultimately receive the property. For example, in a second marriage situation, the decedent may want the property in a Q-TIP trust to pass to the children of a previous marriage after providing income to a surviving spouse.

To set up a Q-TIP, you must file an IRS form 706 within nine months of the first spouse's date of death. If you fail to file this form in that time frame, all of the assets you intended to place in this trust are subject to federal estate taxes. Q-TIPs are tax-saving strategies that can get complex pretty quickly; we suggest you consult an attorney, accountant, or estate planner about these tools if your estate exceeds the maximum amount exempted. (See Chapter 6 for estate tax information.)

Other Types of Trusts

Generation-Skipping Trusts

A generation-skipping transfer (GST) trust is an irrevocable (cannot be changed) arrangement that provides income only—not access to trust principal—to the settlor or the settlor's spouse and/or children. It terminates when all have reached a specified age or died, with trust principal then distributed to grandchildren or grandnieces and grandnephews (hence, generation-*skipping* trust). These types of trusts have tax-saving advantages.

Some people shy away from GST trusts because they are not confident that any financial plan can remain valid through three generations of family—more than 50 years; but these trusts remain popular among very wealthy couples who'd rather preserve their wealth for grandchildren in order to minimize estate taxes. Loopholes in traditional estate tax law made GST trusts very popular in the past, but many of those loopholes have been closed.

Charitable Remainder Trusts

Charitable remainder trusts (CRTs) are best for people who have a lot of money tied up in investments that have appreciated over the years, such as stocks, bonds, a home, or a business. When you sell the asset, you will be liable for a lot of taxes. But if the asset is not providing you with a lot of dividends, interest, or other income you may need to sell the asset and buy another type of investment that generates income for you. With a charitable remainder trust, you create an irrevocable gift of property (example: money, stock, a valuable collectible, or other property) to a tax-exempt charity while you are still alive. Not only do you then receive income from the property, but you control it while you are alive. The tax breaks can be significant. When you die, the property goes to the charity.

There are two types of CRTs. The first is a charitable remainder annuity trust, which is set up to pay income to the donor (you, if you are setting up this type of trust) based on a fixed percentage of the original gift. The second is a charitable remainder unitrust. The income from this trust is based on the annual assessed value of the gift. Both types of charitable remainder trusts are common and relatively easy to set up. Appreciable tax deductions are available, depending on which type of trust you select.

Two examples of how these trusts work are below:

- Anthony Donor, age 65, decides to set up a charitable remainder annuity trust with the National Federation of the Blind. He contacts the Federation's Special Gifts Department in Maryland and decides to donate $100,000 and set up a trust. He asks his brother John to manage the trust for him.
- During Anthony's lifetime John will see to it that Anthony is paid $5,000 each year (5 percent of $100,000). In addition, Anthony can claim a tax deduction of $59,207 in the year the trust is established.

Another scenario:

- Mary Ellen Gift, age 65, sets up a charitable remainder unitrust with $100,000 going to the National Federation of the Blind. She asks her attorney to act as trustee.
- During Mary Ellen's life her attorney will pay her an amount, 5 percent, equal to the annual assessed value of her gift. If the $100,000 unitrust grows to $110,000, Mary Ellen will be paid $5,500. If it grows again to $120,000, she will be paid $6,000 in that year, and so on. Mary Ellen can claim a tax deduction of $48,935 in the year she establishes the unitrust.

The charitable remainder trusts are a tax-wise way to increase your current income—while you provide a generous gift for the future. The donor receives a substantial federal income tax deduction upon the creation of the trust; there is no capital gains tax liability upon the transfer of appreciated property to fund the trust; and the creation of the trust reduces the property that must be administered in the donor's estate, and results in favorable estate tax treatment. If you want more information about CRTs, start by contacting the organization to which you want your trust designated. Large foundations and tax-exempt organizations typically have information on how to set up these types of trusts.

Totten Trusts

A Totten Trust is another term for a pay-on-death account. It is a special type of account set aside for a beneficiary and is usually used to help pay for death-related expenses, such as funerals, taxes, or administrative fees of settling an estate. Pay-on-death accounts can be a welcome relief for families that don't have enough funds to help deal with these death-related costs. Plus, the pay-on-death accounts can pass to named beneficiaries quickly and without going through probate—so there is no delay. So if money needs to be handy soon after a death, pay-on-death accounts can free up needed funds for whatever needs to be paid.

You set up the trust with your financial institution and you designate the person or persons you want to receive the money when you die. You also hope that the person(s) you designate use the funds as you direct. While you are alive, you can do whatever you want with the money in this Totten Trust (it is revocable), including withdrawing some or all of it, and even closing the account or changing the beneficiary. At your death, the trust becomes irrevocable like a living trust.

Pay-on-death accounts are used primarily for bank accounts, such as checking, savings, or certificates of deposit (CD) accounts. You can also designate certain kinds of government securities, including bonds, Treasury bills, and notes to a beneficiary as pay-on-death accounts.

Ask your bank or financial institution about setting up a Totten Trust, or pay-on-death account. Most banks have these forms readily available and can assist you in any questions you might have in regard to these accounts. Your bank can also tell you about any relevant state laws that you should know about, such as any requirements to notify the named beneficiary about the account or the account being frozen for a time period following your death while your estate is being settled.

At your death, the beneficiary can claim the money simply by showing the financial institution the death certificate and personal identification. Until your death, however, the beneficiary has no rights to the money. Again, the benefit of using pay-on-death accounts is that they do not need to go through probate so they are available almost immediately. You name a beneficiary for those funds and that person can receive them at your death without the hassles of waiting for them to go through probate.

Using the Funds to Pay for Funeral Costs. Funeral costs can run amok these days, and it's not unusual for the tab to run more than $10,000, oftentimes more. Burial plots in prime real estate can cost upwards of $30,000 or more. If you want to help pre-plan for your funeral costs (because you really want that elaborate service and to rest in peace on a famous hillside in choice real estate), you can set up a Totten Trust and direct the money to go toward your funeral expenses. You deposit a sum of money equal to today's funeral costs in a savings account, CD, or money market account and name a beneficiary that can carry out your wishes with regard to the use of the funds (you also discuss these wishes with your beneficiary so he or she knows what to do with the funds). Although the money earns interest in the account (hopefully just enough to keep up with inflation), you can also add to it as you like throughout your life (or as you change your plans for your funeral or decide to direct the money for some other use).

Survivors can also pay for your funeral using the proceeds they receive as beneficiaries of your life insurance policy, death benefits from veterans, or Social Security. Whichever way you choose to pre-plan your funeral arrangements, it's a good idea to discuss your plans with any affected beneficiaries and your executor.

Life Insurance Trusts

We explained these kinds of trusts in Chapter 2. Life insurance trusts are legal entities you create for owning life insurance you previously owned and become operational during your lifetime. To minimize estate taxes paid on the proceeds of such a policy, particularly at your death, you will want to consider setting up a life insurance trust, naming an adult friend or family member to serve as trustee. You must transfer the policy to the trust—which must be irrevocable—at least three years before your death. Below is a good example of when you would want to create this kind of trust.

Melanie is a single mother with three children in college and graduate school. Melanie's estate is worth $3.3 million and she also has a life insurance policy that will pay $1 million at her death. She doesn't want these proceeds to be part of her estate, or a lot of estate taxes will be due. Neither does she want to give her policy to just anyone. She wants to remain in control of her policy but make sure that it doesn't become an expensive consequence to her death.

Her tactic: She creates an irrevocable trust for her policy, transferring ownership of the policy to the trust, and she names her best friend, the only person in the world she can depend on, as trustee.

Life insurance trusts are governed strictly by federal law. We recommend consulting with an estate planner or attorney if you think you need to set one of these up.

If you do not create a life insurance trust, and you name a family member as a beneficiary of your policy, the policy does not go through probate at your death. However, the proceeds are included in your estate for federal estate tax purposes. If you name your estate as the beneficiary, then the policy becomes part of your estate and is subject to probate. If your estate will need extra money to pay debts, taxes, or your end-of-life expenses, directing those proceeds to those debts is a good idea. This may mean you designate someone as the beneficiary of those proceeds and tell him or her how you want those funds to be used. Example: You name your wife as beneficiary of your life insurance policy. At your death, she receives those proceeds and uses them to help pay for your last medical bill and your funeral.

Trusts for Pets

We've had many customers leave their entire estates to their beloved pets. A question that we always ask: "How will Buster the cat and Peaches the dog take care of your affairs?" It's not unusual for people to leave everything to their pets in a will and not think about those consequences.

You have two choices when it comes to taking care of your pets in your estate plan: (1) You can arrange for a family member or close friend to care for your pet when you die; or (2) you can set formal arrangements in your living trust or will. If you write in your will or trust who gets your pets, consider leaving some money to that person as well to help pay for caregiving expenses. Despite the wishes of many pet-lovers, the law says you cannot leave assets to an animal. If you try to leave your pets everything you own—or just one asset—the property will become part of your residual estate (remember: your residual estate is the collection of all assets for which you did not name specific beneficiaries) and go to either the beneficiary or beneficiaries named as the residuary beneficiaries or distributed according to your state's laws.

Trusts for pets do exist, and these are separate legal entities. You name a trustee to manage the trust and you direct what happens to your pet at your death. If you truly do not want to leave a pet to someone outright, ask an attorney about these trusts.

States that allow pet trusts include the following:

Alaska	Missouri	North Carolina
Arizona	Montana	Oregon
California	Nebraska	Tennessee
Colorado	Nevada	Utah
Florida	New Jersey	Washington
Iowa	New Mexico	Wisconsin
Kansas	New York	Wyoming
Michigan		

Trusts for Disabled People

If you have any disabled person under your care, you should consult an attorney or estate planner about setting up a special trust for this person. Special needs trusts must be tailored to the specific needs of the disabled person, whether the disability is physical or mental. A person who cannot handle an inheritance will need a trust that names a trustee for managing any assets. Creating such a trust must also take into consideration any government benefits for which the disabled person is eligible and receives.

These trusts must be carefully crafted; knowledge of Medicaid and Supplemental Security Income (SSI) basics is essential to appreciate the drafting idiosyncrasies of the special needs trust. Medicaid and SSI are programs designed for low-income, low-asset individuals, each with independent eligibility criteria setting maximum levels of income and resources the individual can maintain. SSI is a federal cash-assistance program for disabled individuals who have minimal income and resources; it carries automatic coeligibility for Medicaid. While access to food stamps or rental subsidies also may be involved, the predominant concern of the beneficiary is typically medical care. The medical expenses can be significant and, absent public assistance, could not be covered by the child's own funds. What's more, the costs might be so high as to exhaust a trust's principal if it is the primary source of payment (under a traditional standard of principal invasion for the beneficiary's health care).

Consult an attorney who specializes in special needs trusts if you need one.

Educational Savings Plans

When people leave money to children, they often do so in order to help children pay for college or graduate school. An education is an expensive part of life, but a necessary one for which special investment plans exist for the purpose of helping families pay for school. With these types of plans available, you may not need to worry so much about your estate having to foot the entire educational cost. These plans are good for parents who intend to send their children to college at some point. They allow people to designate money for educational purposes with tax-saving advantages. However, if the person to whom these funds are designated never goes to college (or the funds are never used for educational purposes), the special tax treatment is lost.

Qualified Tuition Plans

Every state has its own version of a qualified tuition plan or a 529 plan (of the Internal Revenue Code). These plans are investment accounts that allow you to set aside money—tax-free—for paying for higher education. The money that accumulates and the money used for educational purposes is not taxed. The named beneficiary must be a family member, but that can include cousins. If the money taken out of the account goes toward the beneficiary's education costs, such as tuition, books, and supplies, or equipment necessary for attending a college, graduate school, or vocational school, the money is not taxed.

To place money into a 529 plan, you'll want to avoid contributing more than what trips the federal gift tax, which is $1 million. Couples can contribute double ($2 million).

You must use your state-authorized plan to create and contribute to these accounts. If you want to contribute to a 529 plan that is active in another state, you'll have to check with state laws. Some of these plans are estate tax deductible. Again, check with your state's specific plan to understand how exactly how these plans work and how you can set up one. Remember: These are investment accounts, so they do ebb and flow with the vagaries of the stock market. The managers of these investments accounts vary in the kinds of risk they take.

Coverdell Accounts

Coverdell accounts are not as likeable as 529 plans. They limit the contribution to a beneficiary's account to only $2,000 a year (although this may change), no matter whether that total came from one person or many. Anyone with a six-figure income is not eligible to contribute. And contributions are not tax-deductible. However, the money that accumulates in the account is not taxed, and when it's used for educational purposes, it's also not taxed.

Surviving Spouses

Married couples who set up joint (AB) trusts are each other's successor trustee (sometimes referred to as the continuing trustee). Each spouse names the other as the life beneficiary, which means that the surviving spouse can use and benefit from the decedent's trust for the rest of his or her life, with certain restrictions, but does not have outright ownership of it. How does this work? Let's review:

When the first spouse dies, the mutual trust gets split into two entities—the A trust and the B trust. Technically, both spouses have a B trust, but only one of the couple's B trusts activates, and the spouse who dies first establishes this trust at his or her death. The surviving spouse's assets go into the A trust. When the second spouse dies, the assets in both the A and B trusts go to their final beneficiaries, which are usually the couple's children.

At the death of the first spouse, the surviving spouse divides the living trust assets between the A and B trusts. Both of these trusts follow different rules and must be managed separately.

Managing Trust B

The surviving spouse's trust is the A trust. But as cotrustee, at the death of the first spouse, the surviving spouse must manage trust B. Trust B becomes a distinct taxable entity and the surviving spouse must do the following:

- Divide the assets between trust A and B by deciding which assets go into the irrevocable trust B (the decedent's trust) and the revocable trust A (the survivor's trust)
- Acquire a federal taxpayer ID number for the trust
- Maintain organized and separate tax records
- File separate tax returns for this trust

Although highly unusual, you can name someone else as your successor trustee instead of your spouse. You can also name someone else as initial trustee for your own estate other than yourself while you are living, but this isn't the norm. As settlors of a joint trust, spouses are usually initial trustees (cotrustees), as well as each other's successor or continuing trustees. Each spouse names a successor trustee, typically the same person, for when the second spouse dies.

Surviving spouses may want to consult with an accountant or tax planner when choosing which assets go into which trust at the death of the first spouse. In order to take future income tax and estate tax into consideration when dividing up the assets into both A and B trusts, employing the advice of a professional familiar with your state's laws is a good idea. Your state may have property ownership laws that allow some flexibility with the allocation of shared property, which ultimately translate to tax-saving division. For example, if you and your spouse co-owned property in Montana, but you live in Arizona, you will want to know how best to place that property given Montana's tax codes and related laws. The answers are never clear and easy, which is why having sound professional advice can help your estate's long-term goals. Consider it a wise investment. A professional can tell you what to expect given one division over another, as well as help you understand what you are doing and why from a tax or legal standpoint. An expert can ensure you make the best decisions for you and your family.

> In California and Tennessee, the person who becomes trustee over the B trust (usually the surviving spouse) is required by law to notify the final beneficiaries that trust B is now irrevocable. When the first spouse dies, all beneficiaries named in the first spouse's trust must be notified.

Complicating this division is the situation where one spouse has named different final beneficiaries than the other spouse for shared assets. What if Bruce wants the armoire he shared with his wife to go to Vanessa but his wife names Jessica as beneficiary of that armoire in her trust? How does every item of the shared property get divided fairly, and how can the successor trustee guarantee that all final beneficiaries are treated fairly and equally? This is why talking with an expert about dividing the assets between the two trusts is wise.

Dividing the assets between the two trusts requires some paperwork, including obtaining and recording, if necessary, new title documents that list trust B as the owner of the assets. A schedule listing all property, including assets without a title, becomes attached to the decedent's trust. The surviving spouse does not have to do anything to the survivor's trust other than create a list of assets now in that trust. These new schedules do not need to be notarized or witnessed.

The IRS requires that there is a clear and legally valid record of what assets are in each trust. Technically, each trust should contain 50 percent of shared assets and any separate property owned by each spouse accordingly. The dollar amount of shared assets should be equal.

A taxpayer ID is obtained by filing a simple IRS form, and keeping a clear and organized track record of trust A entails separating your financial paperwork, getting fresh checkbooks and filing systems, and using common sense. If taxes are due on trust B because the gross value of the assets in trust B exceed the personal exemption for the year of the first spouse's death, those taxes must be paid within nine months of the death. In addition to these tax-related responsibilities, the surviving spouse must do the following:

> The death of a spouse is always sudden and troubling. There's a lot of paperwork involved, some of which has nothing to do with taxes and fulfilling estate plans. Although you may want to stay in control of your plans and your estate(s), this is a good time to consult with competent professional advisors who can help you get through this time period and ensure that you don't forget to file a form, pay certain taxes, or do something in his or her fiduciary duty to establish and manage both trusts' property responsibly.

- Distribute the deceased spouse's gifts per trust B's instructions

- Keep all remaining assets of the deceased spouse in the B trust and manage that trust

- Manage the remaining revocable trust (A trust)

Managing the B trust can entail making allowed amendments. A surviving spouse should make any changes to the B trust to reflect changed circumstances. Any property left in a child's trust must also be managed.

Most living trusts allow trustees to hire financial advisors and lawyers, paid for by the trust. Don't be afraid to seek such advice for the benefit of your trust. If you are a surviving spouse and feel insecure with managing your deceased spouse's and your trusts, seek outside help.

It's important to understand that the concept of an AB trust is to split up a couple's estate for tax purposes but allow the surviving spouse to have access to the dead spouse's side of the trust (the decedent's trust) for the rest of his or her life. You don't have to bequeath all of your separate property to beneficiaries and instruct that they receive them at your death. You don't have to leave any specific gifts. If you leave no gifts, all of your assets remain held in the trust.

AB trusts typically grant the surviving spouse broad and sweeping powers as trustee over the dead spouse's trust, which can include selling assets out of it and using those proceeds to live. Here's where the "for the . . . health, education, maintenance, and support" clause comes into play. Any action taken by the surviving spouse—including using trust B's principal—"for the . . . health education, maintenance, and support" of his or her life is okay.

The rights of surviving spouses are so strong that one would think the surviving spouse actually owns the assets in the decedent's trust. Not so. But here's what a surviving spouse can do—usually—with regard to the dead spouse's trust (decedent's trust or trust B):

- Use all the interest and income from the trust's assets

- Use and control all of the trust's assets, such as living in a home and continuing to make improvements on it

- Sell the trust's assets, reinvest the trust's assets, or buy new trust assets in the name of the trust so long as the principal is not exhausted

- Use any of the trust's principal necessary for the health, education, maintenance, and support purposes; this is called invading the trust's principal

Does this mean a surviving spouse can sell the house and buy round-the-world tickets? Probably not. Neither can the surviving spouse make gifts to anyone out of the deceased spouse's trust. This prevents the surviving spouse from changing the deceased spouse's wishes, either by changing the decedent spouse's final beneficiaries or outright giving away assets to someone that the deceased spouse never intended. But the surviving spouse can get away with selling the house in Maine, traveling a little, and eventually buying another home in Florida and placing it in the trust. Some AB trusts add that the surviving spouse can have a right to take $5,000 or 5 percent of the assets in trust B, whichever is greater, once a year for any reason, regardless of how frivolous. Our trusts don't contain this language because we feel that enough of the trust's language allows plenty of room for the surviving spouse to make good decisions for

> If you need to create more complex types of trusts that set stricter restrictions on survivors and beneficiaries, consult an attorney or estate planner.

using trust B to his or her benefit. Determining what is necessary "for the . . . health, education, maintenance, and support" of the surviving spouse is up to the trustee, who is the surviving spouse in most cases. So unless a beneficiary or family member raises hell about how trust funds are being used, the restrictions are close to nil.

As you can see, the trust allows enormous leeway and bases this leeway on a general assumption: that the settlors have faith in and know one another well. Couples who set up joint trusts should know what's important to one another and how each person would want his or her assets to trickle downward in the event of a death. AB trusts are designed to protect the surviving spouse, and make room for the estate to eventually reach final beneficiaries. A certain level of good faith is involved.

Managing Trust A

The surviving spouse's trust remains revocable and flexible. The survivor can do whatever he or she wants with the A trust, including canceling it. Most surviving spouses, however, don't need to change much in their trusts. If the survivor adds new beneficiaries to the trust, the same successor trustee can handle distributing those assets to new beneficiaries. Couples should avoid having two different successor trustees handle their trusts at the death of both spouses. When the second spouse dies, trust A also becomes irrevocable. The successor trustee(s) must distribute both trusts' assets, take care of any children's trusts involved, and handle tax or other trust-related matters.

Successor Trustees

If you read the parts to the living trust in Appendix B that mention the duties of your successor trustee (or, if you look at the Trustee Powers section, which also relates to the powers of your successor trustee), you'll find that he or she retains broad authority over your estate. It's okay for this person also to be a named beneficiary, and they often are. The most important aspect to choosing your successor trustee is naming someone responsible, someone in tune with your family and your affairs (that is, not someone with whom you haven't had a conversation in 15 years), and preferably someone who will have the time, patience, and capability to settle your affairs. This person can reside in another state, but bear in mind that the closer the person lives to you, the easier it will be to take care of business. He or she has a duty to act responsibly and not abuse the trust or in any way act against the best interests of the trust or its beneficiaries. Poorly chosen successor trustees invite lawsuits that can tear an otherwise happy family apart. Among the most important duties of any successor trustee are the following:

- Turning trust property over to named beneficiaries and according to the trust's instructions, which entails obtaining death certificates and dealing with the paperwork and financial institutions or other organizations for distributing those assets
- Managing the trusts of any incapacitated settlors, including making amendments to a couple's AB trust
- Managing children's trusts
- Preparing and filing death tax returns, among other important paperwork duties (that we'll explain in Chapter 7)

Unlike executors for wills and estates that must go through probate, successor trustees don't usually get paid for their trustee tasks. You can, however, set provisions in your living trust that allow your successor trustee to receive reasonable compensation for if and when you become incapacitated or you have children's trusts that need to be managed for a long period of time.

Depending on your state's laws, successor trustees may have to present information about the trust to the beneficiaries. If your state law does not require this disclosure, it's wise for every successor beneficiary to notify beneficiaries and deliver important information. In Chapter 7, we'll go over in detail what happens after a primary trustee's death (and, in the case of a married couple, both spouses) and what a successor trustee must do.

Be cautious about naming more than one successor trustee. Having more than one person with authority over your affairs can create unwanted and unexpected problems—even if you're not around to witness them. While not required, married couples should choose the same successor trustee to manage their estate at the death of the second spouse.

Naming a Bank, Company, or Institution as Successor Trustee

Traditional families and individuals do not normally resort to naming a bank, trust company, or other institution as the successor trustee unless the settlor anticipates serious complications in a convoluted estate. Banks and trust companies won't act like beloved family members when settling an estate, they may not have intimate knowledge of your personal values, and they can also charge fees and drain more out of the estate, leaving less and less to family members. Think long and hard before you name a corporation to handle your affairs. Even if it's hard to think of a competent, responsible, and honest person in your circle of family and friends, keep thinking.

Having said that, however, exceptions to this suggestion do exist in families that are inherently complex or less traditional. Multiple marriages and multiple children of all different ages can create such a situation. You may have reasons to think about naming someone who is dispassionate and disinterested in your estate (who does not care who gets what) and will treat the administration your estate fairly and without prejudice. If this is the case, consider naming a family attorney or an unbiased friend as a successor trustee, and then resort to a company or institution that handles estates.

Another situation that can complicate estate planning is age differences in new marriages. For example, what if a man marries a woman much younger than he, but has several children

---

Minor Details

Second marriages of people with young children present particularly complex estate planning challenges. Selecting an appropriate custodian for a minor needs careful consideration, especially when new spouses arrive and (potentially) create built-in conflicts with the new and blended family. One's choice in an appropriate person to manage a minor child's inheritance should consider the family dynamics and the relationship between the child and the potential custodian. A custodian should always act in the best wishes of the child and not favor one child (such as a biological child) over another (such as a stepchild).

from a previous marriage who are just as old, if not older, than the new wife? Would the children ever see their inheritance if their father sets up a life estate for his new wife and does not make any specific gifts at his death? Finding solutions to cover these potential problems in an estate plan may require the assistance of a professional who knows how to best set up plans for nontraditional or blended families—particularly large ones.

Prenuptials and Second Marriages. While most people commonly associate a prenup with the risk of divorce and a will or living trust with the risk of death, a carefully crafted prenuptial agreement can also prove a powerful tool for managing the disposition of assets. Each spouse can spell out specific bequests while agreeing to forgo certain rights of inheritance. The prenup also enables each spouse to bequeath enough funds to support the survivor, while stipulating that wealth be distributed to chosen inheritors—family, school, or charities. Thus, having a prenup and a living trust that work together can reinforce how a second family's property gets distributed after one spouse dies. This is something to think about if you are contemplating marriage and want to plan your futures together and either reformulate an already existing will or living trust or create one for you and your new spouse. Effective second-family estate planning may sound more complicated, but with the right documents and your wishes spelled out accordingly, it's not all that hard.

For Frequent Travelers. If you do not feel up to the task of managing your living trust while you are alive (as trustee), you can name a company or firm to serve as trustee. This is not very common, but for those who travel a lot—particularly outside the country—and are unable to manage their living trust properly (or just don't want to), naming someone else as trustee may suit your circumstances and desires. This is not an issue for most, however. You can successfully serve as trustee of your own trust, and if you have a joint trust with your spouse, you already have a back-up trustee.

Beneficiaries

Naming beneficiaries in your will or living trust shouldn't be too hard. In fact, this can be the fun part about writing your will or setting up your trust: You get to imagine who gets what and plan for leaving cherished personal possessions to your loved ones.

> If you do name a corporate trustee, be sure to name a successor trustee as well. Many trust departments at banks will refuse to serve if the estate is not of a certain size or if the anticipated cost of serving as trustee would deplete the estate too quickly.

In an AB trust, you can make specific bequests to beneficiaries at your death, but the vast majority of your assets remain in your trust for your surviving spouse to use for the rest of his or her life. Each spouse names final beneficiaries to their assets. In most joint trusts, those final beneficiaries are the same people, and are typically the children of the couple. But in marriages that include children from a previous marriage, one or both spouses may want to name different final beneficiaries for their separate assets. For example, Mark and Sandra each have children from previous marriages. Mark always wanted his children to get his sailboat at his death. Sandra had always dreamed of giving her children her life's work of black and white photographs. In Mark and Sandra's AB trust, they would list these assets as separate property and name their (different) beneficiaries. They can each decide what happens to their separate property at their death. When the first spouse dies, those assets usually become part of the life estate of the surviving spouse to use (but not transfer, sell, or give away) for rest of his or her life; when the second spouse dies, those assets go to the named beneficiaries in the first spouse's trust. The trusts can also specify that bequests to beneficiaries get distributed at the time of death, so if Sandra dies first, she can instruct her photographs to go directly to her children right away as gifts. Otherwise, they will reach her children at the death of Mark (and Mark gets to enjoy them until he goes).

Cobeneficiaries

Let's say you own a small plot of land in a remote area of Colorado. You had always planned on developing the land and building a second home, but that never happened. Now you want to leave that property to your three children. They will be cobeneficiaries. Assuming your children are on good terms with each other, this shouldn't create problems. You name each child in your trust documents and specify how much each will get (percentage of ownership). Don't assume that by naming your children to share an asset means you want each child to receive an equal share. Be very specific in your wording: "To my children, Molly Daniels, Jack Daniels, and Laura Daniels, I give my property at 333 Aspen Way in Colorado *to them in equal shares.*" Or, ". . . to Molly Daniels, Jack Daniels, and Laura Daniels, *share and share alike.*"

You don't have to leave assets to beneficiaries in equal shares. You can give percentages for shares on any one asset. But in some situations, this can create problems, so try to anticipate potential problems, and when necessary, discuss the issues with your family members. You must consider what will happen if your named cobeneficiaries cannot agree how to manage or deal with an inheritance. You can use your trust to give your successor trustee powers over resolving disputes among cobeneficiaries, such as allowing your successor trustee to sell the asset and distributing the proceeds equally among the arguing beneficiaries. You may also want to name alternate cobeneficiaries if one of your named cobeneficiaries dies before you, or you can specifically state what happens to the remaining shares at the death of a cobeneficiary.

Residuary Beneficiaries

The residue of your estate is what's left after taxes and debts are paid and any specific gifts are made. Having a residuary beneficiary ensures that someone gets your assets if you die and your named primary and alternate beneficiaries are not around to receive them, such as in the case that they predecease you. If you keep your trust updated and revise and rename any of your beneficiaries in the event someone predeceases you, naming a residuary beneficiary isn't a big deal. Also, you can state in your living trust that if a beneficiary dies before receiving an asset intended for him or her, that asset should become part of the estate's residue and be distributed equally among the remaining beneficiaries.

Conclusion

You have a lot of choices to make in the construction and successful execution of your living trust. Some of these decisions can conjure up deep emotions. Do you feel overwhelmed? Do you feel as if you are trying to construct a huge research project—that follows a formula and must be written in a very specific way—about your entire life, referencing the people in your life, the things you own, and even the things you owe? Well, you are. But unlike writing a research paper using unfamiliar sources to defend an argument, in living trust documents you use the people you know and the things you own to plan your family's future and, in a way, defend your family's future. Leaving money or assets to heirs is one of the most profound things you can do in life. It's tough—but possible—to do it well.

Here's the easy part: naming yourself as trustee to your own living trust, and naming your spouse as cotrustee if you are creating a joint AB living trust. Choosing beneficiaries beyond your own children can take time, but don't get too bogged down by the formalities of a living trust. You can always change your choices. As the creator (settlor) of your trust, naming the people you include in your trust is the greatest power you have in the entire process. You get to compose the sheet music for your orchestra, then stand in front and serve as conductor. When else or how often can you be such a boss?

We've saved some of the tougher issues to deal with for last: taxes, probate, and other money issues. This is the part of estate planning that turns many people off. The language of estate tax and accounting principles is intimidating and leaves many people wondering how estate planners ever think about mastering this technical area of expertise. In the next two chapters we'll take the mystery out of a lot of estate planning techniques by giving you what you need to know to make good decisions about your plan.

CHAPTER 6

Taxes

Death and taxes are two certainties in life. Taxes dominate most people's thoughts about managing family money. This is true while you are alive and dealing with the annual tax return, or planning your death and dealing with how to distribute your estate and minimize what you owe Mr. Taxman. Issues among family members may be emotional; familial loyalty can be a blessing and a curse; greed and materialism can warp good intentions. But, above all these matters, the taxman wants to be paid every time anyone inherits anything of substantial value.

The goal of any estate planning should include making wise decisions about your assets so that you can pay for your debts and taxes at your death, and have something left over to give to family members. No estate plan can shut the door to the taxman. No matter how much you pay a savvy estate planner to use loopholes in laws or create intricate tax-saving vehicles for your money, no one can prevent your estate from avoiding all taxes (unless your estate is given to charity). But there are ways to minimize those taxes and reduce the bill your estate must pay at your death, or at least delay paying them. If estate planning with tools such as living trusts were not useful for dealing with taxes and finding ways to reduce the taxable estate, then what would be the point? Keep in mind, however, that living trusts are useful beyond tax issues and avoiding probate. Always think of a living trust as a conduit that allows for an orderly distribution according to its terms (that you create).

Many families avoid gift and estate taxes entirely because the amounts of money they leave at their deaths are small enough to qualify for various exemptions (the rules that allow you to keep something without paying taxes on it). We will go through these exemptions in this chapter and show you how they work in your living trust. For example, there is usually no tax if you make a gift to your spouse or if your estate goes to your spouse at your death (note, however, that this does not refer to a joint AB trust that continues to hold the assets of a dead spouse for the life estate of the surviving spouse). But in a joint (non-AB) trust, the death of the second spouse triggers the estate tax. We'll see how an AB trust and a basic joint trust differ with regard to taxes. The tax savings resulting from an AB trust can be quite large.

If you make a gift to someone, currently the gift tax does not apply to the first $11,000 you make to that person per year (this figure is subject to change). You don't even have to file a gift tax return. And, even if tax applies to your gifts of your estate, it may be eliminated by the so-called unified credit. The unified credit is the total credit provided by law that is free of gift tax and/or estate taxation. It applies to both the gift tax and estate tax. But the unified credit is a one-time tool: Any part that you use against the gift tax in one year reduces the amount of credit you can use against gift or estate tax later. We'll see just how this works in this chapter.

The U.S. Tax Code is ugly, complex, and seemingly untouchable. It's worse than the language found in the final draft of your living trust, and it doesn't read like a mystery novel or comedy skit. The Code confuses and bewilders advanced tax specialists every day. There are PhDs in Finance out there who sweat and cry over the Tax Code for a living, and still have issues with it (wouldn't you like that job?). Plus it's vulnerable to changes when Congress decides to pass new laws or the voters decide to elect a new president. Taxes might always reflect politics and political partisanship, but you don't have to worry about those politics; chances are, the most severe and worrisome of taxes will not affect you at all.

Congress likes to change estate tax laws about every five years, which is why it's wise to review your living trust and make any minor adjustments to it every five years. Keeping your trust up-to-date entails reviewing and amending it when any laws that affect the Tax Code or related laws take effect. Your life is also likely to change, so you need to take new circumstances or personal wishes into consideration. This usually means having a tax specialist look over your living trust. You can go to an attorney (who specializes in estate planning) in your area or where you originally set up the trust.

The point here: Don't stress over comprehending the Tax Code and all that it means—or doesn't mean—for you, your family, and your living trust. We give you the basics here and assume you will consult with the proper professionals for assuring you have done what you can to fortify your plans for your family. Leave it to the professionals! When our customers come to us with questions about taxes and numbers and *Can I bury a million dollars I never declared to the IRS in the ground and leave a map to it to my son?* we tell them to speak with a competent tax attorney who is knowledgeable about taxes and estate planning.

Your goal as a living trust creator is to preserve your estate for as long as you can and prepare smartly for those taxes (Mr. Taxman survives everyone, unfortunately!). It can be done, but it requires some work and a little knowledge about rules and laws that involve dollar signs and simple math—but thankfully no calculus or final examinations. How you plan strategically for your family's inheritance will ultimately determine whether you passed life's test. Hopefully, you'll get an A+ and share a legacy with your family for generations to come.

Basics of Tax Law

Four categories of taxes are relevant to you and your estate: the federal estate or "death" tax; any pick-up, inheritance or state death tax; the gift taxes; and income tax. Death taxes are imposed on the transfer of wealth at the time of death or in anticipation of death (transfers made two years prior to death). Some states impose two types of death taxes: inheritance and estate. Some states also have gift taxes, which are closely related to death taxes. Inheritance taxes are state taxes on the right to inherit. While they are theoretically levied on the recipients (named beneficiaries) of assets from an estate, the person receiving an inheritance generally does not pay this tax; it comes out of the estate, as set forth by the will or trust documents. Estate taxes, on the other hand, are levied on the estate of the deceased person before assets are distributed to heirs. Gift taxes are imposed on large transfers of wealth between living people.

Important Distinction

Gift taxes are paid on gifts made during one's life and inheritance taxes are paid after one has died and gifts are made to beneficiaries. Think of gift taxes as "before" and inheritance taxes as "after." The gift tax prevents people from gifting away their estate throughout their lives so at their death, there is nothing left—and nothing left to tax. Most states have an inheritance tax on any property located within that state.

The Federal Estate or Death Tax

This is the tax everyone is afraid of. If it weren't so bad, the word "death" wouldn't sound so negative next to the word "tax." When President Bush first campaigned for office in 2000, one of his selling points was a promise to abolish the federal estate tax. Congress made changes to the tax laws in 2001 that effectively repeal the estate tax over the course of many years. The current federal estate tax laws increase the personal exemption from $1.5 million in 2005 to $2 million in 2006 through 2008. By the year 2010, the estate tax is zero, but then it gets reinstated with a $1 million exemption. The following chart puts this into perspective.

The question mark in the chart below means "who knows?". There is no telling what Congress might do between now and 2011 (when the federal estate tax is suspended for a year) to change this chart and what an estate must pay in terms of taxes. Prepare for future change of plans. Maybe the exemption will rise to $5 million or become unlimited (meaning no estate tax). Until a change happens, you can speculate all you want.

As it stands now, the chart below is how the law sets the exemptions until the year 2011. More than likely, however, Congress will change the rules before the estate tax is totally repealed in 2010, or before it goes back to $1 million in 2011. The new tax laws don't make much sense (but are not on Congress's immediate agenda), so there's no telling when or how the rules will change. You must base your estate planning on today's tax laws and not worry too much about what will happen in the future. As the laws change, you can revise and update your plans. Generally, it's safe to say that Congress will keep a large exemption; and it's unlikely that Congress will continue to keep the tax repealed or restore it to former tax rates.

Estate Tax Exemptions

Year	Estate Tax Exemption	Gift Tax Exemption	Highest Estate and Gift Tax Rate
2005	$1.5 million	$1 million	47 percent
2006	$2 million	$1 million	46 percent
2007	$2 million	$1 million	45 percent
2008	$2 million	$1 million	45 percent
2009	$3.5 million	$1 million	45 percent
2010	no estate tax	$1 million	35 percent (gift tax only)
2011	$1 million (?)	$1 million (?)	55 percent (?)

Whether or not the federal estate tax rides off into the sunset and never returns is unclear. The change in tax laws in 2001 replaced the $675,000 unified gift- and estate-tax credit with a $1 million unified exemption—the amount that each individual can pass free of federal estate tax. This exemption is $1.5 million in 2005 and continues to climb to $3.5 million in 2009. Then estate tax disappears for the year 2010. The new laws also shaved off the top estate-tax rate from 55 percent in 2002 to 45 percent in 2009. As you can see from the chart, the top rate on taxable gifts drops with the estate tax. But when the estate tax drops to zero in 2010, the top gift-tax rate settles at 35 percent, which is the highest income-tax rate. Congress kept the gift tax in 2010 in order to prevent too many lifetime transfers of income-producing property to heirs in lower income-tax brackets to reduce income taxes.

The estate tax exemptions are the amounts you can exempt from estate taxes in the year of your death, so if your entire estate is worth $2 million or less in 2007, the year you die, you don't have to pay any estate taxes. These exemptions are *personal* exemptions. A married couple can exempt twice this amount in their estate, or $4 million in 2006 through 2008, and $7 million in 2009.

Federal estate taxes (and any state-imposed estate taxes) are due within nine months of a person's death. An automatic six-month extension may be requested. (More on this in the next chapter.)

State Taxes

States can impose both inheritance and estate taxes. Inheritance taxes are the oldest and most common form of death tax. They are typically levied at graduated rates based upon the amount of the bequest and upon the relationship between the deceased and the beneficiary. These rates can vary tremendously from state to state. For example, in Indiana, lineal descendants are taxed at rates varying from 1 percent on inheritances of up to $25,000 to 10 percent on amounts of $1.5 million or more. In Pennsylvania, however, they are taxed at a 6 percent rate and non-relatives are taxed at a 15 percent rate, regardless of the amount of inheritance.

Five types of exemptions are usually allowed under the inheritance tax: (1) personal exemptions based on the relationship of the giver and receiver; (2) exemptions of a specified amount allowed for the entire estate; (3) exemptions for property on which a tax already has been paid; (4) exemptions for bequests to charitable, religious or educational institutions; and (5) exemptions for particular types of property.

The personal exemption granted to beneficiaries based upon their relationship to the decedent is the most powerful exemption. Inheritance taxes impose higher taxes for leaving property to distant relatives or friends and encourage leaving estates to immediate family members. In South Dakota, for example, the inheritance of children is taxed at rates varying from nothing on the first $30,000 to 7.5 percent for amounts in excess of $100,000. Surviving children also receive a $3,000 exemption. By contrast, non-relatives are subject to rates ranging from 6 percent to 30 percent and receive only a $100 exemption.

Not all states have inheritance taxes, but those that do can impose a tax on anyone who either owns real estate in that state or any resident of that state that owns real estate elsewhere. State death taxes can have thresholds that are a lot lower than the federal estate tax thresholds. So, your estate can avoid paying federal taxes (because it's lower than the maximum exemption amount) but get hit with state taxes (because it's higher than your state's maximum exemption amount).

Every state benefits from taxable estates. About two-thirds of the states have a pick-up tax law. By virtue of these pick-up taxes, a state can enjoy participation in the federal estate tax. Using this tax, states can take a bite out of the federal tax levy. So, they are generally said to have no inheritance tax. What this really means is these states take part of the amount that is calculated as federal estate tax. The trend in state death taxes has clearly moved in the direction of eliminating traditional taxes and imposing only pick-up taxes.

The states that do not have a pick-up tax instead impose a state death tax, either in the form of an inheritance tax or an estate tax. An inheritance tax is a tax on the assets received by a person (but usually paid for out of the estate). An estate tax is a tax on the assets of the decedent. Like inheritance taxes, state estate taxes can vary significantly from state to state. A will or living trust can affect how taxes are allocated. For example, one can provide that all estate taxes be paid from the residue of the estate and not allocated to specific assets. If the estate taxes are not paid from the estate, however, and the assets are distributed, the IRS can seek to recover from the estate's fiduciary—the executor or successor trustee. The IRS can also proceed against the beneficiaries up to the fair market value of the assets they received.

An important note to make: State death taxes are not in addition to federal estate taxes. Federal law allows an offset for the payment of state death taxes. So don't try to calculate your tax bill. If you need to specifically calculate the tax due, you would be wise to depend on your Certified Public Accountant. All federal and state death taxes are due within nine months of a person's death—but a six-month extension can be granted. If an extension is granted, a payment must be made of the estimated estate taxes that will be due when Form 706 is filed (this is the IRS form that goes with the estate tax payment; see the next chapter for more information).

Another important note to make: The federal estate tax is a tax on the value of the estate as of a particular point in time, as contrasted with an inheritance tax that is based upon the transfer to certain recipients.

States can also impose gift taxes, but many have repealed those taxes. For purposes of understanding gift taxes, however, it's best to focus on the federal gift tax. You probably are not going to be computing any state versus federal gift taxes anyhow. Leave that to the tax and accounting pros. But to get a sense about how you can give gifts during your life, you have to know about gifting.

Gift Taxes

"Gifting" is a great way to reduce the value of your taxable estate. As you can see from the chart, you can gift away a certain amount of property without paying taxes on it. Due to the tax changes of 2001, the federal gift and estate tax have been integrated into one unified tax system, sometimes called the unified credit. Your unified credit is the total amount that the

> States that participate in the pick-up tax include Alabama, Alaska, Arizona, Arkansas, California, Colorado, Connecticut, Delaware, District of Columbia, Florida, Georgia, Hawaii, Idaho, Illinois, Kansas, Maine, Maryland, Massachusetts, Michigan, Minnesota, Mississippi, Missouri, Montana, Nevada, New Mexico, New York, North Carolina, North Dakota, Ohio, Oregon, Rhode Island, South Carolina, South Dakota, Texas, Utah, Vermont, Virginia, Washington, West Virginia, Wisconsin, and Wyoming.

> States with no pick-up tax but impose a separate estate tax are: Indiana, Iowa, Louisiana, Nebraska, New Hampshire, New Jersey, Oklahoma, Pennsylvania, and Tennessee.

law allows you to exempt from taxation. It's a credit against your federal estate taxes. Understanding the unified credit concept, and knowing how much unified credit you've used up, is also a critical factor when considering more advanced estate planning techniques, such as AB trusts. For example, spouses often leave each other all their assets, tax-free. However, when the surviving spouse eventually dies, only his or her unified credit is available. The unified credit of the spouse who died first cannot be used, so it is wasted. But with an AB trust, this complication can be eliminated.

Gifting applies to the transfer—for no compensation—of any property. You make a gift if you give assets (including money)—or the use of or income from property—without expecting to receive something of at least equal value in return (except maybe love). Gifting isn't a hard concept. You do it during birthdays and holidays; you give loved ones things without expecting anything in return. Well, most of us don't expect anything in return.

If you sell something for less than its full value or if you make an interest-free or reduced-interest loan, you may be gifting. The general rule is any gift is taxable, but there are many exceptions to this rule. The following gifts are not taxable:

- The first $11,000 you give to someone in the same year (called the annual exclusion)
- Tuition or medical expenses you pay for someone (called the educational and medical exclusion)
- Gifts to your spouse who is a U.S. citizen
- Gifts to a political organization for its use
- Gifts to tax-exempt charities

A separate $11,000 annual exclusion applies to each person to whom you make a gift. Therefore, you can give up to $11,000 each year to each of any number of people or entities and all those gifts will be tax-free. This $11,000 figure is subject to change as inflation rises. Next year, for example, that exemption can rise to $12,000 depending on the cost of living. By using the Consumer Price Index (CPI), published by the Department of Labor, the federal government determines whether the exemption needs to rise, and if so, it rises in $1,000 increments. A married couple can give away twice this amount per year to the same person, or $22,000 in 2004, tax-free.

You wonder, how does the $1 million gift exemption come into play here? The $1 million gift exemption refers to what you gift away in total throughout your life. If you give $11,000 gifts (or whatever the exemption happens to be that calendar year) to several people for many years, eventually you'll reach $1 million, and thereafter, you will pay a gift tax on any other gifts given. If this lifetime gift tax exemption didn't exist, then people with very large estates would gift away their estate over many years and eventually reduce their estate down to the federal gift exemption amount so that they would pay no taxes at all! If you owe any gift taxes, generally you don't pay these taxes until your death. In other words, your gifting will go through the check-out line at your death, and if you owe anything, your estate will pay for it.

If you do any of the following, you must file a gift tax return on IRS Form 709:

> The gift tax adjustment is determined by measuring the excess of the Consumer Price Index for All Urban Communities, published by the Department of Labor for the preceding year over the Consumer Price Index for 1997. This measurement happens every year.

- You give more than $11,000 during the year to someone other than your spouse
- You and your spouse are splitting the gift
- You give someone other than your spouse a gift that he or she cannot actually possess, enjoy or receive income from until sometime in the future (this would cover some trusts)
- You give your spouse an interest in property that will end by some future event

Gift splitting happens when you and your spouse make a gift to someone and it's considered made half by you and half by your spouse. You have to file a return even if half of the gift is less than $11,000, and you must make the choice to gift split on the gift tax return.

Gifting is a craft all on its own. If you find yourself making several gifts a year in order to reduce the value—and thus the taxable amount—of your estate, then you are among the lucky few who have extra money to throw around. For very large estates, gifting takes discipline and an early start. Gifting works best when you move money gradually to family members over an extended period of time. That's why it's best to keep your gifts during any calendar year under the tax-free limit. If you go over, you either have to pay the IRS some money or use up some of your unified tax credit.

The following is an example of how the unified credit might apply to your gifting strategy. Let's assume you've come into some money in 2006 and you decide you want to do some good in your family and help out your fellow siblings and their children.

You give your sister Marsha a cash gift of $10,000. You also pay the $32,000 hospital bill for your nephew Greg, who was in a bad car accident. You give your other sister Cindy $25,000 and your 19-year-old son Bobby $25,000 to help him get out of debt (ouch!).

When you apply the gift tax exemptions and the unified credit to your generosity, here's what happens:

- Under the medical exclusion, the $32,000 gift to Greg is not taxable at all.
- Under the annual exclusion, the first $11,000 you give someone during the year is not taxable as a gift; thus, your entire $10,000 gift to Marsha, the first $11,000 of the gift you give to Cindy and the first $11,000 of the gift you give to Bobby are not taxable.
- Your total taxable gifts amount to $28,000, which is $14,000 over the annual limit on your gift to Cindy and $14,000 over the annual gift limit on your gift to Bobby. At the standard gift tax rate of 20 percent, you owe the IRS $5,600. And, let's say that after you make all those cash gifts, you don't have the extra $5,600 lying around to write that fat check to the Feds. What do you do? You subtract the $5,600 from your unified credit for 2006 and the amount of the unified credit that you can use in later years is automatically reduced by $5,600.

Income Tax

Income tax is often a concern on two fronts: the beneficiaries that receive assets; and the estate or trust that makes an income. How do taxes come into play here?

The Beneficiaries' "Income." Estates are taxed—not heirs. So when your heirs inherit assets from your estate, they do not have to report those assets as income for tax purposes. However, if they receive *assets that generate income* (example: a brokerage account or rental property), they must include that income on their personal income tax returns. If the trust continues to hold assets that generate income, which are paid to the heirs, the heirs must include such income on their personal taxes. The trust can also retain that income, in which case the trustee must file a tax return for the trust and report that income.

A common misconception is the idea that heirs must get through a tax check-out line similar to a grocery store's check-out line. Taxes are imposed on the estate, so any estate taxes due get paid (by the estate) before any distribution is made to heirs. Once the taxes are paid, the assets pass to the heirs free of estate taxes.

The Estate's Income. An estate's income must be reported annually on either a calendar or fiscal year basis. An estate's fiscal tax year can be any period that ends on the last day of a month and does not exceed 12 months. Normally, the executor (or, in the case of trust, a successor trustee) selects the estate's accounting period when he or she files its first income tax return. Filing this return during the regular income tax return filing date of April 15 (or an extension to October 15) is typical. These returns tax the annual net income earned by the trust and/or estate. Any income a deceased person had a right to receive is included in his or her gross estate and is subject to estate tax. This income is also taxed when received by the recipient (estate or beneficiary). However, an income tax deduction is allowed to the recipient for the estate tax paid on the income.

For review: Trustees of a living trust do not need to file special tax returns for their trust during their life. They file regular tax returns just as they have in the past (before the trust was created). Once an individual dies, or one spouse dies and the B trust becomes irrevocable, special tax returns must then be filed if the value of the estate meets the criteria for taxes. (More on income tax in the next chapter.)

Tax Benefits for Survivors

The Tax Code gives major breaks to married couples and so-called traditional families. Survivors can qualify for certain benefits when they file their own income tax returns. For example, a surviving spouse can usually file a joint return for the year of death and may qualify for special tax rates for the next two years. If the deceased qualified as your dependent (meaning that person was under your care, such as a minor) during part of the year before death, you can claim the exemption for the dependent on your tax return, regardless of when death occurred during the year. This is the same treatment the Code gives to a child born during a tax year. If the deceased was your qualifying child, you may be able to claim the child tax credit.

If your spouse died within the two tax years preceding the year for which your return is being filed, you may be eligible to claim the filing status of qualifying widow(er) with dependent child and qualify to use the married filing jointly tax rates. Generally, you qualify for this benefit if you meet all of the following requirements:

- You were entitled to file a joint return with your spouse for the year of death—whether or not you actually filed jointly
- You did not remarry before the end of the current tax year
- You have a child, stepchild, or foster child who qualifies as your dependent for the tax year

- You provide more than half the cost of maintaining your home, which is the principal place of residence

Dealing with taxes during the year of a death is challenging—and emotional. You have ample reason to get advice from someone who can tell you how to deal with your taxes. In the case of an AB trust, a death that prompts the B trust to activate entails the successor trustee, who is usually the surviving spouse, getting a taxpayer ID and filing separate tax returns on trust B. The paperwork involved isn't too bad, but for a surviving spouse, this task can be overwhelming and add unnecessary grief. The surviving spouse must continue to administer the B trust and file annual trust tax returns. The surviving spouse must also file federal income and estate taxes if they are due on the deceased spouse's estate. Mr. Taxman wants his share of any tax due at the death of an individual, so worrying about this tax and having to take on so much new responsibility at the death of a spouse cannot be easy. Bottom line: Don't be afraid to ask for help.

The Unlimited Marital Deduction

The unlimited marital deduction is the law (in the Tax Code) that says a spouse can leave any amount of property to the surviving spouse free of estate tax—no matter how much that property is worth. How this usually works: You leave the bulk or your assets to your spouse at your death and that transfer is tax-free. However, if by leaving your assets to your spouse, the estate of the surviving spouse swells to an amount that he or she cannot claim entirely as exempt, then taxes will be due at the death of your spouse. This is the problem with not having a trust, or having just a basic shared trust: if one spouse leaves his or her assets to the surviving spouse, the surviving spouse's estate carries all those assets (it literally gets weighted down) and may now have a total value that exceeds the federal tax exemption limit. Couples who have wills but no trust also face this problem. You can will away all of your assets to your spouse at your death and use the unlimited marital deduction, but once your spouse dies, estate taxes will be due if the estate is worth more than the allowable exemptions.

Example: Sue Ellen and Ray share an estate worth $5 million. Sue Ellen dies in 2006, leaving her assets to Ray. No estate tax is due under the marital deduction. Both Sue Ellen and Ray plan on leaving their assets to their two children. Ray dies in 2009, and his estate at that point is worth $5.5 million (the original $5 million plus the appreciation of his assets). In 2009, the personal exemption is $3.5 million, so $2 million is subject to the estate tax. That means the children will receive far less money once the estate tax is paid.

The unlimited marital deduction only works for married people. Life partners, whether gay, lesbian, or heterosexual, cannot use the marital deduction. And, if you are married to a non-U.S. citizen, you are also restricted.

Noncitizen Spouses

If you've married a noncitizen of the United States, you cannot use the unlimited marital deduction to give property to your spouse either in death or while you are alive. Even if you are a bona fide U.S. citizen and your spouse is a legal resident, the laws prevent you from using the unlimited marital deduction. However, before you cancel your wedding plans or urge your spouse to start studying for his citizenship papers, here's what you can do:

- You can make an annual gift to your noncitizen spouse totaling $112,000 without any gift tax or estate tax ramifications (note: this number can change).
- You can both still utilize your personal estate tax exemptions.

Let's look at an example: Erica, a U.S. citizen with quite a lot of assets, marries Joshua, a Canadian who doesn't come into the marriage with a lot of assets. Erica and Joshua set up an AB trust. Over the next eight years, Erica gives the maximum annual gift amount to Joshua without owing taxes. This moves money out of Erica's taxable estate. Joshua dies and his now operational B trust contains the gifted money. His personal tax exemption shelters that money (owes no taxes). As a resident alien, he is entitled to the same personal exemption as a citizen.

Another way to plan an estate between a United States citizen and noncitizen is to have a Qualified Domestic Trust, or Q-Dot. This trust allows for marital deductions. See a lawyer about these kinds of trusts in detail if you are married to a noncitizen and have an estate worth more than your personal exemptions.

How AB Joint Trusts Avoid the Second Tax

The tax on the surviving spouse's estate is sometimes referred to as the second tax. If you are a couple with a combined estate that doesn't meet the tax threshold, which changes given the year of death, then you don't have as much to worry about. You can set up a joint living trust and leave your assets to your spouse at your death. Neither you nor your spouse will have to pay any taxes on an estate that is valued under the estate tax threshold.

Because you cannot know the year in which you die, nor what the exemptions will be or how much your estate will be worth at that unknown point in the future, setting up an AB trust is a smart thing to do. An AB trust set up today prepares you for future wealth and the possibility of your estate exceeding the estate tax threshold. Moreover, with an AB trust you and your spouse can have different final beneficiaries but allow the surviving spouse to have a life estate in your property for the rest of his or her life. Unlike basic mutual trusts, the AB trusts do not combine estates. They keep your spouse's and your estates separate, and when one spouse dies, that estate is subject to tax (but with careful planning you can delay this tax further through the use of a C trust). Let's revisit the example we used above and assume the couple set up an AB trust, rather than using a mutual trust or no trust at all.

Sue Ellen and Ray share an estate worth $4 million. They set up a trust and transfer all of their property into the trust. (Assume neither one has separate property.) Sue Ellen dies in 2006, and the trust splits into A and B. Her B trust owns half, or $2 million of the property, which is the limit of the personal exemption, so no tax is due. Ray's trust owns the other $2 million. Both Sue Ellen and Ray plan on leaving their assets to their two children. Ray dies in 2009, and his trust holds $3 million (the original $2 million plus the appreciation of his assets). In 2009, the personal exemption is $3.5 million, so the second trust can pass tax-free. The children receive both sets of property—from trust A and trust B.

Even though the surviving spouse's trust does not contain the assets from the deceased spouse's estate, nor can the surviving spouse ever own the deceased spouse's trust property, the purpose of an AB trust is to separate the two people's trusts for tax purposes but allow the surviving spouse access to the deceased trust's property for living out the rest of his or her life comfortably. AB trusts make use of both spouse's personal exemptions. If the estates were combined, however, then only one spouse—the second to die—would get to use one personal exemption. Thus, AB trusts allow a couple to double their tax-savings. This may sound ludicrous because you might ask, "Why don't people just split trusts up when one spouse dies? Can't you do that with a regular trust? Isn't that just paperwork to be done?"

Unfortunately, you can't. And you cannot switch a basic joint trust over to an AB trust after the first spouse dies. These are two different kinds of trusts. All of our We The People joints living trusts are AB trusts. Theoretically, a joint mutual trust does get split into two trusts at the death of the first spouse, but solely for the purpose of distributing the assets owned by the deceased spouse's side of the original trust (that is, his separate property and any property shared with the spouse but not going to the spouse). Once the deceased spouse's trust assets have been distributed to named beneficiaries, that trust ceases to exist. The survivor's trust continues to exist as the original revocable living trust, but now it contains assets inherited by the deceased spouse. The survivor's trust has no restrictions on it. The surviving spouse can do whatever he or she wants to the trust's assets, including naming new beneficiaries to assets previously owned by the dead spouse.

Let's compare the difference between a basic joint trust and an AB trust. By comparing the two, you will see how beneficial an AB living trust can be for a married couple.

With a Basic Joint Trust

- Couple co-owns assets worth $3 million.
- Wife owns $300,000 of separate property.
- Husband owns $100,000 of separate property.
- Couple sets up mutual living trust, placing all assets—co-owned and separate—into the trust. The trust owns $3.4 million in property.
- Husband dies in 2006, leaving his $100,000 and $1.5 million in his Trust 1. He specifies in his trust that his brother gets the $100,000 and the rest of his estate goes to his wife. His estate owes no taxes because its value is below the federal estate tax threshold of $2 million for that year. Trust 1's assets get distributed and the trust ends.
- Wife dies in 2007, leaving entire $3.3 million (her $1.5 from the original trust, plus husband's $1.5 carried over to her Trust 2, plus her separate property) to children.
- Estate tax on $1.3 million is due (only $2 million is exempt as a personal exemption).

With an AB Trust

- Couple co-owns assets worth $3 million.
- Wife owns $300,000 of separate property.
- Husband owns $100,000 of separate property.
- Couple sets up an AB living trust, placing all assets—co-owned and separate—into the trust. The trust owns $3.4 million in property.
- Husband dies in 2006, his Trust B owns half of the shared property, or $1.5 million plus his separate property for a total of $1.6 million. His estate owes no tax because it's below the $2 million tax threshold.
- He specifies that his $100,000 goes directly to his son as a gift at his death.
- Wife uses assets remaining in Trust B for the rest of her life. Her Trust A owns $1.8 million dollars ($1.5 from shared property plus $300,000 of separate property).

- Wife dies in 2007, leaving her $1.8 to the children, which is less than the estate tax threshold, so no taxes are due. Husband's Trust B ends here as well, so her husband's assets, which total $1.5 million and are also below the tax threshold, go to the children. No taxes are due.

Notice how a family that creates an AB trust avoids the second tax. In the first example of the basic joint trust, the husband saddles the wife's trust down with the bulk of his estate when he dies. While there is no tax on this transfer using the unlimited marital deduction, the wife is stuck with a large estate at her death, for which taxes will be due. (Alternatively, the first example could reflect an AB trust that distributes the husband's property to his wife at his death. If the husband chooses to give his property to his wife at his death, instead of leaving them in his B trust, he can say so in his trust documents. But this creates an asset-heavy A trust for the surviving wife, which later becomes subject to tax.)

In the second example, the family that uses an AB trust, the trusts remain separate and hold the couple's assets in separate, taxable entities. The husband leaves most of his property in trust B instead of giving it outright to his wife, who's still alive. Both spouses named one another as the life beneficiary of whichever trust becomes the B trust at the death of the first spouse. Here, that means the wife can receive all of the income and has the right to invade (use) the B trust's principal after her husband dies. Each spouse also names final beneficiaries of his or her AB trust. Final beneficiaries receive the property in trust B at the death of the first spouse, the husband, and they also receive the property from trust A at the death of the second spouse. Because these two trusts remain and are managed separately, there's a greater likelihood that they will own property that's worth less than the estate tax threshold. So there is less of a chance that their estates will owe taxes at their death. However, if they do, the amount owed will be less than if their entire estate were part of only one trust.

Make sense? We hope so. It can seem confusing, but when you stop and work through the equation and look at how the charts flow downward—reaching the final beneficiaries— it becomes clear. Take your time and review the material again if you find yourself asking questions.

The Size of Your Estate

Taking inventory of your assets and subtracting your liabilities is how you arrive at your net worth. The size of your gross estate is the total value of your estate's assets subject to estate and gift tax at the time of your death. Another way to see it: The gross estate is the value of your estate before any deductions are made for taxes, funeral expenses, attorneys' fees, or administration costs. When you evaluate your gross estate or net worth, you want to find out how much your estate is over the estate tax threshold, if at all, when you die.

Arriving at this magical number isn't easy. You have to make a few guesses, do some crude appraisal work (with real estate, for example, if you want to know how much your land is worth) and somehow get a ballpark figure that reflects your estate. Don't fret over conducting a scientific experiment to evaluate the size of your estate. Realize that your magic number now is likely to change in the future as your assets change or either appreciate or depreciate in value. This is highly speculative work. And because the laws that govern estate tax (here we go again: the Tax Code) can change in a moment's notice, there's no way to plan today how your estate will fare in the eyes of the law 20 years from now, or whenever you die.

There are too many variables, including the biggest one of all: You don't know when you are going to die. So the best way to plan your estate now is to take three things into consideration:

- What you know about your estate today
- What you know about your tax laws today
- What you know about your health today and your potential to live a long life

Obviously, if you have some reason to believe you won't live for another 10 years, your planning will have a different feel to it. For example, an 85-year-old man setting up an individual living trust—who has acquired the bulk of his estate—will approach his estate planning far differently from a 40-year-old married couple with two small children at home, who are still building their family wealth. While the old man's and the couple's concerns, focuses, and goals may be similar, they will not share the same thinking process.

In Chapter 2 we gave you a list of assets and liabilities to consider when evaluating the size of your estate. Use the charts on the following page as a worksheet for making this rough estimation. (See Figure 6.1.) Again, this should not require complex math. Do what you can to arrive at a roundabout but sensible estimate.

To reiterate: Regardless of whether or not you use a living trust to own the majority of your assets that make up your estate, everyone has an estate. A taxable estate is determined by calculating the gross value of an estate minus various allowable deductions. Once this calculation is made, the IRS uses this number to assess estate taxes. A gross estate includes the total value of all owned assets at the time of your death. The estate also includes the following:

- Life insurance proceeds payable to your estate or to your heirs if you own the policy
- The value of certain annuities payable to your estate or your heirs
- The value of certain kinds of assets transferred out of your estate within three years before you die

The allowable deductions used in calculating the taxable estate include funeral expenses paid out of the estate; debts you owed at the time of your death; and the marital deduction (any property you leave to your spouse). As we saw above, if you have an AB trust with your spouse, there is no need to leave the bulk of your estate to your spouse. Your trust creates a vehicle by which you can leave your estate in your trust for your spouse to use until his or her death, and then pass the property down to final beneficiaries.

An estate that generates a lot of income, for which that income gets passed down to heirs, creates all sorts of tax issues. Gross income of an estate consists of all items of income received or accrued during the tax year. It includes dividends, interest, rents, royalties, capital gains, and income from businesses, partnerships, trusts (yes, including your own), and any other sources. If an estate is going through probate, the executor may find it necessary or desirable to sell all or part of the estate's assets to pay debts and expenses of administration, or to make proper distributions of the assets to the beneficiaries.

Stepped-Up Valuation

Put your thinking cap on for this one. Among the trickier topics to understand about estate planning and taxes is the so-called stepped-up valuation of property—especially, real estate property. The concept of stepped-up valuation emerged with the 1981 Tax Reform Act. The

ESTATE PLANNING CHART

as of _____ 20_____

ASSET	ESTIMATED VALUE	NOTES
Checking account		
Savings account		
Money Market account		
T-bills/notes		
Safety deposit box		
Retirement account		
Brokerage account		
Government bonds & securities		
Life insurance policies		
Real estate		
Automobiles		
Other vehicles (boats, planes)		
Household items		
Artwork, antiques, collectibles		
Tools & equipment		
Valuable animals or livestock		
Money owed to you		
Investments		
DEBTS	**AMOUNT DUE**	**NOTES**
Mortgage		
Home equity loan		
Credit card		
Credit card		
Credit card		
Auto leases/loans		
Other loans		

Figure 6.1

A *basis* relates to the original cost of an asset used to determine the amount of capital gain tax upon its sale. An *adjusted basis* includes improvements, expenses, and damages between the time the original basis (price) is established and transfer (sale) of the asset. "Stepped up basis" means that the original basis of an asset (especially real property) will be stepped up to its current value at the time of the death of the owner, and thus keep down capital gain taxes if the beneficiary of the dead person sells the asset.

goal was to introduce some fairness in estate taxation. Put simply, having a stepped-up basis is a good thing for tax reasons, and typically affects how anyone can inherit real estate. You ask, *What's a stepped-up basis?*

First, the word "basis" refers to how much you can profit from the sale of an asset. For purposes of our discussion on stepped-up basis, we will refer only to real estate; however, a step up in basis is not limited to real estate. Stepped-up valuations can refer to any asset, whether it's real estate or not. In estate planning, people come to understand truly the impact of stepped-up valuations when it comes to real estate.

If you take the purchase price of your real estate (how much you paid for it), and add the amount you've spent on improving that property, and then subtract any depreciation, you arrive at your basis. Second, your taxable profit is the price you can sell your real estate (to someone else) minus your basis.

Example: You buy a home for $180,000 and fix the foundation, add a second story, and make several cosmetic improvements. You spend $85,000 on these improvements (sometimes called capital improvements), and then you can sell the house for $425,000. Your basis is $265,000 ($180,000 + $85,000) and your taxable profit is $160,000 ($425,000 − $265,000).

The law gives inheritors of real estate a break here by "stepping up" the cost basis of any inherited real estate to the market value of the real estate at the death of the owner. So, if you are the owner of the home in the above example and you die, the person who inherits your house inherits a new cost basis of $425,000 and not $265,000. In other words, the inheritor's basis is the market value of the property at your death. If your inheritor sells the house quickly, for $425,000, there is no taxable profit.

Most heirs do not owe capital gains taxes on inherited property when they sell it, but it can happen. Whether the rules revert back in 2011 is anyone's guess. Congress will likely change the rules again—before 2011 hits. Don't worry about computing these numbers and asking

The tax changes made in 2001 affected stepped-up valuation rules as well. The rules are more restricting now. According those changes, the stepped-up basis at death ends with the federal estate tax in 2010. Inheritors in 2010 will receive a stepped-up basis only for inherited property worth a total of $1.3 million when the owner dies, plus an additional $3 million of new basis for the surviving spouse (heirs who are not spouses can add $1.3 million to their tax basis, whereas surviving spouses can add an additional $3 million, for a total of $4.3 million plus the tax basis). In 2010, property worth more than $1.3 million will have the same basis as it had before the death of the owner. In other words, there is no step-up at the death.

too many questions at this point. We know the concept of stepped-up valuation gets confusing and the tax rules coming about don't make much sense to a lot of people—tax professionals included!

Noncommunity Property (Common Law) States and Stepped-up Valuations

In all states but the community property states, any property owned by a married person receives a stepped-up basis at his or her death. The property owned by the surviving spouse, however, does not get the stepped-up basis. If you and your spouse hold property in joint tenancy, when the first spouse dies, the IRS says the surviving spouse can only get a stepped-up tax basis on the half of the property owned by the deceased spouse. The surviving spouse's half does not get a new stepped-up tax basis. If and when that property is later sold, the property owes more tax if it has gone up in value after the joint tenancy was created but before the first spouse died. However, the other half of the property will get stepped-up at the death of the second spouse (assuming the property was not sold before then) and any children who inherit that property will inherit that new basis.

Because of the particular tax advantages afforded people who live in community property states, more states may enact forms of community property laws in the future. Wisconsin was the first state to pass such a statute, and now Alaska has an optional community property system. (Again, the original eight are: California, Arizona, Idaho, Louisiana, Nevada, New Mexico, Texas, and Washington.)

People in the United States are transient, so many can take advantage of community property laws by transferring their assets into a living trust while they reside—albeit temporarily—in one of the community property states, or a state with special provisions for married couples who want their assets to be considered quasi-community property (which means they can transfer their separately-owned assets into the living trust as, effectively, community property). That way, those assets will have the community property benefit of full stepped-up valuation and may also retain the community property characteristic even if the individuals owning those assets move back to noncommunity property states.

If you live in a noncommunity property state and you own property in joint tenancy, you may want to transfer your property into the living trust as "tenancy in common, in equal shares." This may first require that you transfer your title from "joint tenancy" to "tenancy in common, in equal shares," and then transfer that deed to the living trust. Otherwise, the IRS may continue to view your property as being held in joint tenancy within your living trust, and if so, you may face the restrictions inherent to joint tenancy, such as having to leave your share of the property to the joint tenant at your death. On the other hand, if you want to leave some of that property to anyone you wish, it's best to transfer your property into the living trust as "tenancy in common."

For understanding the details and consequences of this scenario, speak with an attorney. The rules related to real property can seem murky and troublesome; don't be afraid. Just know when to ask questions and find someone who can explain your situation to you in easy language. Technically, once you transfer your assets to your living trust, your living trust owns them.

Community Property States

In the community property states, where each spouse owns one-half interest in shared property, both halves of property of both spouses receive a stepped-up basis when one spouse dies.

With a higher stepped-up basis on the entire home, the resulting capital gain is significantly reduced and any taxes due on a subsequent sale of the home are likewise reduced. When the basis on real property goes up, the taxes owed on the sale of the real property go down.

For couples who live in a community property state and who hold assets in joint tenancy, they can use a living trust to solve the problems related to joint tenancy (that is, getting half of a stepped-up valuation at the death of the first spouse as well as the general limitations of joint tenancy discussed earlier), by transferring their property to the living trust as "community property." Joint tenancy is eliminated and the trust owns the property. It's wise to discuss your tax questions and concerns with your tax advisor, as the rules can change at any time. The laws that govern tax and property rules vary state to state, including among the community property states.

Final Note About Stepped-Up Valuation

The subject of buying and selling real estate is an entire book itself. For purposes of planning your estate, it's good to know in general the rules around real estate that have an effect on your estate or your inheritors' ability to inherit your estate's property. Here's the simplest way to look at it: People buy and sell things every day. Hopefully, they buy at a low price and sell at a higher price. The difference is their profit. If, when you buy and sell something, you make a profit on that sale, Mr. Taxman wants some of that profit, too. You can't have all of it. Mr. Taxman calls his share of the profit a capital gains tax.

Your particular circumstances may be different. Always seek the advice of a professional regarding your tax advantages. The main reason for the living trust is avoiding probate. Tax considerations are important, and some savings can be gained by a living trust, but the main purpose is what has already been stated: minimizing the potential burdens—emotional and financial—related to death.

Summation on Taxes

When someone dies, two types of taxes suddenly become a concern: 1) a combo of both federal estate tax and any state taxes, and 2) the annual income tax. At a person's death, Mr. Taxman wants his take in the form of the federal estate tax. But he won't take his share unless the dead person qualifies by way of having an estate worth a certain amount, called a taxable estate. Mr. Taxman allows everyone to exempt a certain amount from his or her estate ($1.5 million in 2005 and $2 million in 2006, and so forth), which changes according to the Tax Code's rules. So if the value of your estate is less than the exemption amount, you have nothing to worry about. Mr. Taxman won't come knocking on your door. If your estate, however, is valued over the amount exempted for your year of death, taxes will be due and must be paid.

If you are married and plan smartly with a living trust, no taxes will be due when the first spouse dies. But once those exemptions are used up, Mr. Taxman will get his share. You cannot run from Mr. Taxman, but you can plan accordingly to minimize what you might owe him. And this is typically achieved through living trusts and consultation with tax experts.

Conclusion

The issue of death or estate taxes is relatively unimportant for the vast majority of American families. They usually do not have enough money at their death to require payment of death

> The most recent changes to tax law are likely to change again before too long. Although most American families are not affected by the federal estate tax, families that own and run small businesses can lose money to this tax. If you own a small business, chances are this tax will prohibit you from passing on your business to your children. A family-owned business stands to lose 55 percent of all its assets when it passes from one generation to the next. That's over half of everything, including land, buildings, equipment, money, and more. Because of this, 70 percent of businesses never make it past the first generation. However, as Congress rehashes the federal estate tax rules, the current limitations of succession in a family may change for the better.

or estate taxes. As a rule, a living trust will not affect or reduce estate taxes. However, in a case where a married couple has in excess of $1.3 million, a different kind of trust may be used to reduce the surviving spouse's exposure to estate taxes. But a trust, in itself, simply cannot completely eliminate all taxes.

You can cry over what you owe in taxes come next April 15, but don't cry over trying to understand taxes related to your estate and how best to minimize them. You'll spend too much time trying to master this topic, and soon enough the rules of the game will change and outdate your knowledge quickly.

You'll find a legal tax break by consulting the people who know the ins and outs of tax laws, namely Certified Public Accountants, financial planners, and tax attorneys. We've given you the groundwork for understanding the basics of how your estate faces taxes, and now when you speak with a professional, you'll have an idea of what's going on and hopefully you can participate in the successful planning of your estate.

Along our journey, we've dropped plenty of messages that say probate is best when avoided. But so many families have to go through probate that we must spend a little time talking about it. It's not so bad for families that are complex or disjointed that necessitate the order and sanity of a court to help them deal with a dead person's estate. Plus, there are many situations that call for accelerated probate proceedings, which can shorten the time it takes a family to go through the probate process. In this next chapter, we turn to the people that survive you and settle your estate. The chapter is particularly useful for those people that a settlor or will-maker has designated as responsible in some way for settling an estate. We give you the information you need to understand probate and get through it successfully (or, at least know what your family may encounter at your death), as well as talk about what exactly happens when a settlor dies. More information about taxes paying certain bills is included. The people you've named in your trust bear many responsibilities, some of which we discussed in Chapter 1. Chapter 7 finishes this discussion.

Settling the Estate

Once you are gone, everything is beyond your control—theoretically. If you have planned well and prepared for your passing, hopefully your wishes survive you. The best advice anyone can give about building and transferring family money is this: Be clear about your wishes. If you keep clear about your financial goals throughout your life, you will have something to pass along to family members or your favorite charity at your death. If you keep clear about your plans for leaving assets and money to family members or charities—via a will or living trust—your loved ones and charities will get what you want them to receive. This is especially true if you have a nontraditional or blended family. The law may not give your family the breaks it gives others—so spelling everything out and using the tools available to you during your life can have a profound impact on the viability of your wishes.

You may have painful or awkward decisions to make about your family and who gets what, but consider it a right of passage in death. To live well, you make essential decisions every day, from the trivial of what to wear and what to eat, to the significant of where to live and how to raise children. To die well, you make essential decisions during your life to prepare for that great What-If, which influences all that you leave behind. To some people, this is a difficult subject to face, but having the courage and strength to prepare for death are extremely admirable qualities. (It is not a question of if but when, unless someone has discovered the keys to immortality.)

The will or living trust you set up during your life does not really have an impact on anyone until you die. In the case of a will, you set forth what you want done at your death. In the case of a living trust, you have a legal entity that owns your assets, but it's more like a ghost that lives with you when you are alive. And you hold the remote control. At your death, your living trust has more meaning and can do things for your family, such as avoid probate and allow for your beneficiaries to receive assets you leave to them without the hassles of dealing with a court or government agency. Your successor trustee will transfer your property as you instructed in your living trust, and this transfer can usually happen quickly.

In this chapter, we give you the details of what happens at your death. We talked a lot about taxes in the previous chapter, but did not necessarily give you the practical how-to information for dealing with their payment and IRS forms. This chapter is good for anyone who has to plan his or her estate, or for the person who has been named an executor or successor trustee to an estate and who needs to know what to do. If your estate goes through the probate process, you'll find useful information for dealing with this special court. No matter how an estate is planned, whether it's with a will, a living trust, or nothing at all, the person or people left to settle a dead person's estate may have a lot to do. Sets of rules accompany every procedure that must occur at the death of an individual. The protocol one must follow is neither obvious nor automatically part of one's basic education. Put simply, most people will have to deal with settling an estate at some point in their lives, but most will not have had any formal education in the subject. *What do I have to do? How do I start the probate process? What forms do I need to obtain?* Let's answer these questions. For people planning their estates, knowing the answers to these questions can help make choosing an executor easier.

Your Executor's or Successor Trustee's Duties

Throughout this book, we've given you details on the roles your executors play in carrying out your wishes. Whether you have a will or living trust, your executors may have quite a to-do list to check off. Dealing with the probate process or following a living trust's instructions can be daunting—and overwhelming. As a condition to being appointed as an executor by a probate court, the executor typically has to sign a written acknowledgment of his duties and responsibilities, and agree to be bound by them. In case a person does not wish to assume these duties and responsibilities, you usually name alternate executors to step into their place. Executors who resign should create notices of their resignation and deliver them to the next one in line to serve. Notices will normally be filed with the court and an accounting rendered of the executor's actions during their tenure. If no one else has been named by your will or living trust, the probate court may have to appoint someone. If you do not want to name an alternate, you can provide in your will or living trust that a resigning executor can appoint someone else to take over. A new appointment should be made in writing, dated, signed, and notarized. Below we will go into the details of probate and how an executor of a will should proceed. Let's finish up our talk about successor trustees.

Initial Duties of an Executor or Successor Trustee

Anyone who assumes the responsibility of carrying out the wishes according to your will or your living trust should follow certain protocol. This includes the following:

- Proving that he or she is entitled to act on behalf of the estate
- Finding and assessing the assets in the estate
- Giving information to beneficiaries

Successor trustees need to appraise the market values of major assets in the trust as soon as possible after the death of the settlor. Some assets are easier to appraise than others. While your state may not stipulate that beneficiaries must be notified promptly or that they should receive specific information regarding the estate, it's always a wise decision for successor trustees to let all beneficiaries of an estate know what is going on. Several states do, in fact, require that successor trustees take certain steps at the death of a settlor. If you live in California, for example, a successor trustee is required by law to notify all beneficiaries of a living trust and all heirs of the settlor once the trust has become irrevocable. This notice must be sent within 60 days after the death, and it must include specific information. If you live in Ohio, a successor trustee is required by law to file an affidavit (another document!) with the county auditor and the county recorder that details any real estate owned by the living trust. And, if you live in Tennessee, successor trustees of AB living trusts must notify the beneficiaries about the details of the living trust. This means the successor trustee can send a copy of the living trust, or an abstract that meets Tennessee's extensive content requirements.

We outlined in Chapter 5 the duties of surviving spouses who take on the role of successor trustee at the death of their spouses. In California and Tennessee, surviving spouses must share information about the living trust at the death of their spouse, specifically information related to the B trust that becomes irrevocable and continues to be managed by the surviving spouse. Surviving spouses with this role must notify the final beneficiaries of the B trust, as well as distribute any assets that are not intended to be part of the surviving spouse's life estate.

Successor Trustee to a Single Living Trust. A successor trustee to an individual's living trust has a relatively easy job: He or she distributes the assets in the trust to the named beneficiaries. The successor trustee also has to file any federal or state estate taxes due and may be responsible for making funeral and burial arrangements. A failure to pay tax liabilities can result in personal liability for the successor trustee (your successor trustee will be responsible for those taxes).

Successor Trustee to a Joint Living Trust. A successor trustee to a joint trust (not an AB trust) also has a relatively easy job. In most cases, the surviving spouse inherited the bulk of the assets from the spouse's death and had a few assets to distribute to named beneficiaries at the death of the first spouse. At the death of the second spouse in a joint trust, the successor trustee simply completes the task of distributing the assets of the trust to final beneficiaries. Note that joint trusts do split into two separate trusts at the death of the first spouse, but most couples make small gifts of specific assets to beneficiaries at their death, and leave the balance of their trust assets to the surviving spouse. So, a joint trust ends when the second spouse dies and all assets from the surviving spouse's trust, which now contains leftover assets from the first spouse to die, get distributed to final beneficiaries. This successor trustee must also file final income tax returns and make sure all estate taxes are paid, if owed. He or she may also have to manage the burial and funeral arrangements.

Example: Andy and Mindy have a joint trust, and they have named Andy's brother Rusty as successor trustee once both Andy and Mindy are dead. Andy and Mindy's trust owns their co-owned assets—a house, their bank accounts, stocks, and major household items. Andy happens to also own valuable separate property (a boat, antiques, and a classic car) that he transfers to the living trust. In their living trust, Andy leaves his separate property to his favorite nephew. Mindy leaves her half of the shared property in the trust to Andy. When Andy dies, Mindy remains as trustee. Theoretically, the shared trust splits into Trust 1 and 2. Trust 1 contains Andy's side of the assets, which include the assets destined to go to his nephew and Andy's half of shared property with Mindy. Trust 1 ends when Andy's nephew gets his inheritance and the balance of Andy's estate is left to Mindy. Trust 2 now owns Mindy's side of the estate plus the assets she inherited from Andy. At her death, those assets go to final beneficiaries Mindy has named. The successor trustee to Andy and Mindy's estate—Rusty—takes control at the death of Mindy and completes this final distribution.

Successor Trustee to an AB Living Trust. A successor trustee in a joint AB living trust must distribute all assets that are still owned by both the A and B trust. This successor trustee must settle the affairs related to the second spouse's death, which entails filing a final income tax return and may include dealing with any burial or funeral arrangements. All estate taxes must be paid as well. Any children's trusts that remain active must be managed.

The Uniform Trust Code

Some states have adopted the Uniform Trust Code (UTC), which requires the successor trustee to keep trust beneficiaries reasonably informed of trust matters. Similar to some of the state requirements of California, the UTC asks that beneficiaries receive a notice within 60 days of the settlor's death that details the successor trustee's identity (name) and contact information (address and phone number). The trustee must also articulate that, at the death of the settlor, the living trust has now become irrevocable and that any beneficiary who wants to see the trust or subsequent reports made by the successor trustee can do so by requesting a copy and any relevant reports.

The UTC applies to the following states: Connecticut, the District of Columbia, Kansas, Maine, Missouri, New Mexico, Nebraska, and Wyoming. More states may adopt this code in the future, so you should check with your local laws regarding the duties of a successor trustee and the rights of beneficiaries. If your state does not enforce the UTC, it may have other rules in place that affect how a successor trustee must execute his or her duties. It's a good idea to notify beneficiaries within 60 days regardless.

How to Transfer Assets to Beneficiaries from a Living Trust

The mechanics of transferring assets to beneficiaries are not that complicated. Part of the reasons for a living trust is the ease with which assets can be distributed quickly at the death of a trust creator. For the most part, trust property left to a surviving spouse in a basic mutual trust remains in the trust and there is no official transfer. In an AB trust, at the death of the first spouse, the trust property in the B trust remains in the B trust (except for a few gifts that might be made by the deceased spouse at his or her death to final beneficiaries right away). Any assets left to young beneficiaries or minors will remain in their respective trusts and be managed according to the trust's instructions and named trustees and/or custodians.

In many ways, transferring ownership from a living trust to a named beneficiary is reversing the process that the original settlor (creator of the living trust) went through to transfer ownership into the trust. This entails (1) preparing new title documents for assets, and (2) dealing with any necessary paperwork to complete the transactions, which usually means contacting various companies or financial institutions that relate to the assets. Examples: mortgage companies, brokerage houses, banks, title companies, private companies, the Office of Patents and Trademarks (for intellectual property), and so on. It's not that difficult, and it's pretty self-explanatory if you find yourself having to settle someone's estate. Picking up the phone and making phone calls will get you on your way to accomplishing the goal. One item a successor trustee must have on hand, however, is copies of the death certificate. When a successor trustee executes these transfers, copies of the settlor's death certificate typically become attached to the transfer. How many copies of a death certificate a successor trustee must obtain depends on how many transfers must be made. It never hurts to obtain more death certificates than one thinks are needed, as one can never know when a death certificate will be requested to complete a certain transaction.

Distributing Real Estate

Any real estate transferred to beneficiaries requires the successor trustee to prepare and sign a new deed that transfers ownership of the property from the trust to the named beneficiary. This entails completing the right deed documents for your state, getting them signed and notarized, and meeting any other state requirements. The new deed must also be recorded, and any transfer tax due must be paid (although these should be small).

The importance of keeping the Trust Instructions up-to-date comes into play here. A successor trustee needs to have updated lists of names and contact information—and who gets what. This is true for all of the assets that must be distributed.

Distributing Bank Accounts, Stocks, Bonds, Mutual Funds, Money Market Accounts

Transferring ownership to the above items out of a living trust requires speaking with the agents and representatives from the financial institutions or companies that house or manage such accounts. For example: If a settlor has money in a brokerage account at Fidelity Investment, the successor trustee would need to contact Fidelity and ask about the forms and necessary documents for transferring ownership. Financial institutions are well-versed and knowledgeable in dealing with living trusts, so they typically know how to guide you through the process without much trouble.

Distributing Other Property with Titles

Any trust property that has a title to it can be transferred to the named beneficiary by creating and signing a new title document that establishes new ownership. For automobiles, a trip to the Department of Motor Vehicles may be necessary. The DMV will provide the forms you need to complete the transaction.

Distributing Assets with No Title

A lot of trust property can have no titles or any formal documents attached to them. Household goods and furniture, heirlooms, special collections, your mother's prized kitchen accoutrements, and your father's wine cellar are some examples. The successor trustee simply hands over the assets to the named beneficiaries. No transfer documents or formalities are required. This is as easy as it gets. Of course, the successor should hand over those

Final Note: Among all these transactions of transferring ownership from a trust to named beneficiaries, copies of the death certificate(s) of the settlor(s) may be required along the way. This is why successor trustees should always get several copies of the death certificates so they can complete their tasks and meet all local, state, and even federal requirements for the proper management and settlement of an estate. The more death certificates a successor trustee has on hand, the quicker the assets can be moved and the faster an estate can be settled. Some estates with a living trust take only a few weeks to settle after the death of the settlor(s). An efficient and competent successor trustee can make this happen!

assets in a timely manner and not hold on to them for months or years. And it's in the successor trustee's best interest to detail the types of assets and have the recipients sign a receipt for them.

The Probate Process

The probate process is the legal process whereby a court oversees the distribution of one's assets and handles any legal matters regarding one's estate. Most probate proceedings take place at the death of an individual who either did or did not create a will. Living trusts usually avoid probate by their design. The probate process averages 9 to 18 months, but it can be considerably longer in some situations. Feuding families can require years of court battles and drawn out probate proceedings. But probate can also be accelerated under certain circumstances:

- The dollar value of the estate is within state limits—which varies widely; in California it's $100,000 whereas in New Hampshire it's $500
- Real estate is or is not involved—it's okay in some states, not in others
- Creditors have been paid or do not object—in some states they are not required to be paid if the estate is less than the state set limit
- The person claiming the estate is legally entitled to it—the will does not indicate someone else as beneficiary
- A specified number of days (usually 30 to 45) have elapsed since the death

The primary purpose of probate is to provide for the orderly management and distribution of assets in accordance with the wishes of the deceased. However, it first has to determine what the wishes of the deceased were before it can order any distributions. The type of probate that an estate may go through depends on the gross value of the entire probatable estate. Formal probate is often costly and time consuming. It is best avoided if possible. The probate legal process includes the following:

- Proving the authenticity of the will
- Appointing an executor or personal representative
- Identifying and inventorying property
- Paying debts and taxes
- Identifying and contacting heirs
- Distributing the remainder according to the will or state law

If there is no named executor of an estate, in some states, as long as the total value of the estate does not exceed the state limit, all a person needs to transfer all of the solely held accounts to his or her name is to fill out a transfer affidavit. This is a form available at all banks, credit unions, insurance companies, or other financial institutions that hold the deceased's assets. The person simply signs the affidavit stating that he or she is the person legally entitled (as spouse or next-of-kin) to inherit the property (cannot be used for real estate) and that there is no court-appointed executor for the estate. A copy of the will and the death certificate may also be required.

Summary Probate (Simple Probate)

The affidavit procedure can be used to transfer bank accounts, insurance policies, securities, and the contents of the safe-deposit box. If the deceased had real estate or if his or her assets exceed the maximum values allowed for transfer by affidavit, a survivor can try another shortened form of probate administration called summary probate administration. This happens when a person asks the probate court to grant him or her (as spouse or next-of-kin) the right to the property. The court will ask that person to provide inventory of the assets and the court will notify all interested parties of a hearing, during which the court will rule whether that person, or someone else, is entitled to the property. In California, for instance, there is a summary administration procedure for the spouse to seek confirmation that the decedent's community property automatically goes to the survivor.

Protecting the Spouse. All states have a minimum family protection allowance that guarantees the spouse and dependent children receive at least some funds for support from the estate—even if they weren't named as designated beneficiaries. The spouse must petition the court soon after the death. The court determines the amount of the allowance, but it may be large enough so that other bequests are reduced or eliminated. If the estate is sufficiently depleted by this allowance, debts including the funeral, court, and probate administration costs may go unpaid. In addition, the spouse may claim a homestead right, which allows the spouse and minor children to stay in the deceased's home for a specified period, even if the house has been bequeathed to someone else. In most states the spouse has the right to choose, within 30 days, whether to take the bequest in the will or the spouse's statutory share.

This share may be greater or less than the amount stipulated in the will. In some states it's one-third or one-half the value of the probate estate. In some states the exact amount of the spouse's share depends on whether the couple has minor children and on how long the couple was married. The spouse may choose the family allowance, the homestead right, and either the statutory share or the willed bequest. Vehicles (cars, motorcycles, boats, RVs, etc.) that belonged solely to the deceased may be informally transferred in some states to a surviving spouse or next-of-kin without going through probate. Call or visit your local DMV for information on changing the title and registration of a vehicle. You may need to sign an affidavit and produce the vehicle's title and registration as well as a copy of the death certificate. If, however, the vehicles exceed the state-imposed maximum values (between $25,000 and $75,000) they may be considered probate assets subject to probate administration.

If after the spouse claims the family protection allowance, the value of the probate assets does not exceed the combined value of the funeral, final health care of the deceased, and probate administration expenses, you may make a summary probate filing. You may close the estate by filing a sworn statement that the value of the estate did not exceed the cost of the family protection allowance and the funeral, health care, and administration expenses; that the distribution of assets is complete; and that a copy of the final statement was sent to all beneficiaries and unpaid creditors. Under this summary filing, you need not pay creditors.

The majority of estates are settled with little or no involvement of the probate court. The value of the deceased's probate assets and whether he or she left any orphaned minors will determine whether the estate must undergo the full probate administration process. If the

Probate Timeline

Prepare and file Petition for Probate: 1 to 2 months

Hearing on Petition for Probate: 2 to 3 months

Issue Letters of Administration, Orders For Probate and Duties & Liabilities: 2 to 4 months

Issue Bond (if ordered): 2 to 4 months

Notice to Creditors: 2 to 4 months

Notice to Dept. of Health Services: 4 to 8 months

Inventory & Appraisement: 4 to 8 months

Pay State/Fed Taxes (if necessary): 6 to 12 months

Allow or reject creditor claims: 6 to 15 months

Possible Preliminary Distributions: 6 to 15 months

Notice to Dept. of Health Services (if deceased received medical): 6 to 15 months

Notice to Franchise Tax Board (if heir is out of state): 6 to 15 months

Claim of exemption (if assets transfer to a minor): 6 to 15 months

Receive final tax letter from State & Federal (if appropriate): 6 to 18 months

File Petition for Final Distribution and Accounting: 8 to 16 months

Hearing on Petition for Final Distribution and Accounting: 9 to 17 months

Order approving Final Distribution and Accounting: 9 to 17 months

Distribution of Assets to Heirs: 9 to 17 months

Final Discharge Order: 9 to 18 months

Final Distribution of Funds: 9 to 18 months

deceased's probate assets were few and he or she had no minor children, the person in charge of settling an estate (customarily called the executor) may be able to avoid or minimize the probate process, providing that there are no objections or contests filed by interested parties to the estate.

The Executor

Whether a person dies with or without a will—with just a few possessions or a vast estate—it may be necessary for that person's

- assets to be inventoried;
- final taxes and debts to be paid; and
- remaining estate to be distributed to the designated beneficiaries.

As we said in the first chapter, the person responsible for these tasks is the executor. Also known as a personal representative or administrator, the executor is usually a friend or relative (but could be a bank or trust company) appointed by the deceased in his or her will or by the probate court to carry out the terms of the will, or if there was no will, the intestacy (next of kin) laws of the state. As we mentioned earlier, executors do not have to be lawyers nor have any special qualifications. However, they are responsible for the initiation and administration of the probate process—if necessary—and management of the estate until it is closed. This process may take anywhere from a few days to a few years, depending on the size and complexity of the estate. Most estates, however, are settled within 12 to 18 months.

At the death of an individual, it may not be necessary to formalize the appointment of the executor with the probate court immediately, because formal probate filing may be avoidable. If the deceased set up his or her assets in a way that allows them to pass directly to those to whom they are intended (through joint ownership, trusts, insurance, and pay-on-death arrangements), one can avoid the tedious and time-consuming probate process.

Whether an estate must undergo formal probate filing has less to do with its actual value than with who owns the assets at the time of death. Probate assets are those owned solely by the deceased at the time of death and not, for example, by a living trust. The executor must also file taxes for the deceased, whether the appointment is formalized or not. Nevertheless, the formal appointment of an executor by the court does not obligate the estate to go through probate; however, it may wind up costing the estate and prove unnecessary if an inventory of assets reveals that nothing requires probate or that probate assets do not exceed the maximum value allowed. This is why an inventory of the assets at the death of an individual is important: A survivor trying to make sense of what to do can first find out if probate is necessary before having the executor formally appointed by the court.

The executor is entitled to a fee for his or her services and reimbursement for all expenses incurred while settling the estate, such as legal and accounting fees. State law sets the amount of the fee. It may be a percentage of the estate. The will may indicate an amount different from that stipulated by the state or it may say that no fee be paid at all to the executor. If the fee listed in the will is less than that stipulated by law, it can be ignored. The fee is taxable as income. In some states, professional fees can be negotiated, as with any other professional services.

To protect the beneficiaries and the creditors of the estate against any negligence or bad behavior on the part of the executor, the will or the court may order the posting of a surety bond (like insurance), which protects the estate from abuse. The cost of the bond is payable with estate funds and premiums are usually based on the value of the estate's assets. Bonds can be arranged through almost any insurance agent. The bond should be canceled as soon as the estate is settled.

Letters of Authority

Once the court confirms the nomination and appointment of the executor, it will issue that person letters of authority, which grant him or her either full or limited authority to act on behalf of the estate, providing access to solely owned assets. As with copies of the death certificate, the executor will need a number of copies of these letters (usually consisting of one page) in order to allow him or her access to each of the deceased's bank and brokerage accounts, CDs and safe-deposit boxes, and other assets.

The responsibility of an executor cannot be underestimated; his or her job really becomes an unselfish tribute to the person who has died. If you are the executor, use the following checklist as a guideline for settling the estate, including carrying out the terms of the will, paying beneficiaries, and paying off any debts or taxes.

Checklist for Executor

- ☑ Locate the will and letter of instruction.
- ☑ Note special instructions regarding anatomical gifts, funeral arrangements, or care of minor children—take immediate and appropriate action.
- ☑ Based on asset inventory, decide if formal probate filing is necessary or if the estate can be settled via small estate transfer procedures.
- ☑ Begin small estate transfer procedures (if possible).
- ☑ File the will at the probate court within 30 days (this does not in itself initiate probate, but it can be done when you file your probate papers).
- ☑ File the necessary papers, including your petition, to the probate court, if necessary (this initiates probate).
- ☑ Confirm appointment as executor (acquire letters of authority).
- ☑ Identify and inventory probate assets.
- ☑ File inventory of probate assets with the court.
- ☑ Contact probate attorney (if necessary).
- ☑ Contact heirs, beneficiaries, and other interested parties.
- ☑ Open estate checking account (consolidate liquid assets).
- ☑ Publish "Notice of Petition to Administer Estate" in local paper.
- ☑ Publish "Notice of Death" in local paper.
- ☑ Send "Notice of Administration" to creditors.
- ☑ Obtain Tax Identification Number (for estate tax filing).
- ☑ Prepare and file final federal, state, and local income tax returns (for deceased and estate, if necessary).
- ☑ File federal, state, and local estate tax returns (if gross estate exceeds $1.5 million for 2005, $2 million for 2005).
- ☑ Settle creditor claims; pay debts and expenses.
- ☑ Notify heirs and beneficiaries of hearings.
- ☑ Distribute balance of probate assets to beneficiaries.
- ☑ File receipts and affidavit for final discharge.
- ☑ Close the estate.

What to Do with the Will

Among a will's most important functions is the distribution of one's assets according to one's wishes. A will can also nominate a guardian for minor or disabled children, which the court must approve in a separate case (it's not always part of an estate's probate proceeding). An executor should file the will as soon as possible with the court so that the court can officially appoint the guardian in accordance to the deceased's wishes. If he or she died without a will and left orphan children, the court will appoint a guardian, usually a blood relative. If the estate is substantial, the will may also name a conservator—a person, bank, or trust company—to manage the inheritance of a minor child until the child reaches the age of maturity. The guardian and conservator (and executor) may or may not be the same person.

As we explained in previous chapters, the will is the vehicle through which the deceased bequeaths his or her assets to the beneficiaries of his or her choosing. He or she can give to family, friends, charities, schools, and foundations or choose not to give to someone; he or she can disinherit one or more children. If no will is in place at the time of death, the state may give as much as three-quarters of the assets to the spouse. If there are no children or grandchildren, half may go to the deceased's parents. If the deceased has no living relatives, the assets will go to the state. (Domestic partners or children who have not been formally adopted will not be entitled to anything under most state laws.) See your local office of the Lambda Legal Defense Fund for more on this. Of course, the will also names the executor. The executor must submit the original will to the court. Most states have laws that require the filing of the original will within 30 to 45 days after its discovery. Neglecting to do so can result in civil or criminal penalties. Filing the will does not necessarily initiate probate. If probate administration is not necessary, the will simply remains on file with the court. Once the executor files the will with the probate court, it will be entered into the public record and the court will make copies available to others.

If the signature appears to be a forged one or if the will does not comply with state law, the will may be contested. The will may also be contested in the following scenarios:

- If it is alleged that the person was mentally impaired—or otherwise lacked testamentary capacity—at the time of signing
- If the person thought he was signing something else
- If he or she was under undue influence or duress when signing

If the court rules that the will is invalid, the estate will be handled as if the deceased died without that invalid document and the state's intestacy laws will dictate who gets what.

Inventorying Assets

An executor's first duty in settling the estate includes taking inventory of the deceased's assets and categorizing them as probate assets and nonprobate assets. Probate assets are those that were owned solely by the deceased at the time of death—such as furnishings, clothing, jewelry, money, homes, and cars. Nonprobate assets, on the other hand, are those that pass to others through joint ownership or by beneficiary designation, such as with insurance. Whether the deceased had any assets subject to probate and their value will determine if formal probate filing with the court is even necessary.

Assets Not Subject to Probate (Nonprobatable) Administration
- Jointly held assets that pass to the surviving owner
- Pay-on-death bank accounts that pass to designated beneficiaries
- Transfer-on-death securities that pass to designated beneficiaries
- Living trust-held assets that pass to designated beneficiaries
- Life insurance proceeds that pass to surviving beneficiaries
- IRA, SEP, and 401(k) retirement accounts that pass to surviving beneficiaries

All nonliquid assets—those that cannot be quickly and easily converted into cash, such as stocks and bank accounts—will require appraisal. An executor is responsible for preserving these nonprobate assets until they can be sold or distributed according to the will or, if no will, to intestacy laws. Retirement accounts and insurance are paid to designated beneficiaries. In addition, any assets held in a living trust are not subject to probate and remain under the control of the trustee or successor trustee, who must hold or distribute them according to the terms of the trust document.

Where to Look for Assets

In addition to a will, the deceased may have left a letter of instruction, which identifies each of his or her assets and liabilities and describes their locations (we discussed this letter in Chapter 2). This document is very helpful to an executor since even a will cannot list everything an individual owned or owed. However, even fewer people than those who write wills (only one-third of Americans) write letters of instruction. If there is no such letter of instruction and the executor does not have intimate knowledge of every financial transaction the deceased may have made, the executor needs to begin a search to identify and assemble all assets and liabilities. Even with such a letter, an executor must look carefully for assets that may have been overlooked or have been acquired after the most recent draft of the letter. Other good places to begin looking for assets are through tax returns, checkbooks, bank statements, and cancelled checks. Through these documents an executor can find information on the following:

- Insurance policies and dividends
- Investments (CDs, IRA, SEP, or 401(k) accounts)
- Charge accounts and loans
- Stock dividend and bond interest payments
- Mortgages/rents (properties owned)
- Taxes/tax refunds (property tax will identify owned properties)
- Utility payments (identifies properties not identified by mortgages or taxes)
- Social Security, veterans, and pension benefits
- Hospital and medical expenses (check with health care insurance for reimbursement)
- Charitable contributions (for filing final tax return)
- Safe-deposit box or post office box (location of box in order to inventory contents)

Mail also provides a good deal of information about a person's assets and liabilities—dividend and pension checks, bank and brokerage statements, utility and tax bills, insurance premiums, charge accounts—and should be sorted as such. According to the law, when the post office learns of a person's death, it will hold the mail for 15 days and then return it to the sender. An executor should have the mail rerouted to the executor's address by filing a change-of-address form with the post office and by providing the postmaster with a copy of the letters of authority. A family member can do the same by providing the postmaster with proper identification and a copy of the death certificate. If the postmaster gets two change-of-address forms from two survivors, the executor will have final authority.

Important Note for Executors: Social Security and VA benefit checks must be returned. Other government checks must be handled in accordance with instructions printed on the documentation that arrives with them or appears on the envelopes. Tax returns become part of the estate and need not be returned. Mail addressed to joint owners should be forwarded to the surviving owner. Letters and personal mail can be answered by family or by means of a death announcement.

Because some funds or banks issue statements only once a year and some insurance premiums are payable annually or semi-annually, it may be a good idea to monitor the mail for six months to a year or so as not to overlook any assets or liabilities. There is no need to delay settling the estate, since it is always possible to reopen probate to settle and distribute newly discovered assets. Remember that taxes may be due and, if so, must be paid on newly discovered assets prior to distribution (otherwise the executor can be personally liable).

Consolidating Assets

All of the deceased's solely held liquid assets—assets that can be quickly and easily converted into cash—such as stocks and bank accounts, should be consolidated into one separate checking account. The executor can then use the money in this account to pay the deceased's taxes, pay off debts, reimburse the administrative expenses as the executor, and pay court costs and any other costs for those the executor hires, such as a legal document assistant (We The People), an attorney, or an accountant to help with settling the estate. The remainder goes to the beneficiaries. Liquid assets include the cash, solely owned bank balances, dividends, proceeds from the sale of estate assets, and any other money that comes into the estate before the administration of probate is finalized. Payroll checks and employee benefits can usually be paid directly to the spouse or next-of-kin. The employer may ask for a copy of the death certificate, and the executor signs an affidavit to authorize the transfer. If the employer complains, the executor can contact the probate court, the state department of labor, or a lawyer. Any securities held solely by the deceased at the time of death can be sold, by the executor, held for later distribution to beneficiaries, or transferred to beneficiaries through small estate transfer procedures. If the executor does not liquidate these funds immediately in hopes of getting a higher yield, the executor should consult with the beneficiaries. Otherwise, the beneficiaries can blame the executor if the securities lose money. If the estate's assets include a large portion of stocks and bonds, the executor should consult an investment counselor at the expense of the estate.

Solely owned accounts receivable payments in the form of royalties, residuals, promissory notes, and so on, are probate assets transferable to beneficiaries designated in the will. In the absence of a specific designation of a beneficiary, these assets will become part of the residue and be distributed as part of it.

Remember: It is the executor's responsibility to protect, maintain, and secure the assets prior to closing the estate. If the deceased owned or ran a business either as a sole proprietor, partnership, or limited liability company (LLC), the will should tell the executor whether his or her intention was to continue the business by bequeathing it to someone, selling it, or continuing in business with the deceased's share being bought out by the surviving partners or shareholders. If the will gives an executor no guidance, the executor can liquidate (sell off) the business. However, the executor should consult the partnership or shareholders agreement to see how death of a partner or shareholder is handled.

The executor appraises nonliquid assets for their inclusion in the inventory filing required by the court. This also helps the executor determine the values before selling or distributing to the beneficiary. Personal property should be either sold or distributed to the entitled beneficiary as soon as possible to eliminate the executor's responsibility and the estate's expense for storing and insuring it. An executor can petition the court for either an early distribution or an order to sell. Real estate requires maintenance and repair as well as insurance, mortgage, taxes, and utility bills until it can be sold or distributed to the beneficiaries. The executor uses the funds in the estate checking account to pay these costs.

The Place of Residence

The deceased's nonliquid assets such as his or her home (or other real estate) if jointly owned pass automatically to the surviving owner (in most cases the spouse). No probate court administration is necessary. However, the surviving owner needs to transfer title to sole ownership by filing a certified copy of the death certificate with an affidavit of death of joint tenant with the register of deeds (land records office) in the county where he or she lives. If the home is held in a living trust, the terms of the trust document will dictate whether the trustee should sell the home, transfer (by deed) to a beneficiary, or keep it in the living trust.

If the home was solely owned by the deceased, it must be entered into probate. It is the executor's responsibility to pay the mortgage—and insurance on the home from estate funds—until the estate is settled. The executor is entitled to reimbursement for any maintenance paid on the home. If the executor sells the home, he or she must pay all real estate related costs—appraisal, closing of sale, etc.—from the estate's funds (those set up in a checking account). The contents of the home—if joint-owned—pass to the surviving owner, except for items determined to be solely owned by the deceased. If such an item is proven (by credit card or sales receipt) to be solely owned by the deceased, it is a probate asset and passes according to the will or state intestacy laws, if there is no will.

Is Probate Necessary?

Once an executor has identified, collected, and appraised the deceased's assets, separated them into probate (solely owned) and nonprobate (jointly owned or passed to beneficiaries) categories, the executor should be able to estimate whether probate administration is necessary or can be avoided. If a guardian or conservator must be appointed, the probate court must be involved, and the sooner the better for the children involved because they can't be left alone until this is sorted out. As noted above, the appointment of a guardian is usually a separate case from the probate of the estate.

The value and complexity of the probate assets is a major factor in determining whether the estate must undergo full administration by the probate court or can be settled less formally through summary or small estate probate administration. Each state has different small estate transfer procedures. The executor needs to inquire with the probate court in the county where the deceased lived at the time of death about eligibility requirements for this type of probate procedure—which may cut your probate process down to a few days rather than several months.

Initiating Probate

To initiate probate when the executor determines that probate is necessary, he or she files the petition at the probate court in the county in the state where the deceased lived. (The executor should not file unless the estate requires probate administration.) The filing process will include a detailed inventory of all probate assets and should be filed within 30 to 60 days after the executor's appointment. The inventory includes fair market values, as of the decedent's date of death, on all of the items listed and any outstanding liens or mortgages.

If a guardian or conservator must be appointed for the protection of the deceased's minor children, or a lawsuit for wrongful death is pending, then the executor must file formal probate proceedings with the court. Likewise, if after conducting the inventory of the person's assets, the executor determines that the estate must undergo the formal probate process because the probate assets are valued above the maximums allowed for small estate settlement, then the executor must officially file a petition to commence formal probate proceedings.

Although the executor normally files the petition, other interested parties such as an heir, beneficiary, or creditor may also do so. The petition should be filed in the county of the state where the deceased lived. If the deceased split his time between a winter home and a summer home, the state where he lived will be determined by the address given in the will and by where he filed income tax, was registered to vote, and had a driver's license. The petition—referred to as the petition to administer estate, petition for commencement of proceedings, or petition for probate of will—is a form that can be found, filled out, and filed at the probate court. Among other things, this petition includes the following:

1. The executor's name and relationship to the deceased

2. The deceased's name, date of death, age, and Social Security number

3. His or her county and state of residence

4. Names and addresses of his or her heirs (surviving spouse and minor children)

5. Date the will was drafted and names of its witnesses

6. The estimated value of the probate assets

A petition to any probate court normally includes many papers—not just one. The actual petition filed is among many papers that must get filed. And as the probate proceeding carries onward, more papers will get filed with the court.

Ancillary (Other) Probate

If a deceased owned property in several states, the executor must file separate probate proceedings in those states (where the property is located). Unless the property was jointly owned (and can transfer without probate), filing separate probate proceedings is the only way to transfer property to beneficiaries or heirs in those states. This requires the executor to contact the probate court in the area where the property is located. There may also be separate inheritance or estate taxes payable to the state where the real estate is located. Probate may also need to be opened in the state where the deceased resided—even if he or she never owned property in that state.

Notifying Interested Parties

Once the probate petition has been filed, the court schedules a hearing to confirm the appointment of the executor and determine whether the will is legally valid and admissible into probate. The executor must notify all interested persons—the deceased's beneficiaries, next-of-kin, and creditors—by sending them a copy of the petition for commencement of

Notifying interested parties and beneficiaries can be tough if the deceased had a previous marriage or was estranged from people. Someone from the deceased's past suddenly can show up and make a legitimate claim. An executor should check with other family members, friends, and the deceased's doctor or clergy. Looking at birth certificates, marriage certificates, death certificates, military records, government (census) records, court (adoption or divorce) records, and the like can also help. If the value of the estate is substantial, the executor may want to consult a genealogist or private investigator to track down any stray heirs who could come forth with a legitimate claim to assets and contest the will.

probate, a copy of the will, and a notice specifying the time, date, and place of the hearing. Any one of these interested persons can file an objection to the appointment of executor or can contest the will. (Contesting the will is not easily done, seriously prolongs the probate process, and costs the estate a great deal. Sometimes it is possible to reach a compromise settlement with the one contesting the will. If the will is thrown out as invalid, the estate will be probated as if there were no will.) A will contest is an uphill battle, as the task of the probate court is to uphold the wishes of the deceased.

Getting Help

As we mentioned in other sections throughout this book, the executor can hire the assistance of others to help in settling the estate. Having a legal document assistant at the executor's disposal to help complete the paperwork and get through the process or an attorney for legal advice and/or to write the occasional letter on the executor's behalf can be very helpful and minimize any waiting time or frustration. Executors should not have to take on the full probate administration and management all on their own. Especially when it comes to large estates or estates that involved complex families (think multiple marriages, blended families, stepchildren, estranged siblings). The more useful assistants an executor has, the more efficient he or she can be. Probate can also be intricate and paperwork-heavy in one state but not in another.

The assets of the estate may also require more management than an executor is inclined to handle. What's more, the probate court system can be confusing, so having someone familiar with property, estate, inheritance, tax, and state laws is very helpful. Therefore, seeking an expert familiar with probate in your state is often at the top of the list of things an executor wants to do.

To find a good legal document assistant or a probate attorney, start by asking friends and family members for recommendations. Ask the clerk of the probate court. Ask your banker. You may even want to consult a lawyer referral service or your state or local bar association for lawyers who specialize in probate law. If you are a member of AARP you may be eligible for free or reduced fee legal services from lawyers who participate in the AARP Legal Services Network. For a list of participating lawyers, visit www.aarp.org/lsn or call (800) 424-3410 for more information and names of attorneys in your area.

Always keep We The People in mind if a store is located in your area. We know how probate works in all the states where we have stores. We help people get through the process step-by-step every day. Probate in California, for example, can be enormously complicated and frustrating. We know exactly how it works and can guide anyone through an uncontested probate proceeding successfully. But for anyone having to deal with a contested probate case, hiring a lawyer is usually necessary.

Tips for Finding a Good Lawyer, If You Need One (Contested Probate Proceedings)

Whether you are an executor or a settlor, finding a good lawyer—or for that matter, just an estate planner or tax specialist or accountant—to assist you should not be an unnerving experience. If you do your due diligence, which means taking reasonable care with and paying attention to a matter, you will find the person you need to get what you want done successfully.

Always meet with a few lawyers before selecting one. Most will meet with you briefly to get acquainted for no charge. Don't let an aggressive attorney choose you as a client. You are the one doing the hiring, and you should find someone you can talk with easily, who understands your needs, and if possible, one you feel you can trust.

When you meet with or call the lawyer, ask if he or she has probate experience, tell him what you need help with, and be sure to discuss fees up front. Choose someone you feel comfortable talking with and make sure that he or she understands your needs. Although many estate attorneys prefer to work for a percentage of the estate, it may serve you—and the estate—better to try to negotiate an hourly fee. If you are organized and do some of the work yourself—notifying beneficiaries, filling out and filing forms—you will make better use of his or her time and save a good deal of money. Use the lawyer's services for big things or purely for legal advice.

Anyone looking for an attorney for help in settling an estate should be sure to find out how much the attorney charges for the services you need. Typically, attorneys charge either a set fee to do a specific task (such as prepare a document), a percentage of the estate, or an hourly rate. Get in writing a detailed statement of the services he or she will provide and the charge for each, including extra costs for filing, appraisers, mileage, copying court documents—before you hire him or her. Confirm the agreement in a formal contract that you can understand. A lot of people sign contracts without knowing what they say—and then get into trouble. If you don't understand a portion of the contract, ask the attorney to explain it to you before signing on the dotted line. In many states, the court dictates the amount—based on the size of the estate—that a lawyer can charge for probate administration. However, it may be less expensive if he or she charges by the hour. Negotiate to pay for only the actual time spent. Or arrange a flat fee for the job. Experts warn that you should be sure you are not being charged the full rate for work done by a paralegal or a student.

The AARP advises that you consider the amount of time it will take to do the work, the difficulty of the legal issue, and the lawyer's experience in figuring out whether a fee is reasonable. A less experienced lawyer may charge less but take longer, while an experienced lawyer may charge more but resolve the matter more quickly. As with all other professional services, the cheapest fee may not be best. If you hire an attorney, you may be able to save on legal fees by using the attorney only in an advisory capacity and handling the rest yourself. Compile and organize all the records, files, forms, and documentation he or she will need to settle the estate. Sometimes an experienced accountant can handle the entire process.

Paying Off Debts

As the person responsible for settling the estate, the executor has to take inventory of the deceased's liabilities (what the deceased still owed or was financially responsible for at his or her death) as well as his or her assets. Although assets jointly owned become the property of the surviving owner, bills incurred jointly—through a joint charge account or credit card—remain the responsibility of both the estate as well as the surviving joint debtor.

Some bills must be paid when due—taxes, insurance, mortgage—otherwise the estate may be jeopardized. State law ranks creditors by priority. The order varies from state to state but usually includes the following at the top of the list:

1. Expenses associated with administering the estate (lawyer fees, court costs, etc.)

2. Taxes

3. Funeral expenses

4. Medical expenses incurred immediately prior to death

An executor pays those at the top of the list first, in full. If an executor pays a low-priority creditor before, say, taxes or funeral expenses, the executor may be held personally responsible for paying the higher ranked creditor later on if the estate runs out of funds. If there are insufficient assets to pay the lower ranked creditors, those creditors get nothing. Even a surviving spouse is under no legal obligation to pay the deceased's debts out of her money, insurance proceeds, jointly owned assets, or even funds from accounts made payable on death. If a surviving wife/executor/successor trustee pays any debts herself, the estate should reimburse her. If, however, she cosigned the credit agreement, she is responsible for the remaining balance.

Creditors' claims can be ignored if there are no probate assets or if the estate is of so little value that it is not required to pay any of its creditors. As mentioned above, some states guarantee a family allowance for the spouse or minor children that is exempt from creditor claims. Estates settled by small estate transfer procedures are usually not required to pay creditor claims.

Notice of Administration

Executors must notify the deceased's creditors by one of two ways: (1) by contacting them directly, or (2) by running a notice in the local newspaper. The notice should state that the will has been admitted into probate and that any claims against the estate must be submitted to the executor or the court within a given time period set by the state (usually within three to four months). The court will tell the executor how long and how often the notice must run. The court will also ask for proof of publication. The notice should include the following information:

- Deceased's name
- Address
- Date of death
- Social Security number
- Executor's name
- Executor's address
- Address of the court

If an executor is unable to pay the creditors because there are not enough funds in the estate, the executor should let the creditors know this. Otherwise, they may continue to hound the executor and demand payment. An executor should not feel embarrassed in such a situation. Most businesses make allowances for nonpayment of debt. The deceased may have had mortgage life insurance or credit card insurance that at death would pay off the balance due. The executor should ask the deceased's mortgage lending company, insurance company, and credit card companies for more information about this insurance coverage.

Any claims that come in after the deadline do not need to be paid. And no claim should be paid before the expiration of the claims deadline; however, once the deadline has passed the executor must pay claims promptly (providing there are enough funds to pay taxes and professional fees). Payment should be made by check from the estate's account. To generate enough funds to satisfy the claims, some assets may have to be sold (example: real estate, stock, bonds). However, the executor should speak with the beneficiaries in order to determine what to sell.

Illegitimate and Unfair Claims. When an executor discovers an illegitimate or unfair claim, it's up to the executor to try and settle the dispute by speaking with the creditor and arriving at a resolution or compromise. If the executor cannot get the creditor to agree, he or she may have to file a formal objection with the court. In this objection, the executor states the reason for the objection and sends a registered copy to the creditor. If the court agrees with the objection, it may intervene on the executor's behalf.

More on Taxes (Ugh!)

Paying the Deceased's Taxes

We saw in Chapter 6 how complex and intimidating taxes can be. But paying taxes is one of the most important tasks that an executor has when settling an estate. In fact, the subject of taxes is so daunting and the task of dealing with taxes can be so cumbersome, that this is why many executors rely on other professionals to help manage it all and get it done correctly. Executors who can manage an estate up until taxes are due have done well for themselves, but there is nothing wrong with surrendering to the aid of a good tax professional when the time is right.

Remember: Payment of taxes takes priority over any other debts. Taxes must be paid on time. An executor cannot distribute assets to the beneficiaries before paying the taxes due or he or she will be held personally responsible for the taxes owed.

If the value of the estate is high or probate is complicated, an executor should consult with an accountant or tax lawyer who is familiar with the tax laws in the state and county where the deceased lived. As with hiring any lawyer, the more organized the executor is and the more information the executor can

The value of good tax advice cannot be over- or underestimated. Even if an executor hires professional help, the executor is personally responsible for filing the returns and paying the taxes. If an executor uses an accountant, no one can be blamed but the executor for any delay in filing. The IRS won't buy it.

provide the accountant, the less time it will take him or her to do the needed work and the less it will cost the estate.

Which Taxes Must Be Paid? The types of taxes an executor is required to file depend on the deceased's income, the value of the overall estate, as well as the estate and inheritance tax requirements of the state and county where the deceased lived and filed taxes. When handling the deceased's taxes, the following must be filed:

- Personal federal, state, and local income tax
- Federal, state, and local estate tax
- Federal, state, and local income tax on the estate (if any)

Other taxes that may have to be filed include the following:

- Gift tax (Form 709)
- Fiduciary income tax (Form 1041)

(Note: The executor should also obtain Form 712 from the insurance company on any life insurance policies.)

These tax returns must also be filed in the case of a living trust. Filing these returns is the responsibility of both the successor trustee and the executor named in the will, but usually this is the same person. In other words, the same person typically serves as both executor and successor trustee. If two different people were named to do these tasks, the estate could be more complicated and hard to settle quickly. Generally, it's best to name the same person as executor and successor trustee. Note also that when there is a living trust, at the death of the individual, the assets left out of the trust get poured into the living trust via the pour over will. The personal representative (or executor) of the pour over will handles this task. Assets that get poured into the living trust at the death are probate assets—they may have to go through the probate court under certain circumstances.

Filing Deadlines. Federal and state (if any) estate taxes are due on the ninth month anniversary of the decedent's date of death. An automatic six-month extension may be requested. If requested, however, a payment must be made of the estimated estate taxes that will be due

---

For information about filing tax returns on an estate, call the Internal Revenue Service (IRS) and ask for Publication 559 (Survivors, Executors and Administrators), which outlines in detail an person's responsibilities regarding tax filing as a survivor or executor of an estate. It also offers information about tax benefits for survivors. You can also get access to other information on their web site at www.irs.gov, and download many forms. Other publications you may find helpful include Instructions for Form 706 and Federal Estate and Gift Taxes or Form 448. You can download all of these materials and access other essential information on the IRS's web site.

Special rules apply to members of the Armed Forces who die in or as a result of active duty in a combat zone. The IRS also has special provisions for public safety workers killed in the line of duty and for victims of terrorist actions. For more information contact the IRS.

when the IRS form (Form 706) is filed. Federal and state income tax returns are filed similar to regular income tax returns, on the fifteenth day of the fourth month after the close of the year, or April 15. An extension to October 15 may also be requested.

Personal Income Tax

To reiterate: The deceased's final federal, state, and local income tax returns need to be filed. The deceased's final income tax return should include all income earned in the year of death up until the date of death. These taxes are due on April 15 following the year of the death, just as they would be normally. An extension can be requested for filing by October 15 (six months later). Final tax returns for the deceased cannot be filed electronically. A paper tax return (Form 1040) must be filed in the IRS center for the place where the deceased lived. If the deceased failed to file an income tax return for any years preceding death, the executor will need to file for those years, too.

If, for example, Martha died in March of 2005 and had not yet filed in April for taxes due on 2004, the executor will have to complete the filing and pay the 2004 taxes as well. Even if the deceased had no taxable income for the year, a return should still be filed. A refund may be due if taxes were paid on wages, pension, or annuities. In addition, medical and dental expenses, if paid within a year of the death, can be deducted from the deceased's final individual income tax return. Surviving spouses who are used to filing joint returns can do so again for the year in which the loved one died. A spouse with dependent children may file jointly for an additional two years after the death. Or the spouse can choose to file separately.

As we detailed earlier, there may be advantages to filing jointly. The surviving spouse may offset income received after the deceased's death against deductions claimed by the deceased. Moreover, the surviving spouse who files a joint return qualifies for special tax rates for the two years following the death—unless he or she remarries. Consult with a tax specialist about the advantages and disadvantages to filing jointly.

Estate Income Tax

We started talking about estate income tax in the previous chapter. Whether there is a living trust owning most of an estate's assets or not, income taxes must be paid on any estate that generates an income. Even though someone has died, an estate can generate income through rental properties, interest, royalties, and so on (see list below). Both federal and state income tax returns must be filed for such income; these returns tax the annual net income earned by a living trust and/or estate.

For Estates without a Living Trust. If the assets of an estate do not earn income during the probate administration process period, there is no need to file a federal income tax return on behalf of the estate. But if the estate is large and takes time for probate administration, it is likely that the estate made money. If it made more than $600 between the time of the deceased's death and the time all assets are distributed, then the executor needs to file federal income tax for the estate. In order to file on behalf of the estate, the executor must apply for an employer identification number (EIN) for the estate and complete IRS form SS-4 (Application for an Employer Identification Number), obtainable from the post office or Social Security office. It takes four weeks by mail or can be done immediately by phone. The EIN functions like a Social Security number. This is the same task a surviving spouse with an AB trust must do at the death of the first spouse in order to pay for any taxes due on the B trust.

For Estates with a Living Trust. A living trust may avoid probate, but taxes must still be paid if the value of the estate meets the criteria. Besides the federal and state (if any) estate tax returns, the successor trustee (the executor here) may have to file income tax returns, such as the following:

- Final federal income tax return (and state, if any) for the deceased settlor
- Final federal income tax return (and state, if any) for the B trust after both spouses die

Remember: The surviving spouse, who normally is named as cotrustee and initial successor trustee, takes care of filing the tax returns on the B trust until he or she dies. At the death of the second spouse, the then-successor trustee must finish up the income tax returns for as long as the estate generates an income.

Employer Identification Number. An executor needs to enter the EIN on tax returns, statements, and documents filed on behalf of the estate. If interest or dividends are payable to the estate, the estate's EIN number must be provided to the payer and used on the Form 1099 to report the interest. It is the executor's responsibility to give the EIN to those who file Form 1099 in connection with the estate. The estate income tax is reported on Form 1041. An executor is also required to file a Notice Concerning Fiduciary Relationship (IRS Form 56) if he or she is appointed to act in a fiduciary capacity for another. A fiduciary is a person acting for another person. An executor or personal representative is a fiduciary. Fiduciaries need the EIN to file the Form 56, and they need to notify the IRS when their responsibilities as fiduciary are completed.

Taxable income on the estate consists of all income received during the tax year and includes the following:

- Dividends
- Interest
- Rents
- Royalties
- Gains from the sale of property
- Income from business
- Partnerships
- Trusts
- Other sources

There is no exemption for dependents or medical or funeral expenses. However, losses from the sale of property, net operating losses, and some casualty and theft losses can be deducted if not also claimed on the federal estate tax return. The cost of administering the estate can be deducted from the gross estate, either on the estate's income tax return or on the federal estate tax return, but not on both. The estate's income tax return must be filed annually on either a calendar- or fiscal-year basis. You may file at the IRS location nearest your home or workplace.

Federal Estate Tax

We went through how federal estate tax works in Chapter 6. To review: If the value of the deceased's taxable estate exceeds $1.5 million in 2005 ($2 million in 2006) you must pay federal estate tax and file an estate tax return (Form 706). The value of the estate is based not only on solely owned (probate) assets, but on all assets including those that are exempt from probate administration, such as the following:

- The deceased's share of jointly owned assets
- Life insurance, payable to the estate or to heirs
- Annuities paid to estate or heirs
- Benefits from retirement accounts and pension plans
- Assets held in any trusts, such as a living trust
- Assets held in pay-on-death or transfer-on-death accounts
- Lifetime gifts made within three years of the death
- Gifts made at the time of the death
- The deceased's interest in community-owned property

When itemizing the assets that comprise the gross estate and assessing fair market values for each, it's best for an executor to assess those values when the total reduces the amount of the tax. As we said previously, the value of the deceased's assets can be determined either at the date of the death or six months thereafter, so an executor should use whichever total is less. For example, let's say you are executor of Aunt Tess's estate. You figure that her estate is worth $1.45 million at the time of her death, but six months later it's worth $1.55 million. She died in 2005 when the federal estate tax exemption limit is $1.5 million, so you use the figure obtained at her death so her estate remains under the tax threshold.

Because of the unlimited marital deduction from the gross estate, the value of an estate can be reduced enough to eliminate having to pay the tax. All assets that pass directly to the surviving spouse—by bequest, inheritance, joint-ownership, revocable living trust, and pay-on-death and transfer-on-death accounts, or as proceeds of life insurance—are exempt from the estate tax. Additional deductions include funeral and burial expenses, administration expenses, debts owed at the time of death, mortgages, income taxes, property taxes, uninsured losses incurred during the estate settlement, charitable bequests, and state death taxes. Once all allowable deductions have been subtracted from the gross estate, the result is the taxable estate.

A tentative estate tax is then computed on a sliding scale based on the value of the taxable estate. Once the tentative tax has been calculated, the unified gift and estate tax credit—a credit of $555,800 in 2005 and $780,800 in 2006 through 2008—may be applied.

Reminder: A credit is allowed for any gift taxes previously paid on lifetime gifts made by the deceased of $11,000 (or $22,000 with the consent of the spouse). These credits may reduce or eliminate the estate tax completely. If, after the unlimited marital deduction has been taken and the unified gift and estate tax credit have been applied, the value of the estate is still greater than $1.5 million in 2005 ($2 million in 2005), federal estate taxes must be paid. The executor must fill out and file IRS Form 706 within nine months of the date of death. Attached to this form are a copy of the will, the death certificate, and state certification of payment of death taxes. United States residents may mail the form to the IRS Center in Cincinnati, Ohio 45999. If an executor fails to pay the tax when it is due, or misreports the value of the estate, the executor will be subject to severe penalties. If the executor cannot pay the tax because he or she has distributed assets to the beneficiaries, the beneficiaries will be personally liable for the tax!

State and Local Estate, Inheritance, and Income Taxes

Consult an accountant, tax attorney, or state and local tax laws to find out about filing estate income tax requirements for the state and local area where the deceased lived. As we explained in the previous chapter, most states have either

- an inheritance tax—payable by each beneficiary (or out of the estate via instructions in the will or living trust); or
- an estate tax—payable by the estate.

The tax may be applicable regardless of how small the estate is. Taxes are due to the state in which the deceased resided—not where the beneficiaries live. Certain beneficiaries may be exempt—spouse, children, grandchildren. The will may state that the tax be paid by the estate on behalf of the beneficiary. Regardless of how the tax is paid, the executor must ensure that all taxes are paid. Otherwise, the IRS can go after the beneficiaries to recover its owed money by ordering the beneficiaries to pay back up to the fair market value of the assets they received from the estate.

> Tax laws and forms are revised and updated frequently. It may help to have the advice and counsel of a certified public accountant (CPA) or tax attorney. Contact your local IRS office or access the IRS web site at www.irs.gov for information. To order forms and publications to assist you with tax filing call (800) 829-3976.

Distributing the Assets and Closing the Estate

Once an executor has inventoried the assets, paid the taxes and debts including all probate administration costs, and gotten permission from the court, he or she can distribute the remaining assets to the beneficiaries. In order to do this, the court may require the executor to submit a plan for distribution of assets for approval. The court may share or ask the executor to share the plan with other interested parties. It may take 30 days or more before the court approves or rejects a plan for disbursement. If the court or other interested party files an objection, the court may make changes to the plan and force the executor (by a court order) to distribute the assets accordingly.

When distributing the assets, the executor uses the estate's checking account, which was set up to sell certain assets, to write checks to the entitled beneficiaries. Cancelled checks prove distribution of assets to the court. When distributing other assets, the executor needs to get receipts signed by the beneficiaries, which proves to the court that the executor has distributed the assets according to the will (or the state law).

When distributing real estate or other personal property, an executor may use a court order assigning residue that describes the property and specifies the beneficiary and delivers the order to the beneficiary. In many states it is customary for the final order of distribution to be recorded in the county where the estate's real property is located. For titled items, like a car, the executor fills out the transferor's portion of the certificate of title. The executor then delivers the title to the beneficiary with copies of the death certificate and a letter of authority (which basically says the executor is in charge of this transaction). Once the executor distributes all of the assets, he or she may submit a final accounting to the court. Each state has different procedures for closing an estate, but in general an executor may close by filing a sworn statement or by petition.

A sworn statement says that the executor has fulfilled his duties, such as published a notice to creditors and distributed probate assets. It also says that all beneficiaries and creditors are aware of the closing and have received an accounting of the administration. An executor cannot file a sworn statement unless he or she has served as executor for at least six months.

Closing by petition also requires that all interested parties be notified of the closing, including beneficiaries, creditors, and heirs. A hearing is then held by the court during which the court rules on the distribution of the assets, the executor's fees and expenses, and whether to discharge the executor and close the estate.

Either way, once the executor has been discharged, he or she no longer has fiduciary authority over any new probate assets that may be discovered. If a survivor discovers new probate assets after the close of the estate, that survivor (who may or may not have been the executor during the administration of the estate) must obtain a court order to reopen the deceased's estate in order to transfer ownership. A survivor can also petition the court to appoint another executor (the same one or a new person) to handle any newly discovered assets.

The Unlisted Responsibilities

As with most to-do lists people have to check off, there are always extra or inherent things to do that are not necessarily listed. This is true for everyday lists and official ones like that of an executor's to-do list. If you are an executor and you find yourself having to manage more than what you ever expected, realize that it's okay to ask for informal help from other family members. For example, you may feel personally responsible for handling the funeral, burial, memorial service, and any special instructions listed in a letter of instruction, will, or trust documents, but feel overwhelmed by it all. You can hire professionals and seek the advice of experts to help settle an estate, but still feel overwhelmed by some of the other, less official but equally as taxing chores to do in reaching the same goal: closing an estate.

An executor must also worry about swindlers and other dishonest people who like to arrive on the scene at the death of an individual and try to abuse the estate. Example: Funeral homes can act abusively and take advantage of a person's vulnerabilities that normally follow a death in the family. They do this by quoting enormous prices or getting people to think they need to buy expensive caskets, have lavish memorials, or order death certificates through them. In fact, some funeral directors can act more like luxury car salesmen than compassionate and reasonable sellers in the death industry. A funeral home may charge $13 for one copy of a death certificate (and suggest that you buy more than 100 copies!) when you can obtain the same certificate from the registrar for $10 and probably do well with 10 to 15 copies. When grief and exhaustion set in, the executor becomes even more vulnerable to dodgy characters. With so many official tasks, having to worry about these extra issues adds to the stress. This is when knowing how to delegate is key. And as an estate planner, choosing an executor who can do this well is your key to your estate plan's overall success.

Conclusion

We hope that the contents of this book inspire you to take charge of your future, as well as that of your family. We also hope that we have taken the mystery out of wills and living trusts. They are documents that do not discriminate and can accomplish many goals for any kind of person. Whether you are a single person with just a few assets or part of a large family with lots of children, complex relationships, and large assets, everyone has a right to plan for his or her passing and think about what it means for loved ones—those left behind.

Estate planning is not a tool for the rich and famous. It's better to think of estate planning as the golden key to your legacy. That's right—your *legacy.* Leaving a legacy is perhaps the ultimate goal of every human being, the ultimate quest in life, the ultimate sign of having lived successfully and done all that one can possibly do.

Life is full of options, decisions, and choices. Life is also full of rules, codes, and procedures. To combine these two sets of realities in a way that gives you the freedom and flexibility to do what you want (within your legal limits) but still remain in control of your own destiny—and the destiny of your loved ones—is what wills and living trusts are designed to do. You may not be able to make every decision or have your way every time, either in life or beyond, but you can maximize that potential. You can enhance the lives of many. And you can secure your legacy into the future.

The last two chapters answer the most commonly asked questions and define many terms that you may encounter on your journey toward creating your will or living trust.

CHAPTER 8

Frequently Asked Questions

This chapter is dedicated entirely to answering the most frequently asked questions. We've organized the chapter according to topic, so you can easily locate a set of questions that pertains to one subject.

Customers who enter our stores are full of questions when they first contemplate a will or living trust. They are starving for answers and sometimes feel embarrassed that they have to ask them. There's nothing to be embarrassed about, however. No one gets a lengthy course in estate planning unless you go to school to study that subject in particular. Estate planning is not a high school requirement or a popular elective in college. People who don't deal with estate planning in their daily lives do not know what it's about. And it's typically not knowledge you pick up along the way, like you do when buying a house or balancing your checkbook. Even lawyers who don't deal with estate planning have questions!

Please note: Generally speaking, there are many exceptions to the various rules. Many questions can be hard to answer in one manner because options may exist depending on state law. One state's way of handling probate, for example, may be entirely different from another state's procedure. For answers tailored to your specific needs, consult with your tax advisor, a local estate planner, or even a We The People store to find out what some of your choices may be. (Check Appendix C to see if there is one close to you.) Because estate planning involves many layers of knowledge—tax, formal documents, legal issues, accounting, and so on—it's best to seek the advice when you need it and never hesitate to act on that advice for the benefit of your overall plan. Remember: Self-knowledge and competent advice are the two key ingredients to a successful plan.

Basic Questions about Estate Planning

What is estate planning?

Estate planning involves two actions:

1) Putting in writing the names of the people you would want to take care of your children, your finances, and your health care if you couldn't do so anymore (and telling them what you would want them to do) while you are still alive.

2) Using the appropriate legal documents so that at your death, the money and things you've worked so hard to acquire goes to whomever you wish, instead of being divided among family according to state law.

Estate planning does not eliminate taxes, but it can help you minimize what you owe through careful planning and the use of certain vehicles, such as an AB trust, to manipulate the exemptions and deductions that the law allows for keeping money in your family.

What is an estate?

Everyone—rich and poor—has an estate. An estate is everything you own and owe. If you were to create a list of your assets (what you own) and your liabilities (what you owe), that list comprises your estate.

What is a will?

Simply put, a will is a statement that indicates your desire about the distribution of your estate following your death. A will is a way to extend your intent and decisions about financial matters into the future of your family for their benefit. A generic will is often called a Last Will and Testament. There are many types of wills, from hand-written (holographic) wills to the more formal documents that get witnessed, notarized (sometimes), and treated in an official manner. States have different rules for what constitutes a valid will. To be valid, the will must be signed by the person who made it (testator), dated, and witnessed by two people (except in Vermont, which requires three). The witnesses should be disinterested (have no relation to the will maker), and in some states, a gift to a witness is void, but the will is valid.

What is a living trust?

A living trust is a document that declares your intention to hold your assets as a "trustee of your trust." Technically, you no longer own the property; your trust owns it. You are called the trustee, which does not modify your ability to buy property, borrow against the property, or sell the property. The benefit of a trust is that the assets you place in it do not have to go through probate at your death. You name beneficiaries of the trust's property, and it can get distributed quickly under normal circumstances.

How are a will and a living trust different?

Both a will and a trust provide the means for you to distribute your property to the persons you choose when you pass away. The most significant difference is that a will must be proven in court through a costly process called probate. A living trust does not require the involvement of the court and does not incur probate or attorney fees.

If I have a living trust, why do I also need a will?

The type of will that is used with a living trust is called a pour over will, because its job is to pour (transfer) assets into the living trust if the assets were not transferred to the trust previously.

What is probate?

Probate is the process of proving a will. It is a public process handled by the courts (probate court). Probate refers to the court oversight of the distribution of your assets and legal issues related to the settlement. Probate is like a legal holding cell where assets and debts are accounted for, taxes are paid, and what's left is distributed to the beneficiaries named in the will, or if there is no will, to the heirs specified by state law.

What happens if I die without a will or living trust?

If you die without planning for the distribution of your assets in a will or through a living trust, you are said to have died intestate. This means that the court must oversee the distribution of your assets and appoint someone to settle your estate. Every state has laws of intestacy, which tell who gets what when somebody dies without a will. These laws prioritize your next of kin, and dictate how much each person is entitled to receive based on your relationships to these family members. Laws of intestacy focus on blood relatives and do not include your best friends, old roommates, or other people that you may want to leave gifts to. This is why having a will or living trust is a good idea: They let you leave what you want to whom you want, so that the state does not make these decisions for you.

How can I name guardians for my minor children?

You can name guardians for minor children for their person and/or estate through a will or living trust. In either document, you nominate someone who can take care of your children in the event it is needed when you die. The court ultimately must approve of and appoint this person as the guardian. You can also name a custodian for anyone that receives a gift from you but whom you think is not ready to control or manage that gift until a certain age.

I am not married. I have no children. I am not rich. Do I still need a will or living trust?

Only you can decide whether or not you need a will or living trust. They are not required. These legal instruments are good for single people, married people, the young, the old, the rich, and the people who are still building their estate and plan to acquire more assets throughout their lives. You may not own a large home or have a lot of valuable possessions to distribute at your death now, but if you set up a will or living trust today, you begin to plan your future and can change your will or living trust as your circumstances change. It's much easier to plan for your death when you are young rather than wait until you are 85. Starting your plan today with a will or living trust gets you in the mode of managing a document that can do a lot for your family at your death, but which does not require a lot of maintenance during your life.

Questions about Wills

What does a will do?

A will is a legal document designating the transfer of your property (both real property and personal property) after you die.

Do I need a lawyer to make my will?

Probably not. You just need to know what you own and whom you want your property to go to when you die.

Do I need to file my will with a court or in public records somewhere?

No. Keep your will in an accessible place and be sure the person in charge of settling your affairs (your executor) knows where it is.

What is an executor/executrix?

An executor/executrix is the person who oversees the distribution of your assets in accordance with your will.

Does my will prevent probate?

A will does not prevent or avoid probate. All the assets passing through the will, over a certain dollar amount, also pass through probate. As previously emphasized, probate is expensive, time consuming, and open to the public's viewing. The majority of people choose to avoid it. You can avoid the problems of probate with a revocable living trust.

Who has to witness my will?

States vary on the answer to this question. Most require at least two competent witnesses to sign your will. In some states, you may have to obtain a third witness's signature and/or get the will notarized. Most states require the witnesses to be at least 18 years old, but a few allow a 16-year-old to witness a will's signing.

Can I give specific instructions about how I want to be buried and memorialized?

Yes, but your will normally does not contain this information. You can write a letter of instruction that supplements your will but is informal and can be changed whenever you like. In your letter of instruction, you can give specific instructions about your funeral, the location of important documents, passwords to computers, and write anything you want about your assets and your life for your survivors to know.

Can I change my will?

Yes. You can make changes to your will as you see fit throughout your life by adding a codicil to it that clearly states your changes. Depending on how your state deals with codicils, they may need to be witnessed and/or notarized. They are formal amendments to formal wills. For significant changes, however, you may want to redo your entire will.

I am married. Do I write a joint will with my spouse?

No. It is best not to create a joint will as you would a joint living trust. If you are married, you and your spouse each write wills that are mirrors of each other (reciprocal wills). But they are treated separately and remain separate entities. Joint wills are not a good idea.

Why can't I just tell someone what to do in the event of my death?

You can. But if a dispute emerges over your assets, such as your siblings or children fighting over who gets what, the court will have to deal with their lawsuits and this prolongs the time and increases the costs it takes to settle your affairs. By planning with a will, you hope to prevent disputes and save your family unnecessary pain and anguish. In your will, you name an executor to take control of settling your estate at your death. The court will likely give this person the authority to carry out your wishes. Also, by creating a will, you start to think about how you would want your family members to deal with certain issues related to your death (example: last rites or nothing, burial or cremation). While these requests are not part of your official will, you can create another, less formal document that tells your survivors how and where, for example, you want your funeral to happen. Your survivors are saved the worry over what to do in the event of your death. Having clear instructions written down is much better than leaving it to the whims of your survivors who may or may not agree with one another.

Questions about Probate

Why do so many people say probate is bad?

Probate gets a bad reputation because it tends to take a long time (between 9 and 18 months, sometimes much longer). When family members begin to file lawsuits (because they are upset over how an estate gets divided, for example), the probate process takes longer and continues to drain money from the estate as attorneys get involved. If you are at the mercy of the probate court in settling an estate, you are likely paying attorneys and executors fees for their hard work throughout the process. Probate is easier—and much cheaper—in some states than others. You can avoid probate by creating a living trust, so the assets owned by the trust do not have to go through the probate court and your beneficiaries can receive their gifts relatively quickly and easily.

How much does probate cost?

An exact cost to probate is incalculable. Probate fees vary across the states. In California, for example, the fees for probate are set by statute as follows: 4 percent on the first $15,000; 3 percent on the next $85,000; 2 percent on the next $900,000; and 1 percent on the next $9,000,000. If you add other costs related to settling an estate, such as attorney fees and executor fees, the price climbs. And the longer probate takes, the higher the numbers climb.

Are there other ways to settle an estate other than going through probate?

Unless you set up certain legal instruments for dealing with the distribution of your assets at your death, you cannot avoid probate. A living trust is a legal instrument that avoids probate. Owning property in joint tenancy is another way to avoid probate. When one owner dies, the other joint tenant(s) automatically becomes the full owner of the property and it does not go through probate. You may qualify for faster probate proceedings if, for example, the value of the estate is below a certain amount set by your state. For example, in California an estate valued less than $100,000 may not have to go through the formal probate process. In New Hampshire, however, the state limit is only $500. Other exceptions to the rules of formal probate proceedings will apply in your state. Depending on the value of your estate, or the asset that must be transferred, there may be simple forms of the probate process that can transfer assets easily and quickly.

Do probate courts routinely give spouses and children an automatic right to a certain amount of assets from a deceased spouse's estate?

Yes. All states have a minimum family protection allowance that guarantees the spouse and dependent children receive at least some funds for support from the estate—even if they weren't named as designated beneficiaries. The spouse must petition the court soon after the death. The court determines the amount of the allowance, but it may be large enough that other bequests are reduced or eliminated. If the estate is sufficiently depleted by this allowance, debts—including the funeral, court, and probate administration costs—may go unpaid.

What is a homestead right?

A spouse may claim a homestead right, which allows the spouse and minor children to stay in the deceased's home for a specified period, even if the house has been bequeathed to someone else. Example: A man has bequeathed his home to his son from a previous marriage. When he dies, his surviving second wife can remain in the home for a specified period of time, sometimes for the rest of her life, at which point the son inherits the house.

If my estate has to go through probate, should my executor be an attorney?

No. Your named executor need not be an attorney or have any experience in settling an estate. Pick someone who you think is responsible and who understands your personal values. You want to name an executor who can best carry out your wishes and who will be able to deal with your family members at your death without much trouble. In other words: Choose someone close to you, but welcomed by your family. Only in extreme circumstances do you need to name a family attorney, company, or firm that specializes in administering an estate.

How can I avoid probate?

How property is owned has a lot to do with whether or not probate is necessary. Property owned by a living trust does not have to go through probate. Property owned in joint tenancy does not have to go through probate. Exceptions to the formal probate process may apply given the value of your estate. For example, if your estate is below a certain value (set by your state), you may qualify for summary probate, which is a shorter version of the formal probate process. Probate is different in every state, and some forms of probate are not all that bad. No matter whether you have to go through probate or not, the administration of every estate entails certain paperwork, procedures, and processes—with or without a will or living trust.

Questions about Living Trusts

Will I need an attorney to advise me concerning my living trust?

Attorneys provide important services and advice concerning the law. An attorney is not needed to set up your living trust unless you have a large, complicated estate. However, your living trust should be an attorney-drafted document. So if you do not go to an attorney well-versed in drafting living trusts, you still need to be sure that your living trust meets the same standards. For example, all of our living trusts at We The People are attorney-drafted documents.

Does the living trust protect me against my creditors?

No, the living trust does not act as a shield to protect you from your creditors.

Must a special income tax return be filed while I am alive with a living trust?

No special income tax forms are required as long as a married couple or one individual alone is receiving all the income from the trust.

Can I transfer money while I'm still alive through gifts without them being taxed?

Yes. There is usually no tax if you make a gift to your spouse or if your estate goes to your spouse at your death. If you make a gift to someone else, the gift tax does not apply to the first $11,000 you give that person each year ($22,000 for a couple making the gift).

Will my disability affect my living trust?

Included in many living trust packages are two important documents: (1) the Durable Power of Attorney for Finances; (2) the Designation for Health Care Agent, or Durable Power of Attorney for Healthcare. These documents allow you to select an individual of your choice to act during your absence or physical incapacity. Should you become disabled, your agent can make decisions on your behalf including the management of your trust.

Will I have to rewrite my living trust if I change my mind or wish to amend my trust?

Included in many living trust packages are minutes of trust, or special trust instructions, which are used to instruct your successor trustees concerning specific wishes. You may use the trust instructions to change or amend your trust. In instances where major modifications are needed, such as changing your beneficiaries, you may need to amend your living trust.

If I set up a trust, is a will also required?

Yes, a pour over will is drafted along with your living trust. It acts as a safety net for all of your smaller assets. The pour over will picks up those assets at the time of your death and transfers them into the trust.

Is it necessary to put personal property into the trust?

Household items of nominal value need not be put into the trust. They will be handled by the pour over will. The gross value of the assets kept outside of the living trust, however, should total less than the amount that triggers the formal probate process in your state. For example, if you must go through the formal probate process in your state if your assets exceed $100,000, then you want the sum of your assets outside of your living trust to total less than $100,000 at your death.

Must I transfer all of my assets into the living trust?

No, but to avoid probate and achieve your objectives, you will want to transfer all of your large assets into the living trust. Only those assets placed into the trust avoid probate. Normally, personal checking accounts and automobiles are not transferred into the living trust.

Does a living trust make sense for a single person?

Yes, a living trust is just as effective for a single person as it is for a married individual. This includes widows, widowers, single men, and single women.

Does a living trust make sense for an estate less than $1.5 million?

Yes, an individual can still avoid the problems of probate. On an estate valued at $300,000, probate fees can be as high as $18,000 or more. Living trusts can be set up for any size estate.

Is the living trust a recent idea?

No, it has been in existence for hundreds of years.

Does the living trust prevent me from borrowing on assets within the trust?

No, the trust does not restrict your rights to borrow in any way, although the lenders will want to examine a copy of the trust documents.

Why didn't my attorney tell me about the living trust?

Most attorneys are not knowledgeable about living trusts. You also may have told your attorney that you were interested in a will, a less expensive instrument.

Why doesn't everyone have a living trust?

The majority of people don't have the knowledge or information about living trusts. People often don't plan for the future and hesitate to discuss what happens at death.

Is a living trust revocable or irrevocable?

A living trust can be either revocable or irrevocable. Revocable means you can cancel or change its terms. Irrevocable means it cannot be changed.

What rights does the surviving spouse have in living trust assets?

If the surviving spouse is the trustee in a joint living trust, he/she has the right to sell, buy, or transfer any of the living trust's assets. The surviving spouse has the freedom to do whatever he/she sees fit.

How will my living trust avoid probate?

A revocable living trust is designed to ensure your estate does not require court supervised probate. Probate is the process in which the court supervises the distribution of your estate after death. You select a trustee to succeed you after your death. Your Declaration of Trust states your desires. The trustee you select to carry out your desires can transfer your assets to your beneficiaries immediately, without having to wait for court direction.

Who can be a trustee?

During your lifetime you are your own trustee. You may wish to select a professional trustee to manage your assets in trust. However, a professional trustee, such as a bank, trust company, or title company is not required by law. Normally, persons with living trusts act as their own trustees. However, someone with a large estate who does not want the headaches of managing certain assets may choose to contract with a professional trustee or another person to manage his or her affairs. In some cases, persons who travel outside the country a good deal of the time hire professional trustees to make sure their affairs are handled according to their needs and desires. Like anything else, professional trustees can also be costly. More importantly, trustees who handle your affairs after death need clear direction from you to enable them to distribute your estate correctly. In your trust package, great care should be taken to ensure that your trustees have the authority to distribute your estate as well as to protect against anyone who may wish to alter your intentions.

What are settlors, trustees, and beneficiaries?

By creating your living trust, you are a settlor (creator of the trust). As stated above, you are normally the trustee (boss of the trust) of your own estate during your lifetime. Likewise, during your lifetime you are also the beneficiary.

If I am settlor, trustee, and beneficiary, is there really a living trust created?

Certainly. A living trust results by designating a successor trustee who will administer your estate according to your wishes after death. You can think of your trust as a substitute for a will. A will does not take effect until after your death and it requires probate by the court. A living trust takes immediate effect when you fund it with your assets (transfer assets to your trust); it then becomes a dynamic instrument for your personal estate plan.

What is the difference between a funded and unfunded living trust?

Your living trust will not take effect until you execute it by signing all of the necessary papers, obtaining witness signatures, and getting it notarized (depending on your specific state's requirements). However, even then your trust will remain unfunded until you transfer your assets into it. The trust must own something, so it's pointless to do all the initial trust paperwork and then get lazy about completing the task of transferring assets into your trust (with a little more paperwork).

What assets are most important to place into my living trust?

You want your trust to own as many of your major assets as possible. Examples of trust assets include: real estate, brokerage accounts, stocks and securities, certain bank accounts (not your day-to-day accounts), Treasury bills and bonds, business interests, partnerships, royalties, copyrights, intellectual property (example: patents), boats, heirlooms, valuable collections, antiques, household furnishings and goods, jewelry, and so on. You can transfer as many assets as you want to your trust.

How do I transfer assets into the living trust?

It is simple to transfer your assets into your trust. For example, you can transfer your real property from your current ownership to your trust with a deed. The law does not consider such a transfer to be a sale for the purpose of reassessing your property for tax purposes. In addition, you may contact your bank or other institution where you hold assets and direct them to rename your assets and accounts as belonging to your trust. Your trust is considered funded after your assets are transferred to it. For assets that do not have a title to them, such as a family heirloom or valuable baseball card collection, you list those assets in the schedule of the trust and you create an Assignment of Interest document that officially transfers the asset into the living trust.

I owe money on some assets, such as my house. I have a mortgage. Can I still place it in my trust?

Yes. If you still owe money on an asset you want to place into your living trust, such as a house, boat, car, or large-ticket item, you can still transfer the asset and your beneficiary will inherit the debt as well (the mortgage or loan).

What assets do I keep out of my living trust?

You want your living trust to own most of your major assets. Any assets that are not included in your living trust will get poured into it at your death through the pour over will, but those assets may be subject to probate. Assets you may not want to include in your trust during your life include the following:

- Small assets you buy and sell frequently or that you don't intend to have forever
- Your personal bank accounts that you use frequently, such as a checking and savings account from which you draw money

- Small items that would be too cumbersome to list and that can be handled by your pour over will

- Insurance policies, including life insurance, and annuities with named beneficiaries

- Individual Retirement Accounts (IRAs, 401(k)s, and profit-sharing plans)

- Pay-on-death bank accounts

What do I do to bequeath particular assets to particular persons following my death?

In a revocable living trust, you can specify, at the creation of your trust, that you wish certain assets to go to certain persons or organizations upon your death. As a working document, your trust allows you to designate in your trust just what your desires are. The Trust Instructions of your trust are included in your trust package and they remain with your trust as a permanent part of your trust administration.

Can I ever change my mind?

Yes. You have complete control over your revocable living trust and all the property you transfer to it. You can:

1. Sell, mortgage, or give away property in the trust
2. Put ownership of the trust property back in your own name
3. Add property to the trust
4. Change the beneficiaries
5. Name a different successor trustee
6. Revoke the trust completely

If you are married and create the trust together, both spouses must consent to changes, although either of you can revoke the trust entirely.

How do I change my trust?

For major changes to your trust, you create an Amendment that is signed, witnessed, and may have to be notarized in your state. You can generally change items in your Trust Instructions without making formal amendments, because your Trust Instructions make up part of the documents outside of your actual trust document, as they comprise the personal instructions you leave for your successor trustee. If, however, you need to change anything in the legal body of your living trust, you will need to make formal amendments. If you make massive changes, you may want to create new trust documents. Adding and removing assets to and from the trust does not require new trust documents. Consult a professional if you are unsure whether you should use amendments or recreate your entire living trust document.

What is a pour over will?

Since it is impractical to include everything you own in your trust by deed, account, or name, you include in your package a simple pour over will. Unlike the normal Last Will and Testament you may be accustomed to, the pour over will simply directs your named executor to pour over any assets that you failed to include in your trust for distribution under the terms of your living trust. Typically, a conscientious trustee of his or her trust will have already transferred all major assets into the living trust so that no probate is necessary when transferring the remaining assets. You may wish to think of the pour over will as a housekeeping implement for your estate.

What does a power of attorney for finances accomplish?

When you create a living trust, a legal entity is established for the maintenance and care of your estate and assets. In the event that you leave the country or become incapacitated, the durable power of attorney for finances allows you to designate an individual to act on your behalf in managing your affairs, usually on a temporary basis. In an extreme example, such as an incapacity, a durable power of attorney will enable your designee to transfer many of the remaining assets to your trust. You typically want to have two durable powers of attorney— one for financial decisions and one for healthcare decisions.

What does a durable power of attorney for healthcare decision mean?

As an option, you may choose to include a healthcare power of attorney in your trust package. This allows a person of your choice to make medical decisions in the event you are physically unable to make decisions or give consent to treatment yourself.

Will my living trust avoid taxes?

No! However, different taxes can have different results depending on the size of the estate and the circumstances existing at the time of your death. For example, if you have income-producing property in your trust, during your lifetime you will be taxed on the income in the same manner as if it were property held by you without a trust. If you have a particularly large estate, it may be helpful to consult with an estate planner or CPA to maximize your estate and to avoid the untimely payment of taxes. Your living trust is an important tool in the overall estate plan.

How do I name my living trust?

Although you can get creative, the best way to name a living trust is to use your full legal name and include the date (as UTD for "under trust dated") when you first signed it. Examples:

- The Ernest Hemingway Living Trust, UTD January 14, 1943; Ernest Hemingway, Trustee.
- The Ira and Linda Distenfield Living Trust, UTD June 22, 1995; Ira Distenfield and Linda Distenfield, Settlors and Cotrustees.

How old must a child be in order to be a successor trustee?

The minimum age for a successor trustee is 18 years.

Questions about the AB Living Trust

What's the difference between a joint living trust and an AB joint trust?

An AB joint living trust protects monies in the estate to a greater extent than a generic joint trust. When a married couple uses an AB trust, theoretically it's as if they are setting up two trusts under one umbrella (see question below; the AB trust is a single entity). At the death of the first spouse, the main trust splits into two—the A and the B trust. The B trust becomes the owner of the deceased's property and the A trust remains the surviving spouse's trust. The B trust becomes irrevocable at the death of the first spouse, but the surviving spouse can use the B trust for the rest of his or her life. This, thus, creates a life estate for the surviving spouse. At the second spouse's death, both trusts' contents get distributed to their final beneficiaries, usually the couple's children. From a tax-savings standpoint, the AB trust allows both spouses to claim their personal exemption because the trusts remain separate. Under a basic joint living trust, on the other hand, at the death of the first spouse, those assets, if they go to the surviving spouse using the unlimited marital deduction, saddle the surviving spouse's trust with so much sudden wealth that at the second spouse's death, he or she has a greater likelihood of having to pay estate tax.

Is an AB trust actually two different trusts?

An AB trust is one trust while both spouses are living and even after a spouse dies. The terms trust A and trust B are used to differentiate between the decedent's share of the assets (trust B) and the survivor's share of the assets (trust A). Only at the death of the first spouse does the distinction between the A part of the AB trust and the B part have any significance. Other than the A and B parts, which are used to apportion assets, the living trust is a single entity. Assets identified as being in the B trust are thereafter insulated from further estate taxes.

Is there any way to cancel the irrevocable B trust once in effect?

No. However, the surviving spouse may spend all the income and principle of the B trust for maintenance, education, support, and health. So, in essence, the surviving spouse may utilize the entire B trust assets.

What are the beneficial rights of the surviving spouse to the decendent's B trust?

The surviving spouse is the beneficiary of the decedent's B trust (and the decedent's C trust, where appropriate). The tax code specifically provides that the surviving spouse has three rights:

- The right to all of the income
- The right to all of the principal that is necessary to maintain the same standard of living as before the decedent passed away
- The right to $5,000 or 5 percent of the assets (in the B trust only), whichever is greater— once a year for any reason

These three rights in effect give the surviving spouse the right to use the funds in the decedent's B and C trusts without restriction. However, the one thing that the surviving spouse cannot do is change the beneficiaries designated in the decedent's B and C trusts or jeopardize the beneficiaries' rights to the assets in the decedent's B and C trusts. Such a restriction is very appropriate when a husband and wife have been married before and each have children from former marriages. For example, the surviving spouse may not reach into the B and/or C trust, take out $100,000, go to Las Vegas, and then gamble away the money. The decedent's children have a right to say, "Mother, you effectively took that $100,000 from your side—the Surivivor's A trust." The surviving spouse also does not have the right to reach into the decedent's B and C trusts, take out funds, and move them to the A trust so that, at the death of the surviving spouse, a greater share of the estate goes to the heirs of the surviving spouse.

What are the rights of the surviving spouse to the assets in trust A?

Since the assets in the survivor's trust A are the assets of the surviving spouse, the surviving spouse may do anything with these assets, including removing the assets and canceling the trust. Trust A remains revocable at the death of the first spouse, whereas trust B becomes irrevocable.

What is a C trust?

A married couple with considerable assets (more than $2 million worth) can set up an AB trust with an additional C trust. The C trust, which is also called a Q-TIP trust (for Qualified Terminal Interest Property), is a way to put off paying any estate taxes until after the second spouse dies. It's a legal instrument that prevents a surviving spouse from having to any pay taxes due on the deceased's B trust at the spouse's death. Payment is postponed until after the second spouse dies, but the second spouse has full use of those assets as a life estate until death.

Taxes

What is the death tax and will it affect my estate upon my death?

The death tax is an estate tax levied on estates worth more than a certain amount. In 2005, that amount is $1.5 million. In 2006 through 2008, the federal estate tax exemption is $2 million. The vast majority of American families do not have enough money at their death to require payment of death or estate taxes. Repealing this death tax is a hotly contested issue today, as Congress has passed changes to the tax laws that suspend all death taxes for the year 2010. This is likely to change again.

States can also impose death taxes in the form of an inheritance or pick-up tax. Generally, estate taxes are taxes imposed on property as it transfers from the dead to the living, so they are essentially transfer taxes. Because taxes are only levied on the property owned at the time of death, estate planning includes techniques to transfer legal ownership of property while you are alive to minimize the amount of property owned at your death and, thus, reduce that amount of taxes owed.

What taxes affect my estate at my death? What taxes concern me and my family?

Four categories of taxes are relevant to you and your estate: the federal estate or death tax; any pick-up, inheritance, or state death tax; the gift taxes; and income tax. Death taxes are imposed on the transfer of wealth at the time of death or in anticipation of death (transfers made two years prior to death). Some states impose two types of death taxes: inheritance and estate. Some states also have gift taxes, which are closely related to death taxes. Inheritance taxes are state taxes on the right to inherit. Most all of these taxes are paid out of the estate—not by family members or beneficiaries.

Will I lose any of my income tax deductions by placing my assets in a living trust?

No. You do not lose tax deductions by placing your assets in a living trust. A living trust is invisible as far as income is concerned. A revocable living trust has absolutely no impact upon income taxes from either an income or expense viewpoint. With a living trust, you continue to file your Form 1040 Individual Income Tax Return, as you always have in the past.

If I put my home in a living trust, can I still deduct my mortgage interest?

Yes. Since a revocable living trust has no impact upon income taxes and since you are still in control of your assets, you continue to file your income and expenses—including your mortgage interest—on your Form 1040 income tax return, as you have done in the past.

Do I need a federal tax number for the trust?

No. A federal tax number is not needed for a trust for a married couple until one of the settlors (trustors) dies, or both settlors resign as trustees or become incompetent. For a trust for a single person, a federal tax number will be required after the settlor dies.

I heard that Congress has changed the tax rules. What does that mean and how does it affect me?

Congress changes the rules occasionally, so you must plan to the best of your ability today with today's tax rules. One cannot predict what changes will occur in the future. Congress last made major changes in 2001, when it repealed the federal estate tax by increasing the exemption rule (what you can keep without being taxed) on a scale. In the 2010, the estate tax will be zero. The new rules also changed the top-rate estate tax rate (the percentage that rich people owe) as well as the gift tax rate. Whether or not the federal estate tax rides off into the sunset and never returns is unclear. The vast majority of American families, however, are not affected by the federal estate tax because they don't own enough to meet the threshold at which taxes are due.

What are gift taxes? If I leave money to my daughter, will I be taxed?

You are allowed to give gifts up to a certain value in your lifetime to whomever you want without being taxed. Currently, you have a $1 million lifetime limit. Once you go over that limit, you are taxed on the overage, or how much you go over the $1 million. Example: You give gifts that total $1.2 million in your lifetime. You owe a gift tax on that $200,000. You also have an annual limit of $11,000 to the same person in the same year, a limit that may change in the future depending on the cost of living. Couples can give $22,000 a year without being taxed. (See a tax advisor for more details.)

Some gifts are never taxed, such as gifts that pay for medical or educational expenses, gifts to your spouse, gifts to tax-exempt charities, and gifts to a political organization.

Can I file a joint tax return in the year my spouse dies?

Yes. In fact, you may find a few tax breaks in the tax code as the surviving spouse. Consult with your tax advisor about these benefits.

What is the unlimited marital deduction?

The unlimited marital deduction is the law (in the Tax Code) that says a spouse can leave any amount of property to the surviving spouse free of estate tax—no matter how much that property is worth.

Taxes confuse me. I don't understand how they work or what I can to do minimize taxes when I plan my estate. What can I do?

Seek the advice of a good tax specialist, such as your accountant, financial or estate planner, or an attorney who can explain things to you in language that you can understand. Before paying for any advice or service, however, make sure the person has experience particularly in estate planning and your tax burdens given the options you have when planning your estate. Not all attorneys and accountants have knowledge or much experience in this field. Find someone who does.

Where can I find information about filing taxes?

Besides consulting with an accountant, for information about filing tax returns on an estate, call the Internal Revenue Service (IRS) and ask for Publication 559 (Survivors, Executors and Administrators), which outlines in detail a person's responsibilities regarding tax filing as a survivor or executor of an estate. It also offers information about tax benefits for survivors. You can also get access to other information on their web site at www.irs.gov, and download many forms. Other publications you may find helpful include Instructions for Form 706 and Federal Estate and Gift Taxes or Form 448. You can download all of these materials and access other essential information on the IRS's web site.

Odds and Ends to Estate Planning

What's the difference between an heir and a beneficiary?

An heir is someone who acquires property at the death of another, based on the rules of descent and distribution, namely, being the child, descendant, or other closest relative of the dearly departed. It also has come to mean anyone who takes (receives something) by the terms of the will. An heir cannot be determined until the moment of death of the person leaving the property, since a supposed beneficiary (heir apparent) might die first.

A beneficiary is a broad definition for any person or entity (like a charity) who is to receive assets or profits from an estate, a trust, an insurance policy, or any instrument in which there is distribution. Beneficiaries are named in wills and living trusts, whereas an heir might not be named but later receives a share of assets due to state laws of succession.

Where do I register my living trust documents?

The living trust document does not have to be registered anywhere, but some states do allow you to officially register it. At the death of the settlor(s), the only person who has a right to see the document is the successor trustee. It's up to you whether or not you want to register your living trust (and can in your state). It's also up to you whether or not you choose to show it to anyone during your life. You may want to share it with your successor trustee, but you do not have to share it with everyone named in the living trust.

The name of the living trust is submitted only to the IRS, in order to request a tax identification number for the trust at the death of the first spouse. You do not need to report the trust's name, however, to the IRS until you need that number to pay taxes on the trust.

What happens if my daughter divorces or remarries and changes her name?

One of the nice aspects of a properly written living trust is that your daughter's name does not make any difference. In your living trust, you identify your children as your children. No matter what name the children may go by in the future, they are still your children. However, it is always a good practice to update all pertinent information in your trust, including changes of names and new addresses and telephone numbers. This saves a successor trustee a lot of time in finding heirs and beneficiaries. Tracking them through several name changes and relocations can be difficult for the person trying to settle an estate or make distributions from a living trust. You can make these informal changes in your Trust Instructions by noting the name change and any other pertinent information, such as contact information and the name of her new spouse.

What's the difference between an administrator and a personal representative?

A personal representative is the same as an executor—the person you name to carry out your wishes in a will or living trust. In a living trust, your personal representative is usually your successor trustee (or your surviving spouse as cotrustee of your joint trust). When a court has to appoint someone to settle an estate because there was no will or living trust, the term administrator is used instead of executor. But the roles are the same.

How can I be sure that my executor or successor trustee does what I want him or her to do?

You will never know whether or not your executor carries out your wishes as you planned. But the nature of a will or living trust allows you to decide who gets to carry out your wishes. So, pick someone that you think is up to this task and whom you trust. Spouses who set up a joint living trust typically name each other as initial successor trustees, and they trust that each will carry out the other's wishes. Two or three children acting together as successor cotrustees can sometimes be better than only one child, particularly when there is a question about the proper way to handle various aspects of an estate. Successor cotrustees tend to monitor each other.

Does a pour over will have to be probated?

Probate is not necessarily required unless the assets that are subject to probate total more than a certain amount, usually set by state law. For example, an estate in California with assets that total less than $100,000 does not have to go through the formal probate process. But if they total more than $100,000, then a probate of the assets and an administration of the assets proceed.

How often should I review and/or amend my will or living trust?

Plan to review your will or living trust every five years or so as circumstances change. Your personal situation may change, such as the addition of children, a move to another state, the death of family members (beneficiaries), or the acquisition/selling of major assets. Other situations can affect your will or living trust, such as tax laws, and state or federal laws. You want your plan to be as up-to-date and reflect your current circumstances as much as possible.

Does my will or living trust remain valid in other states? What if I move?

Every state recognizes official wills and living trusts created in other states. However, if you move to a new state, it is wise to have a professional planner or tax specialist review your will or living trust to ensure that it meets your new state's laws. You should revise and amend your will or living trust according to your new state's laws. This will make it easier for your named executor (or successor trustee) to carry out your wishes easily at your death. Alternatively, you can visit a We The People store and we can help you bring your documents up to standard in the new state. At the least, you want to make sure your documents meet minimum state requirements.

What is a living will?

It is a document that lets your family members know what type of care you do or do not want to receive should you become incapacitated.

What is a power of attorney for healthcare?

A power of attorney for healthcare is a document that authorizes someone you name to act in accordance with your medical intentions.

What is a financial durable power of attorney?

It is a document that authorizes someone you name to act in accordance with your financial intentions.

What does durable power of attorney mean?

An agent (person) with durable power of attorney is someone who legally can make decisions for you on your behalf while you are alive. Documents that name an agent with durable power of attorney are separate documents that we include in our estate planning packages. You can name an agent for durable power of attorney for finances (making financial decisions on your behalf) and for healthcare (making healthcare decisions on your behalf). The same person can hold both powers of attorney. The word durable means that they can still make decisions for you in the event you become incapacitated (example: You get Alzheimer's). Note that agents with durable power of attorney have no powers once you are dead. They are alive when you are alive, and they are effectively dead (powerless) when you are dead.

I live in a community property state. How does that affect my estate planning?

If you live in one of the eight community property states, you must follow your state's system of marital ownership. Wisconsin also has similar laws, and if you sign a community property agreement in Alaska, you may as well consider yourself in a community property state. In these states, all property acquired during your marriage is considered 50/50 between you and your spouse. In other words, each of you owns one-half interest in all shared property. This affects how you can give away property in your estate planning. You cannot, for example, give away your spouse's half of shared property. Many laws, some of which are state-specific, revolve around community property, so seek advice from a professional who knows about this topic if you live in a community property state.

What is a living will?

States have different names for the document that says you do or do not want to be placed on life support or receive extreme medical care that technology can provide at the end of your life to prolong it. Some states call these documents health care directives. They are directed to the doctors, so your family members don't have to be put in the position of guessing whether or not you would have wanted to receive life support. This document allows you to make specific instructions about how your life ends (example: whether you would want to receive pain medication to the extent it hastens your death). In some states, this document may include your agent for durable power of attorney for medical care. In other states, the agent for durable power of attorney is named in a separate document.

Does a living trust protect my estate from nursing home costs?

No. Living trusts do protect your estate from the need for a probate and a conservatorship and may in some cases save taxes, but they cannot shield your estate from nursing home costs. For information on ways to protect your estate from nursing home costs, consult an estate planning specialist.

What is a conservatorship?

A conservatorship is a court process whereby the court appoints a person or entity to be in charge of your affairs if you are unable to do so.

CHAPTER 9

Estate Planning Terms

The following is an alphabetical list of terms you are likely to encounter during your estate planning process. Most of these terms have already been defined and described throughout the book. Others you may come across as you navigate your own particular state's planning customs and laws. These definitions are simplified. Refer to the chapters in this book for more detailed explanations and examples.

Abatement. When there are not enough probate assets to satisfy all bequests in the will. If not addressed in the will, statutory law dictates the priority order in which bequests will be reduced or eliminated to make up the difference.

AB Trust. A special kind of joint (mutual) trust for a couple who wants to minimize estate taxes. The AB trust is one legal entity that splits into two trusts at the death of the first spouse. The surviving spouse can use the deceased spouse's trust assets for the rest of his or her life, but cannot change the names of the deceased spouse's final beneficiaries. At the death of the second spouse, the assets in both the A trust and B trust go to each of their final beneficiaries.

Ademption. When a bequeathed asset is no longer in the estate. The beneficiary may have received the bequest during the deceased's lifetime, or if it was given or sold to someone else before the death, the beneficiary gets nothing.

Administration of Estate. Supervision of a decedent's estate by an executor/administrator and the court.

Administrator. One given the authority to settle the estate of the decedent. Also called an executor or personal representative. The person given the authority to settle your estate at your death. The term administratrix can also be used interchangeably. Both these words usually refer to court-appointed people when there is no will specifically stating someone.

Adult. A person 18 years of age or older.

Affidavit. A document that proves something; a sworn statement in writing that is signed under oath and in the presence of a notary public. An *affidavit of trust* proves your trust document exists.

Affidavit of Trust. This is the document in your living trust that is the evidence of your living trust. It's proof that your trust exists. Sometimes called an abstract of trust or certification of trust, your affidavit of trust is a summary of your trust that you can show to anyone who requests proof of your trust. For example, a bank may want to see your trust documents when you transfer titles of accounts; you may not want to show the entire living trust to them, and the affidavit of trust may satisfy the bank's request. States may have different versions of an affidavit of trust, which take state laws into consideration. Some states have laws that stipulate what must be included on these documents to be official.

Amendment. A change or alteration to a document.

Annuity. A type of policy that pays an amount of money (also called an annuity) yearly or at other regular intervals. Annuities are sometimes referred to as upsidedown life insurance policies because they insure against the risk of living too long. Payments are made periodically during one's lifetime (or for a defined period of time).

Assets. Everything you own, including real estate and personal possessions. Assets and property are interchangeable words.

Assignment. Giving your interest to someone/something else. When you fund your trust by transferring property into it, you may have to use Notices of Assignment that officially transfer ownership of your interest in property to the trust.

Basis. The price paid for property. This term is related to taxes. It has to do with how much a piece of property is worth and takes into consideration any profit or loss made on the property upon its sale.

Beneficiary. One entitled to profit, benefit, or advantage from a contract or estate. A person who receives any assets from a will or living trust is a beneficiary. There are many types of beneficiaries (example: lifetime beneficiaries, primary beneficiaries, residuary beneficiaries). An *alternate beneficiary* is someone who receives any assets as a result of the primary beneficiary's death.

Bequeath. The act of giving any asset, especially through the terms of a will. The gift bequeathed is called the *bequest.*

Bond. A written guaranty or pledge that is purchased from a bonding company (usually an insurance firm) or by an individual as security (called a bondsman) to guarantee some form of performance by an individual. A bond guarantees that an executor, for example, will not steal or mismanage funds from a will or living trust. If the executor does not carry out his or her responsibilities (both legal and ethical) and abuses his or her powers as executor, the bond will help pay for any injuries suffered by anyone as a result. Example: An executor uses money from an estate to take a vacation to Tahiti instead of giving that money to a named beneficiary. The bonding company will replace that money, up to a certain limit.

Bypass Trust. Another term for the AB living trust. Also called the *marital bypass trust.*

Capital Gains. The difference between the sale price and the original cost (plus improvements) of property. Example: You buy a house in 1967 for $40,000 and you sell it in 2005 for $650,000. Your capital gain is $610,000, which is subject to the capital gains tax.

Charitable Remainder Trust (CRT). A type of trust set up that designates a charity as the final beneficiary but while you are alive you receive income from the trust and control it. This type of trust has tax-saving advantages.

Children's Trust. A type of trust set up for a child who cannot manage assets until a certain age. Children's Trusts can be set up within a living trust.

Codicil. A written document or amendment to a will.

Common Law Marriage. A state recognition of marriage if a couple has lived together for a certain period of time and intends to marry officially. Only a few states recognize common law marriages.

Common Law States. All the states except for the community property states.

Community Property. A form of property ownership between a husband and wife—recognized in only a few states: Arizona, California, Idaho, Louisiana, Nevada, New Mexico, Texas, Washington, and Wisconsin. You can also sign a community property agreement in Alaska. Specific community property laws differ greatly among the states, but they all share a defining feature: All property acquired during the marriage by either spouse is automatically split, so that each spouse owns a separate, undivided one-half interest.

Conservator. A person appointed to act on behalf of another person.

Conservatorship. A formal proceeding in which the court appoints a person to act on behalf of another in business and/or personal matters.

Contingent Beneficiary. One entitled to profit from a contract or estate only upon the occurrence of a specific event; usually one who receives assets at the death of the primary or lifetime beneficiary.

Convey. To transfer. Example: You convey title to property from you to your living trust.

Corpus. Principal assets that may earn income.

Creditor. A person or company to whom you owe money. Creditors include lenders on homes and other large assets.

Crummay Powers. The power of a beneficiary of a life insurance trust to demand immediate ownership of a policy, thus qualifying the gift as a present interest which may be excluded from gift taxes.

Custodian. Someone who is named to take care of assets going to a beneficiary (usually a child) who is not old enough to manage those assets. In states that enforce the Uniform Transfers to Minor Act, custodians are the people who manage the property until the minor reaches the age at which state law says he or she can receive the property. In some states, one can specify at which age the assets are to be received. Custodians act like trustees over the minor's assets and can usually use the assets toward the health, education, and support of the minor.

Death Taxes. Another term for the federal estate tax. Some states also impose death taxes as well as inheritance taxes.

Debtor. A person who owes money.

Deceased Spouse. A spouse who has died. Deceased spouse usually refers to the first spouse to die.

Decedent. A deceased (dead) person.

Deed. The legal document that transfers ownership of real property. A deed transfers the title that records that ownership. See *warranty deed* and *quit claim* and *grant deed.*

Deed of Trust or **Mortgage.** A document (record) showing debt tied to property. See *mortgage.*

Descendants. Persons who follow a decedent in line of descent.

Escheat. The right of the state to succeed to property (real or personal) where there is no heir.

Estate. The total of your assets and liabilities, real and personal property.

Estate Tax. A tax levied on the value of an estate. There are federal and sometimes state death taxes, often referred to as inheritance taxes. Estate tax is a federal tax on the transfer of a dead person's assets to the heirs and beneficiaries. Although technically a transfer tax, it is based on the amount in the decedent's estate (including distribution from a trust at the death) and can include insurance proceeds. Certain exemptions apply to the estate tax.

Executor. The person you name in your will to carry out your wishes at your death and distribute your assets. This person is typically a friend, relative, bank, or trust company.

Failure to Issue. To die without lineal descendants.

Fiduciary. A person acting for another person. From the Latin *fiducia,* meaning "trust." A person (or a business, like a bank or stock brokerage) who has the power and obligation to act for another (often called the beneficiary) under circumstances that require total trust, good faith, and honesty. Examples of fiduciaries: trustee of a trust, business advisors, attorneys, guardians, administrators of estates, real estate agents, bankers, stockbrokers, title companies, or anyone who undertakes to assist someone who places complete confidence and trust in that person or company.

Funding a Trust. Transferring legal ownership of property to a trust. You name your trust as owner of that property. A living trust is meaningless unless it owns at least one asset.

Generation-Skipping Trust (GST). An irrevocable arrangement that provides income only, not access to trust principal, to the settlor or the settlor's spouse and/or children. It terminates when all have reached a specified age or died, with trust principal then distributed to grandchildren or grandnieces and nephews (hence, generation-*skipping* trust). This kind of trust has some tax-saving advantages.

Gift. Any property given to a person or organization, either during one's lifetime or by will or by living trust at one's death.

Gift Tax. A tax levied on gifts of property to supplement estate and inheritance tax. Exemptions and exceptions to the tax may apply.

Grant Deed. The document that transfers title to real property or a real property interest from one party (grantor) to another (grantee). See also *quit claim* and *warranty deed.*

Grantor. A person who creates a living trust. Another term for *trustor* and *settlor.*

Guardian. A person named in a will or living trust to care for minor children in the event the legal parent dies or is no longer able to care for the minors.

Heir. One who inherits property. A person entitled to receive property by state intestacy laws if the deceased did not make arrangements for distributing property before death.

Heir Apparent. One who is sure to succeed to the estate if he or she survives the ancestor.

Heir Testamentary. One to whom property is left by will.

Heredity Succession. Title by descent.

Holographic Will. A will written, signed, and dated entirely in the handwriting of the creator without any witnesses necessarily. Also called *holographic will* in some states.

Incapacity. The condition or state of being incapable of handling one's own affairs, either by mental or physical inability.

Inchoate Interest. An interest that has not vested; an expectancy to receive an interest in an estate at some future time.

Income. Value earned by principal assets. Example: rental income from rental properties; dividends from investments.

Inherit. To receive property from someone who dies.

Inheritance Tax. A tax levied on the recipients of gifts from an estate. These taxes are imposed by some states (and sometimes referred to as state death or estate taxes), but they are typically paid out of the estate (and not by the beneficiaries). Inheritance taxes are taxes imposed on property received by inheritors.

Instrument. Another term for document, particularly in a legal sense.

***Inter Vivos* Trust.** Another term for a living trust. *Inter vivos* means "within one's life" or "between the living" in Latin.

Intestate. Dying without a valid will.

Intestate Succession. The process of distributing property based on the relationship between the deceased and his or her survivors. If a person dies without a will or without specifying how his or her estate should get distributed, the laws of the state dictate how that property gets passed down to survivors. Those closest to the deceased, such as the spouse and children, get a greater share. Parents of the deceased, siblings, nieces, nephews, and other next-of-kin get their share on a sliding scale. State laws that govern intestate succession are also called the *laws of intestacy*. They are also used when an heir is omitted from a will.

Irrevocable Trust. A trust that cannot be changed or canceled.

Issue. Lineal descendants.

Joint Tenancy. A holding of property by several persons in such a way that any one of them can act as owner of the whole and take the property by survivorship. When one owner dies, the remaining joint tenants automatically become owners of the deceased owner's share. Joint tenant interest in property avoids probate. So when a joint tenant dies, his or her share does not have to go through probate—it goes directly to the other joint tenant(s).

Kin. Related by blood.

Lapse. When the beneficiary dies after the testator but before the execution of the will, his or her bequest lapses. The will may have named a contingent beneficiary or stipulate that the property may become part of the residue and remainder clause. Or if neither exists, it will be distributed according to the state's intestacy laws.

Last Will and Testament. An instrument (legal document) whereby one makes a disposition (distribution) of his or her property to take effect after his or her death.

Lawful Heirs. Those designated by law to take by descent.

Lawful Issue. Descendants.

Legal Heirs. Next of kin.

Legatee. One to whom property is left by will.

Letter of Attorney. Another term for power of attorney.

Letter of Instruction. An informal document written in addition to a formal will that gives specific instructions about one's estate, such as where items are located, how one wants to be buried, or any information not described in the will.

Letters of Authority. Letters issued by a court empowering the executor of a will to act. Also referred to as letters of testamentary.

Letters of Testamentary. Letters issued by a court empowering an executor of a will to act. Also referred to as letters of authority.

Life Estate. An interest in property whose duration is measured by the life of a person.

Life Insurance Trust. Legal entities you create for owning life insurance you previously owned and which become operational during your lifetime. These types of trusts help minimize estate taxes paid on the proceeds of such a policy at your death.

Life Interest. An interest in property that is to terminate at the death of the holder of the interest or some other designated person.

Lineal Decedents. Individuals related by blood following a line of descent from generation to generation.

Liquid Assets. Assets that can be turned into cold, hard cash quickly. Cash itself is a liquid asset.

Living Trust. A document that distributes your estate after death and avoids the probate process. A living trust is set up while you are alive and remains under your control until your death. Also called an *inter vivos* trust. Creators of living trusts are called the settlors, grantors, and trustors. They are also lifetime beneficiaries of their living trusts.

Living Will. A document that formally expresses your wishes to forgo extraordinary medical treatment when you become terminally ill.

Marital Deduction. Exempts from the estate tax all property passing from one spouse to the other by reason of gift or death. The unlimited marital deduction allows property to pass from one spouse to the other tax free, no matter how much the property is worth. If the spouse receiving the property is not a U.S. citizen, certain restrictions may apply.

Minor. A person under legal age. In most states, a minor is legally defined as anyone under the age of 18.

Mortgage. A document that attaches a piece of property to a debt as security (collateral) for payment of the debt. Example: You buy a house and borrow money from a lender to make the purchase. The lender uses the house as security for the loan. If you don't pay back that loan, the lender can seize the property. Mortgages may have different names in different states, such as a *trust deed* or *deed of trust.* (Fourteen states use a deed of trust [or trust deed] as a mortgage. These states include: California, Illinois, Texas, Virginia, Colorado, Georgia, Alaska, Arizona, Idaho, Mississippi, Missouri, Montana, North Carolina, and West Virginia. Under the deed of trust system, title is technically given to a trustee to hold for the lender, who is called a beneficiary.)

Motion. A document asking the court do something. Example: You file a motion to the probate court asking it to appoint an administrator to an estate.

Net Estate. The net value of an estate, or the value of the gross estate minus debts and liabilities. The net estate is calculated by taking the value of all assets and subtracting all debts of the person who died, including funeral costs, expenses of administering the estate, and any other allowable deductions. The federal estate tax (and/or state inheritance tax where it exists) is then based on the net estate value.

Partnership Agreement. Written agreement laying out the terms of the relationship.

Pay-on-death Account. An account, usually a bank account, that names a beneficiary to receive the assets in the account when the account's owner dies. Pay-on-death accounts avoid probate.

Perfect Trust. An executed trust, signed by the settlor(s).

Personal Property. All assets except for real estate (land and buildings attached to land). Personal property includes personal possessions, bank accounts, cash, insurance policies, a small business, jewelry, pets, collections, heirlooms, and so on.

Personal Representative. Another term for executor.

Pour Over Will. Instrument that provides that property not previously transferred into a trust is to be transferred at the death of the settlor.

Power of Attorney. Giving someone else the authority to act on your behalf. A *durable power of attorney* gives someone else the authority to act on your behalf even if you become incapacitated.

Powers of Appointment. Power vested in an individual to make decisions affecting disposition and distribution of assets.

Prenuptial Agreement. Setting out the terms of the division of assets and debts and the management of property during marriage.

Pretermitted Heir. The child of a person who has written a will in which the child is not left anything and is not mentioned at all. After the death of the parent, a pretermitted heir has the right to demand the share he or she would have received as an heir under the laws of distribution and descent.

Principal. Another term for trust corpus. Property owned by the trust, particularly assets of value that earn income.

Probate. The court-supervised process by which assets are distributed when someone dies and debts and taxes are paid. Also, the process of proving a will.

Probate Assets. Any and all assets that must go through probate. Assets owned by a living trust do not normally have to go through probate. Assets jointly owned normally do not have to go through probate. But assets outside of a living trust or that are not jointly owned usually go through probate and are thus called probate assets.

Probate Court. Court established for the administration of the estate of decedents and the control of the adoption and guardianship of minors.

Property. Everything you own, both real and personal. This term is interchangeable with *assets*.

Q-Tip Trust. A type of trust that allows a surviving spouse to delay payment of estate taxes on the deceased spouse's estate until he or she dies as well. Q-Tip is short for qualified terminal interest property, or the C Trust.

Quit Claim. A real property deed that transfers (conveys) only that interest in the property in which the grantor has title. Commonly used in transfers of title or interests in title. Quit claim deeds are also used to clear up questions of full title when a person has a possible but unknown interest in the property. Quit claims are used in some states to transfer ownership of real property, but quit claims alone do not necessarily guarantee good title. States can also use *warranty deeds* or *grant deeds* to transfer (and warranty) titles.

Real Property. Land, real estate.

Recording. The process of filing a copy of a deed with the county land records office. By recording your deed with the County Recorders or Recorders of Deeds, you create a public record of who or what owns property.

Remainder. Property that remains after the initial distribution of an estate.

Remainderman. Persons designated to receive property following the initial distribution of the estate.

Residue. What remains in an estate after all specific gifts (bequeaths) have been made. A residuary beneficiary is one who receives any assets from an estate—by a will or trust—otherwise not given away to someone else.

Revocable Trust. A trust in which a contingent interest is given to another and in which the settlor retains a present interest, ownership, and control. A revocable trust can be changed or canceled.

Right of Survivorship. The right of a survivor to take ownership of a deceased's property. In terms of joint tenancy, the right of a surviving joint tenant to take ownership of a deceased joint tenant's share of the property. A couple can also own community property with right of survivorship, which means that at the death of one spouse, the surviving spouse automatically owns the deceased spouse's half of the shared property.

Sensitive Trustee. A trustee or successor trustee who is also a beneficiary.

Separate Property. Property owned by one spouse only. In community property states, separate property is all property not considered community property. Example: A husband who comes into a marriage with previously owned assets, such as an heirloom or interest in a business. Those assets are separately owned property.

Settlor. Trustor, one who creates a trust. Also called a *grantor.*

Sprinkling Power. The power vested in a trustee to distribute income to others in a discretionary manner. A sprinkling trust authorizes the trustee to decide how to distribute trust income or principal among different beneficiaries.

Stepped-up Basis. A tax issue that relates to how property gets valued for tax purposes. Under current law, inherited property gets stepped up to the market value at the time of death, so if the asset is sold right away, there are fewer (or no) capital gains.

Succession. The taking of property by inheritance or will or by operation of law.

Successor Trustee. Individual who succeeds to the power to manage trust assets. A successor trustee can also be a company, firm, or institution.

Surviving Spouse. The spouse who outlives his or her spouse. The second spouse to die.

Survivor. A person who outlives another.

Taking Against the Will. All states have some form of a family protection allowance, which guarantees the surviving spouse (and sometimes children) gets a certain share of a deceased spouse's estate. If a surviving spouse chooses to take the statutory share instead of accepting what he or she would inherit through the deceased spouse's will, the surviving spouse is taking against the will.

Taxable Estate. The property subject to taxation.

Tenancy by the Entirety. A holding of property similar to joint tenancy, but for married couples only. If you hold property in tenancy by the entirety, you cannot transfer your portion of the property without your spouse's consent, whereas with joint tenancy you can. Upon your death, your portion of the property goes to your surviving spouse. Tenancy by the entirety is available in only a handful of states.

Tenancy in Common. Ownership by more than one person in such a way that each owns an individual share. People who own property by tenancy in common can do whatever they want to their share by sale, gift, will, or trust. At a co-owner's death, his or her share can go to any named beneficiaries—and not to the other co-owners.

Testamentary Trust. A trust created by the terms of a will. A testamentary trust differs from a living trust, which comes into being during the lifetime of the creator of the trust, usually from the time the declaration of trust is signed. Example: In your will you direct a trust to commence at your death to hold the assets for your children until they reach a certain age.

Testate. Dying with a valid will or other valid instrument for transferring property.

Testator. A person who dies leaving a valid will. He or she is said to have died testate.

Title. A document that proves ownership of property, real or personal.

Totten Trust. Another term for a pay-on-death account.

Trust. A right of property (real or personal) held by one party for the benefit of another. A legal arrangement whereby one party (the trustee) controls property given by another party (the settlor, grantor, or trustor) for the benefit of a third party (the beneficiary). An entity created to hold assets for the benefit of certain persons or entities.

Trustee. One appointed to manage a trust. A trustee can be a person, institution, or firm.

Trustor. One who creates the trust; the grantor, settlor.

Unified Credit. The total credit provided by law that is free of estate taxation.

Uniform Simultaneous Death Act (USDA). When there is no sufficient evidence that persons have died otherwise than simultaneously, it is presumed that each died before the other for determining inheritance.

Uniform Transfers to Minors Act (UTMA). A law imposed in most states that provides a method for transferring property to minors and managing that property until the minor reaches a certain age. States that apply the UTMA set their own age at which a minor can receive property outright. Until the minor reaches that age, a custodian must be appointed to manage those assets.

Vested. An unconditional right to or interest in property.

Warranty Deed. A deed to real property that guarantees that the seller owns clear title, which can be transferred (conveyed). A *grant deed* generally is a warranty deed, while a *quit claim deed* is not.

Will. A statement that spells out your wishes at your death, specifically your desires about the distribution of your assets. Also called a *Last Will and Testament.* To be valid the will must be signed by the person who made it (testator), dated (but an incorrect date will not invalidate the will), and witnessed by two people (except in Vermont, which requires three). In some states the witnesses must be disinterested, or in some states, a gift to a witness is void but the will is valid. There are many types of wills: *holographic wills* are hand-written; *noncupative wills* are spoken (oral) wills, and so on.

Last Will and
Testament Samples

LAST WILL AND TESTAMENT
OF
GREGORY BROWN

I, GREGORY BROWN, of San Luis Obispo County, being of lawful age, sound mind and memory, and under no restraint, do publish this, my Last Will and Testament, and revoke all other wills and codicils heretofore made by me.

I am married to CAROLINE BROWN. I am the father of CORY BROWN.

ARTICLE 1

1.01 All expenses, fees, costs, and taxes related to this estate shall be paid from the probate estate assets, and all gifts and bequests shall be paid from the net distributable estate.

ARTICLE 2

2.01 I give, devise, and bequeath my entire estate, real or personal, or mixed, of every kind and nature, and wherever situated, which I may own or hereafter acquire or have a right to dispose of at my death to my wife, CAROLINE BROWN.

2.02 If CAROLINE BROWN predeceases me, I give, devise, and bequeath my entire estate, real or personal or mixed, of every kind and nature, and wherever situated, which I may own or hereafter acquire or have a right to dispose of at my death to my daughter, CORY BROWN. If CAROLINE BROWN and CORY BROWN both predecease me, I give, devise, and bequeath my entire estate to SANDRA SMYTHE.

ARTICLE 3

3.01 I nominate and appoint my wife, CAROLINE BROWN, to be the Executrix of this my Last Will and Testament, granting unto her full power and authority to sell and convey any or all of my estate, real and personal, or mixed, upon such terms and prices as she may deem proper, without obtaining any prior order of the court. I also grant her full power and authority in the settlement of my estate, to compromise,

____GB

adjust, and settle any and all debts and liabilities due to or from my estate, for such sums, and upon such terms and conditions as she shall deem best.

    3.02   In the event that CAROLINE BROWN shall for any reason decline to serve, or fail to qualify for any reason, or having qualified and been appointed, fail to complete the administration of my estate, then I nominate my daughter, CORY BROWN, to be the Alternate or Successor Executor.

    3.03   I direct that no bond or surety shall be required of any Executor named herein. If any beneficiary in any manner, directly or indirectly, contests or attacks this instrument or any of its provisions, any share or interest given to that contesting beneficiary under this instrument is revoked, and shall be disposed of in the same manner provided herein, as if that contesting beneficiary had predeceased me.

    IN WITNESS WHEREOF, I have hereunto subscribed my name, and acknowledge and publish this instrument as my Last Will and Testament, consisting of two pages including this page in the presence of the undersigned witnesses, on _____, 2005.

_____
GREGORY BROWN

    We hereby certify that the above named GREGORY BROWN subscribed his name thereto this day in our presence, and to us declared the same to be his Last Will and Testament, and that we subscribe our names hereto as witnesses, at his request, and in his presence, and that at the time of the signing, that he was of sound and disposing mind and not under any restraint, to the best of our knowledge and belief. We declare under penalty of perjury that the foregoing is true.

    WITNESS our hand and signature in San Luis Obispo, California, on _____, 2005.

Witness signature_____
Print name_____
Residing at _____
_____

Witness signature_____
Print name_____
Residing at _____
_____

CODICIL TO THE WILL
OF
DEBRA CLOSE

I, DEBRA CLOSE, a resident of Santa Barbara County, California declare this to be the first codicil to my will dated December 1, 1988.

It is my wish that Article 3 be amended to delete THELMA JONES as Alternate Personal Representative and substitute in her place and stead JOYCE J. JOHNSON.

In all other respects I confirm and republish my Will dated December 1, 1988.

I subscribe my name to this codicil this _____ day of _____2004, at Santa Barbara, California and do hereby declare that I sign and execute this codicil willingly, that I execute it as my free and voluntary act for the purposes therein expressed and that I am of the age of majority or otherwise legally empowered to make a codicil and under no constraint or undue influence.

_____
DEBRA CLOSE

On this _____ day of _____, 2004, declared to us, the undersigned, that this instrument was the codicil to the Will dated December 1, 1988 and requested us to act as witnesses to it. DEBRA CLOSE thereupon signed this codicil in our presence, all of us being present at the same time. We now, at Santa Barbara, California, request, in the presence of each other and in the presence of DEBRA CLOSE, subscribe our names as witnesses and declare we understand this to be DEBRA CLOSEís codicil and that to the best of our knowledge DEBRA CLOSE is of the age of majority, or is otherwise legally empowered to make a codicil and is under no constraint or undue influence.

We declare under penalty of perjury that the foregoing is true and correct, this _____ day of _____, 2004 at Santa Barbara, California.

Witness _____
Residing at _____
_____

Witness _____
Residing at _____
_____

Living Trust Samples and Additional Documents

THE MILLER FAMILY LIVING TRUST

ARTICLES OF THE TRUST
CONTENTS

CONTENTS

THE MILLER FAMILY LIVING TRUST

REVOCABLE LIVING TRUST AGREEMENT

DATED: _____, 2005

Between: GEORGE M. MILLER and ILENE MILLER, as Settlors

And: GEORGE M. MILLER and ILENE MILLER, as Trustees

GEORGE M. MILLER and **ILENE MILLER,** residents of the State of California, County of Santa Barbara, establish a Trust upon the conditions and for the purposes hereafter set forth.

ARTICLE ONE

Section 1.01. <u>Trust Estate Defined and Trust Purpose</u>

All property hereafter transferred or conveyed to and received by the Trustee to be held pursuant to the terms of this instrument is herein called the "Trust Estate" and shall be held, administered, and distributed by the Trustee as provided in this Trust Agreement. The Settlors shall transfer and deliver to Trustee the property described in the various schedules accompanying this Trust. Such title and interests the Trustee has received or may hereafter acquire in that property and such other property as may hereafter be added to the Trust, shall be vested in the Trustee.

The primary Trust purposes shall be to provide for the health, support and maintenance of the Settlors during their lifetime, in their accustomed manner of living. The secondary Trust purposes shall be to permit the Settlors to provide funds for the reasonable health, support, and education of the Settlors' designated beneficiaries.

Section 1.02. <u>Definitions</u>

As used in this Declaration of Trust,
a)   The term "husband" shall mean **GEORGE M. MILLER**.
b)   The term "wife" shall mean **ILENE MILLER**.
c)   The term "settlor" shall refer individually and collectively to Husband and Wife.
d)   The term "trustee" shall mean the person appointed to administer the Trust.
e)   The terms "child" and "children" as used in this Declaration shall mean the lawful issue of Settlor, and shall include children hereafter born to or legally adopted by Settlor. The terms "issue," "next-of-kin," "heirs," "child," "children" or any other class designation shall not include stepchildren, foster children, half-bloods or persons born out of wedlock, unless otherwise specifically designated as a beneficiary of this Trust. Said definition shall also apply to any testate or intestate beneficiary or potential beneficiary. The names of the children of the Settlor currently living are: **GEORGE MELVIN MILLER** and **SCOTT C. MILLER**.
f)   The Term "beneficiary" shall mean the person or persons for whose benefit assets are held in Trust.

Visit www.wethepeopleforms.com and enter WTPEP as your password to access this document, as well as many other useful forms.

Section 1.03. <u>Trustee Designation</u>

GEORGE M. MILLER (Husband) and **ILENE MILLER** (Wife)are hereby designated as Co-Trustees. Should either **GEORGE M. MILLER** or **ILENE MILLER** become unable because of death, incapacity, or other cause, to serve as such Co-Trustee, or should either resign as such Co-Trustee, before the natural termination of this Trust, the remaining Co-Trustee, **GEORGE M. MILLER** or **ILENE MILLER**, shall thereafter serve as sole Trustee as provided for in this Declaration. Furthermore, the Co-Trustees shall have the authority to designate either Husband or Wife to deal with particular assets because of their special knowledge of that asset. This designation shall be evidenced by a written agreement signed by both the Settlors and Trustee, a copy of which shall be appended to this Agreement. The term "Trustee" as used in this Declaration shall refer collectively to **GEORGE M. MILLER** and **ILENE MILLER** so long as they shall serve as such Co-Trustees and thereafter to such of them as may serve as sole Trustee. This Paragraph is subject to the provisions contained in Section 9.01.

Section 1.04. <u>Additions to Trust Properties</u>

a)   At any time during the continuance of this Trust the Trustee, in the Trusteeís sole discretion after consideration of the possible tax consequences thereof to all concerned, is authorized to receive additions of cash or other properties to the Trust, subject to any conditions to which the Trustee may agree, from any source whatsoever without limitation, whether by gift, will, or otherwise. However, the Trustee shall accept all assets which any person or persons may give, devise, and/or bequeath by last will and testament to this Trust hereunder as well as all assets which may be transferred to this Trust pursuant to the expressed provisions of any other Trust document or documents of any kind.

b)   Furthermore, at any time any person or persons may designate this Trust as the beneficiary, primary or contingent, of any insurance, pension, or other death benefit, relating to the life of anyone (such designation to be presumed to be revocable unless it is expressly irrevocable) and, until such benefit matures by reason of death. The Trustee shall have no responsibility whatsoever with respect thereto, it being intended that, unless and until the Trust which is designated beneficiary of such death benefit becomes the owner of the insurance proceeds involved (or other source of such benefit), such Trust arrangement shall be operative only with respect to such net proceeds as actually become payable by reason of death.

Section 1.05. <u>Separate and Community Property Remain As Such</u>

All property now or hereafter conveyed or transferred to the Trustee pursuant to this Declaration, which was community property, quasi-community property, or separate property at the time of such conveyance or transfer, shall retain its character respectively, as community property, quasi-community property, or the separate property of the Settlor transferring such property to the Trust.

For the purpose of devise or distribution to the beneficiaries of the Settlor who owns such separate property, all property listed on the accompanying "Husband's Separate Property Schedule" shall be allocated to the beneficiaries of the Settlor/Husband listed on his schedule. All property listed on the accompanying "Wife's Separate Property Schedule" shall be allocated to the beneficiaries of the Settlor/Wife listed on her schedule. Final distribution of the property listed on these accompanying schedules, if not otherwise noted herein, shall be at the death of the surviving spouse.

All other Trust property acquired during the Settlors' marriage, unless included in either the "Husband's Separate Property Schedule" or "Wife's Separate Property Schedule," shall retain the nature of its previous character and shall be distributed according to the terms of this Trust Agreement.

Section 1.06. <u>Amendment and Revocation</u>

a) At any time and from time to time during the joint lives of the Settlors, the Settlors jointly as to community property, and either Settlor as to his or her separate property, may alter, modify or amend the Trusts created by this Agreement in any respect by a duly executed instrument in writing delivered to the Trustee.

b) During the joint lifetimes of the Settlors, this Trust may be revoked in whole or in part with respect to community property by an instrument in writing signed by either Settlor and delivered to the Trustee and the other Settlor, and with respect to separate property by an instrument in writing signed by the Settlor who contributed that property to the Trust delivered to the Trustee. Any property withdrawn from the Trust Estate by reason of any revocation shall be delivered by the Trustee to the Settlor or Settlors revoking the Trust.

c) If this instrument is revoked with respect to all or a major portion of the assets subject to this instrument, the Trustee shall be entitled to retain sufficient assets reasonably to secure payment of liabilities lawfully incurred by the Trustee in the administration of the Trust, including Trustee's fees that have been earned, unless the Settlors shall indemnify the Trustee against loss or expense.

d) From and after the death of the first Settlor, the Surviving Settlor shall have the power to amend or revoke the Survivor's Trust (as hereinafter described), in whole or in part by an instrument in writing delivered to the Trustee; the Decedent's Trust (as hereinafter described), may not be amended or revoked by any person.

e)   Except as otherwise provided in this Agreement, on the death of either Settlor, the designation of beneficiaries of specific gifts and separate property of that deceased Settlor in the Trusts created by this Trust Agreement shall become irrevocable and not subject to amendment or modification.

f) No Trustee shall incur any liability or responsibility either (i) for failing to act in accordance with such instrument (ii) for acting in accordance with the provisions of this Trust Agreement without regard to such instrument, until he or she has received a copy of such revocation instrument.

g) Upon the death of both of the Settlors, this Agreement shall become irrevocable.

h) The rights of revocation, withdrawal, alteration, and amendment reserved by Settlors in this Article may be exercised by the Settlor(s) and by any duly appointed agent acting on his or her behalf.

ARTICLE TWO

Section 2.01. Trust Income

During the joint lives of the Settlors, the Trustee shall at least annually, unless otherwise directed by both Settlors in writing, pay to or apply for the benefit of Husband and Wife, all of the net income from the Trust Estate in the same proportions as each of their respective interests in the Trust Estate.

Section 2.02. Protection of Settlor in Event of Incapacity

During the joint lives of the Settlors, should either Settlor become incapacitated as defined in Section 2.03 below, the Trustee may, in the Trustee's discretion:

a)   Pay to or apply for the benefit of the incapacitated Settlor such amounts of the principal of the Trust Estate, up to the whole of the community estate and the separate property of such Settlor, as the Trustee may, from time to time, deem necessary or advisable for his or her use and benefit. However, the Trustee shall not make payments from the community estate without first obtaining the written approval of the Settlor not so disabled. Any payments made pursuant to this paragraph from the community estate shall be community property.

b)   Pay the entire net income of the Trust Estate in monthly or other convenient installments to the remaining competent Settlor, or

c)   Apply such portion of the net income, up to the whole thereof, of the Trust Estate as the Trustee may deem in his or her absolute discretion reasonable and proper for the benefit of the Settlor so adjudged to be incompetent or unable to manage his or her own affairs.

d)   Declare void and without effect any attempt by the incompetent Settlor to exercise the reserved rights of revocation, amendment, withdrawal of assets, control over Trustee, etc., unless a court of competent jurisdiction determines otherwise or a Settlor's disappearance constitutes incapacity under Section 2.03 c) and the Settlor has reappeared.

Section 2.03. Incapacity

In the event that any Trustee or any beneficiary hereunder comes into possession of any of the following:

a)   A court order, which such Trustee or beneficiary deems to be jurisdictionally proper and still concurrently applicable, holding a person to be legally incapacitated to act on his or her own behalf or appointing a conservator or guardian to act for him or her, or

b)   Duly executed, witnessed, acknowledged written certificates at least one of which is then unrevoked, of two licensed physicians (each of whom represents that he or she is certified by a recognized medical board), each certifying that such physician has examined a person and has concluded that, by reason of accident, or mental deterioration, or similar cause, such person has, at the date thereof, become incapacitated to act rationally and prudently in his or her own financial best interests, or

c)   Evidence which such Trustee or beneficiary deems to be creditable and still currently applicable that a person has disappeared, is unaccountably absent, or is being detained under duress where he or she is unable effectively and prudently to look after his or her own best interests, then in that event and under those circumstances:

i)   Such person shall be deemed to have thereupon become incapacitated, as that term is used in and for all of the purposes of this instrument, and

ii)   Such incapacity shall be deemed to continue until such court order, certificates, and or circumstances have become inapplicable or have been revoked.

Any physician's aforesaid certificate may be revoked by a similar certificate to the effect that the person is no longer thus incapacitated executed either (i) by the originally certifying physician or (ii) by two other licensed, board certified physicians. No Trustee shall be under any duty to institute any inquiry into a person's possible incapacity, but the expense of any such inquiry reasonably instituted may be paid from the Trust assets.

Payment for such inquiry refers both to a reasonable inquiry as to the incapacity of such individual and to that inquiry as to the revocation of such a certificate.

Section 2.04. Principal Invasion

During the joint lives of the Settlors, should the net income of assets contained in this Trust be insufficient to provide for the care, maintenance or support of the Settlors as herein defined, the Trustee may, in the Trustee's absolute discretion, pay to or apply for the benefit of the Settlors, or either of them such amounts from the principal of the Trust Estate as the Trustee may in the Trustee's absolute discretion, from time to time deem necessary or advisable for the care, maintenance or support of the Settlors. As used in this section, the term "care, maintenance or support of the Settlors" shall mean:

a)   The providing of proper care, maintenance and support for the Settlors, or either of them, during any period of illness, or other want or necessity;

b)   The maintenance of the Settlors in the manner of living to which they, and each of them, are accustomed on the date of this Declaration.

Section 2.05. Residence

If the Settlors' residence property is a part of the Trust, the Settlors shall have possession and full management of it and shall have the right to occupy it, rent free. The Trustee shall be responsible for the maintenance of the property and for all taxes, liens, assessments and fire insurance premiums from the Trust to the extent such assets are available for such payment. At such time as the Settlors direct or when it is no longer used by the Settlors as a residence, it may be sold and the Trustee is hereby authorized to purchase another residence or a life tenancy in a retirement facility for use by the Settlors as the Trustee may select. The cost of the new residence or the retirement facility may exceed the proceeds from the sale of the former residence.

ARTICLE THREE

Section 3.01. Provisions After First Death

On the death of either Settlor leaving the other Settlor surviving him or her, the Trustee shall collect all insurance proceeds payable to the Trustee by reason of such death, all bequests and devises distributable to the Trust Estate under the terms of the last Will of the deceased Settlor, and shall divide the entire Trust Estate into two or more separate trusts to be known and herein designated as the "Survivor's Trust" and the "Decedent's Trust."

Whenever the Trustee is directed to make a distribution of Trust assets or a division of Trust assets into separate trusts or shares on the death of a Settlor, the Trustee may, in the Trustee's discretion, defer such distribution or division until six months after the Settlor's death. When the Trustee defers distribution or division of Trust assets, the deferred division or distribution shall be made as if it had taken place at the time prescribed in this Declaration in the absence of this paragraph and all rights given to the beneficiaries of such Trust assets under other provision of this Declaration shall be deemed to have accrued and vested as of such prescribed time.

Section 3.02. The Survivor's Trust

The principal or Trust Estate of the Survivor's Trust shall consist of all the interest in each and every assets held by the Trustee pursuant to this Declaration on or by reason of the death of the deceased Settlor not allocated to the Decedent's Trust pursuant to Section 3.03 of this Agreement.

Notwithstanding the provisions of this Trust Agreement regarding Trustee's powers:
1. The Settlor(s), by written instrument delivered to the Trustee, may require the Trustee of the Survivor's Trust to dispose of unproductive property or direct the Trustee's to convert unproductive property to productive property.
2. The Trustee shall invest and reinvest the assets of the Survivor's Trust in such manner that the aggregate return of all investments of the Trust shall be reasonable in light of then-existing circumstances.

Section 3.03. The Decedent's Trust

The principal or Trust Estate of the Decedent's Trust shall consist of assets equal in value to the maximum amount, if any, that can pass free of federal estate tax by reason of the unified credit available to the estate of the deceased Settlor, after considering any adjusted taxable gifts and bequests by will or other disposition which do not qualify for the marital deduction made by the Settlor, and all charges to the principal of the estate which are not deducted in computation of the federal estate tax of the estate of the deceased Settlor; provided however, that the allocation to the Decedent's Trust shall be satisfied with assets valued as of the date of allocation or distribution; provided further that any assets in the Trust Estate which do not qualify for the federal estate tax marital deduction shall be first used to satisfy the allocation to the Decedent's Trust.

Notwithstanding the provisions of this Trust Agreement regarding Trustee's powers:
1. The Settlor(s), by written instrument delivered to the Trustee, may require the Trustee of the Decedent's Trust to dispose of unproductive property or direct the Trustee to convert unproductive property to productive property.
2. The Trustee shall invest and reinvest the assets of the Decedent's Trust in such manner that the aggregate return of all investments of the Trust shall be reasonable in light of then-existing circumstances.

Section 3.04. Last Expenses

On the death of the first of the Settlors to die, the Trustee shall pay, either from the income or principal of the Decedent's Trust or partly from income of the Decedent's Trust, as the Trustee in the Trustee's absolute discretion may determine, the expenses of the deceased Settlor's last illness, funeral and burial expenses, and any inheritance, estate or death taxes, that may be due by reason of the deceased Settlor's death, unless the Trustee in his or her absolute discretion, determines that other adequate provisions have been made for the payment of such expenses and taxes. All estate, inheritance, transfer, succession and any other taxes, plus interest and penalties thereon (death taxes) which become payable by reason of the deceased Settlor's death, upon property passing under this instrument, shall be paid without reimbursement from the recipient and without reapportionment. All death taxes upon property not passing under this instrument shall be apportioned in the manner provided by law.

Section 3.05. Distributions from Survivor's Trust

a)   Income
        The Trustee shall pay to or apply for the benefit of the Surviving Settlor the net income of the Survivor's Trust in quarterly, or more frequent installments.
b)   Principal
        If the Trustee considers such income insufficient, the Trustee shall also pay to or apply for the benefit of the Surviving Settlor such sums out of the principal of the Survivor's Trust as the Trustee in the Trustee's discretion, shall consider necessary for the Surviving Settlor's health, support, comfort, enjoyment, and general welfare.
c)   Right of Withdrawal
        In addition, the Trustee shall pay the Surviving Settlor, as much of the principal of the Survivor's Trust as he or she shall request in writing.

3.06.   Distributions from Decedent's Trust

a)   Income
        On the death of the deceased Settlor, the Trustee shall pay to or apply for the benefit of the Surviving Settlor and the net income of the Decedent's Trust.

b)   Principal
        The Trustee shall also pay and apply for the benefit of the Surviving Settlor such sums out of the principal of the Decedent's Trust that the Trustee, in the Trustee's sole discretion, considers necessary for the Surviving Settlor's health, education, support and maintenance in accordance with the Surviving Settlor's accustomed standard of living at the date of the deceased Settlor's death.
        Payments out of principal to the Surviving Settlor shall be made first out of the Survivor's Trust until it is exhausted, and thereafter out of the Decedent's Trust.

ARTICLE FOUR

Section 4.01.   Second Death

Upon the death of the Surviving Settlor, the principal of the Survivor's Trust and any accrued and undistributed income of the Survivor's Trust, shall be distributed by the Trustee in such a manner and to such persons, including the estate, the creditors, or the creditors of the estate of the Surviving Settlor, as the Surviving Settlor shall direct by specific reference in his or her special trust instructions.

Section 4.02.   Payment of the Second Death Expenses

On the death of the Surviving Settlor, the Trustee shall pay either from the income or principal of the Survivor's Trust, as the Trustee in his or her absolute discretion may determine, the expenses of the Surviving Settlor's last illness, funeral, burial, and any inheritance, estate or death taxes that may be due by reason of the inclusion of any portion of the Trust Estate in the Surviving Settlor's estate, for the purposes of any such tax, unless the Trustee in his or her absolute discretion determines that other adequate provisions have been made for the payment of such expenses and taxes.

Section 4.03.   Trust Income and Principal Distribution

a)   Upon the death of the Surviving Settlor, the Trustee shall distribute the tangible personal property of the Settlor set forth on the special trust instructions accompanying this Trust which are incorporated herein by this reference, to the beneficiaries designated therein. In the event that the Settlors have not deposited written instructions with the Trustee concerning disposition of personal effects or if such instructions do not concern the disposition of all the Settlors' personal effects, then the personal effects not otherwise disposed of shall be distributed among the Settlors' beneficiaries set forth below in subsection b), in such equitable manner as may be determined between them. The Trustee shall lend whatever assistance the Trustee deems advisable or appropriate to facilitate the distribution of personal effects. If the Trustee determines, due to a dispute or conflict among the beneficiaries, that a sale is in the best interests of the beneficiaries, the Trustee may, in the Trustee's sole discretion, sell the personal effects and distribute the sales proceeds as set forth below in subsection b).

b)   Unless stated otherwise, the Trustee shall divide and distribute the net income and principal of the Trust Estate (consisting of the Decedent's Trust and Survivor's Trust(s) subject to Section 4.02) for the benefit of the Settlors' named beneficiaries as follows:

GEORGE MELVIN MILLER 50%
SCOTT C. MILLER 50%

If one of the beneficiaries named above is deceased at the time of distribution, the entire Trust Estate shall be distributed to the surviving beneficiary.

c) If any beneficiary, to whom the Trustee is directed in a preceding provision hereof, to distribute any share of the Trust principal, is under the age of 25 years when the distribution is to be made, the beneficiary's share shall vest in interest indefeasibly, but the Trustee may, in his or her discretion, continue to hold it as a separate Trust for such period of time as Trustee deems advisable, for matters including college or vocational training, but not after the time the beneficiary reaches the age of 25 years. In the meantime, the Trustee may use as much of the income and principal as Trustee determines to be required, in addition to the beneficiary's other income, from all sources known to Trustee, for reasonable support, comfort, and education. The Trustee has discretion to add any excess income to the principal. Unless otherwise specified in this Section, the Trustee may distribute income to a beneficiary at any time if, in the Trustee's sole discretion, such a distribution would reduce federal or state income taxes that would be paid on income produced by the trust estate and would be beneficial to the beneficiary entitled to receive said income.

d) When each beneficiary reaches the age of twenty-five (25) years, the Trustee shall distribute to each beneficiary One Hundred Percent (100%) of the then balance of the principal of his or her share of the Trust Estate.

e) Except as otherwise specifically provided above in subsection b), if any beneficiary for whom a share of the Trust Estate has been set aside should fail to survive the above distribution, then the Trustee shall distribute one hundred percent (100%) of the balance of such deceased beneficiary's share of the Trust Estate, in equal shares, to the issue then living of the deceased beneficiary, by right of representation, to be held in Trust for such beneficiary's issue until each such beneficiary attains the age of twenty-five (25) years. If there should be no such surviving issue, then all of the balance of such deceased beneficiaryís share of the Trust Estate shall be added to the other shares set aside for the benefit of the Settlors' other living beneficiaries as hereinabove provided, including proportionately both the distributed and the undistributed portions of each such share, to be held, administered and distributed as a part of other shares. If all beneficiaries fail to survive the above distribution, then their shares of the Trust Estate shall be divided equally among said beneficiaries' surviving issue to be held in Trust until each of said issue attains the age of twenty-five (25) years. Notwithstanding the foregoing, in the event of any distribution to issue of a deceased child, if in that child's estate plan a trust is established for the benefit of said deceased child's issue, the assets which would otherwise be distributed hereunder directly to such issue of such deceased child may, instead, be distributed to the trustee of such trust, to be held, administered and distributed as set forth therein for the benefit of such issue.

f) If all of the Settlors' beneficiaries and their issue should fail to survive final distribution of the Trust Estate, all of the Trust Estate not disposed of as hereinabove provided shall be distributed one-half (1/2) to the persons who would then be **GEORGE M. MILLER**'s beneficiaries and the other one-half (1/2) to the persons who would then be the beneficiaries of **ILENE MILLER**. The identities and respective shares of the aforesaid beneficiaries to be determined in accordance with intestate succession laws of the State of California then in effect relating to the succession of separate property not acquired from a predeceased spouse. If either of the Settlors has no such heirs, then all of the Trust Estate shall be distributed to the aforesaid beneficiaries of the other.

Section 4.04.   Principle of Representation

Should a beneficiary predecease the Surviving Settlor's death that beneficiary's interest shall then be distributed to the surviving issue of such deceased beneficiary in equal shares on the principle of representation.

Section 4.05.   Simultaneous Death

Should both Settlors die simultaneously or under any circumstances rendering it difficult or impossible to determine which Settlor predeceased the other, each Settlor shall, for the purpose of disposing of his or her separate property be deemed to have predeceased the other Settlor.

ARTICLE FIVE

Section 5.01.   NonIncome-Producing Property

During the joint lives of **GEORGE M. MILLER** and **ILENE MILLER**, the Trustee is authorized to retain in the Trust for so long as the Trustee may deem advisable and in the best interest of such Trust, any property received by the Trustee from the Settlors, or from either of them separately, whether or not such property is of the character permitted by law for the investment of trust funds. After the death of the deceased Settlor, the Trustee may retain any such property in the Trust at his or her sole discretion, (subject to Section 5.07 of Article 5 herein). Such property shall otherwise be distributed to those beneficiaries defined in Section 4.03.

Section 5.02.   Trustee Powers

The Trustee shall have all powers conferred upon a Trustee by the law of the State of California for the orderly administration of the Trust Estate. If any property is distributed outright under the provision of this instrument to a person who is a minor, distribution may be made under the California Uniform Gifts to Minors Act until said beneficiary attains age 25; any fiduciary acting under this instrument may name a custodian and distribute the property to the custodian.

The Trustee shall with respect to any and all property, which may at any time be held by the Trustee in Trust, pursuant to this Agreement, whether such property constitutes principal or accumulated income, have power, exercisable in the Trustee's absolute discretion, at any time and from time to time, on such terms and in such manner as the Trustee may deem advisable, to:

a) Sell, convey, exchange, convert, improve, repair, partition, divide, allot, subdivide, create restrictions, easements or other servitude thereon, operate and control;

b) Lease for terms within or beyond the term of the Trust and for any purpose, including exploration for the removal of gas, oil and/or other minerals; and enter into any covenants and agreements relating to the property so leased, or any other improvements which may then or thereafter be erected on such property;

c) Mortgage, encumber or hypothecate for any Trust purpose by mortgage, deed of trust, pledge or otherwise;

d) Carry insurance of such kinds, and in such amounts, at the expense of the Trust, as the Trustee may deem advisable;

e) Commence or defend at the expense of the Trust such litigation with respect to any Trust or any property of the Trust Estate, as Trustee may deem advisable and, further employ, for reasonable compensation payable by any such Trust, such counsel as the Trustee shall deem advisable for that purpose;

f) Invest and reinvest the Trust funds in such property as the Trustee, in the exercise of reasonable business judgment, may deem advisable, whether or not such property is of the character specifically permitted by law for the investment of trust funds; provided, however, that the Trustee is not authorized to invest or reinvest the funds in property which is nonproductive of income; provided further that in the event that any income-producing property of the Trust subsequently becomes nonproductive property, the Trustee is authorized to transfer such investment to property which is productive of income (this subject to Section 5.01 herein);

g) Vote by proxy or otherwise, in such manner as Trustee may determine to be in the best interests of the Trust, any securities having voting rights held by the Trustee pursuant to this Agreement;

h) Pay any assessments or other charges levied on any stock or other security held by Trustee in Trust pursuant to this Agreement;

i) Exercise or not exercise, as Trustee may deem best, any subscription, conversion, or other rights or options which may at any time attach, belong or be given to the holders of any stocks, bonds, securities or other instruments held by it in Trust pursuant to this Agreement;

j) Participate in any plans or proceedings for the foreclosure, reorganization, consolidation, merger or liquidation of any corporation or organization that has issued securities held by Trustee in Trust pursuant to the terms of this Agreement, to deposit securities with and transfer title or securities on such terms as Trustee may deem in the best interest of the Trust to any protective or other committee established to further or defeat any such plan or proceeding;

k) Buy, sell, trade and deal in options, precious metals, stocks and bonds, and securities of all nature including short sales, and for such purpose to maintain and operate margin accounts with brokers and in connection therewith to borrow money and pledge any and all stocks, bonds, securities and contracts for the future delivery thereof held or purchased by the Trustee with such brokers as security for loans and advances made to Trustee; and to permit securities to be held in the name of a nominee; and to maintain credit cards and debit cards in the name of the Trust in connection with any brokerage account.

l) Enforce any mortgage or deed of trust, or pledge held by Trustee in Trust pursuant to this Agreement, and at any sale under any such mortgage, deed of trust or pledge, to bid and purchase at the expense of the Trust any property subject to such security instrument;

m) Compromise, submit to arbitration, release with or without consideration, and otherwise adjust any claims in favor or against the Trust provided for in this Agreement.

n) Distribute gifts of up to the maximum amount under Internal Revenue Code Section 2503(b) that may be excluded from gift taxes per year for each Settlor then living out of principal or interest, in any portion of the two that the Trustee, in his or her sole discretion, deems advisable. Such distributions by the Trustee shall be deemed a revocation of the Trust with respect to sufficient funds to make the gifts and the Settlors shall be deemed to have received such funds. Thereafter, the Trustee's payments of said sums to the donee(s) shall be deemed to be made as the Settlors' agent and not as Trustee under this Declaration notwithstanding the fact that said payment is made directly from the Trust.

o) Manage any business interest and use the general assets of the Trust for the purpose of the business and invest additional capital in, or make loans to, such business.

p) Subject to any limitations expressly set forth in this Declaration and faithful performance of Trustee's fiduciary obligations, do all acts, take all such proceedings, and exercise all such rights and privileges as could be done, taken or exercised by an absolute owner of the Trust property.

q) A Trustee may resign at any time without court approval.

Section 5.03. Power to Borrow

The Trustee shall have the power to borrow money for any Trust purpose (including borrowing from the probate estates of the Settlors for the purpose of paying taxes) on such terms and conditions as the Trustee may deem proper, from any person, firm or corporation, and shall have the power to repay such borrowed money.

Section 5.04. Power to Loan to Trust

The Trustee is authorized to loan or advance Trustee's own funds to the Trust provided for in this Agreement for any Trust purpose and to charge for such loan or advance the rate of interest that Trustee, at the time such loan or advance is made, would have charged had such loan or advance been made to a person not connected with the Trust having at least a net worth equal to the value of the principal of the Trust. Any such loan or advance shall be repaid from the income or principal of the Trust as in the discretion of the Trustee appears for the best interest of the Trust and its beneficiaries.

Section 5.05. Purchase of Securities

The Trustee is authorized to purchase securities or other property from the probate estates of the Settlors with or without security to the executor or other representative of the estate of the Settlor. The Trustee is further authorized to make loans and advancements to the probate estates of the Settlors, again, with or without security to the executor or other representative of the estate of the Settlor.

Section 5.06. Manner of Holding Title

The Trustee may hold securities or other property held by Trustee in Trust pursuant to this Agreement in Trustee's name as Trustee, in Trustee's own name without a designation showing it to be Trustee, in the name of the Trustee's nominee, or the Trustee may hold such securities unregistered, in such condition that ownership will pay by delivery.

Section 5.07 Settlors' Residence

After the death of the first Settlor, the Trustee is authorized to retain in any Trust or Trust for personal use of the Surviving Settlor, any property occupied by the Settlor as his/her principal place of residence at the time of death of the first Settlor to die, for so long as the Surviving Settlor may desire to occupy the residential property; during such retention, the Trustee shall pay, from either the income or principal of the Trusts as the Trustee may deem in the best interests of such Trusts and their beneficiaries, all taxes and assessments levied or assessed against such property, and all costs of keeping such property properly insured, maintained and repaired. The Surviving Settlor shall not be obligated for the payment of rent. On written request of the Surviving Settlor, the Trustee may sell such property and replace it with other property, including a life tenancy in a retirement facility, to be retained in Trust in the same manner as the replaced residence property, suitable in the Trustee's judgment as a residence for the Surviving Settlor. The cost of the new residence or the retirement facility may exceed the proceeds from the sale of the former residence.

ARTICLE SIX

Section 6.01   Direction to Minimize Taxes

In the administration of the Trust hereunder, its fiduciaries shall exercise all tax-related elections, options, and choices which they have in such manner as they in their sole but reasonable judgment (where appropriate, receiving advice of tax counsel), believe will achieve the overall minimum in total combined present and reasonably anticipated (but appropriately discounted) future administrative expenses and taxes of all kinds, upon not only such Trust, but also its beneficiaries, the other Trusts hereunder and their beneficiaries and Settlor's probate estate. Without limitation on the generality of the foregoing direction (which shall to that extent supersede the usual fiduciary duty of impartiality), such fiduciaries shall not be accountable to any person interested in any Trust or in Settlor's estate for the manner in which they shall carry out this direction to minimize overall taxes and expense (including any decision they may make not to incur the expense of detailed analysis of alternative choices) and, even though their decisions in this regard may result in increased tax or decreased distribution to the Trust, to the estate, or to one or more beneficiaries, there shall in no event be any compensation readjustments or reimbursements between the Trust hereunder or any of the Trust or estate accounts or beneficiaries by reason of the manner in which the fiduciaries thus carry out said direction.

Section 6.02.   Power to Waive Recovery of Taxes

The Settlors' Personal Representatives and the Trustee shall have the discretionary power to waive the right to recover taxes paid pursuant to Internal Revenue Code Section 2207A or any successor statute.

ARTICLE SEVEN

Section 7.01. Incontestability

The beneficial provisions of this instrument (and of the Settlors' last wills and testaments) are intended to be in lieu of any other rights, claims, or interests of whatsoever nature, whether statutory or otherwise, except bona fide pre-death debts, which any beneficiary hereunder may have against or in a Settlor's estate or the properties in Trust hereunder. Accordingly, if any beneficiary hereunder asserts any claim (except a legally enforceable debt), statutory election, or other right or interest against or in a Settlor's estate, a Settlor's Will, or any properties of this Trust, other than pursuant to the express terms hereof or of said Will, or directly or indirectly contests, disputes, or calls into question, before any court, the validity of this instrument or of said will, then:

a)   Such beneficiary shall thereby absolutely forfeit any and all beneficial interests of whatsoever kind and nature which such beneficiary might otherwise have under this instrument and the interests of the other beneficiaries hereunder shall thereupon be appropriately and proportionately increased and/or advanced,

b)   All of the provisions of this instrument, to the extent that they confer any benefits, powers or rights whatsoever upon such claiming, electing or contesting beneficiary, shall thereupon become absolutely void and revoked, and

c)   Such claiming, electing, or contesting beneficiary, if then acting as a Trustee hereunder, shall automatically cease to be a Trustee and shall thereafter be ineligible either to select, remove, or become a Trustee hereunder.

The foregoing shall not be construed, however, to limit the appearance of any beneficiary as a witness in any proceeding involving this instrument or said will, nor limit any beneficiary's appearance in any capacity in any proceeding solely for the construction of either of said documents.

Section 7.02   Disinheritance

Except as otherwise provided herein, **GEORGE M. MILLER** and **ILENE MILLER** have intentionally omitted to provide for any other of their heirs living at the time of their deaths.

ARTICLE EIGHT

Section 8.01.   <u>Accrued Income on Termination of Beneficial Interest</u>

Except as specifically provided herein, whenever the right of any beneficiary to payments from the net income or principal of the Trust provided for in this Agreement shall terminate either by reason of death or other cause, any accrued net income of such Trust undistributed by the Trustee on the date of such termination, shall be held, administered, and distributed by then Trustee in the same manner as if such income had accrued and been received by the Trustee after the date such beneficiary's right to receive payments from such Trust terminated.

Section 8.02.   <u>Distribution in Kind or Cash</u>

On any division of the assets of the Trust Estate into shares or partial shares, and on any final or partial distribution of the assets of the Trust Estate, the Trustee, in his or her absolute discretion, may divide and distribute undivided interests of such assets, or may sell all or any part of such assets and make division or distribution in cash or partly in cash and partly in kind. The decision of the Trustee, either prior to or on any division or distribution of such assets, as to what constitutes a proper division of such assets, of the Trust Estate, shall be binding on all persons in any manner interested in any Trust provided for in this Declaration.

Section 8.03.   <u>Spendthrift Provision</u>

Neither the principal nor the income of the Trusts hereunder shall be available for the debts of a beneficiary. Except as otherwise expressly provided for in this Agreement, no beneficiary of any Trust shall have any right, power or authority to alienate, encumber or hypothecate his or her interest in the principal or income of such Trust in any manner, nor shall such interests of any beneficiary be subject to claims of his or her creditors or liable to attachment, execution or other process of law. The limitations herein shall not restrict the right to exercise any power of appointment or the right to disclaim.

ARTICLE NINE

Section 9.01. <u>Trustees</u>

The following shall act as Trustees in the following order of succession:

a) The undersigned, **GEORGE M. MILLER** and **ILENE MILLER**

b) The survivor of the undersigned as Trustee of the Survivor's Trust, and Decedent's Trust.

c) At the death, incapacity, or resignation of the undersigned, then **GEORGE MELVIN MILLER** as First Successor Trustee. Should the First Successor Trustee fail or decline to serve, then **JUDY SANDERS** shall serve as Second Successor Trustee. They are to serve without bond.

d) A Trustee chosen by the majority of beneficiaries, with a parent or legal guardian voting for minor beneficiaries; provided, however, that the issue of any deceased beneficiary shall collectively have only one vote.

ARTICLE TEN

Section 10.01.   Perpetuities Savings Clause

Notwithstanding any other provision of this instrument, every Trust created by this instrument, or by the exercise of any power of appointment created by this instrument, shall terminate no later than 21 years after the death of the last survivor of the undersigned and their children and grandchildren who are alive at the creation of the Trust. For purposes of this perpetuities savings clause, a Trust shall be deemed to have been created on the date the Trust becomes irrevocable or the date of death of the Settlor, whichever occurs first. If a Trust is terminated under this section, the Trustee shall distribute all of the principal and undistributed income of the Trust to the income beneficiaries of the Trust in the proportion in which they are entitled (or eligible, in the case of discretionary payments) to receive income immediately before the termination. If that proportion is not fixed by the terms of the Trust, the Trustee shall distribute all of the Trust property to the persons then entitled or eligible to receive income from the Trust as a class, in the manner provided in California Probate Code Section 240.

ARTICLE ELEVEN

Section 11.01. <u>Governing Law</u>

It is not intended that the laws of only one particular state shall necessarily govern all questions pertaining to all of the Trust hereunder. Rather;

a) The validity of the Trust hereunder, as well as the validity of the particular provisions of this Trust, shall be governed by the laws of whatever state having any sufficient connection with such Trust which will support such validity.

b) The meaning and effect of the terms of this Trust instrument and of any other Trust instrument related hereto shall be governed by the laws of the state under which the initial Trust instrument was created, that is, California State in the case of this instrument, and such other state as may be designated in the governing instrument of any Trustee receiving an appointment hereunder.

c) The administration of the Trust hereunder shall be governed by laws of the state in which the Trust is then being administered (based on the location of the principal office of the Trustee then having custody of that Trust's principal assets and records), which state's courts shall have exclusive jurisdiction over that administration of the Trust with respect to any period during which it was thus administered in that state.

The foregoing shall apply even though the situs of some Trust assets or the home of the Settlor, a Trustee, or beneficiary may at some time or times be elsewhere.

Section 11.02 Invalidity of Any Provision

Should any provision of this Declaration be or become invalid or unenforceable, the remaining provisions of this Declaration shall be and continue to be fully effective.

Section 11.03 Successor Trustees

Any successor Trustee taking office pursuant to Article Nine of this Declaration shall forthwith succeed to all title of the prior Trustee and shall have all the power, rights, discretion and obligations conferred on such Trustee by this Declaration.

All rights, titles and interest in the property of the Trust shall immediately vest in the successor Trustee(s) at the time of appointment. The prior Trustee shall, without warranty, transfer to the successor Trustee(s) the existing Trust property.

No successor Trustee(s) shall be under any duty to examine, verify, question, or audit the books, records, accounts, or transaction of any preceding Trustee; and no successor Trustee shall be liable or responsible in any way for any acts or defaults of any predecessor Trustee, nor for any loss or expense from or occasioned by anything done or neglected to be done by any predecessor Trustee. A successor Trustee shall be liable only for his/her own acts and defaults.

WE, AND EACH OF US, CERTIFY THAT:

1. We, and each of us, have read the foregoing Revocable Living Trust Agreement;

2. The foregoing Revocable Living Trust Agreement correctly states the terms and conditions under which the Trust Estate is to be held, managed, administered and disposed of by the Trustee,

3. We, and each of us, approve such Revocable Living Trust Agreement in all particulars; and

4. As the Trustee named in such Revocable Living Trust Agreement, we and each of us, approve and accept the Trusts and terms provided for in such Agreement.

Executed on this _____ day of _____, 2005, at Santa Barbara, CA

BY: _____   **GEORGE M. MILLER**, TRUSTEE

BY: _____   **ILENE MILLER,** TRUSTEE

BY: _____   **GEORGE M. MILLER**, SETTLOR

BY: _____   **ILENE MILLER,** SETTLOR

Declaration and Acknowledgment of Notary Public

STATE OF CALIFORNIA

COUNTY OF SANTA BARBARA

On _____ before me, _____, personally appeared **GEORGE M. MILLER** and **ILENE MILLER,** _____ personally known to me -OR- _____ proved to me on the basis of satisfactory evidence to be the persons whose names are subscribed to the within instrument and acknowledged to me that they executed the same in their authorized capacities, and that by their signatures on the instrument the persons, or the entity upon behalf of which the persons acted, executed the instrument.

WITNESS my hand and official seal.

_____
Signature of Notary Public

Declaration of Intent

THE MILLER FAMILY LIVING TRUST

The undersigned, **GEORGE M. MILLER** and **ILENE MILLER** as Trustees of **THE MILLER FAMILY LIVING TRUST**, declare that all property listed in the Schedule of Trust Property, hereby incorporated by reference, as amended from time to time, and all other property transferred to **THE MILLER FAMILY LIVING TRUST**, and all such assets shall belong to **THE MILLER FAMILY LIVING TRUST** and not to **GEORGE M. MILLER** and **ILENE MILLER** individually. Except to the extent of interest provided in the trust documents and this declaration, they have no personal interest in any such properties. It is the intention of **GEORGE M. MILLER** and **ILENE MILLER** that this declaration shall constitute confirmation of trust ownership and shall be binding on the heirs, successors, executors, administrators, and assignees of **GEORGE M. MILLER** and **ILENE MILLER**.

IN WITNESS WHEREOF, the undersigned have executed this instrument on this the _____ day of _____, 2005.

_____
GEORGE M. MILLER

_____
ILENE MILLER

Declaration and Acknowledgment of Notary Public

STATE OF CALIFORNIA

COUNTY OF SANTA BARBARA

On _____ before me, _____, personally appeared **GEORGE M. MILLER** and **ILENE MILLER**, _____ personally known to me -OR- _____ proved to me on the basis of satisfactory evidence to be the persons whose names are subscribed to the within instrument and acknowledged to me that they executed the same in their authorized capacities, and that by their signatures on the instrument the persons, or the entity upon behalf of which the persons acted, executed the instrument.

WITNESS my hand and official seal.

_____
Signature of Notary Public

POUR OVER WILL

I, **GEORGE M. MILLER**, a resident of California, hereby make, publish, and declare this to be my Last Will and Testament and revoke all Wills and Codicils previously made.

I, **GEORGE M. MILLER** declare that I am married to **ILENE MILLER** and have two children. The names of my children are **GEORGE MELVIN MILLER** and **SCOTT C. MILLER**.

Article I
I give the entire residue of my estate to the trustee then in office under the trust designated as **THE MILLER FAMILY LIVING TRUST**, established on the _____ day of _____, 2005, of which I am the Settlor and Trustee. I direct that the residue of my estate shall be added to, administered, and distributed as part of that trust, and any lawful amendments thereto made before my death. It is not my intent to create a separate trust by this Will, or to subject the trust or the property added to it to the jurisdiction of the probate court.

Article II
If the disposition in Article I is inoperative, invalid, fails, or is revoked for any reason, I incorporate herein by reference the terms of the trust as executed on this date, without giving effect to any amendments made subsequently. I bequeath and devise the residue of my estate to the trustee named in this trust, to be held, administered, and distributed as provided in this trust instrument.

Article III
I hereby nominate **ILENE MILLER** to be the Personal Representative of this Will. In the event that **ILENE MILLER** is unable or declines to serve, I nominate **GEORGE MELVIN MILLER** to be Alternate Personal Representative. The Personal Representative shall have full power and authority to carry out the provisions of this Will. These powers shall include, but are not limited to, the managing and operating of any property and business belonging to my estate during probate.

If any part of this Will is held to be void, invalid, or inoperative, I direct that such voidness, invalidity, or inoperativeness shall not affect any other part of this Will, and the remainder of this Will shall be carried into effect as if such part had not been contained herein.

The Personal Representative shall serve without bond.

Signed on this the _____ day of _____, 2005, Santa Barbara, CA

_____
GEORGE M. MILLER

Declaration of Witnesses

On this date written below, **GEORGE M. MILLER**, the undersigned, declared to us that this instrument, including the page signed by us as witnesses is the Last Will and Testament of **GEORGE M. MILLER** (hereafter, "Settlor/Testator"), who, at the Settlor/Testator's request and in the Settlor/Testator's presence, and in the presence of each other now subscribe our names as witnesses.

We declare under penalty of perjury that the foregoing is true and correct and that this declaration was executed on this the _____ day of _____, 2005, at Santa Barbara, CA

WITNESSES:

_____   _____
Witness Signature   Witness Signature

_____   _____
Print Name   Print Name

_____   _____
Street Address   Street Address

_____   _____
City/State/Zip Code   City/State/Zip Code

Self Approved Affidavit

STATE OF CALIFORNIA

COUNTY OF SANTA BARBARA

    I, **GEORGE M. MILLER**, (Settlor/Testator) and, _____ and _____, (Witnesses), respectively, whose names are signed to the attached or foregoing instrument, being first duly sworn, do hereby declare to the undersigned authority that the Settlor/Testator signed and executed the instrument as the Settlor/Testator's Last Will, that the Settlor/Testator signed willingly (or directed another to sign it for him), and that he executed it as a free and voluntary act for the purposes therein expressed and that each of the witnesses, in the presence and hearing of the Settlor/Testator, signed the Will as witnesses and that to the best of their knowledge the Settlor/Testator was at the time 18 or more years of age, of sound mind, and under no constraint or undue influence.

_____
GEORGE M. MILLER

_____
Witness Signature

_____
Witness Name (Print)

_____
Witness Signature

_____
Witness Name (Print)

    On _____ before me, _____, personally appeared **GEORGE M. MILLER**, _____ personally known to me -OR- ____ proved to me on the basis of satisfactory evidence to be the person whose name is subscribed to the within instrument and acknowledged to me that he executed the same in his authorized capacity, and that by his signature on the instrument the person, or the entity upon behalf of which the person acted, executed the instrument.

    WITNESS my hand and official seal.

_____
Signature of Notary Public

POUR OVER WILL

I, **ILENE MILLER**, a resident of California, hereby make, publish, and declare this to be my Last Will and Testament and revoke all Wills and Codicils previously made.

I, **ILENE MILLER**, declare that I am married to **GEORGE M. MILLER** and have two children. The names of my children are **GEORGE MELVIN MILLER** and **SCOTT C. MILLER**.

Article I

I give the entire residue of my estate to the trustee then in office under the trust designated as **THE MILLER FAMILY LIVING TRUST**, established on the _____ day of _____, 2005, of which I am the Settlor and Trustee. I direct that the residue of my estate shall be added to, administered, and distributed as part of that trust, and any lawful amendments thereto made before my death. It is not my intent to create a separate trust by this Will, or to subject the trust or the property added to it to the jurisdiction of the probate court.

Article II

If the disposition in Article I is inoperative, invalid, fails, or is revoked for any reason, I incorporate herein by reference the terms of the trust as executed on this date, without giving effect to any amendments made subsequently. I bequeath and devise the residue of my estate to the trustee named in this trust, to be held, administered, and distributed as provided in this trust instrument.

Article III

I hereby nominate **GEORGE M. MILLER** to be the Personal Representative of this Will. In the event that **GEORGE M. MILLER** is unable or declines to serve, I nominate **GEORGE MELVIN MILLER** to be Alternate Personal Representative. The Personal Representative shall have full power and authority to carry out the provisions of this Will. These powers shall include, but are not limited to, the managing and operating of any property and business belonging to my estate during probate.

If any part of this Will is held to be void, invalid, or inoperative, I direct that such voidness, invalidity, or inoperativeness shall not affect any other part of this Will, and the remainder of this Will shall be carried into effect as if such part had not been contained herein.

The Personal Representative shall serve without bond.

Signed on this the _____ day of _____, 2005, at Santa Barbara, CA

_____
ILENE MILLER

Declaration of Witnesses

On this date written below, **ILENE MILLER**, the undersigned, declared to us that this instrument, including the page signed by us as witnesses is the Last Will and Testament of **ILENE MILLER** (hereafter, "Settlor/Testator"), who, at the Settlor/Testator's request and in the Settlor/Testator's presence, and in the presence of each other now subscribe our names as witnesses.

We declare under penalty of perjury that the foregoing is true and correct and that this declaration was executed on this the _____ day of _____, 2005, at Santa Barbara, CA

WITNESSES:

_____
Witness Signature

_____
Print Name

_____
Street Address

_____
City/State/Zip Code

_____
Witness Signature

_____
Print Name

_____
Street Address

_____
City/State/Zip Code

Self Approved Affidavit

STATE OF CALIFORNIA

COUNTY OF SANTA BARBARA

    I, **ILENE MILLER** (Settlor/Testator) and, _____ and _____, (Witnesses), respectively, whose names are signed to the attached or foregoing instrument, being first duly sworn, do hereby declare to the undersigned authority that the Settlor/Testator signed and executed the instrument as the Settlor/Testator's Last Will, that the Settlor/Testator signed willingly (or directed another to sign it for her), and that she executed it as a free and voluntary act for the purposes therein expressed and that each of the witnesses, in the presence and hearing of the Settlor/Testator, signed the Will as witnesses and that to the best of their knowledge the Settlor/Testator was at the time 18 or more years of age, of sound mind, and under no constraint or undue influence.

                                                         _____

                                                          ILENE MILLER

                                                          _____

                                                          Witness Signature

                                                          _____

                                                          Witness Name (Print)

                                                          _____

                                                          Witness Signature

                                                          _____

                                                          Witness Name (Print)

      On _____ before me, _____, personally appeared **ILENE MILLER,** _____ personally known to me -OR- _____ proved to me on the basis of satisfactory evidence to be the person whose name is subscribed to the within instrument and acknowledged to me that she executed the same in her authorized capacity, and that by her signature on the instrument the person, or the entity upon behalf of which the person acted, executed the instrument.   **WITNESS** my hand and official seal.

                                                          _____

                                                          Signature of Notary Public

AFFIDAVIT OF TRUST
The following Living Trust is the subject of this Affidavit:

GEORGE M. MILLER and **ILENE MILLER**, Trustees, or their successor in trust, under **THE MILLER FAMILY LIVING TRUST** dated this _____ day of _____, 2005, and any amendments thereto.

The names of the current Trustees of the trust agreement are as follows:

Name: GEORGE M. MILLER, 714 Main Road, Santa Barbara, CA 93105
Name: ILENE MILLER, 714 Main Road, Santa Barbara, CA 93105

The trust is currently in full force and effect.

Attached to this Affidavit and incorporated in it are selected provisions of the trust including the pages naming the initial trustees, creating the trust, trusteeís powers (see Article 5), statement of revocability of the trust (see Article 2), the designation of the successor trustee (see Article 9), third party indemnification (see Power of Attorney), and a copy of the signature pages signed and notarized.

The trust provisions are of a personal and private nature and set forth the distribution of the trust property. **They do not modify** the powers of the Trustee.

The signatories of this Affidavit are currently the acting Trustees of the trust and declare that the foregoing statements and the attached trust provisions are true and correct, under penalty of perjury.

This Affidavit is dated _____.

_____
GEORGE M. MILLER

_____
ILENE MILLER

Witnesses:

_____   _____

STATE OF CALIFORNIA
              } s.s.
COUNTY OF SANTA BARBARA

Subscribed and sworn to (or affirmed) before me this _____ day of _____ 2005, by **GEORGE M. MILLER** and **ILENE MILLER**.

_____
Signature of Notary Public

Trustee Instructions

Managing Your Revocable Living Trust

The "Trustee" is responsible for managing the trust assets. As the Trustee of your own Revocable Living trust your responsibilities for managing your assets do not differ significantly. You are the owner of your assets, whether the assets are in your trust or not. You can control, sell, or borrow against your property just as you always could.

You should always strive to keep careful records of all transactions that affect your Revocable Living Trust. There are specific tax requirements that should be addressed with your accountant or CPA to maximize the efficiency of your trust estate.

Especially important are the actions you take to designate what assets you wish directed to your identified individual beneficiaries. You may have requested that certain percentages of your estate should be passed on to specified individuals or members of your family. However, your Trust Instruction information can be utilized to make specific bequests as well. For example, you may have indicated that your estate should be divided equally to "share and share alike" among your children at your death. You can use your Trust Instructions to pass specific assets of your trust to individual children.

Broad and sweeping powers are given to you as trustee, but you should always exercise prudence in managing your assets. Your Revocable Living Trust is your basic estate plan which will provide the foundation for a well organized estate.

Your Trust Estate

As Trustee, you hold your assets in trust for your own benefit during your life. When you place assets in your trust you should identify those assets as belonging to "**THE MILLER FAMILY LIVING TRUST, GEORGE M. MILLER** and **ILENE MILLER**, Trustees." This simply means that your trust owns the assets and you own the trust.

To transfer real property to your trust, simply utilize a "Quit Claim Deed," which can be easily recorded with your County Recording office or other local government entity. Personal property, such as bank accounts, etc., can be transferred by contacting the office, bank, or corporation involved. Of course, some description of such assets should be recorded in your Trust Instructions.

SCHEDULE A (COMMUNITY PROPERTY LIST)

Our home at 714 Main Street, Santa Barbara, CA

Our certificate of Deposit at the Bank of America on State Street, Santa Barbara, CA

SCHEDULE B (ILENE MILLER's Sole and Separate Property)

My mother's diamond ring

SCHEDULE C (GEORGE M. MILLER's sole and separate property)

My grandfather's fishing gear

SCHEDULE OF TRUST PROPERTY AND ADDITIONAL INFORMATION
The following property, both real and personal, has been allocated by **GEORGE M. MILLER** and **ILENE MILLER** to **THE MILLER FAMILY LIVING TRUST** as indicated below:

Personal Property:

1. Date of Allocation   _____
   Location of Property   _____

2. Date of Allocation   _____
   Location of Property   _____

Real Property:

1. Date of Property Transfer   _____
   Description of Trust Property   _____
   Location of Trust Property   _____

2. Date of Property Transfer   _____
   Description of Trust Property   _____
   Location of Trust Property   _____

Professional Consultants and Advisors:

Physician   _____

Physician   _____

Dentist   _____

Attorney   _____

Accountant   _____

Broker   _____

Investment Advisor   _____

Clergy   _____

Other   _____

Other   _____

Location of Documents:

1. Item: Trust Documents
    Location _____

2. Item: Copy of Trust Documents
    Location _____

3. Item: Life Insurance Policies
    Location _____

4. Item: Cemetery Plot Information
    Location _____

5. Item: Bank Account Records
    Location _____

6. Item: Deeds to Real Property
    Location _____

7. Item: Rental Property Records
    Location _____

8. Item: Motor Vehicle Registration
    Location _____

9. Item: Tax Records
    Location _____

10. Item: Stock/Bond Certificates
    Location _____

11. Item: Broker Account Records
    Location _____

12. Item: Other Investment Records
    Location _____

13. Item: Birth Certificate
    Location _____

14. Item: Marriage Certificate
    Location _____

15. Item: Citizenship Papers
    Location   _____

16. Item: Divorce/Separation Documents
    Location   _____

17. Item: Military Discharge Papers
    Location   _____

18. Item: Adoption Papers
    Location   _____

19. Item: Passports
    Location   _____

20. Item: Annuity Contracts
    Location   _____

21. Item: IRA Plan Records
    Location   _____

22. Item: Keogh Plan Records
    Location   _____

23. Item: Safe Deposit Box Information
    Location   _____

24. Item: Safe Combination
    Location   _____

25. Item: Partnership Agreements
    Location   _____

26. Item: Notes and Loan Agreements
    Location   _____

27. Item: Record of Stored and Loaned Property
    Location   _____

28. Item: Employment Records
    Location   _____

29. Item: Educational Records
    Location _____

30. Item: Miscellaneous
    Location _____

31. Item: Miscellaneous
    Location _____

32. Item: Miscellaneous
    Location _____

33. Item: Miscellaneous
    Location _____

34. Item: Miscellaneous
    Location _____

35. Item: Miscellaneous
    Location _____

36. Item: Miscellaneous
    Location _____

37. Item: Miscellaneous
    Location _____

38. Item: Miscellaneous
    Location _____

39. Item: Miscellaneous
    Location _____

40. Item: Miscellaneous
    Location _____

ADDITIONAL ITEMS:

Liabilities: List all of your liabilities below, including the names and addresses of the institutions or individuals to whom the debt or debts are owed.

1. Name of Individual/Institution
   Address _____
   Account Number _____
   Amount _____
   Date _____

2. Name of Individual/Institution
   Address _____
   Account Number _____
   Amount _____
   Date _____

3. Name of Individual/Institution
   Address _____
   Account Number _____
   Amount _____
   Date _____

4. Name of Individual/Institution
   Address _____
   Account Number _____
   Amount _____
   Date _____

5. Name of Individual/Institution
   Address _____
   Account Number _____
   Amount _____
   Date _____

6. Name of Individual/Institution
   Address _____
   Account Number _____
   Amount _____
   Date _____

7. Name of Individual/Institution
   Address _____
   Account Number _____
   Amount _____
   Date _____

Insurance Policies:

    List all of your insurance policies below, including life, automobile, homeowners, real estate, equipment, disability, medical and dental.

1.   Name of Company   _____

         Address   _____

         Policy Number   _____ Premium _____

         Name of Insured   _____

         Type of Insurance   _____

         Name of Beneficiary   _____

2.   Name of Company   _____

         Address   _____

         Policy Number   _____ Premium _____

         Name of Insured   _____

         Type of Insurance   _____

         Name of Beneficiary   _____

3.   Name of Company   _____

         Address   _____

         Policy Number   _____ Premium _____

         Name of Insured   _____

         Type of Insurance   _____

         Name of Beneficiary   _____

4.   Name of Company   _____

         Address   _____

         Policy Number   _____ Premium _____

         Name of Insured _____

         Type of Insurance _____

         Name of Beneficiary _____

5.   Name of Company   _____

         Address   _____

         Policy Number   _____ Premium _____

         Name of Insured   _____

         Type of Insurance   _____

         Name of Beneficiary   _____

6.   Name of Company   _____

         Address   _____

         Policy Number   _____ Premium _____

         Name of Insured   _____

         Type of Insurance   _____

         Name of Beneficiary   _____

BURIAL INSTRUCTIONS

Below, please indicate your specific desires with regard to burial instructions and donation of anatomical gifts:

Burial Instructions for: **GEORGE M. MILLER**
Date of Birth:
Mortuary:
Address:
City/State/Zip:
Phone Number:

SPECIAL INSTRUCTIONS:

DONATION OF ANATOMICAL GIFTS

Donate Specific Organs to:

Organs to be donated: (list specific organs)

Acknowledgment:

Print Name   **Signature**   **Date**

BURIAL INSTRUCTIONS

Below, please indicate your specific desires with regard to burial instructions and donation of anatomical gifts:

Burial Instructions for: **ILENE MILLER**
Date of Birth:
Mortuary:
Address:
City/State/Zip:
Phone Number:

SPECIAL INSTRUCTIONS:

DONATION OF ANATOMICAL GIFTS

Donate Specific Organs to:

Organs to be donated: (list specific organs)

Acknowledgment:

Print Name   **Signature**   **Date**

TRUST INSTRUCTIONS

Attention Trustee and Successor Trustee: This is a record of **THE MILLER FAMILY LIVING TRUST**, referred to as Trust Instructions. These Trust Instructions are the instructions to the Successor Trustee on the distribution desires of **GEORGE M. MILLER** and **ILENE MILLER**. Each item included below, provided each is signed and dated by the Settlor/Testator, constitutes an important element of this Revocable Living Trust, established on the _____ day of _____, 2005.

*** SEE AFFIDAVIT OF TRUST

Directions to be taken:

If at the time of my death, any of our children are minors and a guardian is needed, We nominate our good friend, Judy Sanders to be the guardian of their estate and their person.

Date: 3/5/05   Signed: *George M. Miller*
Date: 3/5/05   Signed: *Ilene Miller*

We give the antique rocking chair and our condo to our son, George Melvin Miller.

Date: 3/12/05   Signed: *George M. Miller*
Date: 3/12/05   Signed: *Ilene Miller*

Directions to be taken:

Signed:
Dated:

INFORMATION SHEET

In case of emergency, it is important that individuals holding powers of attorney for management of the assets of this Revocable Living Trust, agents holding power to make health decisions, executors and successor trustees are notified. You may wish to list their names, addresses and telephone numbers below.

Successor Trustee: **GEORGE MELVIN MILLER**
Address: 714 Main
City: Santa Barbara
State: CA   Zip Code: 93105
Telephone Number: (805) 555-3820

Alternate Successor Trustee: **JUDY SANDERS**
Address: 2106 Spring Street
City: Redding
State: CA   Zip Code: 96004
Telephone Number: (530) 555-8989

Alternate Conservator: **GEORGE MELVIN MILLER**
Address: Same as above
Telephone Number: (805) 555-3772

Alternate Agent for Health Care: **GEORGE MELVIN MILLER**
Address: Same as above
Telephone Number: (805) 555-3772

ADDITIONAL DOCUMENTS

DURABLE POWER OF ATTORNEY FOR PROPERTY MANAGEMENT
(California Probate Code Section 4401)
TO PERSON EXECUTING THIS DOCUMENT:

NOTICE: THE POWERS GRANTED BY THIS DOCUMENT ARE BROAD AND SWEEPING. THEY ARE EXPLAINED IN THE UNIFORM STATUTORY FORM POWER OF ATTORNEY ACT (CALIFORNIA PROBATE CODE SECTIONS 4400-4465). IF YOU HAVE ANY QUESTIONS ABOUT THESE POWERS, OBTAIN COMPETENT LEGAL ADVICE. THIS DOCUMENT DOES NOT AUTHORIZE ANYONE TO MAKE MEDICAL OR OTHER HEALTH CARE DECISIONS FOR YOU. YOU MAY REVOKE THIS POWER OF ATTORNEY IF YOU LATER WISH TO DO SO.

1. DESIGNATION OF AGENT. I, **GEORGE M. MILLER**, of 714 Main Road, Santa Barbara, CA 93105 do hereby designate and appoint **ILENE MILLER**, whose address is 714 Main Road, Santa Barbara, CA 93105, to be my agent (attorney-in-fact) to act for me in any lawful way with respect to the following subjects.

2. TO GRANT ALL OF THE FOLLOWING POWERS INITIAL (#15) ONLY, FOR THE LIMITING OF POWERS INITIAL ONLY THOSE POWERS WHICH YOU ARE GRANTING TO YOUR AGENT.

_____	(1)	Real estate transactions
_____	(2)	Tangible personal property transactions
_____	(3)	Bond, share, and commodity option transactions
_____	(4)	Banking & other financial institution transactions
_____	(5)	Business operating transactions
_____	(6)	Insurance operating transactions
_____	(7)	Retirement plan transactions
_____	(8)	Estate, trust, & other beneficiary transactions
_____	(9)	Claims and litigations
_____	(10)	Tax matters
_____	(11)	Personal & family maintenance
_____	(12)	Benefits from Social Security, Medicare, Medicaid or other governmental programs, or civil or military services
_____	(13)	Records, reports, and statements
_____	(14)	Full and unqualified authority to my agent to delegate any or all of the foregoing powers to any person or persons whom my agent shall select
_____	(15)	All of the powers listed above.

3. DURATION. This Power of Attorney shall exist for an indefinite period of time even though I become incapacitated, unless I have specified otherwise.

4. NOMINATION OF AGENT. I nominate, as the agent of the estate, **ILENE MILLER**, whose address is written herein above. In the event that **ILENE MILLER** is unable or declines to serve, I nominate **GEORGE MELVIN MILLER** to serve as alternate agent of the estate.

5. RELIANCE. I agree that any third party who receives a copy of this document may act under it. Revocation of the power of attorney is not effective as to a third party until the third party has actual knowledge of the revocation. I agree to i ndemnify the third party for any claims that arise against the third party because of reliance on this power of attorney.

DATE AND SIGNATURE OF PRINCIPAL

I, **GEORGE M. MILLER**, sign my name to this Power of Attorney on this _____ day of _____, 2005, at Santa Barbara, CA

_____
GEORGE M. MILLER
Social Security #

BY ACCEPTING OR ACTING UNDER THE APPOINTMENT, THE AGENT ASSUMES THE FIDUCIARY AND OTHER LEGAL RESPONSIBILITIES OF AN AGENT.

Certificate of Acknowledgment of Notary Public

STATE OF CALIFORNIA

COUNTY OF SANTA BARBARA

On _____ before me, _____, personally appeared **GEORGE M. MILLER**, _____ personally known to me -OR- _____ proved to me on the basis of satisfactory evidence to be the person whose name is subscribed to the within instrument and acknowledged to me that he executed the same in his authorized capacity, and that by his signature on the instrument the person, or the entity upon behalf of which the person acted, executed the instrument.

WITNESS my hand and official seal.

_____
Signature of Notary Public

DURABLE POWER OF ATTORNEY FOR PROPERTY MANAGEMENT
(California Probate Code Section 4401)
TO PERSON EXECUTING THIS DOCUMENT:

NOTICE: THE POWERS GRANTED BY THIS DOCUMENT ARE BROAD AND SWEEPING. THEY ARE EXPLAINED IN THE UNIFORM STATUTORY FORM POWER OF ATTORNEY ACT (CALIFORNIA PROBATE CODE SECTIONS 4400-4465). IF YOU HAVE ANY QUESTIONS ABOUT THESE POWERS, OBTAIN COMPETENT LEGAL ADVICE. THIS DOCUMENT DOES NOT AUTHORIZE ANYONE TO MAKE MEDICAL OR OTHER HEALTH CARE DECISIONS FOR YOU. YOU MAY REVOKE THIS POWER OF ATTORNEY IF YOU LATER WISH TO DO SO.

     1. DESIGNATION OF AGENT. I, **ILENE MILLER**, of 714 Main Road, Santa Barbara, CA 93105, do hereby designate and appoint **GEORGE M. MILLER**, whose address is 714 Main Road, Santa Barbara, CA 93105, to be my agent (attorney-in-fact) to act for me in any lawful way with respect to the following subjects.

     2. TO GRANT ALL OF THE FOLLOWING POWERS INITIAL (#15) ONLY, FOR THE LIMITING OF POWERS INITIAL ONLY THOSE POWERS WHICH YOU ARE GRANTING TO YOUR AGENT.

_____	(1) Real estate transactions
_____	(2) Tangible personal property transactions
_____	(3) Bond, share, and commodity option transactions
_____	(4) Banking & other financial institution transactions
_____	(5) Business operating transactions
_____	(6) Insurance operating transactions
_____	(7) Retirement plan transactions
_____	(8) Estate, trust, & other beneficiary transactions
_____	(9) Claims and litigations
_____	(10) Tax matters
_____	(11) Personal & family maintenance
_____	(12) Benefits from Social Security, Medicare, Medicaid or other governmental programs, or civil or military services
_____	(13) Records, reports, and statements
_____	(14) Full and unqualified authority to my agent to delegate any or all of the foregoing powers to any person or persons whom my agent shall select
_____	(15) All of the powers listed above.

     3. DURATION. This Power of Attorney shall exist for an indefinite period of time even though I become incapacitated, unless I have specified otherwise.

     4. NOMINATION OF AGENT. I nominate, as the agent of the estate, **GEORGE M. MILLER**, whose address is written herein above. In the event that **GEORGE M. MILLER** is unable or declines to serve, I nominate **GEORGE MELVIN MILLER** to serve as alternate agent of the estate.

5. RELIANCE. I agree that any third party who receives a copy of this document may act under it. Revocation of the power of attorney is not effective as to a third party until the third party has actual knowledge of the revocation. I agree to i ndemnify the third party for any claims that arise against the third party because of reliance on this power of attorney.

DATE AND SIGNATURE OF PRINCIPAL

I, **ILENE MILLER**, sign my name to this Power of Attorney on this _____ day of _____, 2005, at Santa Barbara, CA

_____
ILENE MILLER
Social Security #

BY ACCEPTING OR ACTING UNDER THE APPOINTMENT, THE AGENT ASSUMES THE FIDUCIARY AND OTHER LEGAL RESPONSIBILITIES OF AN AGENT.

Certificate of Acknowledgment of Notary Public

STATE OF CALIFORNIA

COUNTY OF SANTA BARBARA

On _____ before me, _____,
personally appeared **ILENE MILLER**, _____ personally known to me -OR- ____ proved to me on the basis of satisfactory evidence to be the person whose name is subscribed to the within instrument and acknowledged to me that she executed the same in her authorized capacity, and that by her signature on the instrument the person, or the entity upon behalf of which the person acted, executed the instrument.

WITNESS my hand and official seal.

_____
Signature of Notary Public

ADVANCE HEALTH CARE DIRECTIVE
(California Probate Code Section 4701)

Explanation

You have the right to give instructions about your own health care. You also have the right to name someone else to make health care decisions for you. This form lets you do either or both of these things. It also lets you express your wishes regarding donation of organs and the designation of your primary physician. If you use this form, you may complete or modify all or any part of it. You are free to use a different form.

Part 1 of this form is a power of attorney for health care. Part 1 lets you name another individual as agent to make health care decisions for you if you become incapable of making your own decisions or if you want someone else to make those decisions for you now even though you are still capable. You may also name an alternate agent to act for you if your first choice is not willing, able, or reasonably available to make decisions for you. (Your agent may not be an operator or employee of a community health care institution where you are receiving care, unless your agent is related to you or is a coworker.)

Unless the form you sign limits the authority of your agent, your agent may make all health care decisions for you. This form has a place for you to limit the authority of your agent. You need not limit the authority of your agent if you wish to rely on your agent for all healthcare decisions that may have to be made. If you choose not to limit the authority of your agent, your agent will have the right to:

a) Consent or refuse consent to any care, treatment, service, or procedure to maintain, diagnose, or otherwise affect a physical or mental condition.

b) Select or discharge health care providers and institutions.

c) Approve or disapprove diagnostic tests, surgical procedures, and programs of medication.

d) Direct the provision, withholding, or withdrawal of artificial nutrition and hydration and all other forms of health care, including cardiopulmonary resuscitation.

e) Make anatomical gifts, authorize an autopsy, and direct disposition of remains.

Part 2 of this form lets you give specific instructions about any aspect of your health care, whether or not you appoint an agent. Choices are provided for you to express your wishes regarding the provision, withholding, or withdrawal of treatment to keep you alive, as well as the provision of pain relief. Space is also provided for you to add to the choices you have made or for you to write out any additional wishes. If you are satisfied to allow your agent to determine what is best for you in making end-of-life decisions, you need not fill out Part 2 of this form.

Part 3 of this form lets you express an intention to donate your bodily organs and tissues following your death.

Part 4 of this form lets you designate a physician to have primary responsibility for your health care.

After completing this form, sign and date the form at the end. The form must be signed by two qualified witnesses or acknowledged before a notary public. Give a copy of the signed and completed form to your physician, to any other health care providers you may have, any health care agents you have named. You should talk to the person you have named as agent to make sure that he or she understands your wishes and is willing to take the responsibility.

You have the right to revoke this advance health care directive or replace this form at any time.

****

PART 1

POWER OF ATTORNEY FOR HEALTH CARE

(1.1) DESIGNATION OF AGENT: I designate the following individual as my agent to make health care decisions for me: **ILENE MILLER** whose address is 714 Main Road, Santa Barbara, CA 93105, and telephone number is (805) 555-3772.

If I revoke my agent's authority or if my agent is not willing, able, or reasonably available to make a health care decision for me, I designate as my first alternate agent: **GEORGE MELVIN MILLER** whose address is 714 Main Road, Santa Barbara, CA 93105, and telephone number is (805) 555-3772.

(1.2) AGENT'S AUTHORITY: My agent is authorized to make all health care decisions for me, including decisions to provide, withhold, or withdraw artificial nutrition and hydration and all other forms of health care to keep me alive, except as I state here:

_____
_____
_____

(Add additional sheets if needed.)

(1.3) WHEN AGENT'S AUTHORITY BECOMES EFFECTIVE: My agent's authority becomes effective when my primary physician determines that I am unable to make my own health care decisions unless I initial the following line. **If I initial this line _____, my agent's authority to make health care decisions for me takes effect immediately.**

(1.4) AGENT'S OBLIGATION: My agent shall make health care decisions for me in accordance with this power of attorney for health care, any instructions I give in Part 2 of this form, and my other wishes to the extent known to my agent. To the extent my wishes are unknown, my agent shall make health care decisions for me in accordance with what my agent determines to be in my best interest. In determining my best interest, my agent shall consider my personal values to the extent known to my agent.

(1.5) AGENT'S POSTDEATH AUTHORITY: My agent is authorized to make anatomical gifts, authorize an autopsy, and direct disposition of my remains, except as I state here or in Part 3 of this form:

_____
_____
_____

(Add additional sheets if needed.)

(1.6) NOMINATION OF CONSERVATOR: If a conservator of my person needs to be appointed for me by a court, I nominate the agent designated in this form. If that agent is not willing, able or reasonably available to act as conservator, I nominate the alternate agents whom I have named, in the order designated.

PART 2

INSTRUCTIONS FOR HEALTH CARE

If you fill out this part of the form, you may cross out any wording you do not want.

(2.1) END-OF-LIFE DECISIONS: I direct that my health care providers and others involved in my care provide, withhold, or withdraw treatment in accordance with the choice I have initialed below:

_____ (a) Choice Not To Prolong Life - I do not want my life to be prolonged if:

(1) I have an incurable and irreversible condition that will result in my death within a relatively short time;

(2) I become unconscious and, to a reasonable degree of medical certainty, I will not regain consciousness, or

(3) the likely risks and burdens of treatment would outweigh the expected benefits, OR

_____ (b) Choice To Prolong Life- I want my life to be prolonged as long as possible within the limits of generally accepted health care standards.

(2.2) RELIEF FROM PAIN: Except as I state in the following space, I direct that treatment for alleviation of pain or discomfort be provided at all times, even if it hastens my death:

_____

_____

_____

(Add additional sheets if needed.)

PART 3
DONATION OF ORGANS AT DEATH
(OPTIONAL)

(3.1) Upon my death (initial each applicable line):

_____ (a) I give any needed organs, tissues, or parts, OR

_____ (b) I give the following organs, tissues, or parts only. _____

_____

_____ (c) My gift is for the following purposes (cross out any of the following you do not

want):

        (1) Transplant

        (2) Therapy

        (3) Research

        (4) Education

PART 4
PRIMARY PHYSICIAN
(OPTIONAL)

(4.1) I designate the following physician as my primary physician:

Name	Address	Telephone

OPTIONAL: If the physician I have designated above is not willing, able or reasonably available
to act as my primary physician, I designate the following physician as my primary physician:

Name	Address	Telephone

****

PART 5

(5.1) EFFECT OF COPY: A copy of this form has the same effect as the original.

(5.2) SIGNATURE: Sign and date the form here:

_____   _____

(date)   (Signature)

                                                 GEORGE M. MILLER

                                                   714 Main Road

                                                   Santa Barbara, CA 93105

STATE OF CALIFORNIA

COUNTY OF SANTA BARBARA

On _____ before me, _____,
personally appeared **GEORGE M. MILLER**, _____ personally known to me -OR- ____
proved to me on the basis of satisfactory evidence to be the person whose name is subscribed to
the within instrument and acknowledged to me that he executed the same in his authorized
capacity, and that by his signature on the instrument the person, or the entity upon behalf of
which the person acted, executed the instrument.

               WITNESS my hand and official seal.

                                           _____

                                           Signature of Notary Public

(5.3) STATEMENT OF WITNESSES: I declare under penalty of perjury under the laws of California (1) that the individual who signed or acknowledged this advance health care directive is personally known to me, or that the individual's identity was proven to me by convincing evidence, (2) that the individual signed or acknowledged this advance directive in my presence, (3) that the individual appears to be of sound mind and under no duress, fraud, or under influence, (4) that I am not a person appointed as agent by this advance directive, and (5) that I am not the individual's health care provider, an employee of the individual's health care provider, the operator of a community care facility, an employee of an operator of a community care facility, the operator of a residential care facility for the elderly, nor an employee of an operator of a residential care facility for the elderly.

First witness

Second witness

_____

_____

(print name)

(print name)

_____

_____

(address)

(address)

_____

_____

(city)   (state)

(city)   (state)

_____

_____

(signature of witness)

(signature of witness)

_____

_____

(date)

(date)

(5.4) ADDITIONAL STATEMENT OF WITNESSES: At least one of the above witnesses must also sign the following declaration:

I further declare under penalty of perjury under the laws of California that I am not related to the individual executing this advance health care directive by blood, marriage, or adoption, and to the best of my knowledge, I am not entitled to any part of the individual's estate upon his or her death under a will now existing or by operation of law.

_____   _____

(signature of witness)   (signature of witness)

PART 6
SPECIAL WITNESS REQUIREMENT

(6.1) The following statement is required only if you are a patient in a skilled nursing facility– a health care facility that provides the following basic services: skilled nursing care and supportive care to patients whose primary need is for availability of skilled nursing care on an extended basis. The patient advocate or ombudsman must sign the following statement:

STATEMENT OF PATIENT ADVOCATE OR OMBUDSMAN

I declare under penalty of perjury under the laws of California that I am a patient advocate or ombudsman as designated by the State Department of Aging and that I am serving as a witness as required by Section 4675 of the Probate Code.

_____   _____

(date)   (Signature)

_____   _____

(address)   (Print your name)

_____

(city)   (state)

ADVANCE HEALTH CARE DIRECTIVE
(California Probate Code Section 4701)

Explanation

You have the right to give instructions about your own health care. You also have the right to name someone else to make health care decisions for you. This form lets you do either or both of these things. It also lets you express your wishes regarding donation of organs and the designation of your primary physician. If you use this form, you may complete or modify all or any part of it. You are free to use a different form.

Part 1 of this form is a power of attorney for health care. Part 1 lets you name another individual as agent to make health care decisions for you if you become incapable of making your own decisions or if you want someone else to make those decisions for you now even though you are still capable. You may also name an alternate agent to act for you if your first choice is not willing, able, or reasonably available to make decisions for you. (Your agent may not be an operator or employee of a community health care institution where you are receiving care, unless your agent is related to you or is a coworker.)

Unless the form you sign limits the authority of your agent, your agent may make all health care decisions for you. This form has a place for you to limit the authority of your agent. You need not limit the authority of your agent if you wish to rely on your agent for all healthcare decisions that may have to be made. If you choose not to limit the authority of your agent, your agent will have the right to:

a)   Consent or refuse consent to any care, treatment, service, or procedure to maintain, diagnose, or otherwise affect a physical or mental condition.

b)   Select or discharge health care providers and institutions.

c)   Approve or disapprove diagnostic tests, surgical procedures, and programs of medication.

d)   Direct the provision, withholding, or withdrawal of artificial nutrition and hydration and all other forms of health care, including cardiopulmonary resuscitation.

e)   Make anatomical gifts, authorize an autopsy, and direct disposition of remains.

Part 2 of this form lets you give specific instructions about any aspect of your health care, whether or not you appoint an agent. Choices are provided for you to express your wishes regarding the provision, withholding, or withdrawal of treatment to keep you alive, as well as the provision of pain relief. Space is also provided for you to add to the choices you have made or for you to write out any additional wishes. If you are satisfied to allow your agent to determine what is best for you in making end-of-life decisions, you need not fill out Part 2 of this form.

Part 3 of this form lets you express an intention to donate your bodily organs and tissues following your death.

Part 4 of this form lets you designate a physician to have primary responsibility for your health care.

After completing this form, sign and date the form at the end. The form must be signed by two qualified witnesses or acknowledged before a notary public. Give a copy of the signed and completed form to your physician, to any other health care providers you may have, any health care agents you have named. You should talk to the person you have named as agent to make sure that he or she understands your wishes and is willing to take the responsibility.

You have the right to revoke this advance health care directive or replace this form at any time.

****

PART 1

POWER OF ATTORNEY FOR HEALTH CARE

(1.1) DESIGNATION OF AGENT: I designate the following individual as my agent to make health care decisions for me; **GEORGE M. MILLER** whose address is 714 Main Road, Santa Barbara, CA 93105, and telephone number is (805) 555-3772.

      If I revoke my agent's authority or if my agent is not willing, able, or reasonably available to make a health care decision for me, I designate as my first alternate agent: **GEORGE MELVIN MILLER** whose address is 714 Main Road, Santa Barbara, CA 93105, and telephone number is (805) 555-3772.

(1.2) AGENT'S AUTHORITY: My agent is authorized to make all health care decisions for me, including decisions to provide, withhold, or withdraw artificial nutrition and hydration and all other forms of health care to keep me alive, except as I state here:

_____

_____

_____

(Add additional sheets if needed.)

(1.3) WHEN AGENT'S AUTHORITY BECOMES EFFECTIVE: My agent's authority becomes effective when my primary physician determines that I am unable to make my own health care decisions unless I initial the following line. **If I initial this line _____, my agent's authority to make health care decisions for me takes effect immediately.**

(1.4) AGENT'S OBLIGATION: My agent shall make health care decisions for me in accordance with this power of attorney for health care, any instructions I give in Part 2 of this form, and my other wishes to the extent known to my agent. To the extent my wishes are unknown, my agent shall make health care decisions for me in accordance with what my agent determines to be in my best interest. In determining my best interest, my agent shall consider my personal values to the extent known to my agent.

(1.5) AGENT'S POSTDEATH AUTHORITY: My agent is authorized to make anatomical gifts, authorize an autopsy, and direct disposition of my remains, except as I state here or in Part 3 of this form:

_____

_____

_____

(Add additional sheets if needed.)

(1.6) NOMINATION OF CONSERVATOR: If a conservator of my person needs to be appointed for me by a court, I nominate the agent designated in this form. If that agent is not willing, able or reasonably available to act as conservator, I nominate the alternate agents whom I have named, in the order designated.

PART 2
INSTRUCTIONS FOR HEALTH CARE

If you fill out this part of the form, you may cross out any wording you do not want.

(2.1) END-OF-LIFE DECISIONS: I direct that my health care providers and others involved in my care provide, withhold, or withdraw treatment in accordance with the choice I have marked below:

_____ (a) Choice Not To Prolong Life - I do not want my life to be prolonged if:

(1) I have an incurable and irreversible condition that will result in my death within a relatively short time;

(2) I become unconscious and, to a reasonable degree of medical certainty, I will not regain consciousness, or

(3) the likely risks and burdens of treatment would outweigh the expected benefits, OR

_____ (b) Choice To Prolong Life- I want my life to be prolonged as long as possible within the limits of generally accepted health care standards.

(2.2) RELIEF FROM PAIN: Except as I state in the following space, I direct that treatment for alleviation of pain or discomfort be provided at all times, even if it hastens my death:

_____

_____

_____

(Add additional sheets if needed.)

PART 3

DONATION OF ORGANS AT DEATH

(OPTIONAL)

(3.1) Upon my death (initial each applicable line):

_____ (a) I give any needed organs, tissues, or parts, OR

_____ (b) I give the following organs, tissues, or parts only. _____

_____

_____ (c) My gift is for the following purposes (cross out any of the following you do not want):

        (1) Transplant

        (2) Therapy

        (3) Research

        (4) Education

PART 4

PRIMARY PHYSICIAN

(OPTIONAL)

(4.1) I designate the following physician as my primary physician:

Name	Address	Telephone

OPTIONAL: If the physician I have designated above is not willing, able or reasonably available to act as my primary physician, I designate the following physician as my primary physician:

Name	Address	Telephone

****

PART 5

(5.1) EFFECT OF COPY: A copy of this form has the same effect as the original.

(5.2) SIGNATURE: Sign and date the form here:

_____   _____

(date)   (Signature)

ILENE MILLER

714 Main Road

Santa Barbara, CA 93105

STATE OF CALIFORNIA

COUNTY OF SANTA BARBARA

On _____ before me, _____,
personally appeared **ILENE MILLER**, _____ personally known to me -OR- ____ proved to me
on the basis of satisfactory evidence to be the person whose name is subscribed to the within
instrument and acknowledged to me that she executed the same in her authorized capacity, and
that by her signature on the instrument the person, or the entity upon behalf of which the person
acted, executed the instrument.

WITNESS my hand and official seal.

_____

Signature of Notary Public

(5.3) STATEMENT OF WITNESSES: I declare under penalty of perjury under the laws of California (1) that the individual who signed or acknowledged this advance health care directive is personally known to me, or that the individual's identity was proven to me by convincing evidence, (2) that the individual signed or acknowledged this advance directive in my presence, (3) that the individual appears to be of sound mind and under no duress, fraud, or under influence, (4) that I am not a person appointed as agent by this advance directive, and (5) that I am not the individual's health care provider, an employee of the individual's health care provider, the operator of a community care facility, an employee of an operator of a community care facility, the operator of a residential care facility for the elderly, nor an employee of an operator of a residential care facility for the elderly.

First witness   Second witness

_____   _____

(print name)   (print name)

_____   _____

(address)   (address)

_____   _____

(city)   (state)   (city)   (state)

_____   _____

(signature of witness)   (signature of witness)

_____   _____

(date)   (date)

(5.4) ADDITIONAL STATEMENT OF WITNESSES: At least one of the above witnesses must also sign the following declaration:

I further declare under penalty of perjury under the laws of California that I am not related to the individual executing this advance health care directive by blood, marriage, or adoption, and to the best of my knowledge, I am not entitled to any part of the individual's estate upon his or her death under a will now existing or by operation of law.

_____   _____

(signature of witness)   (signature of witness)

PART 6

SPECIAL WITNESS REQUIREMENT

(6.1) The following statement is required only if you are a patient in a skilled nursing facility– a health care facility that provides the following basic services: skilled nursing care and supportive care to patients whose primary need is for availability of skilled nursing care on an extended basis. The patient advocate or ombudsman must sign the following statement:

STATEMENT OF PATIENT ADVOCATE OR OMBUDSMAN

I declare under penalty of perjury under the laws of California that I am a patient advocate or ombudsman as designated by the State Department of Aging and that I am serving as a witness as required by Section 4675 of the Probate Code.

_____   _____

(date)   (Signature)

_____   _____

(address)   (Print your name)

_____

(city)   (state)

We the People
Store Addresses

ALASKA

545 E Northern Lights Blvd.
Anchorage, Alaska 99503
(907) 276–3006

ARIZONA

15224 No. 59th Ave.
Glendale, AZ 95306
(602) 942–6777

2815 So. Alma School Rd.
Mesa, AZ 85210
(480) 456-1412

2524 Indian School Rd.
Phoenix, AZ 85016
(602) 340–0290

3329 E. Bell Rd., Ste. 18
Phoenix, AZ 85032
(602) 953–4063

2545 E. Speedway Blvd.
Tucson, AZ 85716
(520) 318–4987

CALIFORNIA

27064 South La Paz Rd.
Aliso Viejo, CA 92656
(949) 425–0630

1137 W. Valley Blvd.
Alhambra, CA 91803
(626) 300–8011

1665 W. Katella Ave.
Anaheim, CA 92802–3021
(714) 772–0449

6332 Beach Blvd.
Buena Park, CA 90621
(714) 523–5000

1172 San Pablo Ave.
Berkeley, CA 94705
(510) 559–3456

649 W. Imperial Hwy.
Brea, CA 92821
(714) 255–9110

356 E. Olive, #101
Burbank, CA 91502
(818) 848–4421

528 Myrtlewood Dr.
Calimesa, CA 92320–1505
(909) 446–1778

21722 Devonshire St.
Chatsworth, CA 91311
(818) 882–7622

4474 Treat Blvd.
Concord, CA 94521
(925) 246–0370

1909 Harbor Blvd.
Costa Mesa, CA 92627–2666
(949) 574–8880

7603A Amador Valley Rd.
Dublin, CA 94568–2301
(925) 479–9600

345 No. 2nd St.
El Cajon, CA 92021
(619) 442–4599

18044 Ventura Blvd.
Encino, CA 91316
(818) 774–1966

1107 4th St.
Eureka, CA 95501
(707) 442–0162

1600 Travis Blvd., Ste. B
Fairfield, CA 94533
(707) 428–9871

12752 Valley View St.
Garden Grove, CA 92845
(714) 934–8382

1415 E. Colorado Blvd.
Glendale, CA 91205
(818) 546–1787

17818 Chatsworth St.
Granada Hills, CA 91344
(818) 363–5837

22551 Foothill Blvd.
Hayward, CA 94541
(510) 728–7600

4479 Hollywood Blvd.
Hollywood, CA 90027
(323) 666–8200

17131 Beach Blvd.
Huntington Beach, CA 92648
(714) 843–6229

698 S. Vermont Ave. #105
(Koreatown)
Los Angeles, CA 90005
(213) 389–2200

1826 W. Ave. J
Lancaster, CA 93534
(661) 726–7646

2115 Bellflower Blvd.
Long Beach, CA 90815
(562) 985–1101

729 W. 7th St.
Los Angeles, CA 90017
(213) 489–1980

5324 Wilshire Blvd.
Los Angeles, CA 90036
(323) 937–2311

2496 Lincoln Blvd.
Marina Del Rey, CA
    90291–5041
(310) 577–8333

2400 Alicia Parkway #1A
Mission Viejo, CA 92691
(949) 951–4411

1347 McHenry Ave.
Modesto, CA 95350
(209) 523–8227

11369 Riverside Dr.
North Hollywood, CA 91602
(818) 762–8647

11755 Imperial Hwy., Ste. 200
Norwalk, CA 90652
(562) 863–1991

3753 Mission Ave.
Oceanside, CA 92054
(760) 754–9059

244 Grand Ave.
Oakland, CA 94610
(510) 452–2324

595 The City Dr. #200
Orange, CA 92868
(714) 634–4885

2400 Saviers Rd.
Oxnard, CA 93033
(805) 487–1210

73121 Country Club Dr.
Palm Desert, CA 92260
(760) 346–7074

2127 El Camino Real
Palo Alto, CA 94306
(650) 324–3800

762 E. Colorado Blvd.
Pasadena, CA 91101
(626) 535–0100

135 Keller St., Ste. C
Petaluma, CA 94952
(707) 769–1639

9030 Foothill Blvd., Ste. 112
Rancho Cucamonga, CA 91730
(909) 466–4500

2968 Churn Creek Rd.
Redding, CA 96002
(530) 222–8747

6519 Magnolia Ave.
Riverside, CA 92506
(909) 369–3591

4211 B Arden Way
Sacramento, CA 95864
(916) 679–6780

517 So. Main St., Ste. 101
Salinas, CA 93901
(831) 771–2029

1435 University Ave.
San Diego, CA 92103
(619) 725–0996

209 North Maclay
San Fernando, CA 91340–2908
(818) 838–3900

411 Divisadero St.
San Francisco, CA 94117
(415) 701–9800

441A Marsh St.
San Luis Obispo, CA 93401
(805) 596–0100

903B Irwin St.
San Rafael, CA 94901–3317
(415) 457–3773

1501 State St.
Santa Barbara, CA 93101
(805) 962–4100

500 Soquel Ave., Ste. B
Santa Cruz, CA 95062
(831) 458–5155

920 South Broadway
Santa Maria, CA 93454
(805) 928- 9700

2922 Wilshire Blvd.
Santa Monica, CA 90403
(310) 264–0517

22933 Soledad Canyon Rd.
Saugus, CA 91350
(661) 255–8488

13565 Ventura Blvd.
Sherman Oaks, CA 91423
(818) 906–0086

4360 Cochran St.
Simi Valley, CA 93065
(805) 526–7351

800 E. Thousand Oaks Blvd.
Thousand Oaks, CA 91360
(805) 371–7575

4727 Torrance Blvd.
Torrance, CA 90503
(310) 370–8399

13732 Newport Ave., Ste. 1
Tustin, CA 92780
(714) 730–5196

7219 Balboa Blvd.
Van Nuys, CA 91406
(818) 989–7431

2827 E. Thompson Blvd.
Ventura, CA 93003
(805) 641–2010

1830 Hacienda Dr. #5
Vista, CA 92081
(760) 941–1604

2061 MT. Diablo Blvd.
Walnut Creek, CA 94596
(925) 407–1010

21904 Ventura Blvd.
Woodland Hills, CA 91367
(818) 704–9394

1648 Westwood Blvd.
W. Los Angeles, CA 90024
(310) 441–5400

COLORADO

3125 28th St.
Boulder, **CO** 80304
(303) 544–1066

14 N. Main St.
Brighton, **CO** 80601
(303) 654–9983

62 E. Arapahoe Rd.
(Arapahoe)
Centennial, **CO** 80122
(303) 991–3651

1806 A Dominion Way
Colorado Springs, **CO** 80918
(719) 590–7779

7115 E. Hampden Ave.
Denver, **CO** 80224
(303) 302–1000

2454 Hwy. 6 & 50
Grand Junction, **CO** 81505
(970) 263–9191

3489 W. 10th St. #C
Greeley, **CO** 80634
(970) 352–5444

3355 So. Wadsworth Blvd.
Lakewood, **CO** 80227
(303) 984–2101

62 E. Arapahoe Rd.
Littleton, **CO** 80122
(303) 991–3651

7330 W. 88th Ave., Ste. E
Westminster, **CO** 80021
(303) 421–0367

CONNECTICUT

1100 Main St.
Newington, **CT** 06111–2910
(860) 665–0540

165 Bank St.
New London, **CT** 06320
(860) 447–9984

281 Connecticut Ave.
Norwalk, **CT** 06854
(203) 852–7006

163 Post Rd.
Orange, **CT** 06477
(203) 795–9978

FLORIDA

1701 No. Federal Hwy
Boca Raton, **FL** 33432
(561) 347–5340

1722 Del Prado Blvd.
Cape Coral, **FL** 33990
(239) 573–7311

101 E. Commercial Blvd.
Fort Lauderdale, **FL** 33334
(954) 491–2990

16050 So. Tamiani Trail
Fort Myers, **FL** 33908
(239) 267–9955

320 Osceola Ave.
Jacksonville Beach, **FL** 32250
(904) 241–2533

3003 So. Tamiami Trail
Sarasota, **FL** 34239
(941) 366–8896

GEORGIA

1524 Church
Decatur, **GA** 30030
(404) 270–9199

561 Forest Parkway
Forest Park, **GA** 30297
(404) 608–0566

HAWAII

564 South St.
Honolulu, **HI** 96813
(808) 548–0379

IDAHO

7974 Fairview Ave.
Boise, **ID** 83704
(208) 658–1745

1587 E. 17th
Idaho Falls, **ID** 93404
(208) 522–5176

ILLINOIS

6218 W. Cermak
Berwyn, **IL**
(708) 484–9200

2411 Ashland
Chicago, **IL** 60614
(773) 529–9900

3210 W. 95th
Evergreen Park, **IL** 60805
708–422–2000

801 E. Ogden Ave.
Naperville, **IL** 60563
(630) 778–9770

KANSAS

7620 Metcalf Ave., Ste. H
Overland Park, **KS** 66204
(913) 383–0505

2243 North Tyler, Ste. 107
(West Wichita)
Wichita, **KS** 67220
(316) 773–2400

410 North Hillside, Ste. 900
(College Hill)
Wichita, **KS** 67214
(316) 685–5759

KENTUCKY

3126 Dixie Hwy.
Erlanger, **KY** 41018
(859)727–6900

MARYLAND

511-C Eastern Blvd.
Essex, **MD** 21221
(410) 780–7084

507 Reisterstown Rd.
Pikesville, **MD** 21208–5303
(410) 580–2036

MICHIGAN

2841 Breton Rd.
Grand Rapids, **MI** 49512
(616) 245–7008

29961 Gratiot Ave.
(Detroit)
Roseville, **MI** 48066
(586) 774–5188

MINNESOTA

2002 Lyndale Ave., So.
Minneapolis, **MN** 55404
(612) 333–3777

MISSISSIPPI

1553 County Line Rd., Ste. 200
Jackson, **MS** 39211
(601) 206–9980

MISSOURI

2722 S. Brentwood Blvd.
Brentwood, **MO** 63144
(314) 963–0600

NEBRASKA

709 No. 48th St.
Lincoln, **NE** 68504
(402) 464–2200

9207 Maple St.
Omaha, **NE** 68134
(402) 502–9898

NEVADA

2300 South Carson St., Ste. 4
Carson City, **NV** 89701
(775) 888–6830

4850 W. Flamingo Rd.
Las Vegas, **NV** 89103
(702) 222–0414

6405–2 So. Virginia St.
Reno, **NV** 89511
(775) 853–4400

NEW JERSEY

107 Broadway
Elmwood Park, **NJ** 07407
(201) 794–6491

534 Bloomfield Ave.
Verona, **NJ** 07044
(973) 857–0057

NEW MEXICO

2828 Carlisle Blvd. N.E.
Albuquerque, **NM** 87110
(505) 889–8900

NEW YORK

133 Wolf Rd.
(Colony)
Albany, **NY** 12205
(518) 435–9110

42–38 Bell Blvd.
Bayside, **NY** 11361
(718) 224–8704

1508 86th St.
Bay Ridge, **NY** 11228
(718) 259–8181

2349 Arthur Ave.
(Belmont)
Bronx, **NY** 10458
(718) 295–5700

92 Willoughby St.
(Downtown Brooklyn)
Brooklyn, **NY** 11201
(718) 855–8585

116–28 Queens Blvd.
Forest Hills, **NY** 11375
(718) 793–4400

1986 Ralph Ave.
(Georgetown)
Brooklyn, **NY** 11234
(718) 968–0022

423B 2nd Ave.
Grammercy Park, **NY** 10010
(212) 213–2700

788 A. Manhattan Ave.
(Greenpoint)
Brooklyn, **NY** 11222
(718) 609–0900

3658 Broadway
Hamilton Heights, **NY** 10031
(212) 281–4800

377 West 125th St.
Harlem, **NY** 10027
(212) 280–3100

519B 207th St.
(Inwood)
New York, **NY** 10034
(212) 942–1600

5661 Broadway
(Kingsbridge)
Bronx, **NY** 10463
(718) 543–5800

796 Ulster Ave.
Kingston, **NY** 12401
(845) 331–5833

470 Hawkins Ave.
Lake Ronkonkoma, **NY** 11779
(631) 467–2667

45–01 Northern Blvd.
Long Island City, **NY** 11101
(718) 392–4300

447 Mamaroneck Ave.
Mamaroneck, **NY** 10543
(914) 835–7800

250 East Houston St.
New York, **NY** 10002
(212) 979–6100

239 W. 72nd St.
New York, **NY** 10023
(212) 501–7700

3478 Jerome Ave.
(Norwood)
Bronx, **NY** 10463
(718) 994–6400

105–28 Cross Bay Blvd.
Ozone Park, **NY** 11417
(718) 845–8300

514 5th Ave.
(Park Slope)
Brooklyn, **NY** 11215
(718) 965–2228

211–36 Hillside Ave.
Queens Village, **NY** 11427
(718) 217–1500

3715 Nostrand
Sheepshead Bay, **NY** 11235
(718) 332–5600

861 Montauk Hwy. #3
Shirley, **NY** 11967
(631) 281–2212

2175 Hylan Blvd.
Staten Island, **NY** 10306
(718) 351–1200

46–14 Queens Blvd.
Sunnyside, **NY** 11104
(718) 472–3800

3427 East Tremont Ave.
(Throgs Neck)
Bronx, **NY** 10465
(718) 863–2200

554 West 181st St.
(Washington Heights)
New York, **NY** 10033
(212) 928–8000

127 Post Ave.
Westbury, **NY** 11590
(516) 333–3306

49 Westchester Sq.
Westchester Square, **NY**
(718) 931–7500

148 Mamaroneck Ave.
White Plains, **NY** 10601
(914) 683–5105

NORTH CAROLINA

624 Tyvola Rd., Ste. 101
Charlotte, **NC** 28217
(704) 665–6353

302-B SE Greenville Blvd.
Greenville, **NC** 27858
(252) 355–8107

4940-C Capital Blvd.
Raleigh, **NC** 27616
(919) 713–0339

OHIO

794 Main St.
Milford, **OH** 45150
(513) 831–3380

OKLAHOMA

3747-B South Harvard
Tulsa, **OK** 74135
(918) 794–0305

OREGON

400 NW Walnut Blvd. #200
Corvallis, **OR** 97330
(541) 738–9872

377 Coburg Rd., Ste. C
Eugene, **OR** 97401
(541) 345–1128

520 S.E. 10th Ave.
Hillsboro, **OR** 97123
(503) 693–8885

PENNSYLVANIA

718 Market St.
(Center City)
Philadelphia, **PA** 19106
(215) 238–8809

2836 Cottman Ave.
Philadelphia, **PA** 19149
(215) 333–8281

34 West Lancaster Ave.
Shillington, **PA** 19607
(610) 796–1250

301 W. Baltimore Pike
Springfield, **PA** 19018
(610) 626–4141

RHODE ISLAND

298 Atwells Ave.
Providence, **RI** 02903
(401) 521–4700

TENNESSEE

8161 Kingston Pike
Knoxville, **TN** 37919
(865) 560–2221

86 Thompson Lane
Nashville, **TN** 37211
(615) 445–3611

TEXAS

13729 Research Blvd., Ste. 850
Austin, **TX** 78759
(512) 996–8558

7726 Forest Lane
Dallas, **TX** 75230
(214) 265–8800

2672 No. Belt Line Rd.
Irving, **TX** 75062
(972) 570–4800

WISCONSIN

4210 E. Washington Ave.
Madison, **WI** 53704
(608) 245–5003

INDEX